THE COMING APOCALYPSE:

WHAT YOU NEED TO KNOW

DANIEL R. PINCKNEY

Updated Edition

ISBN-10: 1477554467
ISBN-13: 978-1477554463

DEDICATION

To my loving and wise wife, Iara. You have encouraged and exposed me to so many new ideas.
Where would I be without you?

CONTENTS

THE END TIME SEQUENCE OF EVENTS: THE BOOK OF REVELATION **PART FOUR**

ACKNOWLEDGMENTS

Special thanks to those who have supported us over the years as we have served in various mission fields. Our ministry abroad would not be possible without you. Likewise a debt of gratitude to the Bavarian International Christian Fellowship, Munich, Germany, for allowing me to research and write this book.

Special recognition goes to my parents, Rev. Earl and Marion Pinckney, who have encouraged me and made helpful suggestions.

Most of all, thanks be to God, the Creator, Revelator and Redeemer. Your love, wisdom, power and grace endure forever!

INTRODUCTION

Great economic uncertainty weighs over Europe with numerous countries in danger of collapsing financially due to overwhelming debt and high unemployment. The future of the Euro is in question. In the United States, investment research advisors Porter Stansberry and Dr. Martin Weiss have put out videos predicting a soon coming end to America as we know it because of its fiscal irresponsibility.

At the start of 2011 and 2012, there were various reports of thousands of birds dropping out of the sky and millions of dead fish washing up on shores in various places around the globe. News organizations such as CNN and Fox News, and I imagine others raised the question if these are not signs of the coming Apocalypse.

2011 was a year with more than its fair share of natural disasters. The most major being the 9.0 earthquake in Japan with the ensuing tsunami and partial nuclear reactor meltdown. There was another devastating earthquake in New Zealand. The US was hit with around 600 tornados in April alone, when the average is 1200 for an entire year. The one that passed through the southeast part of the US was the worst natural disaster in the US since Katrina. Devastating tornados have struck the US much earlier than normal toward the beginning of 2012. Hurricane Sandy in late 2012 combined with the most severe drought in a generation added to the US economic crisis. There has been major flooding in Australia, China, Pakistan and the Mississippi River, and a major mudslide in Brazil whereas other parts of the world suffer drought and famine. Volcanoes around the world have been erupting, and parts of Europe experienced the coldest winter in a thousand years.

2011 and 2012 have also been a hotbed of wars and revolutions. Besides the continuing wars in Iraq and Afghanistan, there have been uprisings and revolt in Tunisia, Egypt, Yemen, Syria and Libya. The Palestinians are notching up the pressure on Israel for Statehood by taking their case to the UN. Israel is increasingly being isolated and boxed in a corner with the constant threats also coming from Iran and lately Turkey.

All three major monotheistic religions – Judaism, Christianity and Islam have writings that point to an eschatological end of time preceded by great moral and spiritual decay combined with economic and meteorological upheavals around the globe. Each religion awaits a Messiah who will make all things right. The Jews look for their Messiah, the Christians claim that the Jewish Messiah has already come once as Jesus of Nazareth and will come again to set up a Kingdom. The Muslims look for the coming Mahdi and the return of Isa (Jesus) who together will persuade or force all unwilling others to convert to Islam so that the world may be united in the belief in Allah and Mohammed as his prophet.

Certainly, the downward spiral in the moral/spiritual arena is evident to all with increased violence, rampant sexual immorality and enormous greed being displayed. Nations in Europe have been facing the need for bailouts and the United States has an unimaginable debt with ever-increasing budget deficits. 2010 was a year of climate shifts with record heat and cold waves being reported in various parts of the world. Airports have had to change runway signs because of the changing magnetic pole causing runways to no longer match their designated coordinates.

One of NASA's 2013 Budget Proposal priorities is to place astronauts on asteroids as a means to protect the earth from possible impact. Reports of UFO sightings are increasing around the globe. Are these indicators of an impending apocalypse? Some interpreted the Mayan calendar as predicting the end of the world on December 21, 2012. Or what about the supposed "Prophecy of the Popes" in 1139 by St. Malachy identifying Pope Francis as the last Pope and that after his papacy the city on seven hills will be destroyed and final judgment will come?

All three monotheistic religions cite the Bible as being their authority – at least part of their authority for what they believe. In addition to the Tanakh, the Hebrew Bible, the Jews lean heavily on the Talmud and Mishna, compilations of Jewish Law and Tradition over the centuries. The Christians hold to both the Old and New Testaments as being the inspired Word of God and the Muslims claim that only those parts of the Bible that have not been corrupted by the Jews and Christians are valid. In addition, the Qur'an and the Hadith are Islamic sacred texts.

Because of the Bible forming a basis in these three religions, I will be looking primarily at what the Bible says regarding the coming End Times. I will refer briefly to the Jewish and Islamic eschatological traditions, but my primary resource will be the Bible. As a Christian, my knowledge is predominantly biblical and thus, both Old and New Testaments will be the major basis for the material in this book. In addition I should add that while I respect other religion's sacred books and will be quoting from them, my personal conviction is that only the Bible is the infallible Word of God. I will be quoting many sources and making personal conjectures, all or some of which may prove to be untrue. However, I believe the Bible will always be true.

While I understand and respect the Jewish concern for not taking God‘s name in vain and thus in Jewish writings, God is written as G-d, I will use the normal Christian way of writing the Name. Likewise, while there are those who believe that Allah is the name of God – the same monotheistic God that Jews and Christians believe in, and indeed, in certain languages such as the Turkish language, some translations of the Bible use the name —Allah when translating the name of God, I share the belief of many Muslims who insist that Allah is not the same God that Jews and Christians worship, and therefore should not be confused as such.

There is a challenge to writing this book. There are a number of audiences I have in mind. I wish to speak to the non-Christian audience, whether, atheist, agnostic, Jew or Muslim, or of any other religion. It is important for them to know where Jews, Christians and Muslims are coming from in regard to this subject. However, I also want to address Christians who are at different levels of their understanding of the Bible. There are those for whom this subject is relatively new, while others have for years been deeply interested in, and indeed can be said to be teachers on the material. Walking the line between providing too much detail for those just getting started and not enough information to support a thesis for the seminary professor is difficult. It is also important that my Christian friends understand the eschatology of the Jewish and Muslim worlds. Many of the decisions made by nations and peoples today are strongly influenced by these eschatological world views.

While the subject of eschatology (study of end time things) has fascinated me for years, I understand that there are a wide variety of interpretations on what the Bible says. What I present here I honestly believe to be what Scripture is teaching, but as there are new things I learn almost weekly, and new ways of looking at texts, I make no claim to being infallible. I welcome interaction and correction where needed.

Daniel R. Pinckney
Munich, Germany

THE KEY TO UNDERSTANDING ALL OF HUMAN HISTORY

PART ONE

1 HISTORY'S FRAMEWORK

Is there a framework for understanding history – past, present and future?

As we look at past human history and think of the future, is there an underlying framework or unifying theme that has determined history, or is it all just a series of random events with no overarching purpose?

I would like to submit that there is a purposeful direction to history, that it is linear (a beginning and an end) rather than cyclical, and that the Bible reveals to us where we came from and where human history is going. The God of the Bible says this:

Isaiah 46:9-10

I am God, and there is no other;
I am God, and there is none like me,
[10] declaring the end from the beginning
and from ancient times things not yet done,
saying, 'My counsel shall stand,
and I will accomplish all my purpose,'

Who is this God? There are many passages where God identifies himself, but this one gives us an idea of who He is, what He has done and what He requires of us:

Isaiah 45:18

For thus says the Lord,
who created the heavens

(he is God!),
who formed the earth and made it
(he established it;
he did not create it empty,
he formed it to be inhabited!):
"I am the Lord, and there is no other."

Isaiah 45:21b -23

And there is no other god besides me,
a righteous God and a Savior;
there is none besides me.
[22] "Turn to me and be saved,
all the ends of the earth!
For I am God, and there is no other.
[23] By myself I have sworn;
from my mouth has gone out in righteousness
a word that shall not return:
'To me every knee shall bow,
every tongue shall swear allegiance.'

This passage tells us that there is only one God – YHVH. The Hebrew Bible is called the *Tanakh* – TaNaKh being an acronym composed from the first Hebrew letters of the three biblical subdivisions: The Torah, or "Teaching", which are the Five Books of Moses, Nevi'im ("Prophets") and Ketuvim ("Writings")[1]. Christians use the same text and call it the Old Testament. The difference in order and names of the books in the Tanakh and the Christian O.T. is due to the Christians following the names and order given by the Jewish translators of the Bible in the 3rd century B.C. from Hebrew to Greek called the Septuagint. They placed the Prophets after the Writings.

In the *Tanakh* this personal name of God was used over 6,800 times. On account of the third of the Ten Commandments (Ex. 20:7), which prohibits the taking of God's name in vain, the Masoretes substituted the vowel markings for *Adonai* under these four Hebrew consonants, Yod, Hey, Vav, Hey, so that God's name would not be pronounced when read. It is not known for sure how God's name sounds, but many have assumed that it would be pronounced as "Yahweh" or "Jehovah." However, since there is no sound of "W" or "J" in Hebrew, perhaps

[1] http://en.wikipedia.org/wiki/Tanakh

"Yahováh," with the accent on the last syllable, is closest to how God's name is pronounced and thus will be the name used in this book.

The text above tells us his name, that he has created all things, that he enjoins all mankind to turn to him and be saved, and that every knee shall bow and every tongue shall swear allegiance to Him. That, in a nutshell, is what history is all about.

Obviously, we know that there is a problem. Not everyone believes this. The majority of humanity does not acknowledge the God of the Bible; they do not believe that He created all things, see no need to turn to Him to be saved and refuse to bow or swear allegiance to Him.

This brings us to the underlying theme of history. God has created this world, but his creation has rebelled against him, wanting to usurp His position, power and glory. History is the story of God's creation, its fall and consequent judgment and God's work of redeeming a people from the consequences of sin's power, punishment and eventual presence, and the reestablishment of His rightful place as God, before whom all will bow and acknowledge Him as Lord.

To Understand the Future, We Must Understand the Past

How did all this happen? When God created this universe in six days, resting the seventh, it was a perfect creation with man as the highest created being:

Genesis 1:26-28

Then God said, "Let us make man in our image, after our likeness. And let them have dominion over the fish of the sea and over the birds of the heavens and over the livestock and over all the earth and over every creeping thing that creeps on the earth."

[27] So God created man in his own image,
in the image of God he created him;
male and female he created them.

[28] And God blessed them. And God said to them, "Be fruitful and multiply and fill the earth and subdue it and have dominion over the fish of the sea and over the birds of the heavens and over every living thing that moves on the earth."

God made man in his image and placed him on earth to rule and judge as his gods – his agents or representatives. Ps 82:1-8 in its context shows men being called "gods", albeit after man's sin, fallen ones.

> God has taken his place in the divine council;
> in the midst of the gods he holds judgment:
> [2] "How long will you judge unjustly
> and show partiality to the wicked? Selah
> [3] Give justice to the weak and the fatherless;
> maintain the right of the afflicted and the destitute.
> [4] Rescue the weak and the needy;
> deliver them from the hand of the wicked."
> [6] I said, "You are gods,
> sons of the Most High, all of you;
> [7] nevertheless, like men you shall die,
> and fall like any prince."
> [8] Arise, O God, judge the earth;
> for you shall inherit all the nations!

In this context, it shows God's sons – "gods" as having both a role of ruling (prince) and primarily that of judging. God is the ultimate King and Judge, but he delegated those roles to man on the earth. In fact, He has given to his saints the responsibility to judge both the world and angels:

1 Cor. 6:2-3

Or do you not know that the saints will judge the world? And if the world is to be judged by you, are you incompetent to try trivial cases? [3] Do you not know that we are to judge angels? How much more, then, matters pertaining to this life!

While man was created in the image of God and given dominion over the earth, he was not the only created order. At some point in time, God had also created heavenly beings – angels. We don't know exactly when this happened, whether it was before or after man was created, but there was a rebellion in heaven. God's highest created angel was not content with his exalted position. He wanted to take God's position, or at least be like God. The leader of that rebellion was Lucifer, or Satan. Here is the record of his rebellion as personified by two kings, the king of Babylon and the king of Tyre:

Isaiah 14:12-15 (NIV)

12 How you have fallen from heaven, O morning star *(Lucifer)*, son

of the dawn! You have been cast down to the earth, you who once
laid low the nations!
13 You said in your heart, "I will ascend to heaven; I will raise my
throne above the stars of God; I will sit enthroned on the mount of
assembly, on the utmost heights of the sacred mountain.
14 I will ascend above the tops of the clouds; I will make myself like
the Most High."
15 But you are brought down to the grave, to the depths of the pit.

Ezekiel 28:12-17 (NIV)
12 "Son of man, take up a lament concerning the king of Tyre and
say to him: 'This is what the Sovereign Lord says: "'You were the
model of perfection, full of wisdom and perfect in beauty.
13 You were in Eden, the garden of God; every precious stone adorned
you: ruby, topaz and emerald, chrysolite, onyx and jasper, sapphire,
turquoise and beryl. Your settings and mountings were made of gold;
on the day you were created they were prepared.
14 You were anointed as a guardian cherub, for so I ordained you. You
were on the holy mount of God; you walked among the fiery stones.
15 You were blameless in your ways from the day you were created till
wickedness was found in you.
16 Through your widespread trade you were filled with violence, and
you sinned. So I drove you in disgrace from the mount of God, and I
expelled you, O guardian cherub, from among the fiery stones.
17 Your heart became proud on account of your beauty, and you
corrupted your wisdom because of your splendor. So I threw you to
the earth;

Satan was unable to raise his throne above the stars of God (angels) in heaven. His desire was to "sit enthroned on the mount of assembly, on the utmost heights of the sacred mountain" in heaven (above the tops of the clouds). He was determined to make himself like the Most High. His was the sin of pride and covetousness and his judgment was to be thrown to the earth and eventually to the depths of the pit.

As we have seen, when God created the earth and man, He gave man dominion over the earth. Satan, unable to obtain dominion in heaven saw his opportunity to fulfill his desire on earth. Just as he lost his exalted place in heaven because of his desire to be like God, he tempted man with the same desire so that man would likewise lose his exalted place of dominion, thus giving Satan the opportunity to usurp man's position here on earth.

Notice the temptation he offered Eve in face of God's prohibition to eat the fruit from one particular tree – the temptation to be like God:

Genesis 3:1-5

Now the serpent was more crafty than any other beast of the field that the Lord God had made.

He said to the woman, "Did God actually say, 'You shall not eat of any tree in the garden'?" [2] And the woman said to the serpent, "We may eat of the fruit of the trees in the garden, [3] but God said, 'You shall not eat of the fruit of the tree that is in the midst of the garden, neither shall you touch it, lest you die.' " [4] But the serpent said to the woman, "You will not surely die. [5] For God knows that when you eat of it your eyes will be opened, and you will be like God, knowing good and evil."

The Bible identifies the serpent:

Rev. 12:7-9

Now war arose in heaven, Michael and his angels fighting against the dragon. And the dragon and his angels fought back, [8] but he was defeated and there was no longer any place for them in heaven. [9] And the great dragon was thrown down, that ancient serpent, who is called the devil and Satan, the deceiver of the whole world— he was thrown down to the earth, and his angels were thrown down with him.

Man's rebellion was essentially the same as Satan's. Adam and Eve were not content with their position as God's highest creation on earth. They wanted to be like God. Down through the ages man has continuously wanted God's place like the king of Tyre:

Ezekiel 28:2

"Son of man, say to the prince of Tyre, Thus says the Lord God:
"Because your heart is proud,
and you have said, 'I am a god,
I sit in the seat of the gods,
in the heart of the seas,'
yet you are but a man, and no god,
though you make your heart like the heart of a god—

The story has not changed. Modern day novelist Dan Brown of *The*

DaVinci Code fame in his recent novel, *The Lost Symbol* has his protagonists say,

"Robert, don't you see? The Ancient Mysteries and the Bible are the same thing."[2] However, what is the message of the Bible according to Dan Brown's characters?

"We've lost the Word, and yet its true meaning is still within reach, right before our eyes. It exists in all the enduring texts, from the Bible to the *Bhagavad Gita* to the Koran and beyond. *All* of these texts are revered upon the altars of Freemasonry because Masons understand what the world seems to have forgotten . . . that each of these texts, in its own way, is quietly whispering the exact *same* message." Peter's voice welled with emotion. "'Know ye not that ye are gods?'"[3] "A wise man once told me," Peter said, his voice faint now, "the only difference between you and God is that *you* have forgotten that you are divine."[4]

Indeed, what does the Bible say the "man of lawlessness", the future Antichrist will say about himself?

2 Thess. 2:3-4

"Let no one deceive you in any way. For that day will not come, unless the rebellion comes first, and the man of lawlessness is revealed, the son of destruction, [4] who opposes and exalts himself against every so-called god or object of worship, so that he takes his seat in the temple of God, proclaiming himself to be God."

This rebellion and seeking to usurp God's rightful place as God and Sovereign over the universe has not only impacted the angelic and human realms, it also impacted the physical earth as animals and nature have been brought under the dominion of the evil one.

Romans 8:20-22

For the creation was subjected to futility, not willingly, but because of him who subjected it, in hope [21] that the creation itself will be set free from its bondage to decay and obtain the freedom of the glory of the children of God. [22] For we know that the whole creation has been groaning together in the pains of childbirth until now.

---

[2] Dan Brown, The Lost Symbol, (New York, NY: Anchor Books, 2010) p. 646.

[3] ibid., p. 647.

[4] ibid., p. 648.

What happened when man sinned was that they forfeited their position as "gods" or rulers of this world to Satan and became his slaves because they chose to obey him rather than God.

Romans 6:16 (NIV)

[16] Don't you know that when you offer yourselves to someone to obey him as slaves, you are slaves to the one whom you obey--whether you are slaves to sin, which leads to death, or to obedience, which leads to righteousness?

Because of their disobedience, there were a number of consequences. Sin, death and evil entered into the world. They were separated from God, and their spirits – that part of them that has communion with God, immediately died. Their bodies were to die later. The consequence was not a temporary one, but rather an eternal separation from God, both while living here on earth as well as in a place of eternal torment known as hell after their physical death.

Rev. 20:12-15

And I saw the dead, great and small, standing before the throne, and books were opened. Then another book was opened, which is the book of life. And the dead were judged by what was written in the books, according to what they had done. [13] And the sea gave up the dead who were in it, Death and Hades gave up the dead who were in them, and they were judged, each one of them, according to what they had done. [14] Then Death and Hades were thrown into the lake of fire. This is the second death, the lake of fire. [15] And if anyone's name was not found written in the book of life, he was thrown into the lake of fire.

Another consequence as mentioned was that they lost their exalted position of dominion over the earth to the serpent – to Satan. He became the god and ruler of this world (2 Cor. 4:4, Jn. 12:31). In fact, see how he tempted Jesus:

Luke 4:5-8

And the devil took him up and showed him all the kingdoms of the world in a moment of time, [6] and said to him, "To you I will give all this authority and their glory, for it has been delivered to me, and I give it to whom I will. [7] If you, then, will worship me, it will

all be yours." [8] And Jesus answered him, "It is written,
" 'You shall worship the Lord your God,
and him only shall you serve.' "

Satan said, "… for it has been delivered to me…" How and by whom? It was delivered to him by man when he chose to obey Satan rather than God.

Notice some of the titles the Bible has for him:

John 12:31

Now is the judgment of this world; now will **the ruler of this world** be cast out.

2 Cor. 4:4

In their case **the god of this world** has blinded the minds of the unbelievers, to keep them from seeing the light of the gospel of the glory of Christ, who is the image of God.

Ephes. 2:2

in which you once walked, following the course of this world, following **the prince of the power of the air**, **the spirit that is now at work in the sons of disobedience**—

1 John 5:19

We know that we are from God, and the whole world lies in the power of **the evil one**.

Hebrews 2:14

Since therefore the children share in flesh and blood, he himself likewise partook of the same things, that through death he might destroy **the one who has the power of death, that is, the devil**, …

History is the story of Satan's stealing man's dominion over the world through the temptation and sin of man, and God's conquest to take that dominion back, liberating the world from Satan's power and returning it to its rightful rule by man. More on that theme will be developed later.

The Key to Unlocking All Human History

After the first couple had eaten the forbidden fruit, God came and pronounced judgment on them. In his judgment on the serpent, we find the theme that explains the purpose and the events of all of human history.

Genesis 3:15 (NASB)

15 And I will put enmity between you and the woman, and between your seed and her seed; He shall bruise you on the head, and you shall bruise him on the heel."

This verse introduces for us the source of conflict in the world. There would be enmity between Satan and his seed and the woman and her seed. This conflict would result in the eventual victory of the seed of the woman over Satan.

There is a commonly held mistaken view that we are all children of God. Jesus dispelled that idea when he was talking with some of the Jewish religious leaders who claimed Abraham as their father:

John 8:44

You are of your father the devil, and your will is to do your father's desires. He was a murderer from the beginning, and has nothing to do with the truth, because there is no truth in him. When he lies, he speaks out of his own character, for he is a liar and the father of lies.

We are not born children of God, but the Christian gospel explains how we can become children of God. Speaking of Jesus, the Apostle John wrote:

John 1:11-12

He came to his own, and his own people did not receive him. [12] But to all who did receive him, who believed in his name, he gave the right to become children of God,

So the verse in Genesis 3:15 tells us that there will be throughout history enmity and conflict between Satan and his children, and the woman, the seed of whom provides the possibility for people to leave Satan's family and kingdom and enter God's family and kingdom.

This verse is also the first prophecy regarding a virgin birth. Women don't have seeds. It is the first prophecy regarding the Messiah who as the seed of the woman, would strike a fatal blow to the head of Satan, the serpent, and Satan would wound the seed of the woman.

Understanding this pronouncement of judgment by God on Satan, one has a framework to understand all of past, present and future history. God told Satan what would happen, and Satan, the rebel, is determined to thwart God's plan and make sure it does not happen. The last chapters of the Bible tell us who will be victorious and everything in between is a record of how this conflict of the ages is playing out. One of the key differences between God and Satan (the want to be god), is that God is omniscient, omnipotent and omnipresent. Satan is powerful, but has none of these three characteristics. In fact, as we shall see, God even uses Satan's bitter schemes against God to accomplish God's own plan.

Only God knows the end from the beginning and only He has the power to make all his purposes come to pass.

Man is not passive or a puppet in this battle of kingdoms and Kings. He is responsible for which kingdom he chooses. Down through history there have been those who have written about the two opposing kingdoms. St. Augustine wrote in his book, *The City of God,* of two cities – a heavenly and an earthly city. In *The Pilgrim's Progress* John Bunyan describes Christian's journey from his "City of Destruction" which is seen as this world, to the "Celestial City" which is the city to come in heaven.

One does not have to wait until death, however, to be in one city or kingdom or the other. When our original parents sinned, they delivered mankind into Satan's kingdom – a kingdom of death and destruction. However, God, in his mercy invites mankind to come to his kingdom of life and blessedness.

The heart of the issue is: who is king – Satan or God, and who are you going to serve. Singer/song writer Bob Dylan expressed it well in his song, "*Gotta Serve Somebody*" The chorus is:

> "But you're gonna have to serve somebody, yes indeed
> You're gonna have to serve somebody
> Well, it may be the devil or it may be the Lord
> But you're gonna have to serve somebody."

All start from birth in the kingdom of darkness and rebellion– the kingdom of Satan, but God urges mankind to turn from that rebellion against his rightful place as God and to embrace his Messiah. He alone is able to save man from the death and destruction that comes by virtue of remaining under Satan's rule, and from the wrath of God against those in rebellion.

THE CONFLICT OF THE AGES: CREATION TO PRESENT

PART TWO

2 SATAN'S STRATEGY UNVEILED: CREATION TO THE FLOOD

SO IF YOU are the devil and God has just told you what your end will be and how it will come about, what would your strategy be? God said that the seed of the woman (the godly seed) would deliver a mortal wound to Satan's head. There would be enmity between Satan's seed and the godly seed. So what would you do?

Eliminate the "Seed of the Woman"

If the godly line from which this future person would come who will deliver a death blow to Satan, could somehow be eliminated, then that person would not be born and Satan would be victorious over God. We see that the devil lost no time putting this strategy into practice. He started with Adam and Eve's first two boys:

1 John 3:10-12

By this it is evident who are the children of God, and who are the children of the devil: whoever does not practice righteousness is not of God, nor is the one who does not love his brother.

[11] For this is the message that you have heard from the beginning, that we should love one another. [12] We should not be like Cain, who was of the evil one and murdered his brother. And why did he murder him? Because his own deeds were evil and his brother's righteous.

Cain, who was of the evil one, a child of the devil, murdered his brother because he was righteous, a child of God.

Though Satan succeeded in bringing about the fall of man, usurping his dominion over the earth and eliminating the first righteous offspring, God raised up another godly line through Seth.

The devil's next strategy to eliminate the godly line almost succeeded and brought about far reaching consequences.

The Rise of the Nephilim

Was there some way to so contaminate the human species that no future godly seed of a woman would be possible? Apparently there was and this is what God's arch enemy sought to do. His strategy? The Nephilim.

Genesis 6:1-7, 11,12 (NIV)

1 When men began to increase in number on the earth and daughters were born to them,
2 the sons of God saw that the daughters of men were beautiful, and they married any of them they chose.
3 Then the Lord said, "My Spirit will not contend with man forever, for he is mortal; his days will be a hundred and twenty years."
4 The Nephilim were on the earth in those days--and also afterward--when the sons of God went to the daughters of men and had children by them. They were the heroes of old, men of renown.
5 The Lord saw how great man's wickedness on the earth had become, and that every inclination of the thoughts of his heart was only evil all the time.
6 The Lord was grieved that he had made man on the earth, and his heart was filled with pain.
7 So the Lord said, "I will wipe mankind, whom I have created, from the face of the earth--men and animals, and creatures that move along the ground, and birds of the air--for I am grieved that I have made them."
11 Now the earth was corrupt in God's sight and was full of violence.
12 God saw how corrupt the earth had become, for all the people on earth had corrupted their ways.

Who or what were these Nephilim? It says they were the offspring of the union of "the sons of God" with "the daughters of men". Who were the sons of God? They are identified in the book of Job:

Job 2:1

Again there was a day when the sons of God came to present themselves before the Lord, and Satan also came among them to present himself before the Lord.

The sons of God are angels. What did they do? They took on human physical forms and had relations with human women. That angels can take on physical appearances is evident by this admonition:

Hebrews 13:2

Do not neglect to show hospitality to strangers, for thereby some have entertained angels unawares.

Peter and Jude speak of judgment on angels in the context of not keeping their proper place and liken their sin to that of Sodom and Gomorrah, an indulging in unnatural sexual desire:

2 Peter 2:4-6

For if God did not spare angels when they sinned, but cast them into hell [Tartaros] and committed them to chains of gloomy darkness to be kept until the judgment; [5] if he did not spare the ancient world, but preserved Noah, a herald of righteousness, with seven others, when he brought a flood upon the world of the ungodly; [6] if by turning the cities of Sodom and Gomorrah to ashes he condemned them to extinction, making them an example of what is going to happen to the ungodly; ...

Jude 1:6-7

And the angels who did not stay within their own position of authority, but left their proper dwelling, he has kept in eternal chains under gloomy darkness until the judgment of the great day— [7] just as Sodom and Gomorrah and the surrounding cities, which likewise indulged in sexual immorality and pursued unnatural desire, serve as an example by undergoing a punishment of eternal fire.

The offspring of these unions were called Nephilim and they were described as the heroes of old, men of renown. They were also noted by their wickedness, corruption and violence. The inclinations of their hearts were only evil continually.

One of the books not included in the Bible, but which had great influence on Judaism is the Book of Enoch. The New Testament writer

Jude acknowledges Enoch, the seventh from Adam as the author. Here is its introduction:

Enoch 1:1-2

The words of the blessing of Enoch, wherewith he blessed the elect and righteous, who will be living in the day of tribulation, when all the wicked and godless are to be removed. And he took up his parable and said --Enoch a righteous man, whose eyes were opened by God, saw the vision of the Holy One in the heavens, which the angels showed me, and from them I heard everything, and from them I understood as I saw, but not for this generation, but for a remote one which is to come.

Peter and Jude quoted from this book and there are multiple phrases from it found in the Bible. Besides the two previous passages just cited in Peter and Jude, here is a direct quote Jude takes from the Book of Enoch:

Jude 1:14-15; (Enoch 1:9)

It was also about these that Enoch, the seventh from Adam, prophesied, saying, "Behold, the Lord came with ten thousands of his holy ones, [15] to execute judgment on all and to convict all the ungodly of all their deeds of ungodliness that they have committed in such an ungodly way, and of all the harsh things that ungodly sinners have spoken against him."

As Enoch lived during the time of the Nephilim, he gives us much more detail regarding these Nephilim and how they came to be:

Enoch 6:1-6; 7:1-6

1. And it came to pass when the children of men had multiplied that in those days were born unto them beautiful and comely daughters. 2. And the angels, the children of the heaven, saw and lusted after them, and said to one another: 'Come, let us choose us wives from among the children of men and beget us children.' 3. And Semjâzâ, who was their leader, said unto them: 'I fear ye will not indeed agree to do this deed, and I alone shall have to pay the penalty of a great sin.' 4. And they all answered him and said: 'Let us all swear an oath, and all bind ourselves by mutual imprecations not to abandon this plan but to do this thing.' 5. Then sware they all together

and bound themselves by mutual imprecations upon it. 6. And they were in all two hundred; who descended [in the days] of Jared on the summit of Mount Hermon, and they called it Mount Hermon, because they had sworn and bound themselves by mutual imprecations upon it.

1. And all the others together with them took unto themselves wives, and each chose for himself one, and they began to go in unto them and to defile themselves with them, and they taught them charms and enchantments, and the cutting of roots, and made them acquainted with plants. 2. And they became pregnant, and they bare great giants, whose height was three thousand ells: 3. Who consumed all the acquisitions of men. And when men could no longer sustain them, 4. the giants turned against them and devoured mankind. 5. And they began to sin against birds, and beasts, and reptiles, and fish, and to devour one another's flesh, and drink the blood. 6. Then the earth laid accusation against the lawless ones.

The Bible and the Book of Enoch are not the only places that record the union of heavenly beings with humans. Many ancient cultures, perhaps the foremost being the Greek one, have what we deem mythological legends of the gods procreating with humans and having mighty offspring such as Hercules. Zeus was said to have married the most beautiful mortal woman, Alcmene who gave birth to Hercules. Hermes ("Messenger of the gods" and called Mercury by the Romans) was said to have been another of Zeus' children who fathered Pan ("all things, all gods"). The original domed Pantheon ("temple for all gods") was built in Rome in 27 BC. This hybrid of angels and humans did not cease with the flood. Indeed, as we will see later, Goliath, the giant whom David killed and many others in Canaan were Nephilim.

As an interesting aside. The text says that Mount Herman was named such because they bound themselves by curses there where these 200 Watcher angels came to comingle with humans. The highest of the three peaks on top of Mount Hermon, which is also the highest mountain in the region, later became the chief temple of the god Baal. Could there be any significance to the fact that this highest peak today is the United Nations' highest permanently manned position in the world?

On the lower slopes of Mount Hermon from which the Jordan River is birthed was the city of Caesarea Philippi. Formerly, its name was Paneas It was the place dedicated to the worship of Pan whose father as we mentioned was Hermes (derived from Hermon?). It was in this city that Jesus asked his disciples who people thought he was. Some thought he was Elijah, others that he was John the Baptist resurrected or one of the prophets. Peter said that Jesus was the Christ, the Son of the living God (Matthew 16:13-16). Note what happened next:

Matthew 17:1-5
And after six days Jesus took with him Peter and James, and John
his brother, and led them up a high mountain by themselves. [2] And
he was transfigured before them, and his face shone like the sun, and
his clothes became white as light. [3] And behold, there appeared to
them Moses and Elijah, talking with him. [4] And Peter said to Jesus,
"Lord, it is good that we are here. If you wish, I will make three tents
here, one for you and one for Moses and one for Elijah." [5] He was
still speaking when, behold, a bright cloud overshadowed them, and a
voice from the cloud said, "This is my beloved Son, with whom I am
well pleased; listen to him."

It is generally thought that Mount Herman, the tallest mountain in Israel, near the borders of Syria and Lebanon, is where Jesus took his three disciples and was transfigured before them. It is as though Jesus stood there in all of his divine splendor and glory to bear witness to the fallen angelic world that he was stepping on their territory and would conquer them.

The angels involved with women were obviously fallen angels, those who had participated with Satan in his rebellion. What effect was there on the human gene pool? While we are not given much information, it can be surmised that the resulting generations of humans would be contaminated in such a way that a natural, 100% human and a godly line without this defect, would be impossible if all the family lines were contaminated by this kind of union.

Satan was almost successful in infecting all the human family lines. But there was one exception:

Genesis 6:8-10
But Noah found favor in the eyes of the Lord.
[9] These are the generations of Noah. Noah was a righteous man,
blameless in his generation. Noah walked with God. [10] And Noah
had three sons, Shem, Ham, and Japheth.

While it may not be conclusive, the word "blameless" in Hebrew is most often translated "without defect" in reference to sacrificial animals needing to be without blemish or defect. If that is the intent of the word here, it would be saying that Noah – and maybe he alone, was the only one left with his family who had not been infected through either direct sexual contact with angels nor had his blood line contaminated with intermarriage with those who had.

Whatever the case, the situation was so grave that God thought it necessary to exterminate all humans save Noah and his family. Again, Satan came close to winning a complete and definitive victory by having all of humanity become his seed, either through fallen angelic procreation or moral wickedness. But God saved a remnant of godly seed alive to begin a new world.

Genesis 6:13-14, 17-18

And God said to Noah, "I have determined to make an end of all flesh, for the earth is filled with violence through them. Behold, I will destroy them with the earth. [14] Make yourself an ark of gopher wood.... [17] For behold, I will bring a flood of waters upon the earth to destroy all flesh in which is the breath of life under heaven. Everything that is on the earth shall die. [18] But I will establish my covenant with you, and you shall come into the ark, you, your sons, your wife, and your sons' wives with you.

Seeds Sown for a Satanic Army

We are told that our primary struggle is against the devil and his unseen forces.

Ephes. 6:10-12

Finally, be strong in the Lord and in the strength of his might. [11] Put on the whole armor of God, that you may be able to stand against the schemes of the devil. [12] For we do not wrestle against flesh and blood, but against the rulers, against the authorities, against the cosmic powers over this present darkness, against the spiritual forces of evil in the heavenly places.

The Bible does not specifically detail the origin of demons. They are different from the fallen angels who operate in the heavenly spheres. Demons seek human or animal bodies to inhabit (Mt. 12:43-45; Lk. 8:30-33) whereas angels can present themselves in human forms when they want.

When the millions of people were destroyed in the flood, the spirits of the Nephilim did not cease to exist. In contrast to the spirits of dead humans who go either to Hades or Paradise until the Judgment Day, it seems they have continued on earth inhabiting humans from generation to generation until the time when they will be judged. In the meantime, their spirits, known as "evil spirits," or "unclean spirits" or "demons" roam here on earth seeking humans to demonize.

Indeed, the Book of Enoch confirms that hypothesis. Enoch records God's judgment on the angels who sinned with these women:

Enoch 15:3-11

3. Wherefore have ye left the high, holy, and eternal heaven, and lain with women, and defiled yourselves with the daughters of men and taken to yourselves wives, and done like the children of earth, and begotten giants (as your) sons? 4. And though ye were holy, spiritual, living the eternal life, you have defiled yourselves with the blood of women, and have begotten (children) with the blood of flesh, and, as the children of men, have lusted after flesh and blood as those [also] do who die and perish. 5. Therefore have I given them wives also that they might impregnate them, and beget children by them, that thus nothing might be wanting to them on earth. 6. But you were [formerly] spiritual, living the eternal life, and immortal for all generations of the world. 7. And therefore I have not appointed wives for you; for as for the spiritual ones of the heaven, in heaven is their dwelling. 8. **And now, the giants, who are produced from the spirits and flesh, shall be called evil spirits upon the earth, and on the earth shall be their dwelling. 9. Evil spirits have proceeded from their bodies; because they are born from men, [[and]] from the holy Watchers is their beginning and primal origin; [they shall be evil spirits on earth, and] evil spirits shall they be called.** [10. As for the spirits of heaven, in heaven shall be their dwelling, but as for the spirits of the earth which were born upon the earth, on the earth shall be their dwelling.] 11. And the spirits of the giants afflict, oppress, destroy, attack, do battle, and work destruction on the earth, and cause trouble: they take no food, [but nevertheless hunger] and thirst, and cause offences. And these spirits shall rise up against the children of men and against the women, because they have proceeded [from them].

The Bible teaches that all humans will be resurrected.

Daniel 12:2

And many of those who sleep in the dust of the earth shall awake, some to everlasting life, and some to shame and everlasting contempt.

While not clear, some scholars believe that the prophet Isaiah spoke of two groups of people: one dying never to live again, and another dying, to be gloriously resurrected. Could it be that the first group, called "lords" who had ruled over them were the Nephilim of old who will not be among those resurrected?

Isaiah 26:13-14

O Lord our God,
other lords besides you have ruled over us,
but your name alone we bring to remembrance.
[14] They are dead, they will not live;
they are shades, they will not arise;
to that end you have visited them with destruction
and wiped out all remembrance of them.

Isaiah 26:19

Your dead shall live; their bodies shall rise.
You who dwell in the dust, awake and sing for joy!
For your dew is a dew of light,
and the earth will give birth to the dead.

Enoch recorded God's judgment on the angels – the Watchers, who had relations with human women. While they would be bound until the day of final judgment when they would be cast into the abyss of fire, the spirits of these Nephilim would be destroyed as cited above in Isaiah 26:14:

Enoch 10:12-15

"...bind them fast for seventy generations in the valleys of the earth, till the day of their judgment and of their consummation, till the judgment that is forever and ever is consummated. 13. In those days they shall be led off to the abyss of fire: 〈and〉 to the torment and the prison in which they shall be confined forever. And whosoever shall be condemned and destroyed will from thenceforth be bound together with them to the end of all generations. 15. **And destroy all**

the spirits of the reprobate and the children of the Watchers, because they have wronged mankind.

In the Apostle's Creed, there is the phrase regarding Jesus: "Was crucified, dead and buried; He descended into hell; The third day he rose again from the dead;" The question is raised regarding where it says in the Bible that he descended into hell and what he did there. We saw the text cited earlier from 2 Peter 2:4 "For if God did not spare angels when they sinned, but cast them into hell [Gk. Tartaros] and committed them to chains of gloomy darkness to be kept until the judgment..." This seems to be the place referred to in the following passage:

1 Peter 3:18-20
For Christ also suffered once for sins, the righteous for the unrighteous, that he might bring us to God, being put to death in the flesh but made alive in the spirit, [19] in which he went and proclaimed to the spirits in prison, [20] because they formerly did not obey, when God's patience waited in the days of Noah, while the ark was being prepared, in which a few, that is, eight persons, were brought safely through water.

It would seem the "spirits in prison" is a reference to the "angels who sinned" being kept in Tartaros, or hell until the day of judgment. He went there to proclaim his triumph and victory over them.

History Repeats Itself

Solomon wrote:

Eccles. 1:9
"What has been is what will be,
and what has been done is what will be done,
and there is nothing new under the sun."

Another way to put it is the refrain, "History repeats itself." The Bible seems to support that general idea. There are numerous times that certain prophecies have dual fulfillments. There is often a type of something or someone, followed by a future antitype. An example of this is the prophecy regarding the "abomination that causes desolation" where God revealed to the prophet Daniel that there would be an event in which the temple sacrifices would cease and the temple would be desecrated (Dan. 8:9-14; 9:27; 11:31-32; 12:11).

That prophecy was fulfilled 400 years later when Antiochus IV Epiphanes, on the fifteenth day of Chislev (December), 167 B.C. set up an altar and idol dedicated to Zeus (Jupiter) in the Jewish temple. Later swine were sacrificed on that altar. Chanukkah is the celebration of the cleansing and rededication of the temple by Judas Maccabeus on December 14, 164 B.C.

However, Jesus said that there would be a future "abomination of desolation" spoken of by the prophet Daniel (Mt. 24:15).

I make this point so that as one reflects on past historical events, one is given some clues as to future events. For example, God destroyed the world by a flood because of the wickedness of mankind, though he saved righteous Noah and his family. The Bible says that though God will not again destroy the world by a flood, there is a coming Day of Judgment on the earth.

Jesus said,

Luke 17:26-30

"Just as it was in the days of Noah, so will it be in the days of the Son of Man. [27] They were eating and drinking and marrying and being given in marriage, until the day when Noah entered the ark, and the flood came and destroyed them all. [28] Likewise, just as it was in the days of Lot—they were eating and drinking, buying and selling, planting and building, [29] but on the day when Lot went out from Sodom, fire and sulfur rained from heaven and destroyed them all—[30] so will it be on the day when the Son of Man is revealed."

Could it be that Jesus is giving us a clue that there will once again be a presence of Nephilim on the earth when he returns? Could the whole UFO phenomena and reports of alien abductions be a repeat of these fallen angelic beings seeking to reinsert themselves into humanity?

3 IDENTIFICATION OF THE GODLY LINE

THOUGH NOAH WAS a righteous man, he was not sinless and the Bible reveals how events surrounding his drunkenness and his son Ham gazing on his nakedness led to one of his grandsons being cursed – Canaan (Gen 9:18-27). Chapter 10 of Genesis records for us the descendants of Noah's three sons, Shem, Ham and Japheth, establishing a table of 72 nations or people groups that began to spread throughout the earth.

The enmity between Satan's seed and the seed of the woman resumed right after the flood. The descendants of Ham – Cush (Sudan), Egypt, Put (Libya) and Canaan (Palestine) and their offspring (settling in areas of Arabia, Iran, Iraq, Syria, Lebanon) eventually had conflict with the offspring of Shem.

The first person of note mentioned in the genealogy was Nimrod.

Genesis 10:8-11

Cush fathered Nimrod; he was the first on earth to be a mighty man. [9] He was a mighty hunter before the Lord. Therefore it is said, "Like Nimrod a mighty hunter before the Lord." [10] The beginning of his kingdom was Babel, Erech, Accad, and Calneh, in the land of Shinar. [11] From that land he went into Assyria and built Nineveh,

Josephus wrote this of Nimrod:

2. "Now it was Nimrod who excited them to such an affront and contempt of God. He was the grandson of Ham, the son of Noah, a bold man, and of great strength of hand. He persuaded them not to ascribe it to God, as if it was through his means they were happy, but to believe that it was their own courage which procured that happiness. He also gradually changed the government into tyranny, seeing no other way of turning men from the fear of God, but to bring them into a constant dependence on his power. He also said he would be revenged on God, if he should have a mind to drown the world again; for that he would build a tower too high for the waters to be able to reach! and that he would avenge himself on God for destroying their forefathers!"[5]

The verb form of the name Nimrod – "nimrodh" means "let us revolt". The word hunter – "tsayid" can mean one who hunts animals or one who hunts men, to enslave them. Nimrod became one who became a mighty tyrant who built Babel (later to be Babylon) as a symbol of revolt against God. When God confused the languages, the project to build a tower to heaven to make a name for themselves in independence from God was abandoned (Gen. 11:1-9). Nimrod then went and built Nineveh, which later became the capital of Assyria. Both cities, Babylon and Nineveh later became the capitals of empires that sought to destroy the people of the godly line.

It is perhaps significant that the word used to describe Nimrod as a "mighty" (Heb. "gibbor") man, hunter, is the same word used to describe the Nephilim in:

Genesis 6:4

The Nephilim were on the earth in those days, and also afterward, when the sons of God came in to the daughters of man and they bore children to them. These were the mighty men who were of old, the men of renown.

It is also the word used to describe the giant Goliath whom David killed (1 Samuel 17:51 – translated "champion"). Could Nimrod have been another Nephilim? If so, how did he get there?

As mentioned, it is unlikely that other angels risked repeating what the Watchers had done. Rob Skiba suggests that while Noah, his wife and children were of a pure line, it is possible that the wife of Ham and possibly the wife of Japheth may have carried Nephilim genes.[6] The

---

[5] Flavius Josephus, Antiquities of the Jews (Grand Rapids, MI: Kregel Publications, 1960), Book 1, Chapter 4, Section 2

[6] http://www.youtube.com/watch?v=FOECn1ZAWu0&feature=related

references to these Nephilim or giants after the flood all seem to come from the line of Ham (Gen. 10:6-20; Num. 13:32-33; 1 Chron. 20:4-8; Dt. 3:11; Am. 2:9).

The Temptation of Secret Knowledge

But is there more to the Tower of Babel that caused God to confuse the languages than just that they were unified and making a name for themselves in independence from God and not filling the earth as He had commanded?

While this is speculation on my part, I would suggest that there was another reason.

What was the devil's temptation to Eve?

Genesis 3:5-6

For God knows that when you eat of it your eyes will be opened, and you will be like God, knowing good and evil." [6] So when the woman saw that the tree was good for food, and that it was a delight to the eyes, and that the tree was to be desired to make one wise, she took of its fruit and ate, and she also gave some to her husband who was with her, and he ate.

The aspect of being like God that appealed to her was that of knowledge – "knowing good and evil." Was Satan making up the story about becoming like God and knowing good and evil? No.

Genesis 3:22-23

Then the Lord God said, "Behold, the man has become like one of us in knowing good and evil. Now, lest he reach out his hand and take also of the tree of life and eat, and live forever—" [23] therefore the Lord God sent him out from the garden of Eden to work the ground from which he was taken.

The Book of Enoch presents one of the key reasons that God's wrath came upon the angels who comingled with humans:

Enoch 8; 9:1, 4, 6; 10:1, 6-8

1. And Azâzêl taught men to make swords, and knives, and shields, and breastplates, and made known to them the metals of the earth and the art of working them, and bracelets, and ornaments, and the use of antimony, and the beautifying of the eyelids, and all kinds

of costly stones, and all colouring tinctures. 2. And there arose much godlessness, and they committed fornication, and they were led astray, and became corrupt in all their ways. Semjâzâ taught enchantments, and root-cuttings, Armârôs the resolving of enchantments, Barâqîjâl, (taught) astrology, Kôkabêl the constellations, Ezêqêêl the knowledge of the clouds, Araqiêl the signs of the earth, Shamsiêl the signs of the sun, and Sariêl the course of the moon. And as men perished, they cried, and their cry went up to heaven . . .

1. And then Michael, Uriel, Raphael, and Gabriel looked down from heaven and saw much blood being shed upon the earth, and all lawlessness being wrought upon the earth. 4. And they said to the Lord of the ages: 'Lord of lords, God of gods, King of kings, and God of the age, 6. **Thou seest what Azâzêl hath done, who hath taught all unrighteousness on earth and revealed the eternal secrets which were (preserved) in heaven, which men were striving to learn**:

1. Then said the Most High, the Holy and Great One spake, … heal the earth which the angels have corrupted, …**that all the children of men may not perish through all the secret things that the Watchers have disclosed and have taught their sons.** 8. And the whole earth has been corrupted through the works that were taught by Azâzêl: to him ascribe all sin.'

What the angelic beings did was to teach the humans eternal secrets preserved in heaven that God had not meant for them to know because the result was further wickedness and man's destruction.

My guess is that Nimrod, one of the post-flood Nephilim, was building a tower, which many scholars think was in the form of a Babylonian Ziggurat temple, for the purpose of accessing the heavenly angelic spheres in order to gain secret knowledge. What was God's reaction to their endeavor?

Genesis 11:5-7

And the Lord came down to see the city and the tower, which the children of man had built. [6] And the Lord said, "Behold, they are one people, and they have all one language, and this is only the beginning of what they will do. **And nothing that they propose to do will now be impossible for them.** [7] Come, let us go down and there confuse their language, so that they may not understand one another's speech."

An angel told the prophet Daniel that at the time of the end, knowledge would increase (Dan. 12:4). We have certainly seen that reality in the past century and knowledge is said to be increasing at exponential rates today. There are secret organizations like the Illuminati and the Freemasons who tout having access to hidden knowledge. Their cryptic symbols are everywhere – the American dollar bill, the US Capital Building, the Washington Monument and other places too numerous to mention.

As mentioned previously, Jesus said that the time of the end before his coming would be as the days of Noah. Part of what brought great destruction to the world was the secret knowledge that the fallen angels imparted to humans. Could that be happening in some way even now? Certainly much of our modern technologies, while having beneficial applications, have also been used for great destruction and evil. Could the great appeal of the future Antichrist be that of disclosing secret knowledge and power to those who pledge their loyalty to him? Might he even present himself as a far more advanced being from another planet coming to "enlighten" mankind?

Lest we think that God is opposed to men gaining knowledge, it is good to remind ourselves that the source of the knowledge and intent of the one revealing it is important. While Satan's intent is for the hidden knowledge to result in destruction, note the contrasting intent and source of God's knowledge:

Col. 2:2-3

that their hearts may be encouraged, being knit together in love, to reach all the riches of full assurance of understanding and the knowledge of God's mystery, which is Christ, [3] in whom are hidden all the treasures of wisdom and knowledge.

Let's get back to tracing the godly line, however.

From the descendants of Shem, there came a man named Terah, **who like so many of all the descendants of Noah, had the knowledge** of God's dealing with Noah, but was a worshiper of idols (Josh. 24:2). Was there anyone through whom a godly line could produce the One who would crush Satan? Here we see how God sovereignly chooses a person. This person was to be claimed as the father of the three great monotheistic religions – Judaism, Christianity and Islam.

God made a special covenant with him which further defined the conflict of the ages – the conflict between Satan's seed and the seed of the woman.

Abraham

Genesis 12:1-3
Now the Lord said to Abram, "Go from your country and your kindred and your father's house to the land that I will show you. [2] And I will make of you a great nation, and I will bless you and make your name great, so that you will be a blessing. [3] I will bless those who bless you, and him who dishonors you I will curse, and in you all the families of the earth shall be blessed."

In addition to this seven part blessing, God included additional promises. He would have innumerable offspring, the land of Canaan would be his and his offspring's as an everlasting possession and God would be his and his offspring's God forever.

Genesis 13:14-16
The Lord said to Abram, after Lot had separated from him, "Lift up your eyes and look from the place where you are, northward and southward and eastward and westward, [15] for all the land that you see I will give to you and to your offspring forever. [16] I will make your offspring as the dust of the earth, so that if one can count the dust of the earth, your offspring also can be counted.

Genesis 15:5
And he brought him outside and said, "Look toward heaven, and number the stars, if you are able to number them." Then he said to him, "So shall your offspring be."

Genesis 17:1-8
When Abram was ninety-nine years old the Lord appeared to Abram and said to him, "I am God Almighty; walk before me, and be blameless, [2] that I may make my covenant between me and you, and may multiply you greatly." [3] Then Abram fell on his face. And God said to him, [4] "Behold, my covenant is with you, and you shall be the father of a multitude of nations. [5] No longer shall your name be called Abram, but your name shall be Abraham, for I have made you the father of a multitude of nations. [6] I will make you exceedingly

fruitful, and I will make you into nations, and kings shall come from you. [7] And I will establish my covenant between me and you and your offspring after you throughout their generations for an everlasting covenant, to be God to you and to your offspring after you. [8] And I will give to you and to your offspring after you the land of your sojournings, all the land of Canaan, for an everlasting possession, and I will be their God."

God's covenant required something of Abraham, however.

Circumcision

Genesis 17:9-10

And God said to Abraham, "As for you, you shall keep my covenant, you and your offspring after you throughout their generations. [10] This is my covenant, which you shall keep, between me and you and your offspring after you: Every male among you shall be circumcised.

This outward act of the removal of the male's foreskin was to symbolize a deeper inward spiritual reality. It symbolized the removal of uncleanness – the removal of sin. God had told Abraham to be blameless. How can a sinful person be blameless? The secret is given in Abraham's response to what God had promised.

Abraham was getting old and his wife was barren and also old. God had promised him innumerable offspring, yet they had no child. Years had gone by since the time of God's promise and humanly speaking it would be impossible to happen. Note the secret to Abraham's being called "righteous".

Faith

Genesis 15:1-6

After these things the word of the Lord came to Abram in a vision: "Fear not, Abram, I am your shield; your reward shall be very great." [2] But Abram said, "O Lord GOD, what will you give me, for I continue childless, and the heir of my house is Eliezer of Damascus?" [3] And Abram said, "Behold, you have given me no offspring, and a member of my household will be my heir." [4] And behold, the word of the Lord came to him: "This man shall not be your heir; your very own son shall be your heir." [5] And he brought him outside and said,

"Look toward heaven, and number the stars, if you are able to number them." Then he said to him, "So shall your offspring be." [6] **And he believed the Lord, and he counted it to him as righteousness.**

Abraham was counted as righteous, blameless, accepted by God because he believed the Lord and that what he had promised he would fulfill. That faith was what made him righteous. The New Testament explains the connection of this with circumcision.

Romans 4:11-12

He received the sign of circumcision as a seal of the righteousness that he had by faith while he was still uncircumcised. The purpose was to make him the father of all who believe without being circumcised, so that righteousness would be counted to them as well, [12] and to make him the father of the circumcised who are not merely circumcised but who also walk in the footsteps of the faith that our father Abraham had before he was circumcised.

It was not just the outward act of circumcision that made Abraham's offspring acceptable to God, it was the inward reality of the faith that validated the symbol. Moses explained to the people that it was a matter of the heart.

Deut. 10:12-16

"And now, Israel, what does the Lord your God require of you, but to fear the Lord your God, to walk in all his ways, to love him, to serve the Lord your God with all your heart and with all your soul, [13] and to keep the commandments and statutes of the Lord, which I am commanding you today for your good? [14] Behold, to the Lord your God belong heaven and the heaven of heavens, the earth with all that is in it. [15] Yet the Lord set his heart in love on your fathers and chose their offspring after them, you above all peoples, as you are this day. [16] Circumcise therefore the foreskin of your heart, and be no longer stubborn.

The New Testament confirms that being a physical descendant of Abraham and being outwardly circumcised is not what makes a person a real Jew. Again, it is a matter of the heart.

Romans 2:28-29

For no one is a Jew who is merely one outwardly, nor is circumcision outward and physical. [29] But a Jew is one inwardly, and circumcision is a matter of the heart, by the Spirit, not by the letter. His praise is not from man but from God.

New Target

Now that God had identified Abraham as the line though which the seed of the woman would come and through whom all the nations of the world would be blessed, Satan's target was narrowed and defined. He would use whatever means possible, including people's own personal weaknesses, to try to destroy Abraham, keep him from having an offspring through Sarah and if that didn't succeed, destroy that offspring.

Four temptations illustrate the enemy's strategy. The first was a famine that caused Abram to go down to Egypt. Because Sarai his wife was so beautiful, he was afraid that he would be killed so they could take her, so he told her to say that she was his sister. She ended up in the Pharaoh's harem. But God protected them and afflicted Pharaoh and his house with great plagues because of Sarai until he understood that she was Abram's and could not have her (Genesis 12:10-20).

Years later Abraham yielded to fear again in the same way with another ruler – Abimelech who also took Sarah into his house. But God warned him in a dream that he would be a dead man if he touched her, because she was Abraham's wife (Genesis 20:1-18). In both of these cases, had these kings succeeded in having relations with her, the promised seed to Abraham through Sarah would have been jeopardized.

Disobedience on Abraham's part brought about another future serious pitfall. God had told him to leave his relatives and household in Ur – the area today known as Iraq, and move to the land of Canaan (today, Israel). Instead, he took his nephew Lot with him. Conflict between their herdsmen, because they both became very wealthy and had large flocks, caused them to separate, Lot choosing the rich, fertile land of Sodom in the Jordan valley, leaving Abraham the less desirable land of the hills. Lot's choice to settle in a wicked city led to his losing everything when Sodom and Gomorrah were destroyed by God. His two surviving daughters after getting him drunk initiated incestuous relations with him, producing Moab and Ammon, whose descendants settled on the east side of the Jordan River and were later to become bitter enemies of Abraham's offspring (Genesis 13, 19).

The most serious consequence of Abraham and Sarah's temporary lapse of faith was Sarah's giving Abraham her Egyptian maid Hagar in order to raise up offspring through her. The result of that union was

Ishmael, the father of the Arabs with whom the Jews have had conflict to this day. Repeatedly down through history, the Arabs have tried to annihilate their half brothers, the Jews. What the angel told Hagar regarding her son can be seen in its fulfillment even today.

Genesis 16:10-12 (NIV)
10 The angel added, "I will so increase your descendants that they will be too numerous to count."
11 The angel of the Lord also said to her: "You are now with child and you will have a son. You shall name him Ishmael, for the Lord has heard of your misery.
12 He will be a wild donkey of a man; his hand will be against everyone and everyone's hand against him, and he will live in hostility toward all his brothers."

Satan used these four moments of weakness on Abraham and Sarah's part to attempt either to keep the promised offspring from coming or setting up seeds of future generations (Moab, Ammon, Ishmael) that would seek to destroy Abraham and Sarah's promised offspring.

The Bible does not say this and so this is pure speculation on my part. Many physical defects, though not all, are attributed in the New Testament to demonic causes. One of a number of examples is when Jesus healed a man who was blind and mute by casting a demon out of him so that he was able to both see and speak (Luke 12:22).

Could it be that Sarai's barrenness was demonically caused so as to thwart God's plan to raise up the godly seed through her line and to keep God's promise to them from being fulfilled? If so, the God of Abraham, Isaac and Jacob – Yahováh - is the same God of power as the God and Father of Jesus Christ. The Hebrew God of the *Tanakh* was able to release those whose physical defects were demonically caused as he likewise did in the New Testament.

A Four Hundred Year Head Start

When God cut a covenant with Abram, he revealed to him something regarding the future of his offspring, which enabled Satan to get a head start in laying plans to keep them from possessing the land promised to them and to try to eliminate them.

Genesis 15:12-16
As the sun was going down, a deep sleep fell on Abram. And

behold, dreadful and great darkness fell upon him. [13] Then the Lord said to Abram, "Know for certain that your offspring will be sojourners in a land that is not theirs and will be servants there, and they will be afflicted for four hundred years. [14] But I will bring judgment on the nation that they serve, and afterward they shall come out with great possessions. [15] As for yourself, you shall go to your fathers in peace; you shall be buried in a good old age. [16] And they shall come back here in the fourth generation, for the iniquity of the Amorites is not yet complete."

We will develop more on this later, but first a couple more important historical foundations.

The Godly Line Further Defined

Abraham and Sarah's miracle child, Isaac – born when he was one hundred years old and she ninety – married Rebekah through whom twins were born, Esau and Jacob. While both were born through the godly line, there was a fork in the road. God chose the one who came second out of the womb rather than the first. This election of God seems unfair for many people, but Scripture presents it as God's sovereign choice.

Romans 9:6-13

... For not all who are descended from Israel belong to Israel, [7] and not all are children of Abraham because they are his offspring, but "Through Isaac shall your offspring be named." [8] This means that it is not the children of the flesh who are the children of God, but the children of the promise are counted as offspring. [9] For this is what the promise said: "About this time next year I will return and Sarah shall have a son." [10] And not only so, but also when Rebecca had conceived children by one man, our forefather Isaac, [11] though they were not yet born and had done nothing either good or bad—in order that God's purpose of election might continue, not because of works but because of his call— [12] she was told, "The older will serve the younger." [13] As it is written, "Jacob I loved, but Esau I hated."

Rebekah and Jacob's trying to fulfill God's promise that Jacob would receive the birthright of the firstborn instead of Esau through deceit and trickery almost cost Jacob his life. When Esau found out that Jacob had stolen the blessing of their father Isaac, he determined he would kill Jacob and Jacob had to flee for his life (cf. Gen. 25:19-34; 27:1-45).

Esau, otherwise known as Edom, settled to the south and east of the Dead Sea, in what today is known as Jordan and extending all the way into Saudi Arabia. Besides marrying two Hittite women, Esau also married a daughter of Ishmael, thus having his offspring become part of the Arab peoples. The descendants of Esau came to be bitter enemies of their brothers, the Jews, and that animosity extends to this day.

Jacob ended up with twelve sons who became known as the Patriarchs of the twelve tribes of Israel. In an encounter with God, Jacob's name was changed to Israel (Gen. 32:22-31). In another attempt to eliminate the godly seed, a severe famine came to the land. However, God again was a step ahead of Satan and intervened by sending a savior ahead of time to Egypt.

Joseph, Jacob's favorite son caused jealousy among his brothers and they sold him into slavery to Egypt. After a time of suffering as a slave and in prison through a false accusation, his gift of interpreting dreams brought him before Pharaoh and he was able to interpret a God-given dream to Pharaoh warning him of the impending famine. Through Joseph's wisdom, they were able to plan accordingly and store up enough grain to weather the seven years of famine and save not only the Egyptians, but also Joseph's family, the sons and families of Israel (Gen. 37-50).

4 THE SAVIOURS

ONE OF THE common themes in the Bible is that God periodically sends saviours to save his people from an impending danger or from tyranny and dominance over them by a foreign power. Repeatedly, however, these saviours have been initially rejected by the very people they were raised to save.

As God had revealed to Abraham, his offspring would be sojourners in a land that was not theirs and they would become slaves and be afflicted for four hundred years. Abraham had Isaac who had the twins, Jacob and Esau. Jacob was the chosen line and he had twelve sons. His favorite son, Joseph had dreams indicating that his brothers and even parents would bow down to him in the future. As we mentioned in the last chapter, because of their jealousy of Joseph, his brothers sold him into slavery in Egypt.

As you can read in the book of Genesis, Joseph went from the prison to the palace as a result of being able to interpret the Pharaoh's dream which warned of a coming seven year famine. God had sent Joseph to Egypt to prepare the country for that famine so that the people, including those of his own family, would be saved.

Joseph became the second in command over Egypt and moved his father and his brothers and their families to Egypt in order to provide for them during the time of famine. However, a new Pharaoh arose who did not know Joseph and rather than being grateful for his having saved his people, Pharaoh became afraid of their multiplication and made slaves out of the descendants of Israel.

Egypt became the first of seven world Empires or Kingdoms that Satan would use to try to annihilate the godly line (Rev. 12; 17:7-14).

Their servitude did not allay the Pharaoh's fears of their numbers and so he instructed that all male Hebrew babies be put to death (Ex. 1). However, God again intervened, preparing another saviour – Moses, by having him adopted into Pharaoh's family (Ex. 2).

At the age of forty, Moses sought to rescue his people, but his own people rejected him and said, "Who made you ruler and judge over us?" (Ex. 2). He ended up having to escape Egypt and spent forty years in the desert tending sheep.

When he was eighty, God revealed himself to Moses as YHVH, or Yahováh and instructed him to go and be God's human instrument to deliver his people from bondage. God would give him power to perform miracles to persuade Pharaoh to let the people of Israel go, but God himself would harden Pharaoh's heart so that he would not let the people go until God's glory would be manifested over the demonic gods of the Egyptians (Ex. 3-4).

The Bible says that when people sacrifice to idols, they are in fact sacrificing to demons (Dt. 32:17; Ps. 106:37).

1 Cor. 10:19-20

"What do I imply then? That food offered to idols is anything, or that an idol is anything? [20] No, I imply that what pagans sacrifice they offer to demons and not to God. I do not want you to be participants with demons."

I will briefly interject a side comment here. We have seen a number of families who have experienced demonic oppression and activity in their homes (constant sicknesses, fears, inability to sleep or to prosper, conflicts, TVs turning themselves on, shadows flitting about, odors and winds moving through the closed house, unseen hands choking people etc.).

In almost every occasion, they have had some sort of idols or pictures of idols or saints in their houses. When they burned them or threw them out and their house was prayed through using the name of Jesus Christ, each time these symptoms all ceased. Having objects of worship, even from ancient cultures and regardless of whether the person worships them or not, opens the door to demonic oppression.

God showed his power and glory over Satan and his demons through the ten plagues, each of them falling on areas of life supposedly protected by Egypt's gods. The tenth and final plague was the killing of the firstborn of every family and animal in Egypt. Through that plague, God instituted a memorial celebration, observed each year by Jews since that time. It is called the Passover. At God's instruction, an innocent, unblemished lamb was to be killed and its blood sprinkled on the doorposts of each Hebrew home. When the angel of death came that night to kill each firstborn, he passed over the homes of those who had the blood of the lamb applied to their doorposts.

This event was to become a picture of what God would do in the future by providing his Son as a Passover lamb, whose blood would be shed on Passover so that those who applied it to themselves by faith, would have the angel of death pass over them.

As God had told Abraham, his descendants would leave the country not their own with great possessions. The Egyptians, after losing their firstborns, could not have them leave fast enough. They showered them with gold and silver and many valuable possessions, perhaps seeking to make up for their guilt of having had them work as slaves for so many generations.

Satan did not give up so easily in his attempt to annihilate or maintain in slavery the line through which the seed of the woman would come to deal him a mortal blow. When Pharaoh realized the full implications of having several million slaves leave his country, he gathered his army and chased them, trapping the Hebrews between mountains on the sides and the Red Sea in front. Again, God showed his power on behalf of his chosen people by opening the sea and having the Israelis walk through on dry ground. When the Egyptian army followed, the sea closed over them, drowning them all (Ex. 14).

God demonstrated his power again on behalf of his people by feeding them with manna and bringing water out of the rocks for what ended up being a period of forty years as they wandered through the wilderness.

The Law

At Mount Sinai, God entered into a covenant relationship with Israel as a nation, giving them the law through Moses. The law was much more than the Ten Commandments. Jewish scholars say there are 613 laws in the Torah – the first five books of Moses. That law was divided into three parts: the moral, ceremonial and civil law.

The most well known part of the law today is the moral law of which the Ten Commandments are a part. They are found listed in two biblical passages, Exodus 20:1-17; Deuteronomy 5:6-21. In summarized form they are as follows:

Ten Commandments

1. You shall have no other gods besides me.
2. You shall not make any images to bow before or serve.
3. You shall not take the name of the Lord your God in vain.
4. Remember the Sabbath day, to keep it holy. Six days are for labor, but on the seventh no labor is to be done.
5. Honor your father and your mother.
6. You shall not murder.
7. You shall not commit adultery.
8. You shall not steal.
9. You shall not bear false witness against your neighbor.
10. You shall not covet.

The ceremonial law prescribed the tabernacle and later temple worship. Laws regarding sacrifices, priests, what was clean and unclean and various Feast Days that were to be celebrated were given in detail. There were seven yearly Feasts and Celebrations that were to be observed by the people of God. These Festivals were to be pictures of a future fulfillment by the Messiah which we will see later. They are listed in Leviticus 23:

Festivals

Passover or Pesach - 14 Nisan (Mar. or Apr.)
Unleavened Bread or Hag HaMatzot - 15-21 Nisan (Mar. or Apr.)
First Fruits or Yom HaBikkurim - 16 Nisan (March or April)
Feast of Weeks or Pentecost or Shavuot - 6 Sivan (May or June)
Feast of Trumpets or Rosh HaShanah - 1 Tishri (Sept. or Oct.)
Day of Atonement or Yom Kippur - 10 Tishri (Sept. or Oct.)
Feast of Booths (Tabernacles) or Sukkot - 15-21 Tishri (Sept./ Oct)[7]

The civil laws were those laws used to govern a society, outlining penalties for infractions of the law and setting up a court system.

The Chosen People

They were to be a unique people in all the earth, chosen by God.

---

[7] Feasts & Holidays of the Bible (Torrance, CA: Rose Publishing, Inc. 2004)

Exodus 19:5-6

"Now therefore, if you will indeed obey my voice and keep my covenant, you shall be my treasured possession among all peoples, for all the earth is mine; [6] and you shall be to me a kingdom of priests and a holy nation."

Deut. 7:6-11

"For you are a people holy to the Lord your God. The Lord your God has chosen you to be a people for his treasured possession, out of all the peoples who are on the face of the earth. [7] It was not because you were more in number than any other people that the Lord set his love on you and chose you, for you were the fewest of all peoples, [8] but it is because the Lord loves you and is keeping the oath that he swore to your fathers, that the Lord has brought you out with a mighty hand and redeemed you from the house of slavery, from the hand of Pharaoh king of Egypt. [9] Know therefore that the Lord your God is God, the faithful God who keeps covenant and steadfast love with those who love him and keep his commandments, to a thousand generations, [10] and repays to their face those who hate him, by destroying them. He will not be slack with one who hates him. He will repay him to his face. [11] You shall therefore be careful to do the commandment and the statutes and the rules that I command you today."

The fact that the Jewish people were specially chosen by God brought upon them a unique weight of responsibility. Not only were they specially targeted by Satan for destruction, but God held them to a higher standard than the other peoples of the world, because they were to represent Him. They were to be a kingdom of priests – representing God to the world and thus were to be a holy nation, and they were to seek to bring the world to God.

Because of this unique relationship with God, they were promised special blessings if they would observe his commandments. However, there would be severe curses for disobedience. The blessings and curses are recorded in Deuteronomy 28.

Deut. 28:1-25

"And if you faithfully obey the voice of the Lord your God, being careful to do all his commandments that I command you today, the Lord your God will set you high above all the nations of the earth. [2]

And all these blessings shall come upon you and overtake you, if you obey the voice of the Lord your God. [3] Blessed shall you be in the city, and blessed shall you be in the field. [4] Blessed shall be the fruit of your womb and the fruit of your ground and the fruit of your cattle, the increase of your herds and the young of your flock. [5] Blessed shall be your basket and your kneading bowl. [6] Blessed shall you be when you come in, and blessed shall you be when you go out.

[7] "The Lord will cause your enemies who rise against you to be defeated before you. They shall come out against you one way and flee before you seven ways. [8] The Lord will command the blessing on you in your barns and in all that you undertake. And he will bless you in the land that the Lord your God is giving you. [9] The Lord will establish you as a people holy to himself, as he has sworn to you, if you keep the commandments of the Lord your God and walk in his ways. [10] And all the peoples of the earth shall see that you are called by the name of the Lord, and they shall be afraid of you. [11] And the Lord will make you abound in prosperity, in the fruit of your womb and in the fruit of your livestock and in the fruit of your ground, within the land that the Lord swore to your fathers to give you. [12] The Lord will open to you his good treasury, the heavens, to give the rain to your land in its season and to bless all the work of your hands. And you shall lend to many nations, but you shall not borrow. [13] And the Lord will make you the head and not the tail, and you shall only go up and not down, if you obey the commandments of the Lord your God, which I command you today, being careful to do them, [14] and if you do not turn aside from any of the words that I command you today, to the right hand or to the left, to go after other gods to serve them.

The first 14 verses of the chapter give the blessings for obedience. The next 54 verses outline the curses that would come on them for disobedience. I have just included the first 10 verses to give a sampling of the woe that would come to them for disobedience.

[15] "But if you will not obey the voice of the Lord your God or be careful to do all his commandments and his statutes that I command you today, then all these curses shall come upon you and overtake you. [16] Cursed shall you be in the city, and cursed shall you be in the field. [17] Cursed shall be your basket and your kneading bowl. [18] Cursed shall be the fruit of your womb and the fruit of your

ground, the increase of your herds and the young of your flock. [19] Cursed shall you be when you come in, and cursed shall you be when you go out.

[20] "The Lord will send on you curses, confusion, and frustration in all that you undertake to do, until you are destroyed and perish quickly on account of the evil of your deeds, because you have forsaken me. [21] The Lord will make the pestilence stick to you until he has consumed you off the land that you are entering to take possession of it. [22] The Lord will strike you with wasting disease and with fever, inflammation and fiery heat, and with drought and with blight and with mildew. They shall pursue you until you perish. [23] And the heavens over your head shall be bronze, and the earth under you shall be iron. [24] The Lord will make the rain of your land powder. From heaven dust shall come down on you until you are destroyed.

[25] "The Lord will cause you to be defeated before your enemies. You shall go out one way against them and flee seven ways before them. And you shall be a horror to all the kingdoms of the earth.

Self Destruction

While Satan had worked through the Egyptian Pharaoh to seek to destroy the godly seed, he had help through the nature of the very people he was trying to destroy. Because of Adam's rebellion, the sin nature was passed on to all mankind and the Hebrews were no exception. They brought upon themselves destruction as a consequence of their own sin and rebellion.

The Torah records how the people's grumbling and complaining, their making a golden calf to worship while Moses was on Mt. Sinai meeting with God, and their rebelling against Moses and Aaron's leadership, all brought God's wrath on them resulting in thousands dying.

The Four Hundred Year Preparation Put to the Test

We mentioned earlier that Satan was aware of the promise made to Abraham that his descendants would be in bondage in another land for 400 years after which they would return and take all the land of Canaan that God had promised to Abraham and his descendants as an everlasting possession.

The devil used a four-fold strategy. He planted Nephilim in the land

– those offspring of fallen angels with human women. As before the flood, the idea was to infect the population with a DNA that would corrupt the human line. The second part of the strategy was to make those inhabitants of the land so strong, especially with the help of these Nephilim, that the Israelis would not be able to defeat them. Third, they were huge and intimidating. Og, king of Bashan (area today known as the Golan Heights) had an iron bed that was 5 meters (16 feet) long and 1,8 meters (6 feet) wide (Dt. 3:11). Their size along with the strong fortified cities would instill fear in the Hebrews and discourage them from attacking. The last part of the strategy, in case the former three did not work, was to cause the people to be so wicked that when the Jews conquered the land, their intermarriage with the people would corrupt them so that God himself would have to destroy them.

The strategy worked, at least for a while. Moses sent out twelve spies, one from each tribe, to spy out the land. After 40 days they returned. Two of the spies, Joshua and Caleb, encouraged the people to go up and take the land because God had promised it to them, but ten of the spies were filled with fear and discouraged the people from going forward.

Numbers 13:30-33

But Caleb quieted the people before Moses and said, "Let us go up at once and occupy it, for we are well able to overcome it." [31] Then the men who had gone up with him said, "We are not able to go up against the people, for they are stronger than we are." [32] So they brought to the people of Israel a bad report of the land that they had spied out, saying, "The land, through which we have gone to spy it out, is a land that devours its inhabitants, and all the people that we saw in it are of great height. [33] And there we saw the Nephilim (the sons of Anak, who come from the Nephilim), and we seemed to ourselves like grasshoppers, and so we seemed to them."

Numbers 14:1-4

Then all the congregation raised a loud cry, and the people wept that night. [2] And all the people of Israel grumbled against Moses and Aaron. The whole congregation said to them, "Would that we had died in the land of Egypt! Or would that we had died in this wilderness! [3] Why is the Lord bringing us into this land, to fall by the sword? Our wives and our little ones will become a prey. Would it not be better for us to go back to Egypt?" [4] And they said to one another, "Let us choose a leader and go back to Egypt."

God's anger was kindled against them. The writer of the book of Hebrews uses that incident to warn us today:

Hebrews 3:7-12
Therefore, as the Holy Spirit says,

"Today, if you hear his voice,
[8] do not harden your hearts as in the rebellion,
on the day of testing in the wilderness,
[9] where your fathers put me to the test
and saw my works [10] for forty years.
Therefore I was provoked with that generation,
and said, 'They always go astray in their heart;
they have not known my ways.'
[11] As I swore in my wrath,
'They shall not enter my rest.' "
[12] Take care, brothers, lest there be in any of you an evil, unbelieving heart, leading you to fall away from the living God.

God's judgment on them was that they would wander through the wilderness for forty years – a year for each day they were spying the land, and that all those 20 years old and up would die in the desert, except Joshua and Caleb. Why?

Hebrews 3:16-19
For who were those who heard and yet rebelled? Was it not all
those who left Egypt led by Moses? [17] And with whom was he
provoked for forty years? Was it not with those who sinned, whose
bodies fell in the wilderness? [18] And to whom did he swear that
they would not enter his rest, but to those who were disobedient? [19]
So we see that they were unable to enter because of unbelief.

It was their unbelief in the promises of God that he would go before them and give into their hand the inhabitants of Canaan. It was unbelief that they would inherit the land. This is a good place to pause and relate one of the most important verses in the Bible:

Hebrews 11:6
And without faith it is impossible to please him, for whoever would draw near to God must believe that he exists and that he rewards those who seek him.

Total Destruction of the Inhabitants of the Land

One of the aspects of the Bible that many modern day people have problems with is God's instruction to the Hebrews to utterly destroy the people of the land of Canaan. That seems so cruel and unfair, we think. But there were at least three good reasons for this instruction.

First, God could not risk allowing the seed of his people to be contaminated with the DNA of the Nephilim, as had almost happened before the flood. Secondly, the people were extremely wicked and their evil had to be dealt with. Their religion would call for them to engage in sexual orgies at their temples and to sacrifice their children alive in the fire to their deity. The third reason, mentioned below, was for the Israelites own self preservation:

Deut. 7:1-6

"When the Lord your God brings you into the land that you are entering to take possession of it, and clears away many nations before you, the Hittites, the Girgashites, the Amorites, the Canaanites, the Perizzites, the Hivites, and the Jebusites, seven nations more numerous and mightier than yourselves, [2] and when the Lord your God gives them over to you, and you defeat them, then you must devote them to complete destruction. You shall make no covenant with them and show no mercy to them. [3] You shall not intermarry with them, giving your daughters to their sons or taking their daughters for your sons, [4] for they would turn away your sons from following me, to serve other gods. Then the anger of the Lord would be kindled against you, and he would destroy you quickly. [5] But thus shall you deal with them: you shall break down their altars and dash in pieces their pillars and chop down their Asherim and burn their carved images with fire.

[6] "For you are a people holy to the Lord your God. The Lord your God has chosen you to be a people for his treasured possession, out of all the peoples who are on the face of the earth.

Did the Hebrews obey God's command to annihilate everyone in the land?

Psalm 106:34-38

They did not destroy the peoples,
as the Lord commanded them,
[35] but they mixed with the nations

and learned to do as they did.
[36] They served their idols,
which became a snare to them.
[37] They sacrificed their sons
and their daughters to the demons;
[38] they poured out innocent blood,
the blood of their sons and daughters,
whom they sacrificed to the idols of Canaan,
and the land was polluted with blood.

The consequences of that disobedience ended up haunting them from the time of Joshua, Moses' successor, to this present day. They had constant warfare with the Philistines and even today, the territory occupied by the Philistines is still occupied by people, the Palestinians, who are seeking to destroy Israel.

Notice how the text says the people of the land worshiped a pagan god and sacrificed their sons and daughters to the demons. That is still the practice today of the people in the land. Every Palestinian family who encourages their child to be a suicide bomber to please Allah – and a former war crimes attorney told me how starting from 2 years of age the Palestinian children are indoctrinated to see the blowing up of themselves to kill the Jews for Allah as a glorious thing – this sacrificing of children to demons continues and the land is polluted with blood.

The people of God have had a history of needing to be saved, and God has repeatedly raised up saviours. God raised up a saviour – Joseph – who was used to keep his people alive by bringing them down to Egypt where he provided for them during the famine. God raised up another saviour – Moses – who would take them out of Egypt and slavery to the land God had promised to give to Abraham and his descendants as an everlasting possession. It was Joshua, whose name means "Yahováh saves", who led them into the Promised Land and was God's instrument to save his people in the many battles against their enemies.

These saviours were types of the ultimate Saviour whom God would send to save his people. Jesus, whose name is the Greek form of Joshua in Hebrew (Yahováh saves) came to save his people through his atoning sacrifice for sins on the cross. Sadly, as has happened down through history, his people did not receive him.

John 1:10-11

He was in the world, and the world was made through him, yet the world did not know him. [11] He came to his own, and his own people did not receive him.

Shortly before Jesus' death, it is recorded:

Luke 19:41-44 (NIV)
41 As he approached Jerusalem and saw the city, he wept over it
42 and said, "If you, even you, had only known on this day what would
bring you peace--but now it is hidden from your eyes.
43 The days will come upon you when your enemies will build an
embankment against you and encircle you and hem you in on every
side.
44 They will dash you to the ground, you and the children within your
walls. They will not leave one stone on another, because you did not
recognize the time of God's coming to you."

That happened in 70 A.D. when the Roman army under Titus destroyed the city.

5 WHO WILL BE WORSHIPED ON MOUNT ZION?

THERE FOLLOWED A dark period in Israel's history after the generation of Joshua. He left Israel with this challenge:

Joshua 24:15
"And if it is evil in your eyes to serve the Lord, choose this day whom you will serve, whether the gods your fathers served in the region beyond the River, or the gods of the Amorites in whose land you dwell. But as for me and my house, we will serve the Lord."

Judges 2:10-19 (NIV)
[10] After that whole generation had been gathered to their fathers,
another generation grew up, who knew neither the Lord nor what he
had done for Israel.
[11] Then the Israelites did evil in the eyes of the Lord and served the
Baals.
[12] They forsook the Lord, the God of their fathers, who had brought
them out of Egypt. They followed and worshiped various gods of the
peoples around them. They provoked the Lord to anger
[13] because they forsook him and served Baal and the Ashtoreths.
[14] In his anger against Israel the Lord handed them over to raiders who
plundered them. He sold them to their enemies all around, whom they
were no longer able to resist.
[15] Whenever Israel went out to fight, the hand of the Lord was against
them to defeat them, just as he had sworn to them. They were in great

distress.
16 Then the Lord raised up judges, who saved them out of the hands of
these raiders.
17 Yet they would not listen to their judges but prostituted themselves
to other gods and worshiped them. Unlike their fathers, they quickly
turned from the way in which their fathers had walked, the way of
obedience to the Lord's commands.
18 Whenever the Lord raised up a judge for them, he was with the
judge and saved them out of the hands of their enemies as long as the
judge lived; for the Lord had compassion on them as they groaned
under those who oppressed and afflicted them.
19 But when the judge died, the people returned to ways even more
corrupt than those of their fathers, following other gods and serving
and worshiping them. They refused to give up their evil practices and
stubborn ways.

Judges 21:25

In those days there was no king in Israel. Everyone did what was right in his own eyes.

Could the United States and formerly Christian Europe be experiencing this cycle?

As we outlined in the Introduction of this book, God's created beings - some angels and all men - have rebelled against God. We would not think it unusual for the seed of Satan to rebel against God, but should not the godly seed be different? God, through the prophet Isaiah painted a picture of his people that was true centuries before he, Isaiah, recorded it:

Isaiah 1:2-9 (NIV)
2 Hear, O heavens! Listen, O earth! For the Lord has spoken: "I reared
children and brought them up, but they have rebelled against me.
3 The ox knows his master, the donkey his owner's manger, but Israel
does not know, my people do not understand."
4 Ah, sinful nation, a people loaded with guilt, a brood of evildoers,
children given to corruption! They have forsaken the Lord; they have
spurned the Holy One of Israel and turned their backs on him.
5 Why should you be beaten anymore? Why do you persist in
rebellion? Your whole head is injured, your whole heart afflicted.
6 From the sole of your foot to the top of your head there is no

soundness-- only wounds and welts and open sores, not cleansed or bandaged or soothed with oil.
7 Your country is desolate, your cities burned with fire; your fields are being stripped by foreigners right before you, laid waste as when overthrown by strangers.
8 The Daughter of Zion is left like a shelter in a vineyard, like a hut in a field of melons, like a city under siege.
9 Unless the Lord Almighty had left us some survivors, we would have become like Sodom, we would have been like Gomorrah.

The period of moral decay during the time of the Judges led to the establishment of the Israelite Monarchy. The first king, Saul, failed in being obedient to God and was rejected. God then chose one to take his place, with whom an amazing covenant was made. The prophet Samuel anointed the young shepherd boy David, of the tribe of Judah to be the next king of Israel. The story of his killing the giant Goliath with his slingshot is almost universally known. Goliath was one of the Nephilim which indicates that the Hebrews had not completely eradicated them. After a period of fleeing for his life from King Saul, who knew that David would be the next king, he eventually took the throne. God's promise to him is one that continues to this day:

2 Samuel 7:11-16

"… the Lord declares to you that the Lord will make you a house. [12] When your days are fulfilled and you lie down with your fathers, I will raise up your offspring after you, who shall come from your body, and I will establish his kingdom. [13] He shall build a house for my name, and I will establish the throne of his kingdom forever. [14] I will be to him a father, and he shall be to me a son. When he commits iniquity, I will discipline him with the rod of men, with the stripes of the sons of men, [15] but my steadfast love will not depart from him, as I took it from Saul, whom I put away from before you. [16] And your house and your kingdom shall be made sure forever before me. Your throne shall be established forever.' "

Psalm 89:35-37

Once for all I have sworn by my holiness;
I will not lie to David.
[36] His offspring shall endure forever,
his throne as long as the sun before me.
[37] Like the moon it shall be established forever,

a faithful witness in the skies." Selah

God blessed and prospered David. Though he would not be the one to build a temple for God, he undertook to supply materials for his son to be able to do so. He gave gold, silver, bronze, iron, wood, precious stones, fine stone and marble – all in large quantities in preparation for the building of God's house. David supplied 7.5 million pounds (3.4 million kilos) of gold and 75 million pounds (34 million kilos) of silver besides the bronze and iron which were too great to be weighed (1 Chron. 22:14). As of this writing in June 2012, with gold selling for close to $1,600 per ounce and silver around $29 per ounce, just the gold and silver was worth $226.8 billion in today's US dollars. Out of David's own personal wealth, he gave an additional 225,000 pounds of gold and 525,000 pounds of silver, or around $6 billion (1 Chron. 29:4). The leaders of Israel also contributed 375,185 pounds of gold and 750,000 pounds of silver, or close to $10 billion. With close to $243 billion in just gold and silver, it would be the most expensive and luxurious building ever built.

David's son Solomon, the wisest and wealthiest king who has ever lived was the one who built the temple in Jerusalem and God's glory filled it at its dedication (2 Chron. 7:1-3). It was built on a special place – the place where Abraham had been about to offer his son Isaac as a sacrifice (Gen. 22). Jerusalem, often called Mt. Zion, was the place that God had chosen as his permanent dwelling place. However, the permanence of the temple was conditional:

2 Chron. 7:11-22

Thus Solomon finished the house of the Lord and the king's house. All that Solomon had planned to do in the house of the Lord and in his own house he successfully accomplished. [12] Then the Lord appeared to Solomon in the night and said to him: "I have heard your prayer and have chosen this place for myself as a house of sacrifice. [13] When I shut up the heavens so that there is no rain, or command the locust to devour the land, or send pestilence among my people, [14] if my people who are called by my name humble themselves, and pray and seek my face and turn from their wicked ways, then I will hear from heaven and will forgive their sin and heal their land. [15] Now my eyes will be open and my ears attentive to the prayer that is made in this place. [16] For now I have chosen and consecrated this house that my name may be there forever. My eyes and my heart will be there for all time. [17] And as for you, if you will walk before me as David your father walked, doing according to all that I have commanded you and keeping my statutes and my rules, [18] then I will establish your royal throne, as I covenanted with David your father, saying, 'You shall not lack a man to rule Israel.'

[19] "But if you turn aside and forsake my statutes and my commandments that I have set before you, and go and serve other gods and worship them, [20] then I will pluck you up from my land that I have given you, and this house that I have consecrated for my name, I will cast out of my sight, and I will make it a proverb and a byword among all peoples. [21] And at this house, which was exalted, everyone passing by will be astonished and say, 'Why has the Lord done thus to this land and to this house?' [22] Then they will say, 'Because they abandoned the Lord, the God of their fathers who brought them out of the land of Egypt and laid hold on other gods and worshiped them and served them. Therefore he has brought all this disaster on them.' "

During Solomon's reign, he ruled over all the territory promised to Abraham as an everlasting possession – from the Euphrates River to the border of Egypt at the Nile River (2 Chron. 9:26; Gen. 15:18-21).

The Cosmic Conflict Over Who Will Be Worshiped On Mt. Zion

Over time there emerged two dominant cities, symbolizing the two kingdoms: Babylon and Jerusalem. Babylon was where man began asserting his collective independence and rebellion against God at the tower of Babel (Gen 11:1-9). It has continued to symbolize humanism in rebellion against God all the way through the Scriptures to the future as expressed in Revelation 17-18 as "Babylon the Great."

Jerusalem, first appearing as the city over which Melchizedek, priest of God Most High was king (Gen 14:18-20), continues throughout Scriptures as Mt. Zion, the holy city where the presence of God dwells, where his people dwell and from which He will reign forever.

As we have outlined, God had chosen Abraham and his descendants to be his holy people and the line through which the seed of the woman would come. He then promised him the land of Canaan, from the Euphrates River to the Nile River as an everlasting possession. God's plan was further narrowed when he chose David and promised that from his seed, there would be a king on his throne forever. The place of God's permanent dwelling, the sacred mountain from where he would be worshiped forever was now made known – Jerusalem, Mt. Zion.

Psalm 48:1-3 (NIV)
1 Great is the Lord, and most worthy of praise, in the city of our God, his holy mountain.
2 It is beautiful in its loftiness, the joy of the whole earth. Like the utmost heights of Zaphon is Mount Zion, the city of the Great King.
3 God is in her citadels; he has shown himself to be her fortress.

The word "Zaphon" is most often translated "north", but it also has another meaning. It was known as the sacred mountain, the residence of El, the chief of the gods of the Phoenicians. The Psalmist is saying that Mount Zion is the sacred mountain, where Yahováh, the God of gods dwells. It is "his holy mountain."

Notice how God shows Isaiah a vision about how Mount Zion in Jerusalem will be established as the chief mountain – the mountain that will be "the joy of the whole earth." It will become the Capital City of the world!

Isaiah 2:1-4 (NIV)
1 This is what Isaiah son of Amoz saw concerning Judah and Jerusalem:
2 In the last days the mountain of the Lord's temple will be established as chief among the mountains; it will be raised above the hills, and all nations will stream to it.
3 Many peoples will come and say, "Come, let us go up to the mountain of the Lord, to the house of the God of Jacob. He will teach us his ways, so that we may walk in his paths." The law will go out from Zion, the word of the Lord from Jerusalem.
4 He will judge between the nations and will settle disputes for many peoples. They will beat their swords into plowshares and their spears into pruning hooks. Nation will not take up sword against nation, nor will they train for war anymore.

So if you are Satan and God has said that Jerusalem – Mt. Zion will be the chief of the mountains in the world, the mountain and city of God from which God will rule the world, what would you want to do?

We noted in chapter one that Satan was not content to be the highest created angel, but that he wanted God's place. He coveted the worship that is due to God alone. He wants to be the god enthroned on Zaphon, the holy mountain and receive adoration.

Isaiah 14:12-14 (NIV)
[12] How you have fallen from heaven, O morning star, son of the dawn! You have been cast down to the earth, you who once laid low the nations!
[13] You said in your heart, "I will ascend to heaven; I will raise my throne above the stars of God; I will sit enthroned on the mount of assembly, on the utmost heights of the sacred mountain.
[14] I will ascend above the tops of the clouds; I will make myself like the Most High."

The word "sacred mountain" above in Hebrew is "Zaphon". Satan insists that **he** will sit enthroned on Zaphon, the mount of assembly. **He** will make himself like the Most High. Once God defined where that sacred mountain was to be, Satan has determined that **he** will be worshiped from that mountain – Mt. Zion.

However, God has promised that position to someone else – his Anointed One – his Messiah, his Son.

Psalm 2:1-12 (NIV)
[1] Why do the nations conspire and the peoples plot in vain?
[2] The kings of the earth take their stand and the rulers gather together against the Lord and against his Anointed One.
[3] "Let us break their chains," they say, "and throw off their fetters."
[4] The One enthroned in heaven laughs; the Lord scoffs at them.
[5] Then he rebukes them in his anger and terrifies them in his wrath, saying,
[6] "I have installed my King on Zion, my holy hill."
[7] I will proclaim the decree of the Lord: He said to me, "You are my Son; today I have become your Father.
[8] Ask of me, and I will make the nations your inheritance, the ends of the earth your possession.
[9] You will rule them with an iron scepter; you will dash them to pieces like pottery."
[10] Therefore, you kings, be wise; be warned, you rulers of the earth.
[11] Serve the Lord with fear and rejoice with trembling.
[12] Kiss the Son, lest he be angry and you be destroyed in your way, for his wrath can flare up in a moment. Blessed are all who take refuge in him.

We as Christians understand this cosmic struggle to be the struggle of the seed of Satan – these kings of the earth, in rebellion against Yahováh and against his Anointed One. The context of this Psalm seems to equate the "Anointed One", or "Messiah", or "Christ" in Greek, to be the Son of Yahováh.

Parallel to Psalm 2 is one of the most quoted Psalms in the New Testament:

Psalm 110:1 A Psalm of David.
The Lord says to my Lord:
"Sit at my right hand,
until I make your enemies your footstool."

In Hebrew, the first "Lord" is "Yahováh" and the second is "Adonai". David writes, "Yahováh said to my Adonai: 'Sit at my right hand until I make your enemies your footstool.'"

The "Anointed One" or Messiah was to be a son of David. Yet in this passage, David, as the father of the Messiah and thus to hold the more exalted position of honor in relation to his son, calls this Son his Lord, or Adonai. Jesus Christ asked the religious leaders of his day how this could be that the Christ, or Messiah could be David's son and Lord (Mt. 22:41-46; Mk. 12:35-37; Lk. 20:41-44). How could David's human son, if he be only human, be sitting at the right hand of Yahováh?

Looking back at Psalm 2 again, we see God – Yahováh – the Lord, installing his Anointed One, or Messiah, or Christ as his King on Mt. Zion. He says that this Anointed One is his Son. This Son is David's Lord or Adonai and is sitting at the right hand of Yahováh until God makes his Son's enemies his footstool. Then Yahováh will give to his Son the nations as an inheritance and he will rule them with an iron scepter. This is a clue to David's future son being both Divine and human.

Indeed, Psalm 110 gives further indications of who this Lord or Adonai is. He is a Priest / King, following in the line of Melchizedek, the King and Priest of Salem, or Jerusalem, who blessed Abram and who received tithes from him (Gen. 14:17-21).

Psalm 110:1-7 (NASB)
1 The Lord says to my Lord: "Sit at My right hand Until I make your enemies a footstool for Your feet."
2 The Lord will stretch forth Your strong scepter from Zion, *saying,* "Rule in the midst of Your enemies."
3 Your people will volunteer freely in the day of Your power; In holy

array, from the womb of the dawn, Your youth are to You *as* the dew.
4 The Lord has sworn and will not change His mind, "You are a priest forever according to the order of Melchizedek."
5 The Lord is at Your right hand; He will shatter kings in the day of His wrath.
6 He will judge among the nations, He will fill *them* with corpses, He will shatter the chief men over a broad country.
7 He will drink from the brook by the wayside; Therefore He will lift up *His* head.

He will rule and judge the nations from Mt. Zion, the Holy Mountain, or Zaphon, as a priest/king crushing his enemies.

That is exactly what Satan wants to do. He wants to install his son on Mt. Zion, to receive worship as god and to rule and judge the nations and crush his enemies. His enemies are God, God's Messiah and the people of God. He will install his "man of lawlessness," "Antichrist," "Beast" in the temple on Mt. Zion in Jerusalem to be worshiped and will successfully wage war on the saints – the people of God. Note the following passages:

2 Thess. 2:3, 4, 9-10

"… the man of lawlessness …, the son of destruction, [4] who opposes and exalts himself against every so-called god or object of worship, so that he takes his seat in the temple of God, proclaiming himself to be God. [9] The coming of the lawless one is by the activity of Satan with all power and false signs and wonders, [10] and with all wicked deception for those who are perishing, because they refused to love the truth and so be saved."

Daniel 9:27

And he shall make a strong covenant with many for one week, and for half of the week he shall put an end to sacrifice and offering. And on the wing of abominations shall come one who makes desolate, until the decreed end is poured out on the desolator."

Rev. 13:5-8

And the beast was given a mouth uttering haughty and blasphemous words, and it was allowed to exercise authority for forty-two months. [6] It opened its mouth to utter blasphemies against

God, blaspheming his name and his dwelling, that is, those who dwell in heaven. [7] Also it was allowed to make war on the saints and to conquer them. And authority was given it over every tribe and people and language and nation, [8] and all who dwell on earth will worship it, everyone whose name has not been written before the foundation of the world in the book of life of the Lamb that was slain.

God however, has promised that he will establish his King, the son of David – his Anointed One – his Son, on Mt. Zion.

Could that be why the Jews, – almost 15 million worldwide, making up only 0.2% of the world's population, and Israel, with only 5.9 million Jews and the city of Jerusalem with a total Jewish and non-Jewish population of 850,000 – are always at the forefront of the world's attention?

Israel is a tiny country, about the same size as New Jersey, USA or around half the size of Switzerland with approximately 20,700 square kilometres (7,992 sq mi), of which the Negev desert covering some 12,000 square kilometres (4,633 sq mi) comprises more than half of the country's total land area. Israel stretches 424 kilometres (263 mi) from north to south, and its width ranges from 114 kilometres (71 mi) to, at its narrowest point, 15 kilometres (9.3 mi).

By size and population, it should be a non-entity. But, "At least 187 Jews and people of half or three-quarters Jewish ancestry have been awarded the Nobel Prize, accounting for 22% of all individual recipients worldwide between 1901 and 2011, and constituting 36% of all US recipients during the same period. In the research fields of Chemistry, Economics, Physics, and Physiology/Medicine, the corresponding world and US percentages are 27% and 39%, respectively. Among women laureates in the four research fields, the Jewish percentages (world and US) are 38% and 50%, respectively. Of organizations awarded the Nobel Peace Prize, 25% were founded principally by Jews or by people of half-Jewish descent. (Jews currently make up approximately 0.2% of the world's population and 2% of the US population.)"[8]

According to the Bible, the land of Israel is the chief battleground between God and Satan, and human history will culminate there.

[8] "Jewish Nobel Prize Winners" <http://www.jinfo.org/Nobel_Prizes.html>

From Golden Age to Subjugation

Israel's golden age under David and Solomon did not last long. Solomon, the builder of the temple was led astray through his own disobedience. Against God's law, he married many foreign wives, who turned his heart from following after Yahováh to idols (1 Kings 11:1-13).

Because of his forsaking the Lord, God raised up adversaries against Solomon, much like the terrorists who are afflicting the United States and the western world today (1 Ki. 11:14ff).

For the sake of David his father, God's judgment did not come in Solomon's days, but rather during his son's reign when most of the kingdom was torn out of his hand. Ten tribes rebelled and formed Israel, a competing and often enemy nation in the north, leaving the descendants of David, Judah, in the south.

The persistent idolatry and evil of Israel in the north, despite many warnings from a multitude of prophets brought eventual judgment from God by the next great world empire. In 722 B.C. the Assyrian king invaded Israel and took the northern ten tribes into captivity (2 Ki. 17).

Though there were a number of godly kings in Judah's history, the people increasingly turned their backs on Yahováh and did not learn the lesson from their brothers in the north. The temple did not serve as their "good-luck charm" and God's wrath came upon them through the king of Babylon, Nebuchadnezzar. Jerusalem and the temple were destroyed and the people taken into captivity in 586 B.C. (2 Ki. 25).

Satan's Kings as God's Servants?

In the book of Revelation, Satan is pictured as "a great red dragon, with seven heads and ten horns, and on his heads seven diadems (crowns)" (Rev. 12:3). The angel explains to the Apostle John what those heads are:

Rev. 17:10

"they are also seven kings, five of whom have fallen, one is, the other has not yet come, and when he does come he must remain only a little while."

The kings represent kingdoms (cf. Dan. 7:17, 23) in opposition to God and his people. Remember that Satan is in the business of seeking to destroy the "seed of the woman". John is told that as of the time of his vision – approx. 95 A.D., five of these kings or kingdoms had fallen, one was currently in existence and there was another one yet to come.

These five kingdoms are generally thought to be the following:

1. Egypt or Ancient Babylon (Nimrod era)
2. Assyria
3. Babylon (Nebuchadnezzar era)
4. Media – Persia
5. Greece

The kingdom in existence during John's writing – the sixth, was Rome, leaving unrevealed the identity of the seventh kingdom. These kingdoms have all persecuted and sought to destroy God's chosen people and have been instruments of Satan, who as we saw previously at the temptation of Jesus, has power over them:

Luke 4:5-7

And the devil took him up and showed him all the kingdoms of the world in a moment of time, [6] and said to him, "To you I will give all this authority and their glory, for it has been delivered to me, and I give it to whom I will. [7] If you, then, will worship me, it will all be yours."

We have seen how there was a Pharaoh of Egypt who sought to destroy the Hebrews by having their male babies put to death. Then Assyria carried off Israel into captivity and succeeded in conquering all of Judah except Jerusalem. The story of King Hezekiah seeking God's help and God's miraculous intervention in having his angel put to death 185,000 Assyrian soldiers in one night is one of history's greatest military reversals (Is. 36-38). We also saw that Babylon destroyed Jerusalem, burning the temple and the city and deporting the survivors in 586 B.C. What about the other empires? Have they really been tools of Satan to try to destroy the chosen seed?

One of the greatest stories in the Bible is that of Queen Esther. During Persian King Xerxes' rule (486 – 465 B.C.), one of his highest nobles, Haman, obtained the kings permission to exterminate all the Jews in the entire Persian Empire. Only the queen's intervention on behalf of her people averted a certain annihilation of the Hebrew people (Book of Esther). The Feast of Purim celebrates that deliverance and is observed even today among Jewish people.

When Greek Alexander the Great conquered the Persian Empire, he was going to destroy Israel because of their refusal to break their oath of allegiance to the Persian King. Circumstances that will be cited later averted that catastrophe, but during the time of his successors, Antiochus IV Epiphanes (175 – 164 B.C.) killed tens of thousands of Jews and set up the first "abomination that causes desolation" by erecting an altar to Zeus in the Jewish Temple and sacrificing a pig on it. Jews led by the Maccabees succeeded in resisting the Greeks and they were able to cleanse and rededicate the Temple in 165 B.C., which is today celebrated as the Feast of Dedication, or Chanukkah (also known as Hanukkah).[9]

The Roman Empire was also used by the enemy of God's people to again destroy Jerusalem, burn the second Temple and scatter the few survivors of the Jews around the world in 70 A.D.[10]

Solomon said:

Eccles. 1:9

What has been is what will be,
and what has been done is what will be done,
and there is nothing new under the sun.

Over the course of Israel's history, it has been the surrounding neighbors that have been bent on Israel's destruction. We see from the following text that even today, there is nothing new. The same players who have repeatedly tried to "wipe them out as a nation", are the ones who today, like Mahmoud Ahmadinejad, president of Iran, threaten to "wipe Israel off the map".

Psalm 83:1-8

A Song. A Psalm of Asaph.

O God, do not keep silence;
do not hold your peace or be still, O God!
[2] For behold, your enemies make an uproar;
those who hate you have raised their heads.
[3] They lay crafty plans against your people;
they consult together against your treasured ones.
[4] **They say, "Come, let us wipe them out as a nation;**

---

[9] Book of Maccabees in the Apocrypha

[10] Op. Cit., Josephus, The Wars of the Jews, Books II – VII

let the name of Israel be remembered no more!"
[5] For they conspire with one accord;
against you they make a covenant—
[6] the tents of Edom and the Ishmaelites,
Moab and the Hagrites,
[7] Gebal and Ammon and Amalek,
Philistia with the inhabitants of Tyre;
[8] Asshur also has joined them;
they are the strong arm of the children of Lot. Selah

The peoples listed then – 10th century B.C. - surrounded Israel. Edom, descendants of Jacob's brother Esau settled, as we noted earlier, in what is today southern Jordan and northwest Saudi Arabia; the Ishmaelites, half brother of Isaac are the Arabs, inhabiting Saudi Arabia and all around the Middle East; Moab, the Hagrites, Gebal, Ammon and Amalek are the peoples east of Israel in what is today Jordan and Syria; Philistia are the peoples in the areas today inhabited by the Palestinians; Tyre is in Lebanon and Asshur refers to Assyria which covered southeastern Turkey, Iraq, Iran, Syria and northern Saudi Arabia. All peoples who today, like 3,000 years ago, are dedicated to Israel's destruction and conspire together to make that happen. Notice how the Psalm identifies them as enemies of the God of the Jews. Indeed, the followers of Islam today are enemies of the God of Abraham, Isaac and Jacob.

So of the seven heads of the dragon, representing Satan and the Empires he has ruled in an effort to do away with the people of God, history has clearly shown that the first six heads or Empires have attempted to exterminate the Jewish people. Should anything different be expected of the seventh head or Empire?

6 THE PROPHETS

THOUGH SATAN IS the god of this world, God and the devil are not equals. As we saw in the last chapter, God uses Satan's minions to serve and perform God's bidding. With Pharaoh, God said this:

Exodus 7:1-5

And the Lord said to Moses, "See, I have made you like God to Pharaoh, and your brother Aaron shall be your prophet. [2] You shall speak all that I command you, and your brother Aaron shall tell Pharaoh to let the people of Israel go out of his land. [3] But I will harden Pharaoh's heart, and though I multiply my signs and wonders in the land of Egypt, [4] Pharaoh will not listen to you. Then I will lay my hand on Egypt and bring my hosts, my people the children of Israel, out of the land of Egypt by great acts of judgment. [5] The Egyptians shall know that I am the Lord, when I stretch out my hand against Egypt and bring out the people of Israel from among them."

Paul records in the New Testament:

Romans 9:17-18

For the Scripture says to Pharaoh, "For this very purpose I have raised you up, that I might show my power in you, and that my name might be proclaimed in all the earth." [18] So then he has mercy on whomever he wills, and he hardens whomever he wills.

After repeated warnings by the prophets to Israel to repent of their sins, God used the Assyrians as his instrument of discipline:

Isaiah 10:5-6

Ah, Assyria, the rod of my anger;
the staff in their hands is my fury!
[6] Against a godless nation I send him,
and against the people of my wrath I command him,
to take spoil and seize plunder,
and to tread them down like the mire of the streets.

Nebuchadnezzar, king of Babylon is another example. God revealed to Jeremiah the prophet that Nebuchadnezzar was his servant and would accomplish God's plan to discipline his people but would then be punished by God for his evil.

Jeremiah 25:1-14

The word that came to Jeremiah concerning all the people of Judah, in the fourth year of Jehoiakim the son of Josiah, king of Judah (that was the first year of Nebuchadnezzar king of Babylon), [2] which Jeremiah the prophet spoke to all the people of Judah and all the inhabitants of Jerusalem: [3] "For twenty-three years, from the thirteenth year of Josiah the son of Amon, king of Judah, to this day, the word of the Lord has come to me, and I have spoken persistently to you, but you have not listened. [4] You have neither listened nor inclined your ears to hear, although the Lord persistently sent to you all his servants the prophets, [5] saying, 'Turn now, every one of you, from his evil way and evil deeds, and dwell upon the land that the Lord has given to you and your fathers from of old and forever. [6] Do not go after other gods to serve and worship them, or provoke me to anger with the work of your hands. Then I will do you no harm.' [7] Yet you have not listened to me, declares the Lord, that you might provoke me to anger with the work of your hands to your own harm.

[8] "Therefore thus says the Lord of hosts: Because you have not obeyed my words, [9] behold, I will send for all the tribes of the north, declares the Lord, and for **Nebuchadnezzar the king of Babylon, my servant,** and I will bring them against this land and its inhabitants, and against all these surrounding nations. I will devote them to destruction, and make them a horror, a hissing, and an everlasting desolation. [10] Moreover, I will banish from them the voice of mirth and the voice of gladness, the voice of the bridegroom and the voice of the bride, the grinding of the millstones and the light of the lamp. [11] This whole land shall become a ruin and a waste,

and these nations shall serve the king of Babylon seventy years. [12] **Then after seventy years are completed, I will punish the king of Babylon and that nation, the land of the Chaldeans, for their iniquity, declares the Lord,** making the land an everlasting waste. [13] I will bring upon that land all the words that I have uttered against it, everything written in this book, which Jeremiah prophesied against all the nations. [14] For many nations and great kings shall make slaves even of them, and I will recompense them according to their deeds and the work of their hands."

Jeremiah 51:11
The Lord has stirred up the spirit of the kings of the Medes, because his purpose concerning Babylon is to destroy it, for that is the vengeance of the Lord, the vengeance for his temple.

If we look at past history, we see a consistent pattern according to the covenant with Abraham:

Genesis 12:3 (NIV)
3 I will bless those who bless you, and whoever curses you I will curse; and all peoples on earth will be blessed through you."

Even those nations which God used to discipline his people, God punished for their mistreatment of his people afterwards. Could it be that this pattern continues today?

The Rise of Prophets

While Abraham (2000 B.C.), Moses (as early as 1450), Samuel (c. 1050-1010), Elijah and Elisha (c. 875-797) and others were called prophets, most of their office involved being a spokesman for God to the people of their generation. God began to raise up writing prophets who would speak and write messages that would address the current situation of their audience as well as to give predictive messages. These first prophetic books appeared in the eighth century B.C. and continued until the fifth century B.C. Among the more noted prophets were Isaiah, Jeremiah, Daniel and Ezekiel.

As alluded to in the Introduction, one of the greatest attestations to the existence of God is that the true God can tell us what will come to pass in the future with 100% accuracy. The proof of a false god and false prophet is that they are not 100% accurate. The accuracy of the predictive messages of these prophetic books attest to their being God-inspired. If some of their prophecies have already come to pass as they predicted, it should give us confidence that those prophecies that speak to yet future events, will likewise come to pass. As recorded above, God revealed to Jeremiah the first year of Nebuchadnezzar's reign, that God would bring Babylon against Judah and destroy it.

Below are examples of the accuracy of prophecy in regard to two very interesting accounts regarding men who saw themselves in the prophetic books written more than a hundred years before they were born. We will look at Cyrus, the Persian King and Alexander the Great.

Cyrus

Isaiah, who ministered from 740-681 B.C. prophesied that Judah and Jerusalem would be destroyed, which happened in 586 B.C. During his ministry God revealed some 200 years beforehand that they would be rebuilt and the name of the king who would authorize it.

Isaiah 44:24-28 (NIV)
[24] "This is what the Lord says-- your Redeemer, ... [26] who carries out the words of his servants and fulfills the predictions of his messengers, who says of Jerusalem, 'It shall be inhabited,' of the towns of Judah, 'They shall be built,' and of their ruins, 'I will restore them,'
[28] who says of **Cyrus**, 'He is my shepherd and will accomplish all that I please; he will say of Jerusalem, "Let it be rebuilt," and of the temple, "Let its foundations be laid."'
Isaiah 45:1-6 (NIV)
[1] "This is what the Lord says to his anointed, to **Cyrus**, whose right hand I take hold of to subdue nations before him and to strip kings of their armor, to open doors before him so that gates will not be shut:
[2] I will go before you and will level the mountains; I will break down gates of bronze and cut through bars of iron.
[3] I will give you the treasures of darkness, riches stored in secret places, so that you may know that I am the Lord, the God of Israel, who summons you by name.
[4] For the sake of Jacob my servant, of Israel my chosen, I summon you by name and bestow on you a title of honor, though you do not acknowledge me.
[5] I am the Lord, and there is no other; apart from me there is no God. I will strengthen you, though you have not acknowledged me,

6 so that from the rising of the sun to the place of its setting men may know there is none besides me. I am the Lord, and there is no other.

Flavius Josephus wrote this of Cyrus:

"Thus saith Cyrus the king: Since God Almighty hath appointed me to be king of the habitable earth, I believe that he is that God which the nation of the Israelites worship; for indeed he foretold my name by the prophets, and that I should build him a house at Jerusalem, in the country of Judea."
2. This was known to Cyrus by his reading the book which Isaiah left behind him of his prophecies; for this prophet said that God had spoken thus to him in a secret vision: "My will is, that Cyrus, whom I have appointed to be king over many and great nations, send back my people to their own land, and build my temple." This was foretold by Isaiah one hundred and forty years before the temple was demolished. Accordingly, when Cyrus read this, and admired the Divine power, an earnest desire and ambition seized upon him to fulfill what was so written; so he called for the most eminent Jews that were in Babylon, and said to them, that he gave them leave to go back to their own country, and to rebuild their city Jerusalem,"[11]

The details God revealed to Isaiah are amazingly accurate. God calls Cyrus "my shepherd". David was also called a king who would shepherd his people Israel. David, as a youth had been a shepherd boy.

Fifth century B.C. Greek historian Herodotus tells of Cyrus' birth:

"[66] Astygages king of the Medes had a daughter whose name was Mandané; and of this daughter, when she was but a child, he dreamed such a dream that he feared exceedingly what might happen to him and to his kingdom by reason of her. Therefore when she grew of age to be married, he gave her not to a man of her own race, but he gave her to a Persian, whose name was Cambyses. And this Cambyses was indeed of a noble house, but of a quiet and peaceable temper. Only because he was a Persian, Astyages held him to be of less account than a Mede, whether he were noble or no.

---

[11] Op. Cit., Josephus, Antiquities of the Jews, Book XI, chpt. I, sec. 1-2:

But in the first year of the marriage King Astyages dreamed another dream of his daughter, which made him yet more afraid than had the former dream. Therefore he sent for the woman, who was now about to bring forth [67] her first-born child, and kept her in the palace, being minded to put to death that which should be born of her, for the interpreters of dreams had signified to him that the son of his daughter should be king in his stead. When therefore she bare Cyrus, for they gave this name to the child, Astyages called to him one Harpagus, who was of his kindred, and faithful to him beyond all other of the Medes, and who had also the care of his household. And when Harpagus was come to him, the King said, "Harpagus, see thou that in the matter which I shall now put in thy charge thou in no wise neglect my commandment, nor prefer others to me, and so in the end bring great sorrow on thyself. Now the matter is this. Thou shalt take this child that Mandané my daughter hath lately borne, and carry it to thy home, and there slay it; and afterwards thou shalt bury it in such fashion as thou wilt."[12]

Harpagus was not willing to kill the child and so he called a herdsman who lived in the mountains and told him to leave the child out in the wilderness so he would be eaten by wild animals. When the herdsman took him to his house and told his wife what he was commanded to do, she absolutely refused to let him do it. She had just given birth to a still born child and they took Cyrus and raised him and presented the remains of the body of their child whom they left out for animals to eat, as proof they had complied with the kings orders.

Cyrus was raised as a shepherd until it was noticed that he had a noble bearing about him and circumstances brought him before the king who inquired of both the herdsman and Harpagus until he got the truth of who Cyrus was. He then took him back into the royal household.

So when Cyrus saw the words written in Isaiah some 200 years previously, calling him "my shepherd," it must have had a great impact on him.

Isaiah 45:1-6 (NIV)

1 "This is what the Lord says to his anointed, to Cyrus, whose right hand I take hold of to subdue nations before him and to strip kings of their armor, to open doors before him so that gates will not be shut:

---

12 Stories of the East From Herodotus, Chapter V: "The Birth and Bringing Up of Cyrus", p. 66-67

2 I will go before you and will level the mountains; I will break down
gates of bronze and cut through bars of iron.
3 I will give you the **treasures of darkness, riches** stored in secret
places, so that you may know that I am the Lord, the God of Israel,
who summons you by name.

Cyrus conquered many kings and nations from India to Turkey. Herodotus described the city of Babylon: "There are **a hundred gates** in the circuit of the wall, **all of bronze** with bronze uprights and lintels."[13]

He conquered the kingdom of Lydia (modern day Turkey) and carried off its treasures, of whom Croesus, Lydia's ruler was said to have been the wealthiest man in the world at that time. The impregnable Babylon, that felt secure from any siege, he conquered without a battle by diverting the Euphrates River and having his soldiers enter the city by night walking in thigh deep water in the middle of the river bed into the city. This happened the very night that the Babylonian vice regent Belshazzar was having a grand banquet and God's hand wrote a message on the wall that Daniel was called in to interpret (Daniel 5). This is what the message said:

Daniel 5:25-28 (NIV)
25 "This is the inscription that was written: MENE, MENE, TEKEL,
PARSIN
26 "This is what these words mean: *Mene*: God has numbered the days
of your reign and brought it to an end.
27 *Tekel*: You have been weighed on the scales and found wanting.
28 *Peres*: Your kingdom is divided and given to the Medes and
Persians."

That very night Belshazzar was killed and the Medes and Persians took over the city. Like Lydia, Babylon had fabulous wealth in their treasuries that Cyrus was able to take.

Alexander the Great

The second example of a ruler reading a prophecy about himself written at least 200 years earlier was when God revealed to the prophet Daniel (605 – 530 B.C.) that Greece would become a world empire. In

---

[13] Ibid., 1. 179

his visions he saw this:

Daniel 7:6
After this I looked, and behold, another, like a leopard, with four wings of a bird on its back. And the beast had four heads, and dominion was given to it.

Daniel 8:5-8
As I was considering, behold, a male goat came from the west across the face of the whole earth, without touching the ground. And the goat had a conspicuous horn between his eyes. [6] He came to the ram with the two horns, which I had seen standing on the bank of the canal, and he ran at him in his powerful wrath. [7] I saw him come close to the ram, and he was enraged against him and struck the ram and broke his two horns. And the ram had no power to stand before him, but he cast him down to the ground and trampled on him. And there was no one who could rescue the ram from his power. [8] Then the goat became exceedingly great, but when he was strong, the great horn was broken, and instead of it there came up four conspicuous horns toward the four winds of heaven.

Daniel 8:20-22
As for the ram that you saw with the two horns, these are the kings of Media and Persia. [21] And the goat is the king of Greece. And the great horn between his eyes is the first king. [22] As for the horn that was broken, in place of which four others arose, four kingdoms shall arise from his nation, but not with his power.

Alexander the Great took over the Persian Empire with breathtaking speed in 12 years, all the way to India, before dying at the age of 33 (323 B.C.). After his death, the empire was divided among four of his generals. When Alexander came to Israel, the high priest was in great fear because he had refused to side with Alexander because of an oath he had given to Darius, the Persian king. Josephus writes:

Now Alexander, when he had taken Gaza, made haste to go up to Jerusalem; and Jaddua the high priest, when he heard that, was in an agony, and under terror, as not knowing how he should meet the Macedonians, since the king was displeased at his foregoing disobedience. He therefore ordained that the people should make supplications, and should join with him in offering sacrifice to God, whom he besought to protect that nation, and to deliver them from the perils that were coming upon them; whereupon God warned him in a dream, which came upon him after he had offered sacrifice, that he should take courage, and adorn the city, and open the gates; that the rest should appear in white garments, but that he and the priests should meet the king in the habits proper to their order, without the dread of any ill consequences, which the providence of God would prevent. Upon which, when he rose from his sleep, he greatly rejoiced, and declared to all the warning he had received from God. According to which dream he acted entirely, and so waited for the coming of the king.

5. And when he understood that he was not far from the city, he went out in procession, with the priests and the multitude of the citizens....And when the Phoenicians and the Chaldeans that followed him thought they should have liberty to plunder the city, and torment the high priest to death, which the king's displeasure fairly promised them, the very reverse of it happened; for Alexander, when he saw the multitude at a distance, in white garments, while the priests stood clothed with fine linen, and the high priest in purple and scarlet clothing, with his mitre on his head, having the golden plate whereon the name of God was engraved, he approached by himself, and adored that name, and first saluted the high priest. The Jews also did all together, with one voice, salute Alexander, and encompass him about; whereupon the kings of Syria and the rest were surprised at what Alexander had done, and supposed him disordered in his mind. However, Parmenio alone went up to him, and asked him how it came to pass that, when all others adored him, he should adore the high priest of the Jews? To whom he replied, "I did not adore him, but that God who hath honored him with his high priesthood; for I saw this very person in a dream, in this very habit, when I was at Dios in Macedonia, who, when I was considering with myself how I might obtain the dominion of Asia, exhorted me to make no delay, but boldly to pass over the sea thither, for that he would conduct my army, and would give me the dominion over the Persians; whence it is that, having seen no other in that habit, and now seeing this person in it, and remembering that vision, and the exhortation which I had in my dream, I believe that I bring this army under the Divine conduct, and shall therewith conquer Darius, and destroy the power of the

Persians, and that all things will succeed according to what is in my own mind." And when he had said this to Parmenio, and had given the high priest his right hand, the priests ran along by him, and he came into the city. And when he went up into the temple, he offered sacrifice to God, according to the high priest's direction, and magnificently treated both the high priest and the priests. And when the Book of Daniel was showed him wherein Daniel declared that one of the Greeks should destroy the empire of the Persians, he supposed that himself was the person intended. And as he was then glad, he dismissed the multitude for the present; but the next day he called them to him, and bid them ask what favors they pleased of him; whereupon the high priest desired that they might enjoy the laws of their forefathers, and might pay no tribute on the seventh year. He granted all they desired.[14]

The Second Temple

In keeping with the prophecy regarding Cyrus made by Isaiah, and the length of time in captivity by Jeremiah we read of this decree in 538 B.C.:

2 Chron. 36:22-23
Now in the first year of Cyrus king of Persia, that the word of the Lord by the mouth of Jeremiah might be fulfilled, the Lord stirred up the spirit of Cyrus king of Persia, so that he made a proclamation throughout all his kingdom and also put it in writing: [23] "Thus says Cyrus king of Persia, 'The Lord, the God of heaven, has given me all the kingdoms of the earth, and he has charged me to build him a house at Jerusalem, which is in Judah. Whoever is among you of all his people, may the Lord his God be with him. Let him go up.' "

Though free to return to their native land, after some seventy years in captivity (may be taken as a round number with the first captives taken in 606/605 B.C. and the first wave to return in 537-535, or as an exact number calculating from the destruction of the temple in 586 to the rebuilt temple in 516 B.C.), the majority of the Jews chose to remain in the Persian Empire. After much opposition by the surrounding peoples, Zerubbabel finally succeeded in having the temple rebuilt in 516 B.C. However, most of the Jews remained in the Persian Empire and did not

[14] Op. Cit., Josephus, Antiquities of the Jews, Book XI, chpt. VIII, sec. 4-5:

return to their homeland.

A Puzzling Prophecy

Most of the Messianic prophecies describe a golden age where a future Davidic king will rule the nations with a rod of iron and Jerusalem will be established as the chief mountain in the world. Two such examples are the following:

Isaiah 9:6-7 (NIV)
6 For to us a child is born, to us a son is given, and the government
will be on his shoulders. And he will be called Wonderful Counselor,
Mighty God, Everlasting Father, Prince of Peace.
7 Of the increase of his government and peace there will be no end. He
will reign on David's throne and over his kingdom, establishing and
upholding it with justice and righteousness from that time on and
forever. The zeal of the Lord Almighty will accomplish this.

We cited Isaiah 2:1-4 earlier which prophesied that the mountain of the Lord's temple would be established as chief among the mountains and all the nations will stream to it.

However, Isaiah presents another picture of the Messiah, not as a conquering king, but as a suffering servant. How can these two conflicting and polar opposite pictures of the Messiah be both true?

Isaiah 52:13-15 (NIV)
13 See, my servant will act wisely; he will be raised and lifted up
and highly exalted.
14 Just as there were many who were appalled at him-- his appearance
was so disfigured beyond that of any man and his form marred
beyond human likeness--
15 so will he sprinkle many nations, and kings will shut their mouths
because of him. For what they were not told, they will see, and what
they have not heard, they will understand.
Isaiah 53:1-12 (NIV)
1 Who has believed our message and to whom has the arm of the Lord
been revealed?
2 He grew up before him like a tender shoot, and like a root out of dry
ground. He had no beauty or majesty to attract us to him, nothing in
his appearance that we should desire him.
3 He was despised and rejected by men, a man of sorrows, and

familiar with suffering. Like one from whom men hide their faces he
was despised, and we esteemed him not.
4 Surely he took up our infirmities and carried our sorrows, yet we
considered him stricken by God, smitten by him, and afflicted.
5 But he was pierced for our transgressions, he was crushed for our
iniquities; the punishment that brought us peace was upon him, and
by his wounds we are healed.
6 We all, like sheep, have gone astray, each of us has turned to his
own way; and the Lord has laid on him the iniquity of us all.
7 He was oppressed and afflicted, yet he did not open his mouth; he
was led like a lamb to the slaughter, and as a sheep before her
shearers is silent, so he did not open his mouth.
8 By oppression and judgment he was taken away. And who can speak
of his descendants? For he was cut off from the land of the living; for
the transgression of my people he was stricken.
9 He was assigned a grave with the wicked, and with the rich in his
death, though he had done no violence, nor was any deceit in his
mouth.
10 Yet it was the Lord's will to crush him and cause him to suffer, and
though the Lord makes his life a guilt offering, he will see his
offspring and prolong his days, and the will of the Lord will prosper
in his hand.
11 After the suffering of his soul, he will see the light [of life] and be
satisfied; by his knowledge my righteous servant will justify many,
and he will bear their iniquities.
12 Therefore I will give him a portion among the great, and he will
divide the spoils with the strong, because he poured out his life unto
death, and was numbered with the transgressors. For he bore the sin
of many, and made intercession for the transgressors.

We have made the point that in the Bible, many prophecies have a dual fulfillment. One comes as a type and the other as the antitype. In this case, the Son of David comes two times. The first time as the suffering servant, to inaugurate the Kingdom of God. The second time, he comes to bring in its fullness.

What did the suffering servant in the passage above accomplish? As these verses make clear, he came as an innocent lamb to be sacrificed as the sin bearer so that the guilty sinner could be forgiven:

4 Surely he took up our infirmities and carried our sorrows, yet we
considered him stricken by God, smitten by him, and afflicted.
5 But he was pierced for our transgressions, he was crushed for our
iniquities; the punishment that brought us peace was upon him, and
by his wounds we are healed.
6 We all, like sheep, have gone astray, each of us has turned to his
own way; and the Lord has laid on him the iniquity of us all.

When John the Baptist saw Jesus, he said this of him:

John 1:29
The next day he saw Jesus coming toward him, and said, "Behold, the Lamb of God, who takes away the sin of the world!

God had chosen his people to be a holy nation. The problem was that down through history they had not been holy. They had rebelled like the seed of Satan. To be righteous, their sins had to be atoned for and that was the role of the suffering servant, the Messiah, in his first coming.

Daniel's Prophecy of the Seventy 'Sevens'

To Daniel was revealed a fascinating prophecy with a time frame that corresponds with the coming of the Messiah as a suffering servant to atone for sins:

Daniel 9:24-27 (NIV)
24 "Seventy 'sevens' are decreed for your people and your holy city
to finish transgression, to put an end to sin, to atone for wickedness,
to bring in everlasting righteousness, to seal up vision and prophecy
and to anoint the most holy.
25 "Know and understand this: From the issuing of the decree to
restore and rebuild Jerusalem until the Anointed One, the ruler,
comes, there will be seven 'sevens,' and sixty-two 'sevens.' It will be
rebuilt with streets and a trench, but in times of trouble.
26 After the sixty-two 'sevens,' the Anointed One will be cut off and
will have nothing. The people of the ruler who will come will destroy
the city and the sanctuary. The end will come like a flood: War will
continue until the end, and desolations have been decreed.
27 He will confirm a covenant with many for one 'seven.' In the middle
of the 'seven' he will put an end to sacrifice and offering. And on a

wing [of the temple] he will set up an abomination that causes desolation, until the end that is decreed is poured out on him".

While there is much debate regarding the details of this prophecy, it is generally accepted by many that "seventy sevens" refers to 490 years. It gives a time table for when the "Anointed One", or Messiah will come. He will come sixty-nine sevens (seven sevens and sixty-two sevens) or 483 years after the issuing of the decree to restore and rebuild Jerusalem.

By the end of the entire 490 years, some amazing things are prophesied regarding the Jews and Jerusalem: Again,

24 "Seventy 'sevens' are decreed for your people and your holy city to finish transgression, to put an end to sin, to atone for wickedness, to bring in everlasting righteousness, to seal up vision and prophecy and to anoint the most holy."

Christians see Jesus as having atoned for wickedness and perhaps bringing in everlasting righteousness (those in Christ have by faith been declared righteous by God -"justified"- by having Christ's perfect record of righteousness credited to their account). However, not all these things were accomplished in their fullness during Jesus' first coming.

Another part of the difficulty is that there were various decrees to restore and rebuild Jerusalem. Cyrus gave one in 538 B.C. (2 Chron. 36:23). Another was given to Ezra by King Artaxerxes in 458 B.C. (Ezra 7:11-26). Still another was given to Nehemiah by king Artaxerxes in 445 or 444 B.C. authorizing him to rebuild the wall of the city and a house for him there (Neh. 2:1-8).

The question is raised as to whether these 490 years are consecutive. After the 483 years (the sixty-two sevens) it says the Messiah would be cut off and have nothing. If, as Christians believe, the Messiah is Jesus Christ, it would be referring to his crucifixion, which happened around 30 to 33 A.D. (depending on the date of his birth). But then, what follows is the destruction of the city of Jerusalem and the temple which occurred in 70 A.D., well after the additional 7 years making a total of 490 years. Many scholars believe the first sixty-nine sevens, or 483 years finished with Jesus' crucifixion – his being "cut off", but that the final seven years picks up in the future, after the "time of the Gentiles" is fulfilled.

Because the Jews rejected Jesus as their Messiah, their branch in the olive tree of faith was cut off and their unbelief ushered in the time of the Gentiles. Note Jesus' prediction of the destruction of Jerusalem given around 32 A.D., almost forty years before it happened:

Luke 21:20-24
"But when you see Jerusalem surrounded by armies, then know that
its desolation has come near. [21] Then let those who are in Judea flee
to the mountains, and let those who are inside the city depart, and let
not those who are out in the country enter it, [22] for these are days of
vengeance, to fulfill all that is written. [23] Alas for women who are
pregnant and for those who are nursing infants in those days! For
there will be great distress upon the earth and wrath against this
people. [24] They will fall by the edge of the sword and be led captive
among all nations, and Jerusalem will be trampled underfoot by the
Gentiles, until the times of the Gentiles are fulfilled.

Paul explains the why of this time of the Gentiles:

Romans 10:21
But of Israel he says, "All day long I have held out my hands to a disobedient and contrary people."

Romans 11:1-2a
I ask, then, has God rejected his people? By no means! For I myself
am an Israelite, a descendant of Abraham, a member of the tribe of
Benjamin. [2] God has not rejected his people whom he foreknew.

Romans 11:11-12; 25-29
So I ask, did they stumble in order that they might fall? By no
means! Rather through their trespass salvation has come to the
Gentiles, so as to make Israel jealous. [12] Now if their trespass
means riches for the world, and if their failure means riches for the
Gentiles, how much more will their full inclusion mean!

[25] Lest you be wise in your own conceits, I want you to
understand this mystery, brothers: a partial hardening has come upon
Israel, until the fullness of the Gentiles has come in. [26] And in this
way all Israel will be saved, as it is written,

"The Deliverer will come from Zion,
he will banish ungodliness from Jacob";

[27] "and this will be my covenant with them
when I take away their sins."
[28] As regards the gospel, they are enemies of God for your sake.
But as regards election, they are beloved for the sake of their
forefathers. [29] For the gifts and the calling of God are irrevocable.

So the last "seven" of the seventy 'sevens', or seven years will begin seven years before the "Deliverer will come from Zion" – referring to the coming of the Messiah, which will be when the time of the Gentiles is fulfilled, which seems to be yet future.

But getting back to the time frame that Daniel set out, we see another complication. The Jewish calendars had twelve 30 day months meaning that a year was composed of 360 days, rather than 365 and a quarter days which is the solar calendar. 483 years of 360 days would be equivalent to 476 solar calendar years. If the starting date is King Artaxerxes' decree to Nehemiah to rebuild the walls of the city in 445 or 444 B.C., then the 483 years, or sixty-nine 'sevens' (476 in solar years) would come out to 31 or 32 A.D. depending on which year the decree was made. That falls in with the time that Jesus was crucified.

This is huge and should give great pause to my Jewish friends as they grapple with Daniel's prophecy. Could Jesus indeed be the Jewish Messiah who came as the suffering Servant that Isaiah prophesied, who would take upon himself our iniquities and as Daniel says, "would atone for wickedness"?

There are scores of prophecies that were literally fulfilled with Jesus, but part of the problem for Jewish people is that he did not fit the picture of a victorious coming king to sit on David's throne and rule over the nations. Again, these point to the dual nature of some of the prophecies. They have been partially fulfilled with the first coming and will be fulfilled in their completeness with his second coming. One example is that of where the Messiah was to be born. The prophet Micah writes:

Micah 5:2
But you, O Bethlehem Ephrathah,
who are too little to be among the clans of Judah,
from you shall come forth for me
one who is to be ruler in Israel,
whose origin is from of old,
from ancient days.

Jesus was born in Bethlehem of Mary, who was a descendant of David and whose husband to be, Joseph, was also of the Davidic lineage. The stumbling block is the term "ruler in Israel". The people of Jesus' time did not see him as a ruler.

Jesus came proclaiming the gospel of the kingdom of God. He came to usher in that kingdom. Jesus was a dividing figure or a turning point in history as illustrated in what he had to say about John the Baptist:

Matthew 11:7-15

As they went away, Jesus began to speak to the crowds concerning John: "What did you go out into the wilderness to see? A reed shaken by the wind? [8] What then did you go out to see? A man dressed in soft clothing? Behold, those who wear soft clothing are in kings' houses. [9] What then did you go out to see? A prophet? Yes, I tell you, and more than a prophet. [10] This is he of whom it is written,

" 'Behold, I send my messenger before your face,
who will prepare your way before you.'

[11] Truly, I say to you, among those born of women there has arisen no one greater than John the Baptist. Yet the one who is least in the kingdom of heaven is greater than he. [12] From the days of John the Baptist until now the kingdom of heaven has suffered violence, and the violent take it by force. [13] For all the Prophets and the Law prophesied until John, [14] and if you are willing to accept it, he is Elijah who is to come. [15] He who has ears to hear, let him hear.

John was the greatest of the Old Covenant Era, but the least person in the kingdom of heaven is greater than he. How? When a person receives Jesus as King of his life through repentance and faith, he is ushered into God's kingdom and has all his sins forgiven and is given the gift of the Holy Spirit. His experience with God is far greater than that of any saint in the Old Testament era.

Besides prophesying his birthplace, many other details of Jesus' life were prophesied hundreds of years before he came. Zechariah prophesied that the Messiah would be betrayed for thirty pieces of silver (Zech. 11:12-13) and that that money would be thrown back into the temple to be given to a potter, which is the price he was paid for his field. Judas was paid thirty pieces of silver to betray Jesus and in remorse he later threw those pieces back in the temple which were used to buy a potter's field for the burial of foreigners (Mt. 26:15; 27:9-10).

David, under the inspiration of the Holy Spirit wrote this:

Psalm 22:14-18
I am poured out like water,
and all my bones are out of joint;
my heart is like wax;
it is melted within my breast;
[15] my strength is dried up like a potsherd,
and my tongue sticks to my jaws;
you lay me in the dust of death.
[16] For dogs encompass me;
a company of evildoers encircles me;
they have pierced my hands and feet—
[17] I can count all my bones—
they stare and gloat over me;
[18] they divide my garments among them,
and for my clothing they cast lots.

Crucifixion as a method of death was not even invented during David's day, but here is a picture of exactly how Jesus died. Though his hands and feet were nailed to the cross, none of his bones were broken, though they did get out of joint by the weight of his body hanging by his hands. His clothes were divided among soldiers by casting lots for them:

John 19:23-24
When the soldiers had crucified Jesus, they took his garments and divided them into four parts, one part for each soldier; also his tunic. But the tunic was seamless, woven in one piece from top to bottom, [24] so they said to one another, "Let us not tear it, but cast lots for it to see whose it shall be." This was to fulfill the Scripture which says,

"They divided my garments among them,
and for my clothing they cast lots."

So the soldiers did these things,

How Will the Jews Recognize the Messiah When He Comes?

The same prophet Zechariah who foretold of the thirty pieces of silver, tells of a future coming of the Messiah when all the nations of the earth have gathered against Jerusalem and Judah to destroy them:

Zechariah 12:1-3 (NIV)
[1] This is the word of the Lord concerning Israel. The Lord, who
stretches out the heavens, who lays the foundation of the earth, and
who forms the spirit of man within him, declares:
[2] "I am going to make Jerusalem a cup that sends all the surrounding
peoples reeling. Judah will be besieged as well as Jerusalem.
[3] On that day, when all the nations of the earth are gathered against
her, I will make Jerusalem an immovable rock for all the nations. All
who try to move it will injure themselves.

Zechariah 12:9-10 (NIV)
[9] On that day I will set out to destroy all the nations that attack
Jerusalem.
[10] "And I will pour out on the house of David and the inhabitants of
Jerusalem a spirit of grace and supplication. They will look on me, the
one they have pierced, and they will mourn for him as one mourns for
an only child, and grieve bitterly for him as one grieves for a firstborn
son.

When Jesus returns to rescue Israel from the nations of the earth bent on her destruction, Israel will see the writer of this prophecy – "the Lord" saying, "They will look on me, the one they have pierced." Who was the one that Israel pierced but Jesus, the Son of God. Then it says, "and they will mourn for him as one mourns for an only child, and grieve bitterly for him as one grieves for a firstborn son." When the Jewish people come to realize that their Messiah, the One they have longed for, is none other than Jesus whom they have rejected for these past two millennia, they will grieve bitterly.

7 THE MESSIAH

IN THE LAST chapter, we raised one of the principle issues that divide Judaism from Christianity. It regards the nature and identity of the Messiah. The Hebrew word *Mashiach* corresponds to the English word *Messiah,* and they both mean "anointed." The belief in a coming Mashiach is part of traditional Judaism. Twelfth century Rabbi Moshe ben-Maimon, called Maimonides, or "The Rambam" (Hebrew acronym for "Rabbi Moshe ben Maimon") formulated thirteen principles of faith, which he considered to be the minimum requirement of Jewish belief. They are summarized as follows:[15]

1. G-d exists
2. G-d is one and unique
3. G-d is incorporeal
4. G-d is eternal
5. Prayer is to be directed to G-d alone and to no other
6. The words of the prophets are true
7. Moses' prophecies are true, and Moses was the greatest of the prophets
8. The Written Torah (first 5 books of the Bible) and Oral Torah (teachings now contained in the Talmud and other writings) were given to Moses
9. There will be no other Torah
10. G-d knows the thoughts and deeds of men

---

[15] Maimonides, Commentary on the Mishnah, Tractate Sanhedrin, chapter 10: Summary, Tracey R Rich, <http://www.jewfaq.org/beliefs.htm>

11. G-d will reward the good and punish the wicked
12. The Messiah will come
13. The dead will be resurrected

While as in Christianity, there are various divisions and interpretations, so too in Judaism. However, this coming Messiah, according to traditional Judaism, will not be divine, but rather a mortal man. Maimonides describes the Messianic age this way:

The Messianic age is when the Jews will regain their independence and all return to the land of Israel. The Messiah will be a very great king, he will achieve great fame, and his reputation among the gentile nations will be even greater than that of King Solomon. His great righteousness and the wonders that he will bring about will cause all peoples to make peace with him and all lands to serve him.... Nothing will change in the Messianic age, however, except that Jews will regain their independence. Rich and poor, strong and weak, will still exist. However it will be very easy for people to make a living, and with very little effort they will be able to accomplish very much.... it will be a time when the number of wise men will increase.... war shall not exist, and nation shall no longer lift up sword against nation.... The Messianic age will be highlighted by a community of the righteous and dominated by goodness and wisdom. It will be ruled by the Messiah, a righteous and honest king, outstanding in wisdom, and close to God. Do not think that the ways of the world or the laws of nature will change, this is not true. The world will continue as it is. The prophet Isaiah predicted "The wolf shall live with the sheep, the leopard shall lie down with the kid." This, however, is merely allegory, meaning that the Jews will live safely, even with the formerly wicked nations. All nations will return to the true religion and will no longer steal or oppress. Note that all prophecies regarding the Messiah are allegorical. Only in the Messianic age will we know the meaning of each allegory and what it comes to teach us. Our sages and prophets did not long for the Messianic age in order that they might rule the world and dominate the gentiles, the only thing they wanted was to be free for Jews to involve themselves with the Torah and its wisdom.[16]

[16] Maimonides, Commentary on Mishnah, Sanhedrin 10:1

According to the Talmud, the Midrash, and the Kabbalistic work, the Zohar, the 'deadline' by which the Messiah must appear is 6000 years from creation. A majority of Orthodox and Hasidic Jews believe that the Hebrew calendar dates back to the time of creation; the year 2012-2013 (the Hebrew New Year being during September or October) of the Gregorian calendar corresponds to the Hebrew year 5773.

There is a kabbalistic tradition that maintains that the 7 days of creation in Genesis 1 correspond to seven millennia of the existence of natural creation. The tradition teaches that the seventh day of the week, *Shabbat* or the day of rest, corresponds to the seventh millennium (Hebrew years 6000 - 7000), the age of universal 'rest' - the Messianic Era.[17]

This would put the coming of the Messiah in the year 2240 A.D according to the Hebrew calendar. The fact that Judaism sees the Messiah as being a human king who will usher in a glorious Messianic age in which Israel is independent and all Jews return to the land, combined with the idea of this happening 6,000 years after Adam, means that for them, Jesus of Nazareth could not have been the Messiah. The Christian teaching of him being the divine Son of God, born of a virgin, suffering an ignominious death, rising from the dead, not ruling gloriously on David's throne, and living thousands of years before the seventh millennium are all insurmountable barriers for most Jews to accept.

The Muslims also have a concept of a Messiah, called the Mahdi. While they believe that Jesus was a prophet of God and that he was born of the virgin Mary, they do not accept his deity or that he died on the cross and was raised from the dead. They believe he ascended directly into heaven without dying. They look forward to his return, not as the Messiah, but as the Mahdi's right hand man, so to speak. He will force everyone to convert to Islam and follow the Mahdi, after which he will die and be buried next to Mohammed, according to Islamic thought. More will be discussed regarding Islamic eschatology in chapter 10.

In the last chapter we presented the idea of the Messiah coming twice: first as a suffering servant, then as a glorious king. But can the Christian concept of the Messiah being divine be substantiated in the Jewish scriptures? In order to answer that, we need to see texts in both the New Testament and the Old Testament to see what the Bible really

[17] Jewish Eschatology, <http://en.wikipedia.org/wiki/Jewish_eschatology>

teaches about who Jesus is, what he did and how that relates to Jewish scriptures.

Perhaps the clearest Old Testament passage that presents the Messiah as being a God-man is found in Isaiah:

Isaiah 9:6-7

For to us **a child is born**,
to us a son is given;
and the government shall be upon his shoulder,
and his name shall be called
Wonderful Counselor, **Mighty God,**
Everlasting Father, Prince of Peace.
[7] Of the increase of his government and of peace
there will be no end,
on the throne of David and over his kingdom,
to establish it and to uphold it
with justice and with righteousness
from this time forth and forevermore.
The zeal of the Lord of hosts will do this.

His humanity is seen by the fact that he is born. His divinity, however, can be surmised by his titles – "Mighty God" and his eternal nature – "Everlasting Father." He is one who will rule on David's throne forever.

The New Testament gives further revelation as to who this Messiah was going to be:

John 1:1-5, 9-14

In the beginning was the Word, and the Word was with God,
and the Word was God. [2] He was in the beginning with God. [3] All
things were made through him, and without him was not any thing
made that was made. [4] In him was life, and the life was the light of
men. [5] The light shines in the darkness, and the darkness has not
overcome it.

The true light, which enlightens everyone, was coming into the
world. [10] He was in the world, and the world was made through
him, yet the world did not know him. [11] He came to his own, and
his own people did not receive him. [12] But to all who did receive
him, who believed in his name, he gave the right to become children
of God, [13] who were born, not of blood nor of the will of the flesh

nor of the will of man, but of God.

[14] And the Word became flesh and dwelt among us, and we have seen his glory, glory as of the only Son from the Father, full of grace and truth.

As we have seen, history is all about Satan and man's rebellion against God and God redeeming a portion of mankind to himself. We said from the beginning that Genesis 3:15 forms the basis for history:

Genesis 3:15 (NASB)
15 And I will put enmity between you and the woman, And between your seed and her seed; He shall bruise you on the head, And you shall bruise him on the heel."

At every turn, Satan and his seed have been dedicated to wiping out the lineage of the woman – the godly seed. God told the devil that the seed of the woman would deal him a deadly head wound, even though Satan would also inflict a wound on him.

Satan's worst nightmare occurred when God's Son took on human form and was born to a simple young Galilean virgin. It was to be no ordinary birth, as an angel explained to Mary:

Luke 1:26-35
In the sixth month the angel Gabriel was sent from God to a city of Galilee named Nazareth, [27] to a virgin betrothed to a man whose name was Joseph, of the house of David. And the virgin's name was Mary. [28] And he came to her and said, "Greetings, O favored one, the Lord is with you!" [29] But she was greatly troubled at the saying, and tried to discern what sort of greeting this might be. [30] And the angel said to her, "Do not be afraid, Mary, for you have found favor with God. [31] And behold, you will conceive in your womb and bear a son, and you shall call his name Jesus. [32] He will be great and will be called the Son of the Most High. And the Lord God will give to him the throne of his father David, [33] and he will reign over the house of Jacob forever, and of his kingdom there will be no end."

[34] And Mary said to the angel, "How will this be, since I am a virgin?"

[35] And the angel answered her, "The Holy Spirit will come upon you, and the power of the Most High will overshadow you; therefore the child to be born will be called holy—the Son of God.

God also communicated to Joseph, her betrothed husband to be, what was happening:

Matthew 1:18-25

Now the birth of Jesus Christ took place in this way. When his mother Mary had been betrothed to Joseph, before they came together she was found to be with child from the Holy Spirit. [19] And her husband Joseph, being a just man and unwilling to put her to shame, resolved to divorce her quietly. [20] But as he considered these things, behold, an angel of the Lord appeared to him in a dream, saying, "Joseph, son of David, do not fear to take Mary as your wife, for that which is conceived in her is from the Holy Spirit. [21] She will bear a son, and you shall call his name Jesus, for he will save his people from their sins." [22] All this took place to fulfill what the Lord had spoken by the prophet:

> [23] "Behold, the virgin shall conceive and bear a son,
> and they shall call his name Immanuel"

(which means, God with us). [24] When Joseph woke from sleep, he did as the angel of the Lord commanded him: he took his wife, [25] but knew her not until she had given birth to a son. And he called his name Jesus.

But Satan was determined to do away with this child who had been prophesied to bring about his eventual demise. We see a picture of this in the book of Revelation:

Rev. 12:1-5

And a great sign appeared in heaven: a woman clothed with the sun, with the moon under her feet, and on her head a crown of twelve stars. [2] She was pregnant and was crying out in birth pains and the agony of giving birth. [3] And another sign appeared in heaven: behold, a great red dragon, with seven heads and ten horns, and on his heads seven diadems. [4] His tail swept down a third of the stars of heaven and cast them to the earth. And the dragon stood before the woman who was about to give birth, so that when she bore her child he might devour it. [5] She gave birth to a male child, one who is to rule all the nations with a rod of iron, but her child was caught up to God and to his throne,

Reading the further context of the same chapter, one sees that the woman is Israel, as personified by Mary and the dragon is Satan. The devil did try to kill Jesus shortly after his birth using Herod, the King, who when he heard from the Wise Men that there had been born "a king of the Jews", he had all the male babies in Bethlehem killed from two years old and younger (Mt. 2). Satan tried numerous other times to kill Jesus – through the people of his own home town (Lk. 4:16-30), the Pharisees, Sadducees and Herodians, who on various occasions plotted to kill him. It is possible that the devil even used the natural elements to try to put Christ to death. There were several times that Jesus was in a boat when a sudden storm came up, so severe that the disciples, who were seasoned fishermen, feared for their lives. This serves as an important principle: Satan has to work through people and nature. God also works through people and nature. In a sense, the battle is fought on the human playing field, even though the forces behind them are in the heavenly and unseen realm.

At the age of 30, Jesus began his public ministry and began to preach, saying, "Repent, for the kingdom of heaven is at hand" (Mt. 4:17). Matthew gives us a summary of his early ministry:

Matthew 4:23-25

And he went throughout all Galilee, teaching in their synagogues and proclaiming the gospel of the kingdom and healing every disease and every affliction among the people. [24] So his fame spread throughout all Syria, and they brought him all the sick, those afflicted with various diseases and pains, those oppressed by demons, epileptics, and paralytics, and he healed them. [25] And great crowds followed him from Galilee and the Decapolis, and from Jerusalem and Judea, and from beyond the Jordan.

While initially popular, when the crowds saw that Jesus was not going to become their king who would free them from Roman tyranny, they rejected him. As we saw in the last chapter, that rejection ushered in the era of the Gentiles. Jesus alluded to this on a number of occasions:

Luke 13:22-30

He went on his way through towns and villages, teaching and journeying toward Jerusalem. [23] And someone said to him, "Lord, will those who are saved be few?" And he said to them, [24] "Strive to enter through the narrow door. For many, I tell you, will seek to enter and will not be able. [25] When once the master of the house has risen and shut the door, and you begin to stand outside and to knock at the door, saying, 'Lord, open to us,' then he will answer you, 'I do not know where you come from.' [26] Then you will begin to say, 'We ate and drank in your presence, and you taught in our streets.' [27] But he will say, 'I tell you, I do not know where you come from. Depart from me, all you workers of evil!' [28] In that place there will be weeping and gnashing of teeth, when you see Abraham and Isaac and Jacob and all the prophets in the kingdom of God but you yourselves cast out. [29] And people will come from east and west, and from north and south, and recline at table in the kingdom of God. [30] And behold, some are last who will be first, and some are first who will be last."

Matthew 21:43
"Therefore I tell you, the kingdom of God will be taken away from you and given to a people producing its fruits."

Finally, the right time came for Satan to strike. The devil entered Judas, one of the twelve and tempted him to betray Jesus to the Jewish High Priests, just as Jesus had predicted on numerous occasions.

Luke 22:3-6
Then Satan entered into Judas called Iscariot, who was of the number of the twelve. [4] He went away and conferred with the chief priests and officers how he might betray him to them. [5] And they were glad, and agreed to give him money. [6] So he consented and sought an opportunity to betray him to them in the absence of a crowd.

Judas betrayed Jesus on the night of the Passover Feast and Jesus was tried in the middle of the night – against all laws, and was sentenced to death. Through pressure brought to bear on Pilate, the Roman governor, he consented in having Jesus crucified, which was carried out that same day, the day of Passover (Jewish days go from sunset to sunset).

Matthew 27:15-26
Now at the feast the governor was accustomed to release for the crowd any one prisoner whom they wanted. [16] And they had then a notorious prisoner called Barabbas. [17] So when they had gathered,

Pilate said to them, "Whom do you want me to release for you: Barabbas, or Jesus who is called Christ?" [18] For he knew that it was out of envy that they had delivered him up. [19] Besides, while he was sitting on the judgment seat, his wife sent word to him, "Have nothing to do with that righteous man, for I have suffered much because of him today in a dream." [20] Now the chief priests and the elders persuaded the crowd to ask for Barabbas and destroy Jesus. [21] The governor again said to them, "Which of the two do you want me to release for you?" And they said, "Barabbas." [22] Pilate said to them, "Then what shall I do with Jesus who is called Christ?" They all said, "Let him be crucified!" [23] And he said, "Why, what evil has he done?" But they shouted all the more, "Let him be crucified!"

[24] So when Pilate saw that he was gaining nothing, but rather that a riot was beginning, he took water and washed his hands before the crowd, saying, "I am innocent of this man's blood; see to it yourselves." [25] And all the people answered, "His blood be on us and on our children!" [26] Then he released for them Barabbas, and having scourged Jesus, delivered him to be crucified.

Satan thought himself to have won the final victory over his arch enemy – the Son of God, by having him put to death. He had been suffering defeat over and over again when Jesus and then his disciples would cast demons out and set people free from Satan's oppression, but now, instead of him receiving the fatal head wound, he had turned the tables so that Jesus would be mortally wounded – so he thought.

What the devil did not realize was that Jesus' death was exactly what had to happen to bring about his own destruction. We read in Hebrews, speaking of Jesus:

Hebrews 2:14-18

Since therefore the children share in flesh and blood, he himself likewise partook of the same things, that through death he might destroy the one who has the power of death, that is, the devil, [15] and deliver all those who through fear of death were subject to lifelong slavery. [16] For surely it is not angels that he helps, but he helps the offspring of Abraham. [17] Therefore he had to be made like his brothers in every respect, so that he might become a merciful and faithful high priest in the service of God, to make propitiation for the sins of the people. [18] For because he himself has suffered when tempted, he is able to help those who are being tempted.

Paul explains further the purpose of Christ's death:

Romans 5:6-11
For while we were still weak, at the right time Christ died for the ungodly. [7] For one will scarcely die for a righteous person—though perhaps for a good person one would dare even to die— [8] but God shows his love for us in that while we were still sinners, Christ died for us. [9] Since, therefore, we have now been justified by his blood, much more shall we be saved by him from the wrath of God. [10] For if while we were enemies we were reconciled to God by the death of his Son, much more, now that we are reconciled, shall we be saved by his life. [11] More than that, we also rejoice in God through our Lord Jesus Christ, through whom we have now received reconciliation.

There is a part that man has to play in this:

John 3:16
"For God so loved the world, that he gave his only Son, that whoever believes in him should not perish but have eternal life.

Jesus had been preaching, "Repent, for the kingdom of God is at hand" (Mt. 4:17). Jesus' death reconciled sinners to God through repentance and faith in Christ and ushered them into God's kingdom, snatching them out of Satan's kingdom.

Though Satan seemed to be the victor in Jesus' death, his death was only a temporary and necessary step to ultimate victory because the grave could not keep Jesus in. He was resurrected the third day and is now seated at God's right hand, interceding for his people. Satan, however, received a mortal head blow from which he will never be able to recover. He is not yet finished and still has a lot of fight in him, but the end is already determined and Jesus won the victory over him, just as God told him in Genesis 3:15. The rest of history, since Jesus' death and resurrection, is the playing out of the final struggle of the devil against God, his people and plans. He wants to take as many people to hell with him as he can.

The New Testament gives a couple of brief summaries of who Jesus Christ is and what he came to do:

Philip. 2:5-11
Have this mind among yourselves, which is yours in Christ Jesus, [6] who, though he was in the form of God, did not count equality

with God a thing to be grasped, [7] but made himself nothing, taking the form of a servant, being born in the likeness of men. And being found in human form, [8] he humbled himself by becoming obedient to the point of death, even death on a cross. [9] Therefore God has highly exalted him and bestowed on him the name that is above every name, [10] so that at the name of Jesus every knee should bow, in heaven and on earth and under the earth, [11] and every tongue confess that Jesus Christ is Lord, to the glory of God the Father.

Col. 1:13-20

He [God the Father] has delivered us from the domain of darkness and transferred us to the kingdom of his beloved Son, [14] in whom we have redemption, the forgiveness of sins.

[15] He is the image of the invisible God, the firstborn of all creation. [16] For by him all things were created, in heaven and on earth, visible and invisible, whether thrones or dominions or rulers or authorities—all things were created through him and for him. [17] And he is before all things, and in him all things hold together. [18] And he is the head of the body, the church. He is the beginning, the firstborn from the dead, that in everything he might be preeminent. [19] For in him all the fullness of God was pleased to dwell, [20] and through him to reconcile to himself all things, whether on earth or in heaven, making peace by the blood of his cross.

The Jewish Feasts Fulfilled in Christ

In Chapter 4 I listed the seven annual Feast Days prescribed for Israel in Leviticus 23. They are again:[18]

Passover or Pesach - 14 Nisan (March or April)
Unleavened Bread or Hag HaMatzot - 15-21 Nisan (Mar. or Apr.)
First Fruits or Yom HaBikkurim - 16 Nisan (Mar. or Apr.)
Feast of Weeks or Pentecost or Shavuot - 6 Sivan (May or June)
Feast of Trumpets or Rosh HaShanah - 1Tishri (Sept. or Oct.)
Day of Atonement or Yom Kippur - 10 Tishri (Sept. or Oct.)
Feast of Booths (Tabernacles) or Sukkot - 15-21 Tishri (Sept./Oct.)

[18] Op. Cit., Feasts & Holidays of the Bible

Were these Festivals to be ends in and of themselves, or did they point to something else to come? The Bible says the festivals are "shadows" of things to come.

Col. 2:16-17

Therefore let no one pass judgment on you in questions of food and drink, or with regard to a festival or a new moon or a Sabbath. [17] These are a shadow of the things to come, but the substance belongs to Christ.

In his first coming, Jesus fulfilled the first four of the seven Old Testament Festivals prescribed in Leviticus 23, sometimes referred to as "God's calendar of redeeming grace" or the "calendar of divine redemption". Some believe it is a calendar of God's redemptive plan for human history.

1. Passover – (Pesach) - 14 Nisan (Lev. 23:4-5; Ex. 12:1-4) which is in March or April. It commemorates God's deliverance of the people of Israel from slavery in Egypt. The Passover lamb had to be sacrificed and the blood applied for the angel of death to pass over their house. Jesus was the Passover Lamb of God who takes away the sin of the world (Jn 1:29) and he was sacrificed exactly on the day of Passover, 14 Nisan.

2. Feast of Unleavened Bread – (Hag HaMatzot) - 15-21 Nisan (Lev 23:6-8; Ex 12:15-20). The cleansing of the house of leaven, which represents sin (Lu 12:1; 1 Cor 5:8) is celebrated starting on the Passover meal where unleavened bread – or "matzot", which is plural for "matzah" bread is eaten. Jesus represented the "bread of life" (Jn 6:32, 35, 41, 48). Leaven represents sin, but Jesus the Messiah is unleavened, or sinless.

3. Firstfruits – (Yom HaBikkurim) - 16 Nisan is the day that the people offered the first ripe sheaf of barley (firstfruits) to the Lord as an act of dedicating the harvest to Him. On the third day after Passover, the priest would wave the sheaf before the Lord. Jesus was raised from the dead on the Feast of Firstfruits which fits in with what Paul tells us in

1 Cor. 15:20-23

"But in fact Christ has been raised from the dead, the firstfruits of those who have fallen asleep. [21] For as by a man came death, by a man has come also the resurrection of the dead. [22] For as in Adam all die, so also in Christ shall all be made alive. [23] But each in his own order: Christ the firstfruits, then at his coming those who belong to Christ."

4. Feast of Weeks, or Pentecost – (Shavuot) - 6 Sivan (Lev 23:15-22) – May or June. This is also known as the Feast of Harvest and is the time to present an offering of the new grain of the summer wheat harvest to the Lord. It is the 50th day after the Sabbath of Passover week, thus the name "Pentecost" and is also always a Sunday, the first day of the week. This is the day that Jesus, exalted in heaven poured out the Holy Spirit on the Church, fulfilling the prophecy in Joel that God would pour out his Spirit on all flesh (Joel 2:28-32). It was also the beginning of the New Covenant (Jer 31:31; Heb 9:14-15) and on that day of Pentecost, there was a gathering in of 3,000 people into the New Covenant Harvest (Acts 2:41).

These first four Festivals are spring festivals. There are three remaining festivals that are fall festivals. Could they point to God's future redemptive plan?

5. Feast of Trumpets – (Rosh HaShanah) – 1 Tishri (Lev 23:23-25) – September or October. This begins the 10 days of repentance leading up to the Day of Atonement. Rosh HaShanah is sometimes referred to as the Day of Judgment. It begins the time when people repent of their sins in hopes that their names will be written in the Book of Life. During the Rosh HaShanah synagogue services, the shofar, or ram's horn – trumpet, is blown 100 times. The Bible refers to Jesus' second coming as a day of judgment.

Rev. 19:11

"Then I saw heaven opened, and behold, a white horse! The one sitting on it is called Faithful and True, and in righteousness he judges and makes war."

2 Tim. 4:1

"I charge you in the presence of God and of Christ Jesus, who is to judge the living and the dead, and by his appearing and his kingdom:"

When does he come?

1 Cor. 15:51-53

Behold! I tell you a mystery. We shall not all sleep, but we shall all be changed, [52] in a moment, in the twinkling of an eye, **at the last trumpet**. For the trumpet will sound, and the dead will be raised imperishable, and we shall be changed. [53] For this perishable body must put on the imperishable, and this mortal body must put on immortality.

Matthew 24:30-31

Then will appear in heaven the sign of the Son of Man, and then all the tribes of the earth will mourn, and they will see the Son of Man coming on the clouds of heaven with power and great glory. [31] And he will send out his angels **with a loud trumpet call**, and they will gather his elect from the four winds, from one end of heaven to the other.

1 Thess. 4:16-17

For the Lord himself will descend from heaven with a cry of command, with the voice of an archangel, **and with the sound of the trumpet** of God. And the dead in Christ will rise first. [17] Then we who are alive, who are left, will be caught up together with them in the clouds to meet the Lord in the air, and so we will always be with the Lord.

Zech. 9:14

Then the Lord will appear over them, and his arrow will go forth like lightning; **the Lord God will sound the trumpet** and will march forth in the whirlwinds of the south.

Based on the fact that Jesus' other redemptive acts were done exactly on the day corresponding to the respective Feast Day, could we conclude that Jesus will return on the 1st of Tishri, the Feast of Trumpets, which is in September or October? In answer to that question, many point to Jesus' statement that "no one knows the day or the hour" (Mt 24:36). However, is there more to his statement than meets the eye? We will look at that later.

6. Day of Atonement – (Yom Kippur) – 10 Tishri (Lev 23:26-32) – September or October. This is the day when the priest makes atonement for sin. It means the reconciliation of God and man and follows the 10 days of repentance beginning with the Feast of Trumpets.

Yom Kippur is the final day of judgment when God judges his people. Notice what follows Christ's future appearance in Jerusalem:

Zech. 12:10-12
"And I will pour out on the house of David and the inhabitants of Jerusalem a spirit of grace and pleas for mercy, so that, when they look on me, on him whom they have pierced, they shall mourn for him, as one mourns for an only child, and weep bitterly over him, as one weeps over a firstborn. [11] On that day the mourning in Jerusalem will be as great as the mourning for Hadad-rimmon in the plain of Megiddo. [12] The land shall mourn, each family by itself …"
Zech. 13:1
"On that day there shall be a fountain opened for the house of David and the inhabitants of Jerusalem, to cleanse them from sin and uncleanness.

If Jesus were to return on the Feast of Trumpets and "they will look on him whom they have pierced", could it be that for the following ten days they will mourn a great mourning of repentance? God will pour out on them a spirit of grace and pleas for mercy as they realize that Jesus is the Messiah they have so stubbornly rebelled against these 2,000 years. On the tenth day, the Day of Atonement, Jesus will open a fountain for them from the temple symbolizing their cleansing from sin and uncleanness.

Zech. 14:4,5-8,9
On that day his feet shall stand on the Mount of Olives that lies before Jerusalem on the east, and the Mount of Olives shall be split in two from east to west by a very wide valley, so that one half of the Mount shall move northward, and the other half southward…..
Then the Lord my God will come, and all the holy ones with him.
[8] On that day living waters shall flow out from Jerusalem, half of them to the eastern sea and half of them to the western sea. It shall continue in summer as in winter.
[9] And the Lord will be king over all the earth. On that day the Lord will be one and his name one.

Ezekiel 47:1
Then he brought me back to the door of the temple, and behold, water was issuing from below the threshold of the temple toward the

east (for the temple faced east). The water was flowing down from below the south end of the threshold of the temple, south of the altar.

Ezekiel 47:12

And on the banks, on both sides of the river, there will grow all kinds of trees for food. Their leaves will not wither, nor their fruit fail, but they will bear fresh fruit every month, because the water for them flows from the sanctuary. Their fruit will be for food, and their leaves for healing."

Joel 3:17-18

"So you shall know that I am the Lord your God,
who dwells in Zion, my holy mountain.
And Jerusalem shall be holy,
and strangers shall never again pass through it.
[18] "And in that day
the mountains shall drip sweet wine,
and the hills shall flow with milk,
and all the streambeds of Judah
shall flow with water;
and a fountain shall come forth from the house of the Lord
and water the Valley of Shittim.

What about the last Feast?

7. Feast of Booths or Tabernacles – (Sukkot) – 15-21 Tishri (Lev 23:33-43) – September or October. This is a week-long celebration of the fall harvest and is sometimes called the Festival of Ingathering. It is also a time to build booths (temporary shelters of branches) to remember how the people of Israel lived under God's care in the wilderness for 40 years (Neh 8:14-17). The celebration is a reminder of God's faithfulness and protection and is referred to as the Season of our Rejoicing.

Two ceremonies were part of the last day of Sukkot. First, the people carrying torches marched around the Temple, then these lights were set around the walls of the Temple, indicating that Messiah would be a light to the Gentiles:

Isaiah 49:6

"I will make you as a light for the nations,
that my salvation may reach to the end of the earth."

Secondly, a priest carried water from the pool of Siloam to the Temple, symbolizing that when Messiah comes the whole earth will know God, "as the waters cover the sea." (Is 11:9) and as a memorial to God's provision of water out of the rock in the wilderness.

John 7:37-38
On the last day of the feast, the great day, Jesus stood up and cried out, "If anyone thirsts, let him come to me and drink. [38] Whoever believes in me, as the Scripture has said, 'Out of his heart will flow rivers of living water.' "

The next morning, while the torches were still burning, he said, …

John 8:12
Again Jesus spoke to them, saying, "I am the light of the world. Whoever follows me will not walk in darkness, but will have the light of life."

Notice the importance of celebrating this Feast after Jesus has set up his throne to rule from Jerusalem:

Zech. 14:16-19
Then everyone who survives of all the nations that have come against Jerusalem shall go up year after year to worship the King, the Lord of hosts, and to keep the Feast of Booths. [17] And if any of the families of the earth do not go up to Jerusalem to worship the King, the Lord of hosts, there will be no rain on them. [18] And if the family of Egypt does not go up and present themselves, then on them there shall be no rain; there shall be the plague with which the Lord afflicts the nations that do not go up to keep the Feast of Booths. [19] This shall be the punishment to Egypt and the punishment to all the nations that do not go up to keep the Feast of Booths.

When Will Christ Return?

That is the question that everyone would like to know, including Jesus' disciples. They asked Jesus,

Matthew 24:3
"Tell us, when will these things be, and what will be the sign of your coming and of the close of the age?"

Later in his discourse Jesus said this:

Matthew 24:36

"But concerning that day and hour no one knows, not even the angels of heaven, nor the Son, but the Father only.

That would seem to indicate that it is foolhardy to attempt to ever know when Jesus will return. However, looking more closely at the text, we may come to a different conclusion.

We have suggested that in fulfillment of the Festival Calendar, Jesus will return on the Feast of Trumpets. That was the only Feast that began on the first day of a month. According to the Jewish lunar calendar, the first sighting of a lunar crescent marked the first day of the month. Wikipedia explains:[19] "The length of a month orbit/cycle is difficult to predict and varies from its average value. Because observations are subject to uncertainty and weather conditions, and astronomical methods are highly complex, there have been attempts to create fixed arithmetical rules. The average length of the synodic month is 29.530589 days. This requires the length of a month to be alternately 29 and 30 days."

In the Jewish tradition, two priests would stand at the pinnacle of the temple looking for the first sign of the lunar crescent. There was a 48 hour window of possibility. Once seen, they would declare the beginning of the Feast of Trumpets. For that reason, it became known as the Feast for which no one knew the day or the hour when it would begin. In saying that, Jesus was actually giving us a clue as to what Festival would mark his coming.

In the whole discourse regarding things to come in the future, Jesus speaks in the future tense. "These things **will** happen …etc." However, in this sentence he is speaking in the present tense. No one knows ***now*** what that day or hour will be. That this uncertainty is not a permanent condition can be shown by the following arguments:

1. The Bible specifies certain things that have to happen before his return:

Matthew 24:14

And this gospel of the kingdom will be proclaimed throughout the

[19] http://en.wikipedia.org/wiki/Lunar_calendar

whole world as a testimony to all nations, and **then the end will come.**

Matthew 24:15

"**So when you see** the abomination of desolation spoken of by the prophet Daniel, standing in the holy place (let the reader understand),…"

Matthew 24:29-30

"**Immediately after the tribulation** of those days the sun will be darkened, and the moon will not give its light, and the stars will fall from heaven, and the powers of the heavens will be shaken. [30] **Then will appear** in heaven the sign of the Son of Man, and then all the tribes of the earth will mourn, and they will see the Son of Man coming on the clouds of heaven with power and great glory.

Matthew 24:32-34

"From the fig tree learn its lesson: as soon as its branch becomes tender and puts out its leaves, you know that summer is near. [33] **So also, when you see all these things, you know that he is near, at the very gates.** [34] Truly, I say to you, this generation will not pass away until all these things take place.

2 Thess. 2:1-3

Now concerning the coming of our Lord Jesus Christ and our being gathered together to him, we ask you, brothers, [2] not to be quickly shaken in mind or alarmed, either by a spirit or a spoken word, or a letter seeming to be from us, to the effect that the day of the Lord has come. [3] Let no one deceive you in any way. **For that day will not come, unless** the rebellion comes first, and the man of lawlessness is revealed, the son of destruction,

2 Thess. 2:7-8

For the mystery of lawlessness is already at work. **Only he who now restrains it will do so until he is out of the way. [8] And then** the lawless one will be revealed, whom the Lord Jesus will kill with the breath of his mouth and bring to nothing by the appearance of his coming.

2 Thess. 2:4

who [the man of lawlessness] opposes and exalts himself against every so-called god or object of worship, so that **he takes his seat in the temple of God, proclaiming himself to be God.**
(This presupposes that a temple has to be built in Jerusalem before this can take place)

2. While the world will be surprised when that day comes, the believers will not be:

1 Thess. 5:1-5

Now **concerning the times and the seasons**, brothers, you have no need to have anything written to you. [2] For you yourselves are fully aware that **the day of the Lord will come like a thief in the night.** [3] While people are saying, "There is peace and security," then sudden destruction will come upon them as labor pains come upon a pregnant woman, and they will not escape. [4] **But you are not in darkness, brothers, for that day to surprise you like a thief.** [5] For you are all children of light, children of the day. We are not of the night or of the darkness.

3. The Bible gives an exact timeline once certain events happen:

Daniel 12:1-2, 6-7

"At that time shall arise Michael, the great prince who has charge of your people. And there shall be a time of trouble, such as never has been since there was a nation till that time. But at that time your people shall be delivered, everyone whose name shall be found written in the book. [2] And many of those who sleep in the dust of the earth shall awake, some to everlasting life, and some to shame and everlasting contempt.....
[6]"**How long shall it be till the end of these wonders?**" [7] And I heard the man clothed in linen, who was above the waters of the stream; he raised his right hand and his left hand toward heaven and swore by him who lives forever that **it would be for a time, times, and half a time**, and that when the shattering of the power of the holy people comes to an end all these things would be finished.

Daniel 12:11-12

And from the time that the regular burnt offering is taken away and the abomination that makes desolate is set up, **there shall be 1,290 days**. [12] Blessed is he who waits and arrives at the **1,335 days.**

Rev. 12:5-6

She gave birth to a male child, one who is to rule all the nations with a rod of iron, but her child was caught up to God and to his throne, [6] and the woman fled into the wilderness, where she has a place prepared by God, in which she is to be nourished for **1,260 days.**

Rev. 12:13-14

And when the dragon saw that he had been thrown down to the earth, he pursued the woman who had given birth to the male child. [14] But the woman was given the two wings of the great eagle so that she might fly from the serpent into the wilderness, to the place where she is to be nourished **for a time, and times, and half a time**.

Rev. 13:5

And the beast was given a mouth uttering haughty and blasphemous words, and it was allowed to exercise authority **for forty-two months.**

Jesus did not know then when the day or hour would be for his return because he did not know when the events he prophesied would take place. However, he said that once the events he mentioned above started happening, the generation alive at that time would not pass away until all those things were fulfilled. From the other passages we can know that once the "abomination that causes desolation" takes place, his coming will be 1260 days, or forty-two months or a time, and times and half a time (three and a half years) later. While it will come as a thief in the night for unbelievers, believers in Christ will not be in the dark for that day to surprise them.

Just as God revealed to Daniel the prophet the year that the Messiah would be cut off – 483 years after the decree to rebuild Jerusalem, so God also revealed to the day - 1290 days after the regular burnt offerings are taken away and the abomination that makes desolate is set up, when something very significant would take place, which I believe, judging from the context, is the resurrection or the rapture. In a later chapter, I will address the differences between the 1260, 1290 and 1335 days.

Therefore, once a certain series of events start happening, we can know when Jesus will return. My belief is that his return will fall on the Feast of Trumpets, three and a half years, or forty-two months, or 1260 days after the abomination that makes desolate is set up in the temple. And as cited before, because of the complexity of the lunar calendar, the exact day and hour will still not be known, though it will most likely fall within a certain 48 hour window.

8 CHRIST TO PRESENT DAY

WITH SATAN UNSUCCESSFUL at defeating his arch enemy, and having received a mortal head wound with Jesus' death and resurrection, did that mean that he would just roll over and die? No. Like a wounded bear, it just made his attacks on God's people and His plan all the more intense.

While the focus of his attention before Christ was on the Jewish people because of the promise that his enemy would come through that line, after Christ's sacrifice, his scope broadened. He has always been called "the accuser of God's people" (Rev. 12:10) and has had as his mode of operation to steal, kill and destroy (Jn. 10:10). He has also been called "the father of lies" (Jn. 8:44).

Now his mission is to try to keep people from coming to a knowledge of the truth and to keep them from entering God's kingdom. His destiny is eternal torment in hell and as has been said, "misery loves company." He wants to take as many as he can with him.

Jesus taught often in Parables and one of them, the Parable of the Sower, he explained this way:

Luke 8:11-12

Now the parable is this: The seed is the word of God. [12] The ones along the path are those who have heard. Then the devil comes and takes away the word from their hearts, so that they may not believe and be saved.

He does everything possible to keep people in darkness:

2 Cor. 4:3-4
And even if our gospel is veiled, it is veiled only to those who are perishing. [4] In their case the god of this world has blinded the minds of the unbelievers, to keep them from seeing the light of the gospel of the glory of Christ, who is the image of God.

Once a person enters God's kingdom, they are not left alone. The Apostle Peter said:

1 Peter 5:8
Be sober-minded; be watchful. Your adversary the devil prowls around like a roaring lion, seeking someone to devour.

Now his enemies are not only the Jewish race, but also the Christians. Jesus was very clear that his followers would face persecution and tribulations. When sending his disciples out on their first missions trip Jesus told them,

Matthew 10:16-18; 21-22
"Behold, I am sending you out as sheep in the midst of wolves, so be wise as serpents and innocent as doves. [17] Beware of men, for they will deliver you over to courts and flog you in their synagogues, [18] and you will be dragged before governors and kings for my sake, to bear witness before them and the Gentiles. .... [21] Brother will deliver brother over to death, and the father his child, and children will rise against parents and have them put to death, [22] and you will be hated by all for my name's sake. But the one who endures to the end will be saved.

But rather than moan about the abuse Christians would be experiencing, Jesus said this:

John 16:33
"In the world you will have tribulation. But take heart; I have overcome the world."

Matthew 5:10-12
"Blessed are those who are persecuted for righteousness' sake, for theirs is the kingdom of heaven.
[11] "Blessed are you when others revile you and persecute you and utter all kinds of evil against you falsely on my account. [12]

Rejoice and be glad, for your reward is great in heaven, for so they persecuted the prophets who were before you.

Jesus taught that as he was treated, so would the world treat his followers:

John 15:18-20

"If the world hates you, know that it has hated me before it hated you. [19] If you were of the world, the world would love you as its own; but because you are not of the world, but I chose you out of the world, therefore the world hates you. [20] Remember the word that I said to you: 'A servant is not greater than his master.' If they persecuted me, they will also persecute you.

As we have seen, the first persecutors were Jesus' own people – the Jews whom he had come to save.

Though they were still loved by God and still his chosen people, God himself would pour out his wrath on them, as he had in the past because of their idolatry, rebellion and disobedience. Formerly his instruments of judgment were other Empires like Assyria, Babylon and Greece. This time because they rejected the Messiah sent to them, the Romans would be the instrument of judgment.

Matthew 23:29-39

"Woe to you, scribes and Pharisees, hypocrites! For you build the tombs of the prophets and decorate the monuments of the righteous, [30] saying, 'If we had lived in the days of our fathers, we would not have taken part with them in shedding the blood of the prophets.' [31] Thus you witness against yourselves that you are sons of those who murdered the prophets. [32] Fill up, then, the measure of your fathers. [33] You serpents, you brood of vipers, how are you to escape being sentenced to hell? [34] Therefore I send you prophets and wise men and scribes, some of whom you will kill and crucify, and some you will flog in your synagogues and persecute from town to town, [35] so that on you may come all the righteous blood shed on earth, from the blood of innocent Abel to the blood of Zechariah the son of Barachiah, whom you murdered between the sanctuary and the altar. [36] Truly, I say to you, all these things will come upon this generation.

[37] "O Jerusalem, Jerusalem, the city that kills the prophets and stones those who are sent to it! How often would I have gathered your

children together as a hen gathers her brood under her wings, and you would not! [38] See, your house is left to you desolate. [39] For I tell you, you will not see me again, until you say, 'Blessed is he who comes in the name of the Lord.' "

Luke 19:41-44
And when he drew near and saw the city, he wept over it, [42] saying, "Would that you, even you, had known on this day the things that make for peace! But now they are hidden from your eyes. [43] For the days will come upon you, when your enemies will set up a barricade around you and surround you and hem you in on every side [44] and tear you down to the ground, you and your children within you. And they will not leave one stone upon another in you, because you did not know the time of your visitation."

Matthew 24:1-2
Jesus left the temple and was going away, when his disciples came to point out to him the buildings of the temple. [2] But he answered them, "You see all these, do you not? Truly, I say to you, there will not be left here one stone upon another that will not be thrown down."

God's judgment on Israel was neither total nor immediate. He graciously offered and still today offers forgiveness. On the Day of Pentecost following Jesus' crucifixion, the promised Holy Spirit came upon Jesus' followers and they began to speak in languages they had never learned before. A great crowd gathered together in Jerusalem in amazement because they were hearing these Galileans speak many foreign languages – languages that Jews from all over the Roman Empire and beyond could understand because many had come to Jerusalem for the Festival. Peter explained the phenomenon to them:

Acts 2:14-24
But Peter, standing with the eleven, lifted up his voice and addressed them, "Men of Judea and all who dwell in Jerusalem, let this be known to you, and give ear to my words. [15] For these men are not drunk, as you suppose, since it is only the third hour of the day. [16] But this is what was uttered through the prophet Joel:

[17] " 'And in the last days it shall be, God declares,
that I will pour out my Spirit on all flesh,

and your sons and your daughters shall prophesy,
and your young men shall see visions,
and your old men shall dream dreams;
[18] even on my male servants and female servants
in those days I will pour out my Spirit, and they shall prophesy.
[19] And I will show wonders in the heavens above
and signs on the earth below,
blood, and fire, and vapor of smoke;
[20] the sun shall be turned to darkness
and the moon to blood,
before the day of the Lord comes, the great and magnificent day.
[21] And it shall come to pass that everyone who calls upon the name of the Lord shall be saved.'

[22] "Men of Israel, hear these words: Jesus of Nazareth, a man attested to you by God with mighty works and wonders and signs that God did through him in your midst, as you yourselves know— [23] this Jesus, delivered up according to the definite plan and foreknowledge of God, you crucified and killed by the hands of lawless men. [24] God raised him up, loosing the pangs of death, because it was not possible for him to be held by it. …
Acts 2:36-41

Let all the house of Israel therefore know for certain that God has made him both Lord and Christ, this Jesus whom you crucified."

[37] Now when they heard this they were cut to the heart, and said to Peter and the rest of the apostles, "Brothers, what shall we do?" [38] And Peter said to them, "Repent and be baptized every one of you in the name of Jesus Christ for the forgiveness of your sins, and you will receive the gift of the Holy Spirit. [39] For the promise is for you and for your children and for all who are far off, everyone whom the Lord our God calls to himself." [40] And with many other words he bore witness and continued to exhort them, saying, "Save yourselves from this crooked generation." [41] So those who received his word were baptized, and there were added that day about three thousand souls.

Prophesied Events from First Century to Present

The early church grew rapidly and was initially predominantly Jewish. In fact, all the apostles and writers of the New Testament were Jewish except Luke. However, after the death of the first Christian martyr,

Stephen, at the hands of the Jewish Sanhedrin or ruling council, persecution scattered Jewish believers abroad. But as mentioned previously, Jesus had told them that this was to occur:

Luke 21:10-19
Then he said to them, "Nation will rise against nation, and kingdom against kingdom. [11] There will be great earthquakes, and in various places famines and pestilences. And there will be terrors and great signs from heaven. [12] **But before all this** they will lay their hands on you and persecute you, delivering you up to the synagogues and prisons, and you will be brought before kings and governors for my name's sake. [13] This will be your opportunity to bear witness. [14] Settle it therefore in your minds not to meditate beforehand how to answer, [15] for I will give you a mouth and wisdom, which none of your adversaries will be able to withstand or contradict. [16] You will be delivered up even by parents and brothers and relatives and friends, and some of you they will put to death. [17] You will be hated by all for my name's sake. [18] But not a hair of your head will perish. [19] By your endurance you will gain your lives.

Jesus prophesied almost forty years beforehand that Jerusalem would be destroyed, that the massive stones of the temple would be thrown down, that the Jews would be scattered among the nations and that Jerusalem would be trampled underfoot by the Gentiles until the times of the Gentiles are fulfilled. He said that his followers would be persecuted and hated for his name's sake and some would be put to death. All the apostles died martyr's deaths except John. What was prophesied regarding Jerusalem happened in 70 A.D. when Titus conquered the city.

As the Roman legions advanced toward Jerusalem, the Jewish believers in Jesus remembered what he had said to do when they saw the armies surrounding Jerusalem and they fled, escaping before the siege. During that time 1 million Jews perished and 100,000 were sold into slavery, captivity, and scattered around the Roman Empire.

When Jesus told the disciples that the stones of the temple would be thrown down, they obviously wanted to know when this would be. They assumed that this would happen at the same time as Christ's return and the end of the age. Jesus gives them an answer, but he does not clarify for them that these three events (temple's destruction, Christ's return and the end of the age) would not happen concurrently.

Or will they? Is it possible that the destruction of the temple in 70

A.D. was a type of a future destruction of a future temple? If we consider the stones of the foundation of the temple mount, those of the "wailing wall" and other places, we see that they are still standing. Could it be that at the time of Jesus' return there will be a total destruction and that as Jesus said, not one stone will be left upon another?

Matthew 24:3-13

As he sat on the Mount of Olives, the disciples came to him privately, saying, "Tell us, when will these things be, and what will be the sign of your coming and of the close of the age?" [4] And Jesus answered them, "See that no one leads you astray. [5] For many will come in my name, saying, 'I am the Christ,' and they will lead many astray. [6] And you will hear of wars and rumors of wars. See that you are not alarmed, for this must take place, but the end is not yet. [7] For nation will rise against nation, and kingdom against kingdom, and there will be famines and earthquakes in various places. [8] All these are but the beginning of the birth pains.

[9] "Then they will deliver you up to tribulation and put you to death, and you will be hated by all nations for my name's sake. [10] And then many will fall away and betray one another and hate one another. [11] And many false prophets will arise and lead many astray. [12] And because lawlessness will be increased, the love of many will grow cold. [13] But the one who endures to the end will be saved.

To a greater or lesser extent, all these signs have been occurring since the time Jesus was here. However, as with birth pains, as the time of the delivery comes closer, the pains grow in frequency, intensity, and in shorter intervals.

Persecutions

Satan's initial tactic to destroy God's people was through persecution, and that has continued in varying degrees to the present.

While the early Church was initially greatly persecuted by the Jews, the Romans stepped in and starting with Nero (37-68 A.D.), who put the blame on the Christians for his burning of Rome in 64 A.D., the state began a systematic persecution of the believers. Already Christianity was viewed as a foreign superstition and under Nero many were put to death – some in the most horrid of ways. Nero would even cover them with oil and burn them alive in his gardens to serve as light for his guests.

Persecution of both Christians and Jews continued under the Roman Emperors to varying degrees until 313 when Constantine signed the *Edict of Milan* extending religious tolerance to Christians. In 380 Christianity was declared the religion of the State.

The enemy of God's people is smart and has used various tactics over the millennia. Instead of persecution diminishing the church, it blossomed during that time, so a new approach had to be employed. Once Christianity became the Religion of the Roman Empire, its decline began. It did not decline in an outward, visible sense. Many great cathedrals, monasteries and Christian orders were founded, but when Christianity became the dominant religion, the church was flooded with pagans who became a part for political expediency and they brought their idolatry with them. Pagan deities were renamed with Christian names – Mary, the apostles, the saints, etc. and idols of virgins and christs and saints were proliferated in the churches. Though Christian in name, many of the people did not have a genuine personal Christian faith. Indeed, the non-Christian behavior and excesses of many of the Popes have been attested to down through the ages.

The persecuted became the persecutors and down through the centuries, the Church persecuted the Jews, calling them "*Christ killers*". While the Crusades (11th-13th Centuries) originally had the goal of liberating Jerusalem and the Holy Land from Muslim rule, Jews became a target as well and thousands were killed by "Christian" Crusaders.

In the 14th century Europe was plagued by "The Black Death", a plague that came from rats and was transmitted to humans through fleas. 25 million died in Europe as a result. As proportionately fewer Jews died than Christians – undoubtedly because of their following Mosaic sanitary and dietary laws - they were accused of being the cause of the plague and tens of thousands were put to death.

The Spanish Inquisition of the late 1400s brought death to many Jews and forced hundreds of thousands to flee to Turkey where strangely they found some tolerance among the Muslims.

While the Protestant Reformation begun by Martin Luther brought a return to the tenets of the true Christian faith, he himself remained strongly anti-semitic after his hope of seeing Jews converted was not realized. Other reformers however, such as John Calvin, saw the importance of the Covenant with Abraham as applying today: "I will bless those who bless you and curse those who curse you." He saw the need to bless the Jews regardless of whether they converted or not because they were specially loved by God and chosen by Him.

Satan's work of "stealing, killing and destroying" the people of God has continued down through history. It was certainly evident in the wars between the Protestants and the Catholics. It would not be an exaggeration to say that millions have died in that conflict over the past 500 years. The atheistic French Revolution also was responsible for the death of multitudes of believers, Catholic and Protestant alike.

Though countless millions of varying beliefs have been killed in the name of Allah since the time of Mohammed, Islam has had a particular hatred toward Jews and Christians and has been one of the foremost persecutors the world has ever known. In fact, families whose members have converted to Christianity consider it a duty of honor to kill these people.

The greatest persecutor of the Jews was, of course, Adolf Hitler and Nazi Germany, killing some 6 million Jews from 1941-1945. Some 2.1 million Christians were killed by Muslims in Turkey in 1915 and space and time does not permit to recount all the genocides of Christians by Communist governments such as the USSR, North Korea and China. Today, the greatest persecution of Christians is occurring in Muslim lands, in India by Hindus and in China. Even in Europe and the Americas – traditionally Christian continents, there is a growing and virulent anti-Christian sentiment.

Jesus' promise: "If they persecuted me, they will persecute you as well" has certainly been true. That his followers would have tribulation is as true today as back in Jesus' time.

False Christs

While there have always been those who claim to be the Christ, the last hundred years have seen an increased number of those who have been able to gather followers such as Unification Church founder Sun Myung Moon (1920-2012), Jim Jones (1931-1978), who led 900 people to commit suicide in Guyana, David Koresh (1959-1993), leader of the Branch Davidians and many others too numerous to list here. Likewise in the Muslim community, there have been many claiming to be the Mahdi, Islam's version of the Messiah.

Lawlessness

Jesus said, "And because lawlessness will be increased, the love of many will grow cold." If we look at many parts of the world today, we see an increased propensity to "call good evil and evil good". Practices, that societies a generation ago would consider so scandalous and shameful that almost no one would publically admit to being involved, are being actively and openly promoted as good, healthy and normal, while those who maintain that there is an absolute standard of right and wrong are vilified as being the evil hate mongers of society.

Crime in the United States is rampant. According to the U.S. Bureau of Justice Statistics (BJS), 7,225,800 people at year end 2009 were on probation, in jail or prison, or on parole — about 3.1% of adults in the U.S. resident population. With only about 5% of the world's population, the U.S. has about a quarter of the world's prison population. In Mexico, more than 50,000 have been killed in the last six years in the drug wars. Russia's mafia is notorious for its violence, making Italy's mafia seem like school children in comparison.

Wars

While there have always been wars, we would have to say that the two world wars of the twentieth century were unparalleled in scope and destruction. Estimates of deaths between the two wars range from a low of 55 to a high of 137 million. Estimates of people killed by Soviet Communist leaders from 1917-1953 range from 8 to 61 million.[20] Mao Tse-tung is reported to have been responsible for 40-70 million deaths of Chinese – during peacetime.[21] Numerous smaller wars were waged in the last century.

Africa has had multiple genocidal tribal and national wars with literally millions dying just in the past 30 years.

Wars, conflicts, revolutions and religious killings in the Middle East and elsewhere are everyday news headlines, making Jesus' prediction that there would be wars and rumors of wars seem like he was talking about today. In Syria alone, more than 20,000 have been killed in 18 months of civil war. Rather than the world becoming more peaceful, the Heidelberg Institute for International Conflict Research published its annual "conflict barometer" for 2011 counting 38 highly violent conflicts worldwide, classifying 20 of them as wars, the most since 1945.[22]

---

[20]http://en.wikipedia.org/wiki/List_of_wars_and_anthropogenic_disasters_by_death_toll

[21] http://en.wikipedia.org/wiki/Mao:_The_Unknown_Story

[22] http://www.dw.de/dw/article/0,,15765187,00.html

Famines have affected various parts of the world and the rising food prices have been catalysts in a number of the revolutions.

Earthquakes

With regard to earthquakes, the chart below shows the increase in earthquake activity both in number and intensity over the past 300 years.

WORLDWIDE EARTHQUAKES – 1700 TO PRESENT[23]

1700 – 1799		
7.0 +	28	
8.0 +	13	
9.0 +	0	
Total	41	Average of about 1 every 2.5 years

1800 – 1899		
7.0 +	73	
8.0 +	39	
9.0 +	3	
Total	115	Average of a little more than 1 per year

1900 – 1999		
7.0 +	728	
8.0 +	161	
9.0 +	0	
Total	889	Average of about 9 per year

2000 – 2012		
7.0 +	187	
8.0 +	15	
9.0 +	2	
Total	204	Average of almost 16 per year

The Land

As we have seen from texts cited before, Daniel and Jesus predicted the destruction of Jerusalem, and that part of God's judgment on his

---

[23] Global Earthquake Search <http://earthquake.usgs.gov/earthquakes/eqarchives/epic/epic_global.php>

people for their turning from Him and their unbelief, was that they would be scattered throughout the whole earth. However, throughout the scripture, there has been a promise of return to the land covenanted to Abraham, Isaac and Jacob.

Persecution of Jews throughout the past two millennia brought a longing among many of them to have a land of their own once again. The founder and leader of the modern Zionist movement, Theodor Herzl had a vision for establishing a Jewish homeland in Palestine, which at that time was under the rule of the Turkish Ottoman Empire until post World War I when it came under the British Mandate.

Herzl convened the first Zionist Congress in Basil, Switzerland in 1897. He later wrote in his diary,

"If I were to sum up the Congress in a word – which I shall take care not to publish – it would be this: At Basle I founded the Jewish State. If I said this out loud today I would be greeted by universal laughter. In five years perhaps, and certainly in fifty years, everyone will perceive it."[24]

Fifty-one years later, and in large part because of the Holocaust, Jewish leader, David Ben Gurion, announced the rebirth of the State of Israel on May 14, 1948 fulfilling a prophesy in Isaiah.

Isaiah 66:8

Who has heard such a thing?
Who has seen such things?
Shall a land be born in one day?
Shall a nation be brought forth in one moment?
For as soon as Zion was in labor she brought forth her children.

An interesting side note is that Abraham, the father of Israel, was born 1,948 years after Adam. The State of Israel was reborn 1,948 years after the second Adam, Jesus Christ.

It would not be exaggeration to say that the most hotly contested piece of real estate in the world today is the land of Israel, or Palestine. In 1800, it is estimated that only 7,000 Jews lived in Palestine, compared

---

24 "World Zionist Organization" <http://en.wikipedia.org/wiki/World_Zionist_Congress>, *The Diaries of Theodor Herzl*, ed. and trsl. Marvin Lowenthal, London, 1958, p. 220 as quoted in Gideon Shimoni: *Historiographical Issues in Conveying Herzl's Legacy*

to 22,000 Christians and 246,000 Muslims. By 1890, those numbers increased to 43,000, 57,000 and 432,000 respectively.[25]

The terrible massacre and plight of the Jews in Europe, and being turned away by many countries where they sought refuge, caused many of the survivors of the war to seek refuge in Palestine. By 1947, the population in Palestine was 630,000 Jews, 143,000 Christians and 1,181,000 Muslims.[26]

Satan lost no time in trying to destroy the covenant people of God in that land. In spite of the 1947 United Nations decision to partition Palestine and give the Jewish people their own homeland, the next day after the declaration of the founding of the State of Israel, they were invaded by the surrounding Arab nations in an effort to destroy them.

Since that time, again, in spite of numerous wars and almost constant rocket attacks and suicide bombers, another prophecy regarding Israel has had a second fulfillment:

Isaiah 43:5-7

Fear not, for I am with you;
I will bring your offspring from the east,
and from the west I will gather you.
[6] I will say to the north, Give up,
and to the south, Do not withhold;
bring my sons from afar
and my daughters from the end of the earth,
[7] everyone who is called by my name,
whom I created for my glory,
whom I formed and made."

The Jewish nation has grown through constant immigration of Jews from around the world. Population estimates for Israel and Palestine at the end of 2010 are 5.7 million Jews and 5.5 million Palestinian Muslims[27] with 331,000 Christians.[28] The Palestinian Central Bureau of

---

[25] "Demographics of Palestine" <http://en.wikipedia.org/wiki/Demographics_of_Palestine>, citing DellaPergola, IUSSP XXIVth General Population Conference in Salvador de Bahia, Brazil, August 18–24, 2001

[26] "Demographics of Palestine" <http://en.wikipedia.org/wiki/Demographics_of_Palestine>

[27] "Palestinian population grew 8-fold since 1948" <http://www.americantaskforce.org/daily_news_article/2011/05/12/1305172800_16>

Statistics estimates that, at current growth rates, Jewish and Palestinian populations are predicted to equal at 6.1 million at end of 2014, and reach 7.2 million Palestinians and 6.7 million Jews at the end of 2020.[29]

Since then, the nation has survived against overwhelming odds in various wars. In 1967, the Jews regained control of Jerusalem after almost 1900 years – since 70 A.D.

Does the Bible give us indications of what is next on the prophetic calendar? I believe the Book of Revelation outlines for us a chronological glimpse into the future. Jesus revealed to the Apostle John what is to take place. The events are given in three sets of progressively more intense judgments on the earth. There are seven seals, seven trumpets and seven bowls of the wrath of God that will be poured out upon the earth. Volumes have been written on just the Book of Revelation alone and it is not in the scope of this book to give a detailed exegesis of the book, but we will look at some of the broad pictures presented. Before getting into Revelation, however, we need to look at some pieces of the apocalyptic pie.

---

[28] CIA World Factbook, 2010, West Bank, Israel, Gaza

[29]Op. Cit., <http://www.americantaskforce.org/daily_news_article/2011/05/12/1305172800_16>

PIECES OF THE APOCALYPTIC PIE

PART THREE

9 THE LAST WORLD EMPIRE

UP TO NOW, we have largely looked at the past. We have seen what explains the conflict of the ages and God's decisive victory over Satan through the death and resurrection of his Son, Jesus Christ. That victory was like the invasion of Normandy during the Second World War. It was the turning point, the victory that spelled the death knell of Hitler, but the war was far from over. We also saw that the biblical prophets are to be trusted; their short to medium range prophecies have been accurately fulfilled. That gives us confidence in the predictions of things yet to come.

In part four of the book we will look at the future sequence of events as outlined in the Book of Revelation, or "The Apocalypse" as some languages call it. But before we do that, it is necessary to address some terms that make up the pieces of this apocalyptic pie. Six major components of the future – the last world empire, the antichrist, the mark of the beast – 666, the great tribulation, the millennium and the rapture, are all key elements to understanding the future, but are also, unfortunately, all elements that are laden with differing viewpoints. We will seek to look more closely at what the Bible says about these issues, what the various interpretations are and then I will present the viewpoint that will form the basis of the conclusions presented in this book. As stated in the introduction, there are fine scholars who differ significantly on these issues and I would not suppose that my conclusions will be free from error, but you can make the judgment yourself as to what is true and what is erroneous after examining the arguments.

The first significant question we will look at is the identity of the last empire prophesied in opposition to God and his people. Again, the ambiguity of scripture on this subject has caused there to be a legion of differing viewpoints. As that empire is not yet clearly and unmistakably identified, at best we can only make a well informed guess.

We looked before at the passage in the book of Revelation 17:9-11 where John saw Satan, the dragon with seven heads and ten horns. The explanation was that the heads were seven kings or kingdoms, five of which had already fallen, one was, which was Rome and there was one still to come. This chapter will seek to discover what is that seventh king or kingdom. Has it already come – is it here now? Or, is it yet to make its appearance on the scene.

The importance of this question is that the Bible indicates that the Antichrist, who will rule the world, will come from this last empire. To look for the future, we have to go back to the past.

Book of Daniel

Daniel is one of the most significant apocalyptic prophets of the Old Testament. We have already looked at some of his prophesies, but to set the stage for the future world empire, we must look there again. Based on passages we have already looked at in Daniel and Revelation, we concluded that the first six empires by the time the Apostle John wrote in 95 A.D. were:

1. Egypt or Ancient Babylon (Nimrod era)
2. Assyria
3. Babylon (Nebuchadnezzar era)
4. Media – Persia
5. Greece
6. Rome
7. ?

What are we told about the seventh empire? Daniel records several dreams and visions that reveal to him future world empires (the dreams start with the Babylonian empire, which is the third of seven, though first of the four that he sees). The first was a dream that Nebuchadnezzar had that only Daniel, through God's revelation, was able to both tell him what his dream was and what it meant. Combined with other visions and dreams he had, the empires of Babylon, Media-Persia and Greece are clearly identified. There is a fourth empire that Daniel sees which is not clearly named, but which most biblical scholars have thought to be Rome, which naturally followed chronologically after the Greek empire.

Daniel 2:40-45

[40] And there shall be a fourth kingdom, strong as iron, because iron breaks to pieces and shatters all things. And like iron that crushes, it shall break and crush all these. [41] And as you saw the feet and toes, partly of potter's clay and partly of iron, it shall be a divided kingdom, but some of the firmness of iron shall be in it, just as you saw iron mixed with the soft clay. [42] And as the toes of the feet were partly iron and partly clay, so the kingdom shall be partly strong and partly brittle. [43] As you saw the iron mixed with soft clay, so they will mix with one another in marriage, but they will not hold together, just as iron does not mix with clay. [44] And in the days of those kings the God of heaven will set up a kingdom that shall never be destroyed, nor shall the kingdom be left to another people. It shall break in pieces all these kingdoms and bring them to an end, and it shall stand forever, [45] just as you saw that a stone was cut from a mountain by no human hand, and that it broke in pieces the iron, the bronze, the clay, the silver, and the gold. A great God has made known to the king what shall be after this. The dream is certain, and its interpretation sure."

Daniel himself later had a vision of four beasts, the first three being clearly indentified in history as mentioned. The fourth was an enigma, however:

Daniel 7:7

[7] After this I saw in the night visions, and behold, a fourth beast, terrifying and dreadful and exceedingly strong. It had great iron teeth; it devoured and broke in pieces and stamped what was left with its feet. It was different from all the beasts that were before it, and it had ten horns.

Daniel 7:16-17

I approached one of those who stood there and asked him the truth concerning all this. So he told me and made known to me the interpretation of the things. [17] 'These four great beasts are four kings who shall arise out of the earth.

This is the same dream that God gave Nebuchadnezzar, but with different imagery. Combining the dreams and visions of Daniel 2, 7 and

8 we see the identities of these kings or kingdoms:

First
Head of gold, 2:38
Lion with eagles' wings, 7:4

Nebuchadnezzar, Babylonian Empire (626 – 539 BC)

Second
Chest & arms of silver, 2:32,39
Bear, 7:5
Ram with two horns, 8:20

Kings of the Medo-Persian Empire (559 – 331 BC)

Third
Middle & thighs of bronze, 2:32,39
Leopard with 4 wings & 4 heads, 7:6
Male Goat with 1 horn; broken & 4 horns came up, 8:5-8

Alexander the Great (336 – 323 BC) and the Greek Empire divided among his 4 generals (323 – 164 BC)

Fourth
Legs of iron, feet & toes partly iron & partly clay, 2:33, 40-43
Ten horns 7:7

Traditional view: - Roman Empire (63 BC – 476 AD)
The Eastern Roman Empire or Byzantine Empire (63 BC – 1453 AD).

NB. The Bible specifically identifies by name the first three kingdoms but does not identify the fourth one, the terrifying beast with iron teeth (Dan. 7:7).

Our interest is primarily in the last kingdom – the one with legs of iron and toes partly of iron and partly of clay. As mentioned above, the traditional view has been that this last kingdom of iron was the Roman Empire and the Ten Toes of iron and clay will be some sort of ten nation revived Roman Empire just before God sets up his kingdom that will never be destroyed. Note the following summary points from the passage in Daniel 2:

Points:

- Fourth kingdom characterized by legs of iron with feet partly of iron partly of clay mixed together meaning that it will be a divided kingdom, partly strong, partly weak, will mix but not hold together.

- Like iron that crushes, the fourth kingdom will crush the previous three kingdoms (Babylon, Medo-Persian, Greek empires).

- A stone cut from a mountain by no human hand will strike the image on its feet of iron and clay, crushing all the previous kingdoms of iron, clay, bronze, silver and gold at the same time and like chaff, they will all blow away so that there is no trace left of them.

- "In the days of those kings" (the ten kings represented by the ten toes) God will set up a kingdom that will never be destroyed or left to another people, and will become a great mountain and fill the earth.

More detail of this last kingdom is given us in Daniel 7.

Daniel 7:7-28

After this I saw in the night visions, and behold, a fourth beast, terrifying and dreadful and exceedingly strong. It had great iron teeth; it devoured and broke in pieces and stamped what was left with its feet. It was different from all the beasts that were before it, and it had ten horns. [8] I considered the horns, and behold, there came up among them another horn, a little one, before which three of the first horns were plucked up by the roots. And behold, in this horn were eyes like the eyes of a man, and a mouth speaking great things.

[9] As I looked,

thrones were placed,
  and the Ancient of days took his seat;
his clothing was white as snow,
  and the hair of his head like pure wool;
his throne was fiery flames;
  its wheels were burning fire.

[10] A stream of fire issued
and came out from before him;
a thousand thousands served him,
and ten thousand times ten thousand stood before him;
the court sat in judgment,
and the books were opened.

[11] I looked then because of the sound of the great words that the horn was speaking. And as I looked, the beast was killed, and its body destroyed and given over to be burned with fire. [12] As for the rest of the beasts, their dominion was taken away, but their lives were prolonged for a season and a time.

[13] I saw in the night visions,

and behold, with the clouds of heaven
there came one like a son of man,
and he came to the Ancient of Days
and was presented before him.
[14] And to him was given dominion
and glory and a kingdom,
that all peoples, nations, and languages
should serve him;
his dominion is an everlasting dominion,
which shall not pass away,
and his kingdom one
that shall not be destroyed.

[15] "As for me, Daniel, my spirit within me was anxious, and the visions of my head alarmed me. [16] I approached one of those who stood there and asked him the truth concerning all this. So he told me and made known to me the interpretation of the things. [17] 'These four great beasts are four kings who shall arise out of the earth. [18] But the saints of the Most High shall receive the kingdom and possess the kingdom forever, forever and ever.'

[19] "Then I desired to know the truth about the fourth beast, which was different from all the rest, exceedingly terrifying, with its teeth of iron and claws of bronze, and which devoured and broke in pieces and stamped what was left with its feet, [20] and about the ten horns that were on its head, and the other horn that came up and before which three of them fell, the horn that had eyes and a mouth that

spoke great things, and that seemed greater than its companions. [21] As I looked, this horn made war with the saints and prevailed over them, [22] until the Ancient of Days came, and judgment was given for the saints of the Most High, and the time came when the saints possessed the kingdom.

[23] "Thus he said: 'As for the fourth beast,

there shall be a fourth kingdom on earth,
  which shall be different from all the kingdoms,
and it shall devour the whole earth,
  and trample it down, and break it to pieces.
[24] As for the ten horns,
out of this kingdom ten kings shall arise,
  and another shall arise after them;
he shall be different from the former ones,
  and shall put down three kings.
[25] He shall speak words against the Most High,
  and shall wear out the saints of the Most High,
  and shall think to change the times and the law;
and they shall be given into his hand
  for a time, times, and half a time.
[26] But the court shall sit in judgment,
  and his dominion shall be taken away,
  to be consumed and destroyed to the end.
[27] And the kingdom and the dominion
  and the greatness of the kingdoms under the whole heaven
  shall be given to the people of the saints of the Most High;
their kingdom shall be an everlasting kingdom,
  and all dominions shall serve and obey them.'

[28] "Here is the end of the matter. As for me, Daniel, my thoughts greatly alarmed me, and my color changed, but I kept the matter in my heart."

Note the following bullet points of this passage:

Points:

- Fourth Beast is terrifying, dreadful, exceedingly strong, with great iron teeth and bronze claws.

- It devours, crushes (breaks in pieces) and tramples down the whole earth.

- It is different from all the previous beasts (kingdoms).

- The Beast has ten horns on his head which means that out of this kingdom ten kings will arise.

- Another king will arise after the ten kings different from the others.
  He uproots or puts down three of the ten kings.
  He seems greater than the other kings.
  He has eyes like the eyes of a man,
  He has a mouth that speaks great things against God,
  He will wear out the saints of the Most High and they shall be given into his hand for "a time, times, and half a time." (3.5 years)
  He will think to change the times and the law.

- The heavenly court will sit in judgment and his dominion will be taken away and destroyed.

- One like a son of man, and the saints of the Most High will be given an everlasting dominion, glory and kingdom, and all the peoples, nations and languages will serve and obey them.

The Book of Revelation

God reveals to the Apostle John in the Book of Revelation similar visions that correspond with that which Daniel saw.

Rev. 13:1-10
And I saw a beast rising out of the sea, with ten horns and seven
heads, with ten diadems on its horns and blasphemous names on its
heads. [2] And the beast that I saw was like a leopard; its feet were
like a bear's, and its mouth was like a lion's mouth. And to it the
dragon gave his power and his throne and great authority. [3] One of
its heads seemed to have a mortal wound, but its mortal wound was
healed, and the whole earth marveled as they followed the beast. [4]
And they worshiped the dragon, for he had given his authority to the

beast, and they worshiped the beast, saying, "Who is like the beast, and who can fight against it?"

[5] And the beast was given a mouth uttering haughty and blasphemous words, and it was allowed to exercise authority for forty-two months. [6] It opened its mouth to utter blasphemies against God, blaspheming his name and his dwelling, that is, those who dwell in heaven. [7] Also it was allowed to make war on the saints and to conquer them. And authority was given it over every tribe and people and language and nation, [8] and all who dwell on earth will worship it, everyone whose name has not been written before the foundation of the world in the book of life of the Lamb that was slain. [9] If anyone has an ear, let him hear:

[10] If anyone is to be taken captive,
to captivity he goes;
if anyone is to be slain with the sword,
with the sword must he be slain.

Here is a call for the endurance and faith of the saints.

Note the following bullet points:

Points:

- The Beast has ten horns with crowns on them. (ten kings reigning)
- It has seven heads with blasphemous names on its heads. (seven kings or kingdoms)
- It was like a leopard (Greece), feet like a bear's (Medo-Persia) and mouth like a lion's (Babylon).
- The dragon (Satan) gave his power, his throne and great authority to the beast.
- One of the seven heads (kings/kingdoms) seemed to have a mortal wound but its wound was healed and the whole earth marveled, followed and worshiped the dragon and the beast.

- The Beast was given a mouth uttering haughty and blasphemous words against God, his name and his dwelling – that is those who dwell in heaven.

- He was allowed to exercise authority for 42 months (3.5 years or "a time, times and half a time").

- He makes war on the saints and conquers them.

- Authority is given the beast over every tribe, people, language and nation.

- All on earth will worship it, whose name has not been written in the book of life from before the world began.

Rev. 17:7-14

But the angel said to me, "Why do you marvel? I will tell you the mystery of the woman, and of the beast with seven heads and ten horns that carries her. [8] The beast that you saw was, and is not, and is about to rise from the bottomless pit and go to destruction. And the dwellers on earth whose names have not been written in the book of life from the foundation of the world will marvel to see the beast, because it was and is not and is to come. [9] This calls for a mind with wisdom: the seven heads are seven mountains on which the woman is seated; [10] they are also seven kings, five of whom have fallen, one is, the other has not yet come, and when he does come he must remain only a little while. [11] As for the beast that was and is not, it is an eighth but it belongs to the seven, and it goes to destruction. [12] And the ten horns that you saw are ten kings who have not yet received royal power, but they are to receive authority as kings for one hour, together with the beast. [13] These are of one mind and hand over their power and authority to the beast. [14] They will make war on the Lamb, and the Lamb will conquer them, for he is Lord of lords and King of kings, and those with him are called and chosen and faithful."

Points:

- There is a beast with seven heads and ten horns.

- There is a beast who was, and is not, and is about to rise from the bottomless pit and go to destruction.

- The seven heads are seven mountains on which the woman (Babylon the Great, mother of prostitutes and of the earth's abominations) sits.

- The seven heads are also seven kings.

- Five kings have fallen, one is (during John's time), and the other had not yet come (during John's time), and when he does come, he must remain only a little while.

- The beast that was and is not is an eighth king, but belongs to the seven and it goes to destruction.

- The ten horns are ten kings who had not yet received royal power (during John's time), but they will receive authority as kings for one hour together with the beast. They are of one mind and hand over their power and authority to the beast. They (the kings) will make war on the Lamb and will be conquered by him because He is the Lord of lords and King of kings.

CONCLUSIONS ABOUT THESE PASSAGES

1. The 4th kingdom (legs iron, feet iron & clay) in Daniel 2, the 4th beast (terrifying, iron teeth) in Daniel 7 and the seventh head (king/kingdom) in Revelation 12, 13 & 17 are the same.

2. Its power, throne and authority come from Satan.

3. It is characterized as a strong, terrifying, dreadful, crushing, trampling down, breaking in pieces kind of kingdom that devours the earth.

4. It is different than all other previous kingdoms.

5. It seems to have had a mortal wound but then is healed causing all to marvel. Or it is a kingdom that was, is not, and will come. It is called an eighth king, though it comes from one of the previous seven kingdoms.

6. Out of this kingdom, ten kings will arise – unified, though in not a strong union. Some kings will be stronger than others.

7. Another king will arise (the eighth) who will overthrow three of the ten kings and who will receive power and authority from the other kings. He will speak blasphemous words against God.

8. All the world will be under this king's authority and will worship him and Satan.

9. This king, along with the other kings, will make war on the saints of God and will conquer them. They will also make war on "the Lamb", but will be destroyed.

10. The "Lamb", or "one like a son of man" will conquer these kings and will set up an everlasting kingdom and will rule, together with the saints, all the nations of the world.

THE IDENTITY OF THIS KINGDOM

As has been mentioned, for most of the last two thousand years, the church has assumed that the kingdom described is the Roman Empire. That is the view point that I had (even more strongly felt after living in Rome for almost 10 years) until relatively recently. Many of the following ideas I picked up from Joel Richardson's *Islam and the End Times*[30] videos. Let me share with you why I now do not think it is the Roman Empire and why I believe the last kingdom is the Islamic Empire.

Reasons why the last empire is not Rome and how Islam fits better:

1. Let us look again at John's description of the beast he saw:

Rev. 13:2:
"And the beast that I saw was like a leopard; its feet were like a bear's, and its mouth was like a lion's mouth. And to it the dragon gave his power and his throne and great authority".

---

[30] Joelstrumpet.com

John clearly identifies the beast with Alexander the Great, the Medo-Persian Empire and Nebuchadnezzar and the Babylonian Empire. The traditional view identifies the unnamed fourth empire – the legs of iron and the terrifying beast with iron teeth as the Roman Empire which started in 63 BC, 158 years before John is writing. John is also writing 25 years after Jerusalem and the temple have been destroyed by the Roman general, Titus.

A question naturally arises. Why did John not also see in his vision of the beast the description of the fourth empire, if that empire was indeed Rome?

2. Rev. 17:9-10 "This calls for a mind with wisdom: the seven heads are seven mountains on which the woman is seated; [10] they are also seven kings, five of whom have fallen, one is, the other has not yet come, and when he does come he must remain only a little while."

The identity of the seven heads being seven mountains has caused many to immediately assume Rome is being referenced here. However, as we will discuss later in more detail, Mecca is also a city with seven mountains. Here we see that the seven headed dragon – Satan, and the beast to whom Satan gives his power, throne and authority, are also seven kings, five of whom had fallen by the time John is writing in 95 AD, one was still in existence (the sixth) and one was still to come (the seventh). It seems obvious that the one during John's writing was the Roman Empire (63 BC – 476 AD), but he does not associate that with Daniel's vision of the fourth beast - the "terrifying beast with iron teeth and ten horns", which is also the "legs of iron and feet of mixed iron and clay".

In John's vision in Rev. 13 and 17, it is the seventh King or kingdom that will be destroyed by the coming of the Lamb who is the King of Kings and Lord of Lords (17:12-14). In Nebuchadnezzar's and Daniel's visions, it is God who destroys the previous kingdoms (statue – Dan. 2) and beasts (Dan. 7) and this occurs during the fourth kingdom and fourth beast. That means that the fourth in the Daniel visions is the same as the seventh in John's vision which would seem to rule out Rome as Rome was the sixth kingdom.

3. There are those who would rebut the previous reason saying that the last kingdom is the Roman Empire resurrected – the kingdom "that was, and is not, and will come". The Roman Empire was the legs of iron (the two legs representing the eastern and western parts of the Roman

Empire); the "feet of iron and clay", or the "ten toes" is a resurrected ten nation confederacy that will arise out of the Roman Empire (the European Union), from which the "Antichrist" will come.

The problem with that view is that John seems to identify the Roman Empire as the sixth. If one says that the ten toes will be the seventh, there is a problem because it says that the beast who was, and is not, and will come, is an eighth king who will come from one of the seven former kingdoms. That means that Rome would have to have been the seventh kingdom, but John identifies it as the sixth, with one kingdom (the seventh) not yet having come – i.e. future to John's time and from which the eighth would most likely come.

4. The Roman view fails to take into consideration the context of Nebuchadnezzar's dream in Daniel 2. It was a revelation of what would happen to his empire after him. Let us look at the maps of the Babylonian, Medo-Persian and Greek Empires. Each succeeding empire swallowed up the territory of the previous empire and took more. The Roman Empire, however, did not even take Babylon except for a few months in 116 AD when Trajan conquered it but then later withdrew. The Roman Empire overlaps only the western parts of the previous empires, but not the central and eastern parts.

Note the following maps:[31] While there is not much overlap of the Roman Empire with the previous three, as we look at the map of the Islamic Empire, we see that it almost totally encompasses all the territories of the first three kingdoms.[32]

---

[31]<http://www.gregwolf.com/mapframe.htm>

[32]<http://www.lib.utexas.edu/Libs/PCL/Map_collection/world_maps/Muslim_Distribution.jpg>

The Babylonian, Persian, Greek and Roman Empires

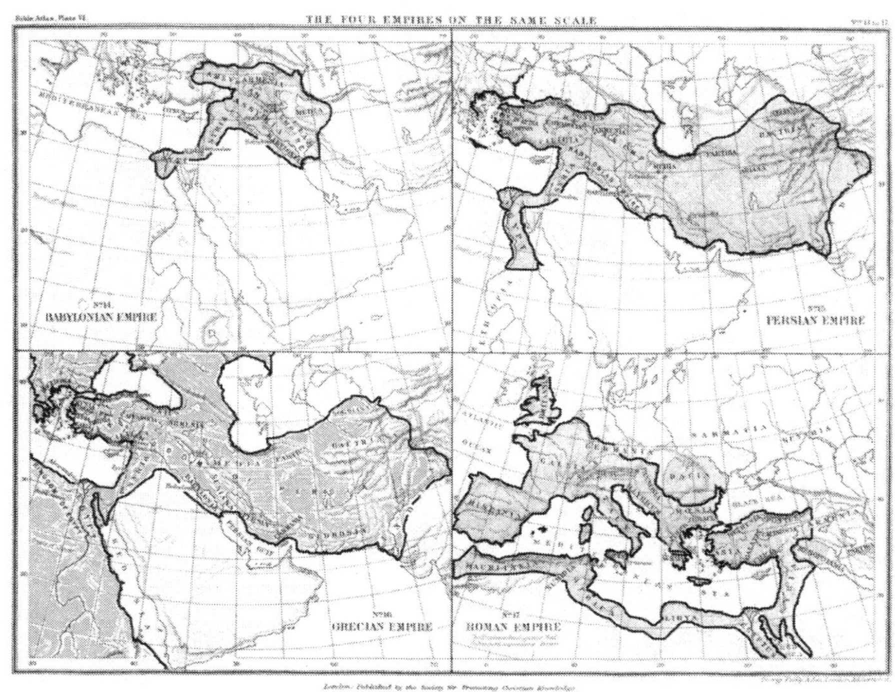

The Islamic Empire

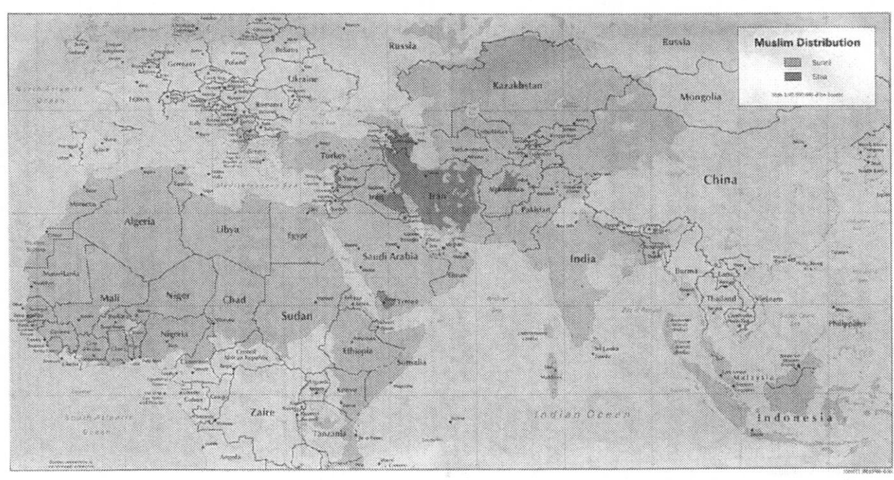

5. Along with the previous reason, Daniel says

Daniel 2:34-35 (NIV)
[34] "While you were watching, a rock was cut out, but not by human hands. It struck the statue on its feet of iron and clay and smashed them.
[35] Then the iron, the clay, the bronze, the silver and the gold were broken to pieces **at the same time** and became like chaff on a threshing floor in the summer. The wind swept them away without leaving a trace. But the rock that struck the statue became a huge mountain and filled the whole earth."

To break in pieces all the four kingdoms at the same time means that they would have to be overlapping kingdoms geographically, which Rome does not do and Islam does.

6. The fourth kingdom or beast is said to be different from all the others and that it crushes, devours, breaks in pieces, like iron, the world.

Joel Richardson cites Michael Savage. In his book The Savage Nation: Saving America from the Liberal Assault on Our Borders, Language and Culture[33] he says that those three things define a people: their borders, language and culture. We can throw in as part of the culture, their religion.

When we look at these aspects of a people and ask the question, "How did Rome treat the Greek Empire?" we see that the borders of the nations were largely left intact. Greek continued being the dominant language of the Roman Empire – in fact, the New Testament was written in Greek and not in Latin. The Romans did not destroy the Greek gods – they embraced them and gave them Latin names. The Greek, Hellenistic culture continued and prevailed in the Roman Empire.

To "crush" means more than crushing militarily. It means crushing or conquering geographically – changing borders, conquering culturally, religiously and changing languages. Islam does all these things. It is very much an Arab supremacist religion and kingdom. Wherever they go and gain the upper hand, they tear down all former symbols and houses of worship of the local people. They force people to learn Arabic to be able to read the Qur'an. Even in present days, they behead

---

[33] As quoted by Joel Richardson in his DVD, *Islam & The End Times*

people who do not convert to Islam. They make the cultures they conquer accept Sharia law. They change the dress and culture of the peoples they conquer.

7. The prophet Isaiah (ch. 24) records a vision of the apocalypse when God will judge the world, save his people and reign on Mount Zion in Jerusalem. Part of the judgment to the earth because of their sin comes through a "curse" that devours earth. In Hebrew, the word "curse" is אָלָה transliterated "alah" (New American Standard Exhaustive Concordance of the Bible). Could this be more than a coincidence connecting the word "curse" with the god of Islam?

Isaiah 24:1, 3, 5-6

Behold, the Lord will empty the earth and make it desolate,
and he will twist its surface and scatter its inhabitants.
The earth shall be utterly empty and utterly plundered;
for the Lord has spoken this word.
The earth lies defiled
under its inhabitants;
for they have transgressed the laws,
violated the statutes,
broken the everlasting covenant.
[6] Therefore a **curse** devours the earth,
and its inhabitants suffer for their guilt;
therefore the inhabitants of the earth are scorched,
and few men are left.

The goal of Islamic Jihad is to force the entire world to convert to Allah and live under Sharia law, or have their heads cut off.

8. Daniel 2:41-43 (NASB)

41 "In that you saw the feet and toes, partly of potter's clay and
partly of iron, it will be a divided kingdom; but it will have in it the
toughness of iron, inasmuch as you saw the iron **mixed** with common
clay.
42 "*As* the toes of the feet *were* partly of iron and partly of pottery, *so*
some of the kingdom will be strong and part of it will be brittle.
43 "And in that you saw the iron **mixed** with common clay, they will
combine with one another in the seed of men; but they will not
adhere to one another, even as iron does not **combine** with pottery.

The New American Standard Exhaustive Concordance of the Bible has this to say regarding the words "mixed" and "combine" in bold in the text above:

Hebrew NASB Number: 6151

Hebrew Word: עֲרַב
Transliterated Word: *arab* (1107d)
Root: (Aramaic) corr. to the root of 6154a;

Definition: *to mix:--*
List of English Words and Number of Times Used
combine (2),
mixed (2).

There seems to be a play on words here. The words "mixed and combine" in Hebrew is "arab". Arabs were viewed as a mixed people – Esau marrying Ishmael's daughter and intermarrying came to produce a mixed people – "arab" and the word became synonymous with "mixed people". It may be there is a hidden "encrypted clue" here for us with regard to the composition of the last ten kings or kingdoms, being made up largely of Arabs.

9. Daniel 2:41 says it will be a divided kingdom. After Mohammed died, there was a dispute over his successor, and the Religion and Empire was divided into what is today known as the Sunni and Shia groups. We see today that most of the violence in Iraq is between these Muslim groups. Notice what the Bible prophesies regarding the great final Battle of Armageddon:

Ezekiel 38:21
I will summon a sword against Gog on all my mountains, declares the Lord God. Every man's sword will be against his brother.

Zech. 14:13
And on that day a great panic from the Lord shall fall on them, so that each will seize the hand of another, and the hand of the one will be raised against the hand of the other.

10. The last Kingdom is the Muslim Empire that conquered the Eastern Roman Empire, or the Byzantine Empire in Constantinople (Istanbul) in 1453. That Muslim Empire led by the Caliphate came to an end in 1924 when the Turkish Ottoman Empire came to an end and Mustafa Kemal Atatürk, the founder of the modern secular Republic of Turkey did away with the Muslim Caliphate. The Caliph is like the Pope of Islam, but is much more. He is a political, military, economic and spiritual leader of all of Islam. There are signs that the Caliphate may soon be revived. All over the Muslim world there is talk of uniting Islam again under a Caliphate. Some see the next Caliph as being the Mahdi or the Twelfth Imam, the Muslim Messiah.

If there is a revival of the Islamic Caliphate, could that be the fulfillment of these passages? Remember, in the Revelation passages describing the beast with seven heads, the heads are kings and/or kingdoms.

Rev. 13:3

One of its heads seemed to have a mortal wound, but its mortal wound was healed, and the whole earth marveled as they followed the beast.

Rev. 13:12-14

It exercises all the authority of the first beast in its presence, and makes the earth and its inhabitants worship the first beast, whose mortal wound was healed. [13] It performs great signs, even making fire come down from heaven to earth in front of people, [14] and by the signs that it is allowed to work in the presence of the beast it deceives those who dwell on earth, telling them to make an image for the beast that was wounded by the sword and yet lived.

Rev. 17:8

The beast that you saw was, and is not, and is about to rise from the bottomless pit and go to destruction. And the dwellers on earth whose names have not been written in the book of life from the foundation of the world will marvel to see the beast, because it was and is not and is to come.

Rev. 17:11

As for the beast that was and is not, it is an eighth but it belongs to the seven, and it goes to destruction.

11. A trait common to each of the first six empires was that of continued expansion through conquest. The leaders of the empires were not content with the territory they had, but sought to subdue other peoples and lands and bring them under their dominion. What can be said about Islam's past practice and future aspirations? In his well researched book, *The Islamic Antichrist*, Joel Richardson quotes a number of passages from the Qur'an, Hadiths and commentaries from well known Islamic scholars regarding Islam's goal of world domination.

Allah's Apostle [Muhammad] said, 'I have been ordered to fight the people till they say: 'None has the right to be worshipped but Allah.'[34]

Fight against those who (1) believe not in Allah, (2) nor in the Last Day, (3) nor forbid that which has been forbidden by Allah and His Messenger (4) and those who acknowledge not the religion of truth (i.e. Islam) among the people of the Scripture (Jews and Christians), until they pay the Jizyah with willing submission, and feel themselves subdued. And the Jews say: 'Uzair (Ezra) is the son of Allah, and the Christians say: Messiah is the son of Allah. That is a saying from their mouths. They imitate the saying of the disbelievers of old. Allah's Curse be on them, how they are deluded away from the truth! (*Surah 9:29-30;* Muhsin Khan)

O ye who believe! Fight those of the disbelievers who are near to you, and let them find harshness in you, and know that Allah is with those who keep their duty (unto Him). (*Surah 9:123;* Pickthall)

Ibn Kathir's commentary on the above verse tracing the early history of Islam and how this was carried out in their conquest of the world can be read at the below website.[35]

One of Islam's greatest scholars, Mawlana Sayid Abul Mawdudi, born in 1905, had this to say about Islam and global domination:

Islam is not a normal religion like the other religions in the world, and Muslim nations are not like normal nations. Muslim nations are very special because they have a command from Allah to rule the entire world and to be over every nation in the world.

---

[34] Sahih Bukhari, Vol. 9, Bk. 84, Nu. 59, narrated by Abu Huraira, <http://www.sahih-bukhari.com/Pages/Bukhari_9_84.php>

[35] Tafsir Ibn Kathir-Quran Tafsir, Surah 9:123, <www.qtafsir.com>

Islam is a revolutionary faith that comes to destroy any government made by man. Islam doesn't look for a nation to be in a better condition than another nation. Islam doesn't care about the land or who owns the land. The goal of Islam is to rule the entire world and submit all of mankind to the faith of Islam. Any nation or power that gets in the way of that goal, Islam will fight and destroy. In order to fulfill that goal, Islam can use every power available every way it can be used to bring worldwide revolution. This is Jihad.[36]

Lest westerners think those sentiments are only those of past Middle Eastern writers, the following is a quote by Omar Ahmed, chairman of the board of CAIR (Council on American-Islamic Relations):

"Islam isn't in America to be equal to any other faith, but to become dominant. The Qur'an should be the highest authority in America, and Islam the only accepted religion on Earth."[37]

Like the six empires before it, Islam, the seventh, is bent on worldwide conquest. Its conquest is on a much larger scale than the previous empires. And like Nimrod, the builder of the tower of Babel, whose aim was to have a one world religion, language and government in rebellion and independence against Yahovàh, so Islam wants the same.

Common Thread

What the seven empires also have had in common is that they have been used by Satan to oppose and seek to destroy the people of God. The same is seen to be true of the Islamic Empire. Besides verses previously quoted from the Qur'an, note the following verses *(Surah)* from the Qur'an and Hadith regarding Islam's position on the Jews and Christians:[38]

Among the Jews are those who distort words from their [proper] usages .... But Allah has cursed them for their disbelief, so they

---

[36] Joel Richardson, The Islamic Antichrist, (Los Angeles, WorldNetDaily, 2009) p.144

[37] Ibid: p. 145

[38] < http://quran.com>

believe not, except for a few. (*Surah 4:46*)

Have you not seen those who were given a portion of the Scripture, [*Islam calls Jews and Christians 'people of the book' because of having received Scripture.*] who believe in superstition and false objects of worship and say about the disbelievers, "These are better guided than the believers as to the way"? Those are the ones whom Allah has cursed; and he whom Allah curses - never will you find for him a helper. (*Surah 4:51-52*)

The punishment of those who wage war against Allah and His Messenger, ... is: execution, or crucifixion, or the cutting off of hands and feet from opposite sides, or exile from the land: (*Surah 5:33*)

O you who believe! do not take the Jews and the Christians for friends; they are friends of each other; and whoever amongst you takes them for a friend, then surely he is one of them; surely Allah does not guide the unjust people. (*Surah 5:51*)

... kill the polytheists [*Christians who believe in the Trinity are among those considered polytheists*] wherever you find them and capture them and besiege them and sit in wait for them at every place of ambush. (*Surah 9:5*)

Narrated Abu Huraira: Allah's Apostle said, "The Hour will not be established until you fight with the Jews, and the stone behind which a Jew will be hiding will say. "O Muslim! There is a Jew hiding behind me, so kill him." [39]

Indeed, since the founding of the modern State of Israel in 1948, it has been involved in seven major wars, besides two *Intifadas* or uprisings on the part of the Palestinians and conflicts in Gaza. The stated goal on the part of many of the forces that have attacked the Jewish State has been to annihilate them. They are as follows:[40]

War of Independence, 1948-1949

---

[39] Sahih al-Bukhari, The Hadith Book,"Fighting for the Cause of Allah (Jihaad)" 52:177

[40] "Wars Involving Israel," <http://en.wikipedia.org/wiki/Wars_involving_Israel>

Sinai War, 1956
Six Days War, 1967
War of Attrition, 1967-1970
Yom Kippur War, 1973
First Lebanon War, 1982
Second Lebanon War, 2006

The nations involved in these wars against Israel give a clue as to who will be involved in future continued conflict. A list of those who have attacked them are as follows:[41]

War of Independence: Egypt, Anglo Egyptian Sudan, Transjordan, Syria, Lebanon, Iraq, Saudi Arabia, Yemen, Holy War Army, Arab Liberation Army, Muslim Brotherhood
Sinai War: Egypt, Palestinian fedayeen
Six Days War: Egypt, Syria, Jordan, Arab Expeditionary Forces: Iraq, Saudi Arabia, Morocco, Algeria, Libya, Kuwait, Tunisia, Sudan, PLO (Palestine Liberation Organization)
War of Attrition: Egypt, USSR, PLO, Jordan, Syria
Yom Kippur War: Egypt, Syria, Arab Expeditionary Forces: Iraq, Jordan, Saudi Arabia, Morocco, Algeria, Libya, Kuwait, Tunisia, Sudan, Lebanon: Other Expeditionary Forces: Pakistan, North Korea, Cuba, Supported by: USSR
First Lebanon War: PLO, Syria, LNRF (Lebanese National Resistance Front), Amal al-Mourabitoun (Lebanese), ASALA (Armenian Secret Army for the Liberation of Armenia), PKK (Kurdistan Workers' Party)
Second Lebanon War: Hezbollah, Amal (Lebanese Shia Movement), SSNP (Syrian Social Nationalist Party), LCP (Lebanese Communist Party), PFLP-GC (Popular Front for the Liberation of Palestine)

In his May 14, 2011 speech before the American Congress, referring to Israel being a democracy, Israeli Prime Minister Benjamin Netanyahu said:

"We're proud that over one million Arab citizens of Israel have been enjoying these rights for decades. Of the 300 million Arabs in the Middle East and North Africa, only Israel's Arab citizens enjoy real democratic rights. I want you to stop for a second and think about that.

[41] Ibid.

Of those 300 million Arabs, less than one-half of one-percent are truly free, and they're all citizens of Israel!"[42]

It is no wonder that Israel does not want to allow more Arabs to become citizens of Israel, where they have the right to vote. Before long, it would cease to be a Jewish State. The prime minister went on to say in his speech:

"So now here is the question. You have to ask it. If the benefits of peace with the Palestinians are so clear, why has peace eluded us? Because all six Israeli Prime Ministers since the signing of Oslo accords agreed to establish a Palestinian state. Myself included. So why has peace not been achieved? Because so far, the Palestinians have been unwilling to accept a Palestinian state, if it meant accepting a Jewish state alongside it.

You see, our conflict has never been about the establishment of a Palestinian state. It has always been about the existence of the Jewish state. This is what this conflict is about. In 1947, the United Nations voted to partition the land into a Jewish state and an Arab state. The Jews said yes. The Palestinians said no. In recent years, the Palestinians twice refused generous offers by Israeli Prime Ministers, to establish a Palestinian state on virtually all the territory won by Israel in the Six Day War.

They were simply unwilling to end the conflict. And I regret to say this: They continue to educate their children to hate. They continue to name public squares after terrorists. And worst of all, they continue to perpetuate the fantasy that Israel will one day be flooded by the descendants of Palestinian refugees.[43]

Is the conflict in the Middle East really about justice for the Palestinians and their having a State of their own or is there something else that is driving this conflict?

As we have cited before, almost four thousand years ago God made a covenant with Abraham and his descendants. The descendants being referred to were the Hebrews, the Jewish line of Abraham, Isaac and Jacob. Note what is said about the land:

---

[42]Noel Shepherd, "Video and transcript of Benjamin Netanyahu's speech to Congress," <http://newsbusters.org/blogs/noel-sheppard/2011/05/24/video-and-transcript-benjamin-netanyahus-speech-congress>

[43] Ibid.

Genesis 17:7-8

And I will establish my covenant between me and you and your offspring after you throughout their generations for an everlasting covenant, to be God to you and to your offspring after you. [8] And I will give to you and to your offspring after you the land of your sojournings, all the land of Canaan, for an everlasting possession, and I will be their God."

Psalm 105:6-11

O offspring of Abraham, his servant,
children of Jacob, his chosen ones!
[7] He is the Lord our God;
his judgments are in all the earth.
[8] He remembers his covenant forever,
the word that he commanded, for a thousand generations,
[9] the covenant that he made with Abraham,
his sworn promise to Isaac,
[10] which he confirmed to Jacob as a statute,
to Israel as an everlasting covenant,
[11] saying, "To you I will give the land of Canaan
as your portion for an inheritance."

As we have repeatedly stated in this book, there is still a battle raging today between Satan and God – between his forces and God's people over the control of Jerusalem. For Satan, not only does he want to rid the world of God's people, he also wants to discredit God by proving him to be a liar. If he can keep the descendants of Abraham out of the land promised to them as an everlasting inheritance, he will show God to be either unfaithful to his covenant or impotent, or both.

Another reason for the cosmic battle over the possession of Israel, and in particular Jerusalem, is that Satan is determined to be worshiped there through his proxy, the Antichrist on the temple mount – the place where God has said that he has set his King – his Son (Ps. 2).

If the city is strictly under Jewish control, the placing of his man in the temple of God where he will proclaim himself to be God, will be complicated. That is why, I believe, there is such a strong movement, not only among Muslims, but also in the broader United Nations world community, for Jerusalem to be an international city, under the administration of the United Nations.

Humanly speaking, it makes perfect sense for there to be two separate, coexisting Jewish and Palestinian states. But human reason must bow to God's eternal decree that that land is to be an everlasting possession for the Jewish people. In fact, God's wrath is prophesied to come upon the nations of the world because they have divided the land. In speaking of the coming "day of the Lord", a day of judgment when God will gather the nations for the great battle of Armageddon, God says this:

Joel 3:1-2

"For behold, in those days and at that time, when I restore the fortunes of Judah and Jerusalem, [2] I will gather all the nations and bring them down to the Valley of Jehoshaphat. And I will enter into judgment with them there, on behalf of my people and my heritage Israel, **because they have scattered them among the nations and have divided up my land**,

2011-2012 pro-democracy uprisings in the Middle East, known as "the Arab spring" have resulted in the further isolation of Israel with increasingly hostile neighbors all around. Does the Bible tell us what will happen to Israel in the future? Will they be destroyed by an Iranian nuclear bomb? Will the nations around unite again in another great war to wipe Israel off the map? We will see the answers to these questions later in the book.

Many in the West have a hard time envisioning Islam having a worldwide power and influence since there are only 2.6 out of 311 million adherents in the US (2010 Religious Census) and comprise of only 6% of Europe's population.[44]

Paul E. Marek shares "**A German's Point of View on Islam**:"[45]

by Paul E. Marek

Wednesday January 2, 2008
from (forwarder) Dr Emanual Tanay
republished Thursday January 3, 2008

---

[44] http://en.wikipedia.org/wiki/List_of_countries_by_Muslim_population

[45] http://www.icjs-online.org/index.php?article=1414

A man whose family was German aristocracy prior to World War II owned a number of large industries and estates. When asked how many German people were true Nazis, the answer he gave can guide our attitude toward fanaticism. 'Very few people were true Nazis 'he said,' but many enjoyed the return of German pride, and many more were too busy to care. I was one of those who just thought the Nazis were a bunch of fools. So, the majority just sat back and let it all happen. Then, before we knew it, they owned us, and we had lost control, and the end of the world had come. My family lost everything. I ended up in a concentration camp and the Allies destroyed my factories.

'We are told again and again by 'experts' and 'talking heads' that Islam is the religion of peace, and that the vast majority of Muslims just want to live in peace. Although this unqualified assertion may be true, it is entirely irrelevant. It is meaningless fluff, meant to make us feel better, and meant to somehow diminish the spectra of fanatics rampaging across the globe in the name of Islam. The fact is that the fanatics rule Islam at this moment in history. It is the fanatics who march. It is the fanatics who wage any one of 50 shooting wars worldwide. It is the fanatics who systematically slaughter Christian or tribal groups throughout Africa and are gradually taking over the entire continent in an Islamic wave. It is the fanatics who bomb, behead, murder, or honor kill. It is the fanatics who take over mosque after mosque. It is the fanatics who zealously spread the stoning and hanging of rape victims and homosexuals. The hard quantifiable fact is that the 'peaceful majority', the 'silent majority', is cowed and extraneous.

Communist Russia was comprised of Russians who just wanted to live in peace, yet the Russian Communists were responsible for the murder of about 20 million people. The peaceful majority were irrelevant. China's huge population was peaceful as well, but Chinese Communists managed to kill a staggering 70 million people. The average Japanese individual prior to World War II was not a warmongering sadist. Yet, Japan murdered and slaughtered its way across South East Asia in an orgy of killing that included the systematic murder of 12 million Chinese civilians; most killed by sword, shovel, and bayonet. And, who can forget Rwanda, which collapsed into butchery. Could it not be said that the majority of Rwandans were 'peace loving'?

History lessons are often incredibly simple and blunt, yet for all our powers of reason we often miss the most basic and uncomplicated of points: Peace-loving Muslims have been made irrelevant by their silence. Peace-loving Muslims will become our enemy if they don't speak up, because like my friend from Germany, they will awaken one day and find that the fanatics own them, and the end of their world will have begun. Peace-loving Germans, Japanese, Chinese, Russians, Rwandans, Serbs, Afghan is, Iraqis, Palestinians, Somalis, Nigerians, Algerians, and many others have died because the peaceful majority did not speak up until it was too late.

Emanuel Tanay,
M.D. Ann Arbor, MI

Summary

The theme of this chapter has been to seek to identify the seventh, (fourth in the Daniel visions) and last kingdom that will be in existence when Christ comes back. For the reasons stated in this session, I believe that the Islamic kingdom or Empire is that seventh kingdom. It ceased to exist as an official empire in 1924, but I believe it will be resurrected and it does not take a stretch of imagination, reading current events, to see how this is very possible and in the not too distant future.[46] Already, without being a unified kingdom, its religion is unifying the nations in their intent to destroy Israel.

---

[46] Again, many of the ideas in this chapter regarding Islam being the last empire, I have taken from Joel Richardson's *Islam and the End Times* DVD

10 THE ANTICHRIST: OLD TESTAMENT ALLUSIONS

EVEN IN NON-RELIGIOUS circles, the term "Antichrist" is known. Who is this Antichrist and what will he do? What will his right-hand man be like? This is what we look at in the next two chapters.

While the term "Antichrist" is a New Testament term, the concept comes from the Old Testament. He is the one who is against, or opposes the Christ, or the Messiah. First, let us look at his various names or titles:

OLD TESTAMENT ALLUSIONS TO THE ANTICHRIST

- "the seed" of the serpent (Gen. 3:15)
- "another horn, a little one, before which three of the first [ten] horns were plucked up by the roots. And behold, in this horn were eyes like the eyes of a man, and a mouth speaking great boasts" (Dan. 7:8)
- "the prince who is to come" (Dan. 9:26)
- "one who makes desolate" (Dan. 9:27)
- "the king" (Dan. 11:36)
- "the Assyrian" (Micah 5:5-6)

The Seed of the Serpent

As we have seen, the unifying theme of history is this conflict between the "seed of the serpent" and the "seed of the woman". Satan has used the kings and kingdoms of the world that have opposed the godly line as his main instruments to strike at God and oppose his plans. It makes sense that Satan's Antichrist will come from one of these empires that has been opposing God and his people.

The Antichrist Prefigured

Often the Bible presents types in history who represent and foreshadow the antitype to come. These are recorded for us in the Bible to give us clues so as to recognize who the fulfillment will be or what event will take place as illustrated in the type. There were various "saviours" in Israel's history that prefigured the Christ, like Joseph, Moses, Joshua and David.

The same is true with the Antichrist. We are given detailed prophesies in Daniel almost four hundred years before they happened of a man named Antiochus IV Epiphanes (175-164 BC), who prefigures the final Antichrist. He was the 8th king of the Syrian or Seleucid dynasty. He was not the legitimate heir to the throne, but his older brother who was, was being held hostage in Rome. While his brother's son was the legitimate successor during his father's imprisonment, Antiochus usurped his throne. Daniel is given a vision regarding this Antiochus who would come out of one of the four kingdoms that divided up Alexander the Great's empire, pictured here as a goat.

Daniel 8:8-14, 21-26

Then the goat became exceedingly great, but when he was strong, the great horn was broken, and instead of it there came up four conspicuous horns toward the four winds of heaven. [9] Out of one of them came a little horn, which grew exceedingly great toward the south, toward the east, and toward the glorious land. [10] It grew great, even to the host of heaven. And some of the host and some of the stars it threw down to the ground and trampled on them. [11] It became great, even as great as the Prince of the host. And the regular burnt offering was taken away from him, and the place of his sanctuary was overthrown. [12] And a host will be given over to it together with the regular burnt offering because of transgression, and it will throw truth to the ground, and it will act and prosper. [13] Then I heard a holy one speaking, and another holy one said to the one who spoke, "For how long is the vision concerning the regular burnt offering, the transgression that makes desolate, and the giving over of the sanctuary and host to be trampled underfoot?" [14] And he said to me, "For 2,300 evenings and mornings. Then the sanctuary shall be restored to its rightful state." .... [21] And the goat is the king of Greece. And the great horn between his eyes is the first king. [22] As for the horn that was broken, in place of which four others arose, four kingdoms shall arise from his nation, but not with his power.

We have already mentioned Alexander the Great in the chapter on the Prophets. When he died after extending his empire from the Mediterranean to the Hindu Kush in India, his empire was divided up among his four generals:

Macedonia & Greece: Cassander
Asia Minor and Thrace: Lysimachus
Syria and Babylon: Seleucus
Egypt, Arabia, Israel: Ptolemy

[23] And at the latter end of their kingdom, when the transgressors have reached their limit, a king of bold face, one who understands riddles, shall arise. [24] His power shall be great— but not by his own power; and he shall cause fearful destruction and shall succeed in what he does, and destroy mighty men and the people who are the saints. [25] By his cunning he shall make deceit prosper under his hand, and in his own mind he shall become great. Without warning he shall destroy many. And he shall even rise up against the Prince of princes, and he shall be broken—but by no human hand. [26] The vision of the evenings and the mornings that has been told is true, but seal up the vision, for it refers to many days from now."

Antiochus IV ("Epiphanes") 175-164 BC
• Made Torah reading punishable by death
• Slaughtered a sow on the Altar
• Erected an idol to Zeus in the Holy of Holies
– "The Abomination of Desolation" Matt 24:15
• The Maccabean Revolt
– 3 years: threw off the yoke of Seleucid Empire
– Rededicated the Temple: 25th of Kislev, 165 BC
• Celebrated as Chanukkah John 10:22

Let us look at the history of this Antiochus Epiphanes ("the Manifest/Conspicuous One"). On his coins he had the inscription "theos epiphanes" on the back, meaning, "god manifest" which probably meant that he considered himself Zeus manifest on earth. As mentioned, he usurped the throne from his older brother's son (his brother, Seleucus IV was being held hostage by the Romans). Daniel 8:9 refers to his success in invading Egypt (170-169 BC) and that he was also successful in putting down rebellions of the Parthians and Armenians in the east. He determined to impose Greek religious and cultural uniformity in his kingdom and brutally suppressed Jewish worship in Jerusalem and throughout Palestine.

Antiochus deposed the Jewish high priest, Onias III in 175 and placed his Hellenizing younger brother Jason in his place. After a period of time, another Jew of the priestly family, Menelaus, bribed Antiochus to appoint him in his place. However, while Antiochus was in Egypt, Jason laid siege to Jerusalem in an effort to take back his position as high priest. On his way back from Egypt, Antiochus saw this rebellion going on and he dealt ruthlessly with the Jews, killing 40,000 men, women and children and selling 40,000 into slavery. He also plundered the temple.

As a result of this brutality and the plundering of the temple, there arose a full-fledged revolt led by the Maccabean family.

The suppression came to a head in December 167 BC when Antiochus, after a second invasion of Egypt, returned from Alexandria in frustration because he had been turned back by the Roman commander. He sent his general Apollonius, with 20,000 troops to seize Jerusalem on a Sabbath. There, he erected an idol of Zeus and desecrated the altar by offering swine on it. This event became known as "the abomination of desolation" which served as a type of a future similar event predicted by Jesus.

Host of Heaven

What is this reference in Daniel 8 to "[10] It grew great, even to **the host of heaven**. And some of the **host** and some of the **stars** it threw down to the ground and trampled on them. [11] It became great, even as great as **the Prince of the host**."? And vs. 25, "And he shall even rise up against **the Prince of princes**"?

The word "host" in Hebrew means army. But it seems in the context of "host of heaven" to refer to angels. The word "host" is also used in the same context as "stars" which are thrown down to the ground. Note the following verses:

Job 38:4,7

"Where were you when I laid the foundation of the earth? ....
[7] when the morning stars sang together
and all the sons of God shouted for joy?

(in Job, the "sons of God" are angels (1:6; 2:1) and in other contexts angels are called "morning stars or stars," Is. 14:12-14)

Rev. 12:4

His tail swept down a third of the stars of heaven and cast them to the earth. And the dragon **(Satan)** stood before the woman who was about to give birth, so that when she bore her child he might devour it.

2 Kings 17:15-17

... They went after false idols and became false, and they followed the nations that were around them, concerning whom the Lord had commanded them that they should not do like them. [16] And they abandoned all the commandments of the Lord their God, and made for themselves metal images of two calves; and they made an Asherah and worshiped all **the host of heaven** and served Baal. [17] And they burned their sons and their daughters as offerings and used divination and omens and sold themselves to do evil in the sight of the Lord, provoking him to anger.

As noted earlier, those who worship idols, worship demons.

Psalm 106:36-38

They served their idols,
which became a snare to them.
[37] They sacrificed their sons
and their daughters to the demons;
[38] they poured out innocent blood,
the blood of their sons and daughters,
whom they sacrificed to the idols of Canaan,
and the land was polluted with blood.

Now this is the most amazing picture of heaven:

1 Kings 22:19-23

And Micaiah said, "Therefore hear the word of the Lord: I saw the Lord sitting on his throne, and all **the host of heaven** standing beside him on his right hand and on his left; [20] and the Lord said, 'Who will entice Ahab, that he may go up and fall at Ramoth-gilead?' And one said one thing, and another said another. [21] Then **a spirit** came forward and stood before the Lord, saying, 'I will entice him.' [22] And the Lord said to him, 'By what means?' And he said, **'I will go out, and will be a lying spirit** in the mouth of all his prophets.' And he said, 'You are to entice him, and you shall succeed; go out and do so.' [23] Now therefore behold, **the Lord has put a lying spirit in the mouth of all these your prophets**; the Lord has declared disaster for you."

This is a picture of fallen angels or spirits standing beside God in heaven. A non-fallen angel would not be able to be “a lying spirit”. They had access to God, as Job 1:6 tells us that Satan came before God with the “sons of God”. But the Bible tells us of a time when they would have no more access:

Rev. 12:7-9

Now war arose in heaven, Michael and his angels fighting against the dragon. And the dragon and his angels fought back, [8] but he was defeated and there was no longer any place for them in heaven. [9] And the great dragon was thrown down, that ancient serpent, who is called the devil and Satan, the deceiver of the whole world— he was thrown down to the earth, and his angels were thrown down with him.

But God has appointed a day of judgment for this host of heaven:

Isaiah 24:21-23

On that day the Lord will punish
 the host of heaven, in heaven,
 and the kings of the earth, on the earth.
[22] They will be gathered together
 as prisoners in a pit;
they will be shut up in a prison,
 and after many days they will be punished.
[23] Then the moon will be confounded
 and the sun ashamed,
for the Lord of hosts reigns
 on Mount Zion and in Jerusalem,
and his glory will be before his elders.

This is a foreshadowing of:

Rev. 20:1-3
Then I saw an angel coming down from heaven, holding in his hand the key to the bottomless pit and a great chain. [2] And he seized the dragon, that ancient serpent, who is the devil and Satan, and bound him for a thousand years, [3] and **threw him into the pit**, and shut it and sealed it over him, so that he might not deceive the nations any longer, until the thousand years were ended. After that he must be released for a little while.

Rev. 20:7-10
And when the thousand years are ended, Satan will be released from his prison [8] and will come out to deceive the nations …. [10] and the devil who had deceived them was thrown into the lake of fire and sulfur where the beast and the false prophet were, and they will be tormented day and night forever and ever.

So, back to this passage about the little horn, who we know from history was Antiochus IV Epiphanes, it says:

"[10] It grew great, even to **the host of heaven**. And some of the **host** and some of the **stars** it threw down to the ground and trampled on them. [11] It became great, even as great as **the Prince of the host**." And vs. 25, "And he shall even rise up against **the Prince of princes**. . ."

This is an example of the passage in Isaiah 14 where it starts talking about the king of Babylon and then the language obviously shifts to refer to Satan. The same is true in Ezekiel 28 where it is an oracle against the king of Tyre, but then directs its language to Satan ("you were in the Eden, the garden of God…" 28:13).

So here, the passage refers to Antiochus, but then some of the language is speaking of Satan who was possessing Antiochus, or was the power ruling through Antiochus. Here it says that Satan (if this interpretation is correct), grew great, even to the host of heaven – the army of the angels of God, and he threw some of them down to the ground (Rev. 12 says he swept a third of them and cast them to the earth). Then it says that he became great, even as great as "the Prince of the host." The interpretation the angel Gabriel gives says the "Prince of the host" is "the Prince of princes," which would have to refer to God

the Son – Jesus. But notice the end of this conflict:
"And he shall even rise up against the Prince of princes, and he shall be broken—but by no human hand." (8:25). So shall it be in the last conflict with the Antichrist.

There is a time period given of 2,300 evenings and mornings.

Daniel 8:13-14

Then I heard a holy one speaking, and another holy one said to the one who spoke, "For how long is the vision concerning the regular burnt offering, the transgression that makes desolate, and the giving over of the sanctuary and host to be trampled underfoot?" [14] And he said to me, "For 2,300 evenings and mornings. Then the sanctuary shall be restored to its rightful state."

There is general disagreement as to whether this is talking about 2,300 days – six and a third years, or 2,300 evening and morning sacrifices, thus being 1,150 days or three years, two months and ten days. Given that the abomination of desolation took place on December 14, 167 BC, three years before its rededication on December 14 (25 Chislev) 164 BC, it seems more likely that the number is 1,150 days. It seems the sacrifices were stopped some months before the actual "abomination of desolation", when swine were sacrificed, and thus accounts for the 1150 days. The significant point is that God presents Daniel an exact number which is fulfilled exactly. This is a clue for us regarding the future days given for the end time Antichrist.

Daniel 11 gives us more detail on Antiochus IV, outlining his conflicts with the Ptolemy rulers of the south. The "abomination of desolation" mentioned in Daniel 8 is again spoken of:

Daniel 11:31-35

[31] Forces from him shall appear and profane the temple and fortress, and shall take away the regular burnt offering. And they shall set up <u>the abomination that makes desolate</u>. [32] He shall seduce with flattery those who violate the covenant, but the people who know their God shall stand firm and take action. [33] And the wise among the people shall make many understand, though for some days they shall stumble by sword and flame, by captivity and plunder. [34] When they stumble, they shall receive a little help. And many shall join themselves to them with flattery, [35] and some of the wise shall stumble, so that they may be refined, purified, and made white, until the time of the end, for it still awaits the appointed time.

The "wise among the people" undoubtedly refers to the Maccabean (also called Hasmonean) family, and in 167 B.C. they led a revolt that established a new, independent kingdom of Israel.

The Apocryphal books of Maccabees record the history of that era:

1 Maccabees 1:41-64 (NRSV)
41 Then the king wrote to his whole kingdom that all should be one
people,
42 and that all should give up their particular customs.
43 All the Gentiles accepted the command of the king. Many even
from Israel gladly adopted his religion; they sacrificed to idols and
profaned the sabbath.
44 And the king sent letters by messengers to Jerusalem and the towns
of Judah; he directed them to follow customs strange to the land,
45 to forbid burnt offerings and sacrifices and drink offerings in the
sanctuary, to profane sabbaths and festivals,
46 to defile the sanctuary and the priests,
47 to build altars and sacred precincts and shrines for idols, to sacrifice
swine and other unclean animals,
48 and to leave their sons uncircumcised. They were to make
themselves abominable by everything unclean and profane,
49 so that they would forget the law and change all the ordinances.
50 He added, "And whoever does not obey the command of the king
shall die."
51 In such words he wrote to his whole kingdom. He appointed
inspectors over all the people and commanded the towns of Judah to
offer sacrifice, town by town.
52 Many of the people, everyone who forsook the law, joined them,
and they did evil in the land;
53 they drove Israel into hiding in every place of refuge they had.
54 Now on the fifteenth day of Chislev, in the one hundred forty-fifth
year, they erected a desolating sacrilege on the altar of burnt offering.
They also built altars in the surrounding towns of Judah,
55 and offered incense at the doors of the houses and in the streets.
56 The books of the law that they found they tore to pieces and burned
with fire.
57 Anyone found possessing the book of the covenant, or anyone who
adhered to the law, was condemned to death by decree of the king.
58 They kept using violence against Israel, against those who were
found month after month in the towns.

[59] On the twenty-fifth day of the month they offered sacrifice on the
altar that was on top of the altar of burnt offering.
[60] According to the decree, they put to death the women who had their
children circumcised,
[61] and their families and those who circumcised them; and they hung
the infants from their mothers' necks.
[62] But many in Israel stood firm and were resolved in their hearts not
to eat unclean food.
[63] They chose to die rather than to be defiled by food or to profane the
holy covenant; and they did die.
[64] Very great wrath came upon Israel.

2 Maccabees 6:1-6 (NRSV)

[1] Not long after this, the king sent an Athenian senator to compel the
Jews to forsake the laws of their ancestors and no longer to live by the
laws of God;
[2] also to pollute the temple in Jerusalem and to call it the temple of
Olympian Zeus, and to call the one in Gerizim the temple of Zeus-
the-Friend-of-Strangers, as did the people who lived in that place.
[3] Harsh and utterly grievous was the onslaught of evil.
[4] For the temple was filled with debauchery and reveling by the
Gentiles, who dallied with prostitutes and had intercourse with
women within the sacred precincts, and besides brought in things for
sacrifice that were unfit.
[5] The altar was covered with abominable offerings that were forbidden
by the laws.
[6] People could neither keep the sabbath, nor observe the festivals of
their ancestors, nor so much as confess themselves to be Jews.

So what again is the significance or importance of knowing something of Antiochus Epiphanes and what he did in the Jewish Temple? It was a precursor of what the Antichrist will do. Here is what Jesus said of a yet future abomination of desolation:

Matthew 24:15-22

"So when you see the abomination of desolation spoken of by the prophet Daniel, standing in the holy place (let the reader understand), [16] then let those who are in Judea flee to the mountains. [17] Let the one who is on the housetop not go down to take what is in his house, [18] and let the one who is in the field not turn back to take his cloak.

[19] And alas for women who are pregnant and for those who are nursing infants in those days! [20] Pray that your flight may not be in winter or on a Sabbath. [21] For then there will be great tribulation, such as has not been from the beginning of the world until now, no, and never will be. [22] And if those days had not been cut short, no human being would be saved. But for the sake of the elect those days will be cut short.

It also gives us a picture of the final theater of battle; that in the end times there will again be a north – south struggle. Later in Daniel 11 the passage shifts from the time of Antiochus Epiphanes to the final Antichrist:

While the Antichrist will most likely not be an exact replica of Antiochus Epiphanes, there are some characteristics that we can note regarding Antiochus that may also be repeated by the coming world ruler.

1. He was the eighth king in the Seleucid Dynasty (the Antichrist is also an eighth king).
2. He came to power illegitimately and was an evil, contemptible person.
3. He used deceit, intrigue, flattery and money to gain power with the help of only a few people.
4. He made treaties that he broke.
5. While people felt secure, he invaded them suddenly, killing tens of thousands and plundering their wealth.
6. He distributed plunder, loot and wealth to his followers.
7. He prospered greatly.
8. He tried to unify everyone in his kingdom to a common culture and religion and put to death those who resisted.
9. He exalted himself as god and placed a statue of Zeus (the god he claimed to incarnate) in the temple, offering swine on God's altar to Zeus and put an end to the temple worship of Yahováh.
10. He sought to destroy the Jewish religion and any Jewish people who did not apostatize.
11. Most of the Jews did leave their faith or compromise their beliefs, including most of the religious leaders and priests, and greatly opposed those who sought to remain true to God.
12. The reason given for his prospering in killing many Jews and putting an end to the sacrifices is because of their rebellion or transgression.

13. There was a definite time period prophesied for his trampling God's people underfoot and desecration of the sanctuary.
14. There were saints who resisted him, many to imprisonment or death, and many insincere joined them and were treacherous.
15. He came to an end without human intervention.

With these points in mind, let us now look at how the Bible describes the end time Antichrist.

One of the characteristics of Biblical prophecy is that a single sentence of prophecy can have part of it fulfilled in one time period and the other part thousands of years later. We have mentioned a case in point when Jesus was quoting from

Isaiah 61:1-2

The Spirit of the Lord God is upon me,
because the Lord has anointed me
to bring good news to the poor;
he has sent me to bind up the brokenhearted,
to proclaim liberty to the captives,
and the opening of the prison to those who are bound;
[2] to proclaim the year of the Lord's favor,
and the day of vengeance of our God;

Jesus stopped short of reading the last phrase "and the day of vengeance of our God;" (Luke 4:17-21). He said to them,

"Today this Scripture has been fulfilled in your hearing."

So far, close to two thousand years are separating the "to proclaim the year of the Lord's favor" and "the day of vengeance of our God."

So, in this passage of Daniel 11, there are very detailed and exact accounts of events following Alexander the Great's death and the rule of Antiochus Epiphanes and the "abomination that causes desolation". All of a sudden, in the middle of the text, there seems to be a shift of characters that so far are separated by more than two thousand years. However, the phrase in verse 35 "until the time of the end" seems to be introducing a shift in persons, with the king in verse 36 not being Antiochus, but rather the end time Antichrist.

Daniel 11:35-45 (NASB)

35 "Some of those who have insight will fall, in order to refine,

purge and make them pure until the end time; because *it is* still *to*
come at the appointed time.
36 "Then the king will do as he pleases, and he will exalt and magnify
himself above every god and will speak monstrous things against the
God of gods; and he will prosper until the indignation is finished, for
that which is decreed will be done.
37 "He will show no regard for the gods [*Elohim* can be gods or God]
of his fathers or for the desire of women, nor will he show regard for
any *other* god; for he will magnify himself above *them* all.
38 "But instead he will honor a god of fortresses, a god whom his
fathers did not know; he will honor *him* with gold, silver, costly
stones and treasures.
39 "He will take action against the strongest of fortresses with *the help*
of a foreign god; he will give great honor to those who acknowledge
him and will cause them to rule over the many, and will parcel out
land for a price.
40 "At the end time the king of the South will collide with him, and [*or*
but] the king of the North will storm against him with chariots, with
horsemen and with many ships; and he will enter countries, overflow
them and pass through.
41 "He will also enter the Beautiful Land, and many *countries* will fall;
but these will be rescued out of his hand: Edom, Moab and the
foremost of the sons of Ammon.
42 "Then he will stretch out his hand against *other* countries, and the
land of Egypt will not escape.
43 "But he will gain control over the hidden treasures of gold and
silver and over all the precious things of Egypt; and Libyans and
Ethiopians [in Hebrew text, "Cushites", which includes the area today
known as the Sudan] *will follow* at his heels.
44 "But rumors from the East and from the North will disturb him, and
he will go forth with great wrath to destroy and annihilate many.
45 "He will pitch the tents of his royal pavilion between the seas and
the beautiful Holy Mountain; yet he will come to his end, and no one
will help him.

Daniel 12:1-13 (NASB)

1 "Now at that time Michael, the great prince who stands *guard* over
the sons of your people, will arise. And there will be a time of distress
such as never occurred since there was a nation until that time; and at
that time your people, everyone who is found written in the book, will
be rescued.

2 "Many of those who sleep in the dust of the ground will awake, these
to everlasting life, but the others to disgrace *and* everlasting contempt.
3 "Those who have insight will shine brightly like the brightness of the
expanse of heaven, and those who lead the many to righteousness,
like the stars forever and ever.
4 "But as for you, Daniel, conceal these words and seal up the book
until the end of time; many will go back and forth, and knowledge
will increase."
5 Then I, Daniel, looked and behold, two others were standing, one on
this bank of the river and the other on that bank of the river.
6 And one said to the man dressed in linen, who was above the waters
of the river, "How long *will it be* until the end of *these* wonders?"
7 I heard the man dressed in linen, who was above the waters of the
river, as he raised his right hand and his left toward heaven, and
swore by Him who lives forever that it would be for a time, times, and
half *a time;* and as soon as they finish shattering the power of the holy
people, all these *events* will be completed.
8 As for me, I heard but could not understand; so I said, "My lord,
what *will be* the outcome of these *events?*"
9 He said, "Go *your way,* Daniel, for *these* words are concealed and
sealed up until the end time.
10 "Many will be purged, purified and refined, but the wicked will act
wickedly; and none of the wicked will understand, but those who
have insight will understand.
11 "From the time that the regular sacrifice is abolished and the
abomination of desolation is set up, *there will be* 1,290 days.
12 "How blessed is he who keeps waiting and attains to the 1,335
days!
13 "But as for you, go *your way* to the end; then you will enter into rest
and rise *again* for your allotted portion at the end of the age."

First of all, it is important to make an observation. We have a clue as to how to interpret future prophecy based on how past prophecy was fulfilled. Daniel wrote hundreds of years before Antiochus and history has shown that what he wrote was fulfilled precisely and literally. The symbolic terms Daniel used are explained in the text and are not fulfilled allegorically, but rather historically. That means that what we read about the future opponent of God will also be fulfilled with the same literal exactness, including the numbers used.

I have cited this because we are talking about what people need to know concerning the coming apocalypse and how to survive. It says of those who were God's people:

Daniel 11:31-35

[32] He shall seduce with flattery those who violate the covenant, but the people who know their God shall stand firm and take action. [33] And the wise among the people shall make many understand, though for some days they shall stumble by sword and flame, by captivity and plunder. [34] When they stumble, they shall receive a little help. And many shall join themselves to them with flattery, [35] and some of the wise shall stumble, so that they may be refined, purified, and made white, until the time of the end, for it still awaits the appointed time.

It should not be surprising for us if this same pattern does not occur again with the final Antichrist. God's people will suffer and stumble, by sword and flame, by captivity and plunder. The purpose from God's perspective, however, is that they be refined, purified and made white.

Now, combining passages we have looked at in Daniel 7:23-27; 8:8-26; 9:24-27 and chapters 11-12, what are some summary observations we can make about this person based on what is revealed in Daniel?

1. Based on our previous chapter, we can say that this "fourth beast, terrifying and dreadful and exceedingly strong, with great iron teeth and which devoured and broke in pieces and stamped what was left with its feet and was different from all the previous beasts" is the Islamic Empire. Taking the description from Nebuchadnezzar's dream of the statue, perhaps the two legs of iron could refer to the two main branches of Islam – the Sunni and Shi'a branches. This kingdom is said to devour the whole earth and tread it down and crush it (*some believe the term 'whole earth' in general OT usage does not refer to the entire inhabited globe but rather the entire territory of the Near and Middle East that in any way relates to the Holy Land).*[47]

2. Out of this Islamic Empire ten kings or leaders or kingdoms will arise. Note how the symbols are used interchangeably: 7:17 'These four great beasts are four **kings** who shall arise out of the earth.' And vs. 23: 'As for the fourth beast, there shall be a fourth **kingdom** on earth,'

---

[47] Frank E. Gaebelein, The Expositor's Bible Commentary, (Grand Rapids, MI: Zondervan, 1984) vol. 7 pg. 93

3. After these ten leaders are manifested, there will come one later who will be different than the others and will subdue or put down three of these leaders or kingdoms.

4. This new leader will appear more imposing or greater than the other kings.

5. He will do as he pleases – perhaps not encumbered by a political system he has to answer to.

6. He will make a firm covenant with the many (i.e. Jews and others?) for seven years.

7. He will appear to be religiously tolerant as evidenced by the fact that the Jews will be offering sacrifices in the temple.

8. His personal religious make-up is that he will show no regard for the gods or God of his fathers. If 'gods' (the term is 'Elohim' which is the plural form for god, but is also used as a singular when referring to 'God' as in Genesis 1) are to be understood, it would mean that he would come from a polytheistic background. If 'God' or 'god' is understood, he could come from a Jewish, Christian or Muslim background. He could be someone like Stalin who began as a candidate for the Russian Orthodox priesthood before turning to Marxism and atheism. Or he could be like so many in the Middle East, a Muslim Jew. Hundreds of years ago, when Jews were forced to convert or have their heads cut off, many chose to recant their Jewish heritage and faith and converted to Islam to save their lives.

The phrase 'he will show no regard for the desire of women (or the love of women)' is hard to understand. Some have suggested it may indicate he will be a homosexual, though the text does not give a clear idea of its meaning. It says he will not show regard for any god, but rather will magnify himself above all gods.

9. In a seeming contradiction it says that he will instead honor a god of fortresses – a god his fathers did not know. This god he will honor with gold, silver, costly stones and treasures. Not until modern times has the concept of atheism been accepted. This seems to indicate that while he does not believe in any god, his god is military strength, for which he will spend a great deal of money.

10. He will take action against the strongest of fortresses with a foreign god. This is not clear whether he uses a god foreign to his background or nation or belief. Perhaps he invokes that god which gains him favor with those he is seeking to conquer. There are those who conjecture that this is a reference to his attacking the USA and Europe, which at this moment are the strongest military powers. He would use Islam, or Allah, a god that he himself does not really believe in, to motivate the people to attack these lands. Interestingly, a friend, who is a corporate executive, had a near death experience with a heart attack and he said that he saw and conversed with Christ or an angel. He also saw the entire East Coast of America in flames from nuclear explosions. It takes little imagination to see how Muslim terrorists would want to attack the US in this way.

11. He will give great honor to those who acknowledge him and will cause them to rule over many and will parcel out land or territories for a price.

12. He will not be unopposed. Egypt will collide with him. The text here is taken two ways by various translations. The "he, i.e. the Antichrist" is referred to as the 'king of the north' (in Biblical parlance usually refers to areas north of Israel like Syria or Assyria or Babylon - Iraq or Iran today - or Turkey) who will attack Egypt with a great army and many ships and in the process will pass through many countries, including Israel (the Beautiful Land). Many of these countries will fall, though what is today Jordan will somehow be rescued from his hand. He will attack other countries and will take the treasures of Egypt as well as bringing Libya and Sudan in submission to him (it could be these are the three countries that he uproots). The other interpretation is that "he" is attacked by both the king of the south and the king of the north, but that he will be victorious over both.

13. Rumors from the East and from the North will disturb him and he will with great wrath go and destroy and annihilate many. His headquarters will be in Israel between the Mediterranean and Dead Seas and Jerusalem. In the book of Revelation, one of the seven seals of judgment foresees a quarter of the world's population dying from wars, famine, pestilence and wild animals. When the sixth trumpet of judgment is sounded, there will be a massive world war in which a third of the world's population will die. Between these two, some three billion people will meet their death. It is possible that what is mentioned

here may involve war with India, China and Russia, which are east and north of Palestine and have great populations.

14. Halfway through the seven year covenant, he will break the covenant and put a stop to sacrifices and grain offerings in the temple and will bring about the abomination that causes desolation.

15. He will speak great boasts and will exalt and magnify himself above every god and will speak out against God and say monstrous things against God.

16. He will wage war with the saints of God through a process of wearing them down – systematic pressure, persecution and opposition and he will overpower them and they will be given over to him for the last three and a half years. This will usher the greatest time of distress and suffering on the Jewish nation in their entire history.

17. He will make alterations in the way of measuring time, perhaps altering the calendar much as in the French Revolution. They sought to do away with the dating based on A.D. (Christ) and dating by the first year of the French Republic. For twelve years this revolutionary calendar was made absolutely obligatory and those who adhered to the Christian (Gregorian) calendar were subject to criminal prosecution. They also changed the months into three 10 day weeks. Likewise the Soviets tried to change the calendar into at first 5 day weeks and then later 6 day weeks.[48]

18. He will intend to make changes in law (much like Muslims are seeking to impose Sharia law in countries around the world).

19. He will prosper until a time of complete destruction when God comes and he is destroyed and thrown into a burning fire (perhaps 1290 days after the stopping of the temple sacrifices and the abomination of desolation – 30 days longer than the three and a half years. As with Antiochus Ephipanes, the sacrifices were stopped first and then later occurred the "abomination that causes desolation." It could be that regular burnt offerings will be taken away 1290 days from the end and the abomination of desolation will occur 30 days later, which would be 1260 days from the end).

---

[48] Ibid. vol.7 p. 94

20. The other kingdoms or kings will have their dominion taken away, but will be allowed to live for a time.

21. God will pass judgment in favor of the saints and the sovereignty, dominion and greatness of all the kingdoms of the earth will be given over to the saints of God and all will serve and obey God. (This will occur perhaps 1,335 days after the abomination of desolation – 45 days after the 1290 days).

Muslim Eschatology

An interesting twist in all this is what Muslims regard as end time events.

"According to Islamic view, Isa (Jesus) son of Mary, was a prophet and messenger of God. It is believed that Jesus was not crucified; instead he was raised bodily. According to many hadith and believed by most Muslims, he will return to Earth. At the time appointed by Allah, Jesus will physically return to this world and aid the Mahdi. According to some sects of Shia Islam, the Mahdi also descends. He will break the cross, kill the swine, slaughter the Dajjal and end all wars, ushering in an era of peace. The messianic era comes after Jesus kills ad-Dajjal, the false messiah antichrist figure in Islam, and defeats his followers.[49]

"Masih ad-Dajjal (Arabic: المسيح الدجّال *al-Masīḥ ad-Dağğāl*, Arabic for "the false messiah") is an evil figure in Islamic eschatology. He is to appear pretending to be *Masih* (i.e. the Messiah) at a time in the future, before Yawm al-Qiyamah (*Judgment Day*), directly comparable to the figures of the Antichrist and Armilus in Christian and Jewish eschatology, respectively.

Dağğāl is a common Arabic word, with the meaning "deceiving", used in the sense of "false prophet". *Al-Masīḥ ad-Dağğāl* with the definite article, refers to "the deceiving Messiah", a specific end-of times deceiver. The term is a literal rendition of the Classical Syriac term for "Antichrist", *Mšīḥā Daggālā*, used in the Syriac Peshitta. Hadith attributed to Muhammad give many signs of the appearance of the Dajjal, … Muhammad is reported to have said: '... Allah is not one eyed while Messiah, Ad-Dajjal is blind in the right eye and his eye looks like a bulging out grape.'

---

[49] "Islamic Eschatology" <http://en.wikipedia.org/wiki/Islamic_eschatology>

It is said that he will have his right eye damaged and the left will be working because knowledge acquired through the right eye can be *nūrī* (means that pertaining to light) and through the left *nārī* (that pertaining to fire). It is also said that he will have the word *kafir* (nonbeliever) on his forehead.

The belief is based around the events prior to the Day of Judgment around the Second Coming of Isa (Jesus), when *Ad-Dağğāl* who is blind in his right eye, shall gather an army of those he has deceived and lead them in a war against Jesus, who shall be accompanied by an army of the righteous.

He will appear somewhere between Syria and Iraq, at which time Prophet Isa (known as Jesus in English) will return and the Mahdi will come, the Dajjal will travel the whole world preaching his falsehood but will be unable to enter Mecca or Medina."[50]

The Bible says that Satan is the master deceiver – the father of lies. Deception is most effective when mixed with truth. As you have seen above, Islam mixes a lot of what the Bible says with sufficient untruths to keep one from salvation. The rejection of Jesus' death and resurrection for our sins is the key message of salvation that must be accepted to enter the kingdom of heaven, but Islam rejects that truth.

Islam speaks of a coming Antichrist – Masih ad-Dajjal who will be blind in his right eye. The God of the Bible reveals to Zechariah that He will raise up a "worthless shepherd" for Israel in the future (Zech. 11:4-17). A possible interpretation of the text is that this "worthless shepherd" will be blind in his right eye and his right arm will be withered.

If this does in fact happen, can you see the implications for Israel? If Israel accepts a leader who is blind or blinded in his right eye, how will he be viewed by the Muslim world? He will be seen as the Antichrist, or Dajjal and will provide the greatest motivation possible for all Muslims to gather in Jihad to invade Israel in order to kill the Antichrist. Could this be the motivation of the invasion and battle of Armageddon?

The continuing passage in Zechariah outlines what will happen with this invasion. It seems that chapter 12 gives a summary – that Israel will be invaded, but they will defeat their enemies. However, chapter 14 gives more detail, explaining that Israel will be defeated at first and occupied, until the real Messiah comes to do battle on their behalf. It is fascinating reading, but we will get to that later. For now, back to the

---

50 "Masih ad Dajjal" <http://en.wikipedia.org/wiki/Masih_ad-Dajjal>

Antichrist.

The Assyrian

One of the possible titles for the Antichrist is that of "the Assyrian" and comes from the prophet Micah. He prophesied leading up to and after the time of the Assyrian invasion of Israel in 722 B.C. and of Judah in 701 B.C.. As mentioned previously, Old Testament prophecies are at times difficult to follow as they shift from their present circumstances to the future, and sometimes very distant future all in the same context.

Micah prophesies judgment on Samaria (the capital of Israel) and Jerusalem (the capital of Judah). But then he speaks of God's glorious restoration (the same text that Isaiah also used) which as the context shows, has not as yet happened:

Micah 4:1-4
It shall come to pass in the latter days
that the mountain of the house of the Lord
shall be established as the highest of the mountains,
and it shall be lifted up above the hills;
and peoples shall flow to it,
[2] and many nations shall come, and say:
"Come, let us go up to the mountain of the Lord,
to the house of the God of Jacob,
that he may teach us his ways
and that we may walk in his paths."
For out of Zion shall go forth the law,
and the word of the Lord from Jerusalem.
[3] He shall judge between many peoples,
and shall decide for strong nations afar off;
and they shall beat their swords into plowshares,
and their spears into pruning hooks;
nation shall not lift up sword against nation,
neither shall they learn war anymore;
[4] but they shall sit every man under his vine and under his fig
tree, and no one shall make them afraid,
for the mouth of the Lord of hosts has spoken.

The text continues to explain that in the day that the above will happen, God will have brought his people back to the land and the Lord would rule over them in Mount Zion forever:

Micah 4:6-7
In that day, declares the Lord,
I will assemble the lame
and gather those who have been driven away
and those whom I have afflicted;
[7] and the lame I will make the remnant,
and those who were cast off, a strong nation;
and the Lord will reign over them in Mount Zion
from this time forth and forevermore.

In the process of this, however, Israel will be attacked by many nations:

Micah 4:11-5:1
Now many nations
are assembled against you,
saying, "Let her be defiled,
and let our eyes gaze upon Zion."
[12] But they do not know
the thoughts of the Lord;
they do not understand his plan,
that he has gathered them as sheaves to the threshing floor.
[13] Arise and thresh,
O daughter of Zion,
for I will make your horn iron,
and I will make your hoofs bronze;
you shall beat in pieces many peoples;
and shall devote their gain to the Lord,
their wealth to the Lord of the whole earth.
Now muster your troops, O daughter of troops;
siege is laid against us;
with a rod they strike the judge of Israel
on the cheek.

The text continues explaining that their deliverance from these invading armies will come from the Messiah who would come from Bethlehem and be the ruler over his people.

Micah 5:2-6
But you, O Bethlehem Ephrathah,

who are too little to be among the clans of Judah,
from you shall come forth for me
one who is to be ruler in Israel,
whose origin is from of old,
from ancient days.
[3] Therefore he shall give them up until the time
when she who is in labor has given birth;
then the rest of his brothers shall return
to the people of Israel.
[4] And he shall stand and shepherd his flock in the strength of the Lord, in the majesty of the name of the Lord his God.
And they shall dwell secure, for now he shall be great
to the ends of the earth.
[5] And he shall be their peace.
When the Assyrian comes into our land
and treads in our palaces,
then we will raise against him seven shepherds
and eight princes of men;
[6] they shall shepherd the land of Assyria with the sword,
and the land of Nimrod at its entrances;
and he shall deliver us from the Assyrian
when he comes into our land
and treads within our border.

The context seems to be saying that this ruler who will rule over and shepherd his people Israel, who would be from Bethlehem (Jesus was born in Bethlehem), will deliver his people from the Assyrian who will invade their land. As this is clearly a Messianic text, the events in the context speak of something far in the future of the Assyrian invasion of Judah in 701 B.C. The Messiah was still to come seven hundred years later and this invasion did not happen during Christ's first coming. This speaks of an Assyrian yet in the future. As we will see in later texts, the Messiah will deliver Israel from the Antichrist at his coming. So it seems that this Antichrist will be an Assyrian.

The modern day territories that comprised the nucleus of Assyria are Iran, Iraq, eastern Turkey, Syria, and northern Saudi Arabia. They also conquered Lebanon, Israel, Jordan and Egypt. The Bible always referred to the invasions of Assyria and Babylon as coming from the north – north of Israel. The lands that Assyria occupied are all Muslim lands today which would seem to give a fairly good idea that this Assyrian will be from a Muslim background.

The Prince to Come

One of the texts used by those who support the idea that the Antichrist will come from a ten nation revived Roman Empire is in Daniel.

Daniel 9:26-27
And after the sixty-two weeks, an anointed one shall be cut off and shall have nothing. And the people of **the prince who is to come** shall destroy the city and the sanctuary. Its end shall come with a flood, and to the end there shall be war. Desolations are decreed. [27] And he shall make a strong covenant with many for one week, and for half of the week he shall put an end to sacrifice and offering. And on the wing of abominations shall come one who makes desolate, until the decreed end is poured out on the desolator."

The reference to the destruction of the city and the sanctuary is clearly referring to the events in 70 A.D. when the Roman armies under Titus destroyed Jerusalem. The "people of the prince who is to come" seems to be referring to the person or prince in verse 27 who is the Antichrist. The obvious deduction is that as it was the Romans who destroyed Jerusalem, this future prince will be from the former Roman Empire.

Jewish historian Flavius Josephus, who was there at the destruction of Jerusalem sheds some interesting light on this, however. Titus gathered his army from Legions that were from the east. Josephus writes:

"for the greatest part of the Roman garrison was raised out of Syria; and being thus related to the Syrian part, they were ready to assist it."[51]

"So Vespasian sent his son Titus from Achaia, where he had been with Nero, to Alexandria, to bring back with him from thence the fifth and the tenth legions, while he himself, when he had passed over the Hellespont, came by land into Syria, where he gathered together the Roman forces, with a considerable number of auxiliaries from the kings in that neighborhood.[52]

---

[51] Op. Cit., Josephus, *The Wars of the Jews,* Book II, Chapt. 13: Sec. 7

[52] Ibid., Book III, Chpt. 1: Sec. 3

2. But as to Titus, he sailed over from Achaia to Alexandria, and that sooner than the winter season did usually permit; so he took with him those forces he was sent for, and marching with great expedition, he came suddenly to Ptolemais, and there finding his father, together with the two legions, the fifth and the tenth, which were the most eminent legions of all, he joined them to that fifteenth legion which was with his father; eighteen cohorts followed these legions; there came also five cohorts from Cesarea, with one troop of horsemen, and five other troops of horsemen from Syria. Now these ten cohorts had severally a thousand footmen, but the other thirteen cohorts had no more than six hundred footmen apiece, with a hundred and twenty horsemen. There were also a considerable number of auxiliaries got together, that came from the kings Antiochus, and Agrippa, and Sohemus, each of them contributing one thousand footmen that were archers, and a thousand horsemen. Malchus also, the king of Arabia, sent a thousand horsemen, besides five thousand footmen, the greatest part of which were archers; so that the whole army, including the auxiliaries sent by the kings, as well horsemen as footmen, when all were united together, amounted to sixty thousand,[53]

The famine in the city of Jerusalem was so severe that many tried to desert the city and cast themselves on the mercy of the Romans. However, as their stomachs were bloated, when they ate, many of their stomachs exploded and gold was found in their bellies. Josephus writes:

So the multitude of the Arabians, with the Syrians, cut up those that came as supplicants, and searched their bellies. Nor does it seem to me that any misery befell the Jews that was more terrible than this, since in one night's time about two thousand of these deserters were thus dissected.[54]

"What! have any of my own soldiers done such things as this out of the uncertain hope of gain, without regarding their own weapons, which are made of silver and gold? Moreover, do the Arabians and Syrians now first of all begin to govern themselves as they please, and to indulge their appetites in a foreign war, and then, out of their barbarity in murdering men, and out of their hatred to the Jews, get it

[53] Ibid., Book III, Chpt. 4: Sec. 2

[54] Ibid., Book V, Chpt. 13, section 4

ascribed to the Romans?" for this infamous practice was said to be spread among some of his own soldiers also. Titus then threatened that he would put such men to death, if any of them were discovered to be so insolent as to do so again;[55]

Indeed, the four specific legions under Titus involved in the taking and destruction of the city and Temple were: Legion XV Apollinaris, Legion V Macedonica, Legion XII Fulminata and Legion X Fretensis. In fact, it was the Tenth Legion in particular that breached the wall and set fire to the Temple. Their soldiers were from Turkey and Syria. Those of the other legions were from Syria, Melitene (Eastern Turkey, Syria) and Moesia (Serbia, Bulgaria).[56]

So the people who actually destroyed the city and Temple were primarily Arabs, Syrians and Turks, all Muslim countries today. This is another clue that the "prince to come" will come from these lands and peoples.

---

[55] Ibid., Book V, Chpt. 13, section 5

[56] Pace, H. Geva, "The Camp of the Tenth Legion in Jerusalem: An Archaeological Reconsideration", IEJ 34 (1984), pp. 247-249

11 THE ANTICHRIST: NEW TESTAMENT ALLUSIONS

NEW TESTAMENT ALLUSIONS TO THE ANTICHRIST

- [24] "For false Christs and false prophets will arise and will show great signs and wonders, so as to mislead, if possible, even the elect. " (Mt. 24:24)
- "one who 'comes in his own name'" (John 5:43)
- "the man of lawlessness is revealed, the son of destruction (perdition)," 2 Thess. 2:3
- "the deceiver and the antichrist" (2 John 1:7)
- "the beast that comes up from the Abyss" (Rev. 11:7)
- "the beast [who] seemed to have had a fatal wound, but the fatal wound had been healed" (Rev. 13:3-8)
- "the beast which … once was, now is not, and will come up out of the Abyss and go to his destruction." …. "the world will be astonished when they see the beast, because he once was, now is not, and yet will come." (Rev. 17:8)
- "The beast who once was, and now is not, is an eighth king. He belongs to the seven and is going to his destruction." (Rev. 17:11)

The Christ

What may seem obvious needs to be underlined. The Antichrist will seek to portray himself as "The Christ", or "The Messiah". Matthew records,

Matthew 24:4-5

And Jesus answered them, "See that no one leads you astray. [5] For many will come in my name, saying, 'I am the Christ,' and they will lead many astray.

Matthew 24:23-27

Then if anyone says to you, 'Look, here is the Christ!' or 'There he is!' do not believe it. [24] For false christs and false prophets will arise and perform great signs and wonders, so as to lead astray, if possible, even the elect. [25] See, I have told you beforehand. [26] So, if they say to you, 'Look, he is in the wilderness,' do not go out. If they say, 'Look, he is in the inner rooms,' do not believe it. [27] For as the lightning comes from the east and shines as far as the west, so will be the coming of the Son of Man.

The Man of Lawlessness

Both Paul and John also record that this person will perform miraculous signs. Paul calls him the "man of lawlessness."

2 Thess. 2:1-12

Now concerning the coming of our Lord Jesus Christ and our being gathered together to him, we ask you, brothers, [2] not to be quickly shaken in mind or alarmed, either by a spirit or a spoken word, or a letter seeming to be from us, to the effect that the day of the Lord has come. [3] Let no one deceive you in any way. For that day will not come, unless the rebellion comes first, and the man of lawlessness is revealed, the son of destruction, [4] who opposes and exalts himself against every so-called god or object of worship, so that he takes his seat in the temple of God, proclaiming himself to be God. [5] Do you not remember that when I was still with you I told you these things? [6] And you know what is restraining him now so that he may be revealed in his time. [7] For the mystery of lawlessness is already at work. Only he who now restrains it will do so until he is out of the way. [8] And then the lawless one will be revealed, whom the Lord Jesus will kill with the breath of his mouth and bring to nothing by the appearance of his coming. [9] The coming of the lawless one is by the activity of Satan with all power and false signs and wonders, [10] and with all wicked deception for those who are perishing, because they refused to love the truth and so be saved. [11] Therefore God sends them a strong delusion, so that they may believe what is false, [12] in order that all may be condemned who did not believe the truth but had pleasure in unrighteousness.

The Beast

Rev. 13:1-4

And I saw a beast rising out of the sea, with ten horns and seven heads, with ten diadems on its horns and blasphemous names on its heads. [2] And the beast that I saw was like a leopard; its feet were like a bear's, and its mouth was like a lion's mouth. And to it the dragon gave his power and his throne and great authority. [3] One of its heads seemed to have a mortal wound, but its mortal wound was healed, and the whole earth marveled as they followed the beast. [4] And they worshiped the dragon, for he had given his authority to the beast, and they worshiped the beast, saying, "Who is like the beast, and who can fight against it?"

The question is raised, who or what is this beast? We see similarities with the description of the dragon, who is identified as Satan:

Rev. 12:3

And another sign appeared in heaven: behold, a great red dragon, with seven heads and ten horns, and on his heads seven diadems.

In the case of the dragon, or Satan, the crowns or diadems are placed on the seven heads. In the case of the beast, the diadems are placed on the ten horns. What do these heads and horns and diadems mean? An angel explains to John (Rev. 17:7-14) that the seven heads are seven kings or kingdoms and the ten horns are ten kings which come out of the seventh kingdom, as we have already seen. The diadems indicate that they are reigning.

First, where does this beast come from? Revelation 12 is a very compressed picture of world history – of Satan, the dragon fighting against Israel, the woman and her offspring. He and his angels are then engaged in a battle with Michael and heaven's angels and is defeated and cast out of heaven to earth. He is thwarted at every turn. This sets the stage for the introduction of two of Satan's helpers – two beasts, or the

Antichrist and the false prophet. They form an unholy trinity in their effort to defeat the divine Trinity.

Rev. 12:17

Then the dragon became furious with the woman and went off to make war on the rest of her offspring, on those who keep the commandments of God and hold to the testimony of Jesus. And he stood on the sand of the sea.

Rev. 13:1

And I saw a beast rising out of the sea, with ten horns and seven heads, with ten diadems on its horns and blasphemous names on its heads.

Rev. 13:11-12

Then I saw another beast rising out of the earth. It had two horns like a lamb and it spoke like a dragon. [12] It exercises all the authority of the first beast in its presence, and makes the earth and its inhabitants worship the first beast, whose mortal wound was healed.

The beast rising out of the sea is also said to come from the bottomless pit, or the abyss where Satan will be chained for a thousand years during Christ's earthly reign (Rev. 11:7; 17:8; 20:1-3).

As we have noted in a previous chapter, the seven heads are said to be both seven mountains on which the prostitute, Babylon the Great is seated (allusion to Rome, but as mentioned before, Mecca also has seven mountains) and seven kings or kingdoms which we have already identified as Egypt, Assyria, Babylon, the Medo-Persian Empire, Greece, Rome and the last being the Islamic Empire. The description in 13:2: "And the beast that I saw was like a leopard; its feet were like a bear's, and its mouth was like a lion's mouth. And to it the dragon gave his power and his throne and great authority," is a description of the Greek, Medo-Persian and Babylon Empires and it shows where each of these seven kingdoms have gotten their power. The dragon, Satan, has given each of them his power, his throne and great authority.

The fact that the diadems or crowns are on the heads when describing the dragon speaks of his historic ruling through the seven kings or Empires down through the ages that have been in hostility to the people of God and have sought to destroy them.

The beast in Revelation 13, however, is shown as having ten crowns on the ten horns and this represents the last of the seven kingdoms.

This is also the feet with ten toes of iron mixed with clay in Nebuchadnezzar's vision. But it is not just the last of the seven, it is the revived, or resurrected king or kingdom – the "beast that you saw was, and is not, and is about to rise…"

"As for the beast that was and is not, it is an eighth but it belongs to the seven, and it goes to destruction." It is an interesting detail that this last king, or Antichrist is an eighth. As mentioned before, Antiochus Epiphanes was also the eighth in his dynasty, though not a legitimate ruler, just as this Antichrist will usurp power from the ten kings or kingdoms.

"And the ten horns that you saw are ten kings who have not yet received royal power, but they are to receive authority as kings for one hour, together with the beast. [13] These are of one mind and hand over their power and authority to the beast." In the Old Testament, this eighth king will root up and cast down three of the ten kings, apparently before getting all of them to give him their power and authority.

In the past, many thought the ten horns would be a ten nation revived Roman Empire such as the European Union. With 27 nations currently in the Union, that does not seem likely. Another possible fulfillment is found in the United Nations Millennium Development Goals Report 2009 where they divide the world into ten regions.[57]

Now that we understand a little better the imagery, let's continue to see more of a description of what this Antichrist or Beast will be like and do.

Rev. 13:5-10

[5] "And the beast was given a mouth uttering haughty and blasphemous words, and it was allowed to exercise authority for forty-two months. [6] It opened its mouth to utter blasphemies against God, blaspheming his name and his dwelling, that is, those who dwell in heaven. [7] Also it was allowed to make war on the saints and to conquer them. And authority was given it over every tribe and people and language and nation, [8] and all who dwell on earth will worship it, everyone whose name has not been written before the foundation of the world in the book of life of the Lamb that was slain. [9] If anyone has an ear, let him hear:

---

[57]http://www.un.org/millenniumgoals/pdf/MDG_Report_2009_ENG.pdf pg. 55

[10] If anyone is to be taken captive,
to captivity he goes;
if anyone is to be slain with the sword,
with the sword must he be slain.
Here is a call for the endurance and faith of the saints."

The theme of this beast speaking haughty and blasphemous words has been said in many of the passages we have cited. He will exalt himself above all gods and claim himself to be God, and that, in God's temple in Jerusalem. Also there is the reoccurring theme of his having power for 42 months, which is the same as "time, times and half a time" or 1260 days (three and a half years based on a 30 day month, 360 day year calendar).

As has been stated before, he will make war on the saints and will conquer them. Some will go into captivity and some will be killed with the sword. Often, scripture is written with terminology understandable to the people of the era in which it was written, but it is interesting that today, Muslims kill their enemies by beheading them with a sword.

We see also that this Beast will have authority over "every tribe and people and language and nation, [8] and all who dwell on earth will worship it, everyone whose name has not been written before the foundation of the world in the book of life of the Lamb that was slain." In this passage, those who worship the Beast are those whose names were not written in God's book of life before the world began. In Thessalonians, the reason is given emphasizing man's responsibility: "because they refused to love the truth and so be saved. [11] Therefore God sends them a strong delusion, so that they may believe what is false, [12] in order that all may be condemned who did not believe the truth but had pleasure in unrighteousness."

John then continues in Revelation 13 introducing the third member of this unholy trinity:

The False Prophet

Rev. 13:11-18

[11] Then I saw another beast rising out of the earth. It had two horns like a lamb and it spoke like a dragon. [12] It exercises all the authority of the first beast in its presence, and makes the earth and its inhabitants worship the first beast, whose mortal wound was healed. [13] It performs great signs, even making fire come down from heaven to earth in front of people, [14] and by the signs that it is

allowed to work in the presence of the beast it deceives those who dwell on earth, telling them to make an image for the beast that was wounded by the sword and yet lived. [15] And it was allowed to give breath to the image of the beast, so that the image of the beast might even speak and might cause those who would not worship the image of the beast to be slain. [16] Also it causes all, both small and great, both rich and poor, both free and slave, to be marked on the right hand or the forehead, [17] so that no one can buy or sell unless he has the mark, that is, the name of the beast or the number of its name. [18] This calls for wisdom: let the one who has understanding calculate the number of the beast, for it is the number of a man, and his number is 666."

It would seem that the False Prophet will be a religious leader, by virtue of his title. In other words, the people will accept him as God's prophet, though from God's point of view, he will be a false one. I have argued that the Beast, or Antichrist, will come from the Islamic world as the last World Empire, even though much of the Church down through the ages have held to the viewpoint that Rome is the last Empire and the Pope will be the Antichrist. But how can a Muslim Antichrist gain the following of a third of the world that call themselves Christians? Will Rome play any part in this final scene?

Prophecy of the Popes

In this context it is worth mentioning the supposed Prophecy of the Popes by Irish Bishop St. Malachy in 1139. It is a list of 112 short Latin phrases said to describe all the future popes beginning with Pope Celestine II (1143-1144) and concluding with the successor of Pope Benedict XVI. The prophecy was lost in the Vatican Archives, but found in 1590 and published in 1595 by Arnold de Wyon, a Benedictine historian, as part of his book *Lignum Vitæ*. There are those who dispute its authenticity, but regardless of its provenance, we have prophetic descriptions of the popes from at least 1595 on.

The quote regarding the last pope goes like this:

Petrus Romanus
In persecution extrema Sanctae Romanae Ecclesiae sedebit Petrus Romanus, qui pascet oves in multis tribulationibus; quibus transactis, civitas septicolis diruetur, et Judex tremendous iudicabit populum suum. Finis.

Translation:

Peter the Roman
"In the final persecution of the Holy Roman Church, there will sit [i.e., as Pope] Peter the Roman, who will pasture his sheep in many tribulations: and when these things are finished, the city of seven hills will be destroyed, and the terrible judge will judge his people. The End."

According to St. Malachy's list of popes, Pope Francis is the last one. A fascinating and well researched book on the subject is Thomas Horn and Cris Putnam's *Petrus Romanus: The Final Pope is Here.*[58] If there is any truth to the "Prophecy of the Popes," could Pope Francis or some other powerful leader within the Vatican throw their weight behind a popular world leader claiming to be the Christ citing his miracles as proof? Only time will tell.

Is the Muslim Messiah the Antichrist?

The Muslims await a messiah called "the Mahdi", or "the Twelfth Imam".

In Shia Islam "the Mahdi symbol has developed into a powerful and central religious idea." Twelver Shia Muslims believe that the Mahdi is Muhammad al-Mahdi, the Twelfth Imam, who was born in 869 CE and was hidden by God at the age of five (874 CE). He is still alive but has been in occultation, "awaiting the time that God has decreed for his return".

According to Moojan Momen, Shia traditions state that the Mahdi be "a young man of medium stature with a handsome face" and black hair and beard. "He will not come in an odd year [...] will appear in Mecca between the corner of the Kaaba and the station of Abraham and people will witness him there.

The Twelfth Imam will return as the Mahdi with "a company of his chosen ones," and his enemies will be led by the one-eyed Antichrist and the Sufyani. The two armies will fight "one final apocalyptic battle" where the Mahdi and his forces will prevail over

---

[58] Thomas Horn & Cris Putnam, *Petrus Romanus:The Final Pope is Here* (Crane, MO: Defender, 2012)

evil. After the Mahdi has ruled Earth for a number of years, Isa will return.

- At-Tirmidhi reported that the Prophet said:

  The Mahdi is from my Ummah; he will be born and live to rule five or seven or nine years. (If) one goes to him and says, "Give me (a charity)", he will fill one's garment with what one needs.

- Abu Dawud also reported a *hadith* about the Mahdi that the Prophet Muhammed said:

  The Mahdi will be of my stock, and will have a broad forehead, a prominent nose. He will fill the earth with equity and justice as it was filled with oppression and tyranny, and he will rule for seven years."[59]

The idea of a seven year rule certainly fits in with what the Bible says about the length of time the Antichrist will be in power.

Daniel 9:27
"And he shall make a strong covenant with many for one week, and for half of the week he shall put an end to sacrifice and offering. And on the wing of abominations shall come one who makes desolate, until the decreed end is poured out on the desolator."

Is There A Time Frame for the Appearance of the Mahdi?

We saw with the Prophecy of the Popes that there is a definite time pinpointed by the prophecy, namely that Pope Francis is the last one. Is there a similar type of time marking prophecy in the Muslim tradition? Authors Horn and Putnam in their book *Petrus Romanus* cite Amir Taheri's op Ed "Obama and Ahmadinejad" published in *Forbes*, October 26, 2008.[60]

---

59 "Mahdi" <http://en.wikipedia.org/wiki/Mahdi>

60 http://www.forbes.com/2008/10/26/obama-iran-ahmadinejad-oped-cx_at_1026taheri_print.html

"Is Barack Obama the "promised warrior" coming to help the Hidden Imam of Shiite Muslims conquer the world?

The question has made the rounds in Iran since last month, when a pro-government Web site published a Hadith (or tradition) from a Shiite text of the 17th century. The tradition comes from *Bahar al-Anvar* (meaning Oceans of Light) by Mullah Majlisi, a magnum opus in 132 volumes and the basis of modern Shiite Islam.

According to the tradition, Imam Ali Ibn Abi-Talib (the prophet's cousin and son-in-law) prophesied that at the End of Times and just before the return of the Mahdi, the Ultimate Saviour, a "tall black man will assume the reins of government in the West." Commanding "the strongest army on earth," the new ruler in the West will carry "a clear sign" from the third imam, whose name was Hussein Ibn Ali. The tradition concludes: "Shiites should have no doubt that *he is with us*."

In a curious coincidence Obama's first and second names--Barack Hussein--mean "the blessing of Hussein" in Arabic and Persian. His family name, Obama, written in the Persian alphabet, reads O Ba Ma, which means "he is with us," the magic formula in Majlisi's tradition."

Antichrist a Person or an Empire or a World Religion?

I have stated before that the seventh head of the dragon is the Islamic Empire and that there will be an eighth that will come from this head, which will be the Islamic Empire revived. This idea has led some to believe that the Beast, or Antichrist is not a person, but rather an Empire, or an anti-God world system or religion such as Islam.

However, it seems that it is very likely that this last figure is a person as well as being an Empire and/or religion. If that is the case, the individual who will be the Antichrist may also personally be mortally wounded and as a counterfeit Christ, present himself as having been resurrected like Christ. We are told that this "man of lawlessness" (2 Thess. 2:4) … opposes and exalts himself against every so-called god or object of worship, so that he takes his seat in the temple of God, proclaiming himself to be God. His destruction, which we have seen in several texts is described as being the destruction of a man. In the passage describing Christ's return from heaven to fight against the Beast and the armies gathered against Jerusalem we read the following:

Rev. 19:19-21

And I saw the beast and the kings of the earth with their armies gathered to make war against him who was sitting on the horse and against his army. [20] And the beast was captured, and with it the false prophet who in its presence had done the signs by which he deceived those who had received the mark of the beast and those who worshiped its image. These two were thrown alive into the lake of fire that burns with sulfur. [21] And the rest were slain by the sword that came from the mouth of him who was sitting on the horse, and all the birds were gorged with their flesh.

This passage seems to clearly identify the two beasts we have seen before as humans. Just as there were two men who went directly to heaven without dying – Enoch (Heb. 11:5) and Elijah (2 Ki 2:11), so these two will go directly into the lake of fire without dying.

Will there be a way to identify who are followers of this Antichrist? Our next chapter deals with one of the most famous and enigmatic subjects – "The Mark of the Beast – 666."

12 THE MARK OF THE BEAST - 666

VARIOUS RELIGIONS have ways of identifying its adherents through outward dress or symbols. Sikh males have a distinctive turban, uncut hair, beard and mustache, and wear a steel or iron bracelet. Muslim women are identified by their head covering. Catholic priests normally wear their distinctive white collar. Will there be a way to distinguish those who are true followers of the Antichrist from those who are not?

One of the most widely speculated passages in the Bible is regarding the "mark of the Beast" found in the text cited in the last chapter (Rev. 13:11-18). We read of this mark in the context regarding the third member of the unholy trinity – Satan, the Beast and the False Prophet:

Rev. 13:11-18

Then I saw another beast rising out of the earth. It had two horns like a lamb and it spoke like a dragon. [12] It exercises all the authority of the first beast in its presence, and makes the earth and its inhabitants worship the first beast, whose mortal wound was healed. [13] It performs great signs, even making fire come down from heaven to earth in front of people, [14] and by the signs that it is allowed to work in the presence of the beast it deceives those who dwell on earth, telling them to make an image for the beast that was wounded by the sword and yet lived. [15] And it was allowed to give breath to the image of the beast, so that the image of the beast might even speak and might cause those who would not worship the image of the beast to be slain. [16] Also it causes all, both small and great, both rich and poor, both free and slave, to be marked on the right hand or the forehead, [17] so that no one can buy or sell unless he has the mark, that is, the name of the beast or the number of its name. [18] This calls for wisdom: let the one who has understanding calculate the number of the beast, for it is the number of a man, and **his number is 666**.

Before speculating on what the number 666 may mean, it is important to see what is clear.

1. No one will be able to buy or sell unless he has the mark, regardless of status in life.
2. The mark will be placed on the right hand or the forehead.
3. The mark will be the name of the beast or the number of its name.
4. Wisdom and understanding are required in order to calculate the number of the beast.
5. The number is the number of a man and his number is 666.
6. There is an association between worshiping the beast and his image and receiving the mark.
7. The work and power of this unholy trinity will be very deceptive because of the miraculous powers they possess:

Rev. 19:20

And the beast was captured, and with it the false prophet who in its presence had done the signs by which he deceived those who had received the mark of the beast and those who worshiped its image. These two were thrown alive into the lake of fire that burns with sulfur.

2 Thess. 2:9-12

The coming of the lawless one is by the activity of Satan with all power and false signs and wonders, [10] and with all wicked deception for those who are perishing, because they refused to love the truth and so be saved. [11] Therefore God sends them a strong delusion, so that they may believe what is false, [12] in order that all may be condemned who did not believe the truth but had pleasure in unrighteousness.

8. There are eternal consequences to those who take this number or name upon themselves.

Rev. 14:9-12

And another angel, a third, followed them, saying with a loud voice, "If anyone worships the beast and its image and receives a mark on his forehead or on his hand, [10] he also will drink the wine of God's wrath, poured full strength into the cup of his anger, and he will be tormented with fire and sulfur in the presence of the holy angels and in the presence of the Lamb. [11] And the smoke of their torment goes up forever and ever, and they have no rest, day or night, these worshipers of the beast and its image, and whoever receives the mark of its name."
[12] Here is a call for the endurance of the saints, those who keep the commandments of God and their faith in Jesus.

While refusing to worship the beast and receive the mark will cause people to not be able to buy or sell and may single them out for imprisonment or death, those who do receive the mark and avoid temporary difficulties and persecution, will be tormented in hell forever.

9. The beast and false prophet will succeed in their war against God's saints:

Rev. 13:7-10

Also it was allowed to make war on the saints and to conquer them. And authority was given it over every tribe and people and language and nation, [8] and all who dwell on earth will worship it, everyone whose name has not been written before the foundation of the world in the book of life of the Lamb that was slain. [9] If anyone has an ear, let him hear:

[10] If anyone is to be taken captive,
to captivity he goes;
if anyone is to be slain with the sword,
with the sword must he be slain.

Here is a call for the endurance and faith of the saints.

10. Those who resist this beast and refuse to worship him and receive his mark because of their faith in Jesus will be victorious over him and will be resurrected and will reign with Christ on earth for a thousand years.

Rev. 12:11

And they have conquered him by the blood of the Lamb and by the word of their testimony, for they loved not their lives even unto death.

Rev. 20:4-6

Then I saw thrones, and seated on them were those to whom the authority to judge was committed. Also I saw the souls of those who had been beheaded for the testimony of Jesus and for the word of God, and who had not worshiped the beast or its image and had not received its mark on their foreheads or their hands. They came to life and reigned with Christ for a thousand years. [5] The rest of the dead did not come to life until the thousand years were ended. This is the first resurrection. [6] Blessed and holy is the one who shares in the first resurrection! Over such the second death has no power, but they will be priests of God and of Christ, and they will reign with him for a thousand years.

So what is this mark and what about the number 666? Many theories have been put forth regarding the mark. Some believe it could be some sort of tattoo. Others have referred to the Universal Product Code which is stamped on all products, each of which features three sixes as end borders and the middle lines.

Others see the mark as being some sort of implanted RFID (radio-frequency identification) tag. Indeed, we were surprised when living in Rome, Italy, to learn that all dogs and cats (and probably other pets) had to have tattoos identifying their owners, which later gave way to microchips based on a passive RFID technology which is about the size of a large grain of rice and is injected under the skin of the pet. This became mandatory law. We could see how the voluntary injection of these chips in people in the US, containing all their medical data, could easily become law under a government that required it.

A manuscript called the *Oxyrhynchus Papyri* has been found dating back to the late third to early fourth century with a fragment of the papyrus of Revelation which instead of giving the number 666, is written as 616. Irenaeus, a second century church father wrote that there was a copy of the book with that number. However, the most reliable and ancient manuscripts, including those who had seen the Apostle John face to face, gave their testimony that the number **was** 666 and not 616. Irenaeus attributed the 616 number as a copyist's error.

Walid Shoebat in his book *God's War On Terror* has proposed that the Codex Vaticanus (350 AD) Greek text of the Book of Revelation where "the supposed Greek letters (Chi Xi Stigma) that are used to translate to the number 666 very much resemble the most common creed of Islam Bismillah (or Basmalah), written in Arabic. Bismillah literally means 'In the Name of Allah' and is followed by the symbol of crossed swords, which is used universally throughout the Muslim world to signify Islam."[61]

For a thorough rebuttal of Walid's proposal see: http://eutychusnerd.blogspot.com/2010/07/mark-of-beast-is-islam-walid-shoebat.html

New technologies are being developed at a rapid pace and so we may not even know at present how this mark will be applied, though a fairly recent technology developed by Professor John Rogers of the University of Illinois certainly could fit the bill. He calls it "epidermal electronics" which is a tiny, bendy computer chip that can be placed on or in the body to monitor critical health data. It can be applied like a band aid or underneath a temporary tattoo and is almost invisible.[62]

Blog writer identified as ICA ("In Christ Alone", a.k.a. "MidnightWatcher") presents a theory that the Mark of the Beast is not to be understood as a literal visible mark on the forehead or right hand, but rather is a figurative or spiritual mark, indicating the person's heart beliefs similar to the seal the angels place on God's servants in the following text:

---

[61] Walid Shoebat and Joel Richardson, God's War On Terror (Top Executive Media, 2008) p. 369.

[62] Scientific Chicago: http://chicagotonight.wttw.com/2013/11/12/skin-electronics. Video interview with John Rogers demonstrating his epidermal electronics

Rev. 7:2-3
Then I saw another angel ascending from the rising of the sun, with the seal of the living God, and he called with a loud voice to the four angels who had been given power to harm earth and sea, [3] saying, "Do not harm the earth or the sea or the trees, until we have sealed the servants of our God on their foreheads."

With regard to the objection that it must be a visible sign because no one will be able to buy or sell if they do not have this mark the ICA blogger continues: "When it comes to the conditions that exist in many Islamic nations for Christians, Dr. Labib Mikhail, a former professor of homiletics from the Faith Mission Bible College in Cairo, Egypt, states that one reason why people are forced to embrace Islam is because of the poverty they will assuredly find themselves in if they do not. "If you don't embrace Islam *you may not find a job*; you may not find an apartment, and *you'll be in financial trouble*" [**4**]. Non-Muslims, particularly Christians and Jews, living in Muslim-dominated countries are finding themselves subjected to an ever increasing wave of discrimination, oppression and persecution at the hands of the Ummah (Islamic Community). Even today a Christian in a Muslim country is often treated as a second-class citizen or worse, unable to serve in the military or police, many cannot work or own a business, or even find a place to live. They cannot own a weapon to defend themselves, nor can they testify against a Muslim in court, etc. etc. etc. [**5**]. And this type of treatment is getting worse, not better."

"In many Islamic nations, for instance, everyone must be given an ID card and this ID card specifies what religion you are, such as "M" for Muslim or "C" for Christian or "J" for Jew. For example, "Christian converts and members of minority religions suffer daily discrimination in Egypt, which restricts their access to work, education, travel and healthcare... Every Egyptian over 16 years old must have an ID card which mentions religious belief". In fact, "an ID card is required for the most basic needs in Egypt — to open a bank account, get a driver's license, obtain a pension cheque, enroll at school, get a job, and even for childhood immunizations..." Some Muslims will convert to another faith other than Christianity, but "Muslims who convert to Christianity account for many more and their treatment is often harsher as they are considered to be apostates, which some Muslims see as punishable by death" [**8**]. And now, since the fall of Hosni Mubarak and the rise of the 'Egyptian Revolution', the situation has worsened dramatically for Jews and Christians. This is where Islamic supremacy veiled in a cloak of 'democracy' will take you in a country where Islam is the overwhelming, dominant religion. It's like Sunni and Shia. It's like iron and clay. Democracy and Islamism will never fully mix."[63]

The Biblical text itself indicates that a number is being referred to, making reference four times to the word, "number" and the number has something to do with the name of the beast:

Rev. 13:17-18
so that no one can buy or sell unless he has the mark, that is, the name of the beast or the **number** of its name. [18] This calls for wisdom: let the one who has understanding calculate the **number** of the beast, for it is the **number** of a man, and his **number** is 666.

A concept widely practiced among the Hebrews and Greeks and also used in the Bible, called "gematria" is almost completely foreign to the western world. It is the system of assigning numerical values to letters, thus giving words or phrases a total numerical value.

I include part of an article written by Keith Newman entitled "Is God a Mathematician?" to explain a little of how gematria works:

"Vital research on this numeric seal was completed by a native of the world's most renowned atheistic nation, Russia. Dr Ivan Panin was born in Russia on Dec 12, 1855. As a young man he was an active nihilist and participated in plots against the Czar and his government. He was a mathematical genius who died a Harvard scholar and a citizen of the United States in 1942.

Panin was exiled from Russia. After spending a number of years studying in Germany he went to the United States where he became an outstanding lecturer on literary criticism.

Panin was known as a firm agnostic - so well known that when he discarded his agnosticism and accepted the Christian faith, the newspapers carried headlines telling of his conversion.

It was in 1890 that Dr Panin made the discovery of the mathematical structure underlining the vocabulary of the Greek New Testament. He

---

[63] http://midnightwatcher.wordpress.com/2011/03/22/the-mark-of-the-beast-what-your-church-may-not-be-telling-you/

was casually reading the first verse of the gospel of John in the Greek: "In the beginning was the Word and the Word was with the God and the Word was God...".

Dr Panin was curious as to why the Greek word for "the"' preceded the word "God"' in one case and not the other. In examining the text he became aware of a number relationship. This was the first of the discoveries that led to his conversion and uncovered the extensive numeric code.[64]

Let's take the number seven as an illustration of the way the patterns work. Seven is the most prolific of the mathematical series which binds scripture together. The very first verse of the Bible "In the beginning God created the heaven and the earth" (Gen 1:1), contains over 30 different combinations of seven.

This verse has seven Hebrew words having a total of 28 letters 4 x 7. The numeric value of the three nouns "God", "heaven" and "earth" totals 777. Any number in triplicate expresses complete, ultimate or total meaning.

The beginning of Matthew's gospel includes a genealogy of Jesus Christ. It begins and is concluded by these verses:

Matthew 1:1

The book of the genealogy of Jesus Christ, the son of David, the son of Abraham.

Matthew 1:17

So all the generations from Abraham to David were fourteen generations, and from David to the deportation to Babylon fourteen generations, and from the deportation to Babylon to the Christ fourteen generations.

The English Standard Version Study Bible has this footnote regarding the "fourteen generations":

Matt. 1:17 **fourteen generations**. Matthew does not mean **all** the generations that had lived during those times but "all" that he included in his list (for he evidently skipped some, such as three

---

64 Keith Newman, "Is God A Mathematician?" <http://www.wordworx.co.nz/panin.html>

generations between Uzziah [Ahaziah] and Jotham in v. 9; cf. 1 Chron. 3:10–12); cf. note on Matt. 1:6b–11. Perhaps for ease of memorization, or perhaps for literary or symbolic symmetry, Matthew structures the genealogy to count 14 generations from each major section. (According to the Jewish practice of *gematria*, the giving of a numeric value to the consonants in a word, David's name would add to D + V + D or 4 + 6 + 4 = 14, and David is the 14th name on the list.)[65]

So, what can we conclude using gematria as a way to calculate who this person will be? The ESV notes on Revelation 13:18 include the following:

"Both "beast" and "Nero Caesar," written in Hebrew characters, add up to 666, but many interpreters expect a future, greater fulfillment in a world ruler who is violently opposed to God and his people."[66]

It seems likely that whoever this end time Antichrist will be, the letters of his name will add up to 666. The question is, in what language? As the New Testament was written in Greek, are we to understand that they will add up when transliterated into Greek? Or perhaps Hebrew? Or is it possible that as English is now the *lingua franca*, as Greek was during the time of Christ, that the gematria will work with the English language? At this point, it is anyone's guess, but when this "man of lawlessness" will appear, by setting himself up in God's temple and proclaiming himself to be god, there will be no doubt as to who he is and it should be able to be shown that his name, using gematria in some language, will total 666.

The Beast and His Mark in Islam

In Islamic eschatology there is also a "Beast" who will give people a mark. He is said to come from the desert near Mecca and will write the word "Kafir" on the foreheads of the unbelievers (in Allah) and on the foreheads of the believers he will write "Mu'min" (true believer). The status of everyone will be clear and the Beast will begin to destroy the unbelievers.

---

65 Op. Cit., ESV Study Bible p. 1821

66 Ibid. p. 2482

“The emergence of the beast:

Among the signs of the Hour will be the emergence of a beast from the earth. It will be very strange in appearance, and extremely huge; one cannot even imagine what it will look like. It will emerge from the earth and shake the dust from its head. It will have with it the ring of Solomon and the rod of Moses. People will be terrified of it and will try to run away, but they will not be able to escape, because such will be the decree of Allah. It will destroy the nose of every unbeliever with the rod, and write the word "Kafir" on his forehead; it will adorn the face of every believer and write the word "Mu'min" (true believer) on his forehead, and it will speak to people.
Allah SWT said:

"And when the Word is fulfilled against them (the unjust), We shall produce from the earth a Beast to (face) them: it will speak to them,'" (al-Naml 27.82)

“Baridah said: "The Prophet (sallallahu alayhe wa sallam) took me to a place in the desert, near Makkah. It was a dry piece of land surrounded by sand. The Prophet (sallallahu alayhe wa sallam) said, 'The Beast will emerge from this place. It was a very small area.’" (Ibn Majah.)

It was reported from Abu Hurairah that the Prophet (sallallahu alayhe wa sallam) said, "The Beast of the Earth will emerge, and will have with it the rod of Moses and the ring of Solomon." It was also reported that he said, "(The Beast) will destroy the noses of the unbelievers with the ring, - so that people seated around one table will begin to address one another with the words "O Believer!" or "O Unbeliever!" (i.e. everyone's status will become clear). (Ibn Majah.)

'Abd Allah ibn 'Amr said, "I memorised a Hadith from the Prophet (sallallahu alayhe wa sallam) which I have not forgotten since. I heard the Prophet (sallallahu alayhe wa sallam) say, 'The first of the signs (of the Hour) to appear will be the rising of the sun from the West and the appearance of the Beast before the people in the forenoon. Whichever of these two events happens first, the other will follow immediately.'" (Muslim).

That is to say, these will be the first extraordinary signs. The Dajjal, the descent of Jesus (alayhe salam), the emergence of Gog and Magog, are less unusual in that they are all human beings. But the emergence of the Beast, whose form will be very strange, its addressing the people and classifying them according to their faith or unbelief, is something truly extraordinary. This is the first of the earthly signs, as the rising of the sun from the West is the first of the heavenly signs."[67]

While God says in the Bible that:

"If anyone worships the beast and its image and receives a mark on his forehead or on his hand, [10] he also will drink the wine of God's wrath, poured full strength into the cup of his anger, and he will be tormented with fire and sulfur in the presence of the holy angels and in the presence of the Lamb. [11] And the smoke of their torment goes up forever and ever, and they have no rest, day or night, these worshipers of the beast and its image, and whoever receives the mark of its name." (Rev. 14:9-12)

The Muslim will eagerly seek to have the Beast put the mark on his forehead identifying him as a true believer in Allah. Indeed, that mark will be the outward symbol of his confession of faith called the *Shahada*, declaring, "There is no god but Allah, and Mohammed is the messenger of Allah."

The world has seen its fair share of great suffering, but as we have seen, there is yet to come a time of difficulty such as the world has never known, nor will it ever experience such tribulation again.

---

[67] "Islamic Network" <http://talk.islamicnetwork.com/archive/index.php/t-158.html>

13 THE GREAT TRIBULATION

AS WE NOTED in chapter 8, tribulation and persecution for the sake of one's faith is nothing new. People of many faiths have suffered when they are in a culture where their faith is not the dominant one. The Bible presents suffering for God and righteousness as being normative. Jesus said in his well known "Sermon on the Mount":

Matthew 5:10-12
"Blessed are those who are persecuted for righteousness' sake, for theirs is the kingdom of heaven.
[11] "Blessed are you when others revile you and persecute you and utter all kinds of evil against you falsely on my account. [12] Rejoice and be glad, for your reward is great in heaven, for so they persecuted the prophets who were before you.

The whole of the New Testament presents suffering for one's faith in Christ as what is to be expected. Note the following passages:

John 16:33
I have said these things to you, that in me you may have peace. In the world you will have tribulation. But take heart; I have overcome the world."

Romans 8:16-18
The Spirit himself bears witness with our spirit that we are children of God, [17] and if children, then heirs—heirs of God and fellow heirs

with Christ, provided we suffer with him in order that we may also be glorified with him.

[18] For I consider that the sufferings of this present time are not worth comparing with the glory that is to be revealed to us.

Philip. 1:29

For it has been granted to you that for the sake of Christ you should not only believe in him but also suffer for his sake,

1 Thessalonians 3:4 (NKJV)

[4] For, in fact, we told you before when we were with you that we would suffer tribulation, just as it happened, and you know.

2 Tim. 3:12

Indeed, all who desire to live a godly life in Christ Jesus will be persecuted,

However, there will come a time when the persecution will become so intense, that the Bible refers to it as "great tribulation" such as the world has never seen and never will see again. Jesus said:

Matthew 24:21-22

For then there will be great tribulation, such as has not been from the beginning of the world until now, no, and never will be. [22] And if those days had not been cut short, no human being would be saved. But for the sake of the elect those days will be cut short.

This seems to coincide with the revelation given to Daniel 500 years before Christ:

Daniel 12:1

"At that time shall arise Michael, the great prince who has charge of your people. And there shall be a time of trouble, such as never has been since there was a nation till that time. But at that time your people shall be delivered, everyone whose name shall be found written in the book.

This seems to also refer to the passage cited earlier in Revelation:

Rev. 12:7-14

Now war arose in heaven, Michael and his angels fighting against the dragon. And the dragon and his angels fought back, [8] but he was defeated and there was no longer any place for them in heaven. [9] And the great dragon was thrown down, that ancient serpent, who is called the devil and Satan, the deceiver of the whole world— he was thrown down to the earth, and his angels were thrown down with him. [10] And I heard a loud voice in heaven, saying, "Now the salvation and the power and the kingdom of our God and the authority of his Christ have come, for the accuser of our brothers has been thrown down, who accuses them day and night before our God. [11] And they have conquered him by the blood of the Lamb and by the word of their testimony, for they loved not their lives even unto death. [12] Therefore, rejoice, O heavens and you who dwell in them! **But woe to you, O earth and sea, for the devil has come down to you in great wrath, because he knows that his time is short!"**

[13] And when the dragon saw that he had been thrown down to the earth, he pursued the woman who had given birth to the male child. [14] But the woman was given the two wings of the great eagle so that she might fly from the serpent into the wilderness, to the place where she is to be nourished for a time, and times, and half a time.

Satan's wrath toward God's people will be directed through his agent – the Beast, or the Antichrist and as we have seen earlier in

Rev. 13:5-10

And the beast was given a mouth uttering haughty and blasphemous words, and it was allowed to exercise authority for forty-two months. [6] It opened its mouth to utter blasphemies against God, blaspheming his name and his dwelling, that is, those who dwell in heaven. [7] Also it was allowed to make war on the saints and to conquer them. And authority was given it over every tribe and people and language and nation, [8] and all who dwell on earth will worship it, everyone whose name has not been written before the foundation of the world in the book of life of the Lamb that was slain. [9] If anyone has an ear, let him hear:

[10] If anyone is to be taken captive,
to captivity he goes;
if anyone is to be slain with the sword,

with the sword must he be slain.

Here is a call for the endurance and faith of the saints.

This "Beast" of the above passage is called "the horn" in Daniel:

Daniel 7:19-27
"Then I desired to know the truth about the fourth beast, which was different from all the rest, exceedingly terrifying, with its teeth of iron and claws of bronze, and which devoured and broke in pieces and stamped what was left with its feet, [20] and about the ten horns that were on its head, and **the other horn that came up** and before which three of them fell, the horn that had eyes and a mouth that spoke great things, and that seemed greater than its companions. [21] As I looked, **this horn made war with the saints and prevailed over them, [22] until the Ancient of Days came,** and judgment was given for the saints of the Most High, and the time came when the saints possessed the kingdom.
[23] "Thus he said: 'As for the fourth beast,

there shall be a fourth kingdom on earth,
which shall be different from all the kingdoms,
and it shall devour the whole earth,
and trample it down, and break it to pieces.
[24] As for the ten horns,
out of this kingdom ten kings shall arise,
and another shall arise after them;
he shall be different from the former ones,
and shall put down three kings.
[25] He shall speak words against the Most High,
and shall wear out the saints of the Most High,
and shall think to change the times and the law;
and they shall be given into his hand
for a time, times, and half a time.
[26] But the court shall sit in judgment,
and his dominion shall be taken away,
to be consumed and destroyed to the end.
[27] And the kingdom and the dominion
and the greatness of the kingdoms under the whole heaven
shall be given to the people of the saints of the Most High;

their kingdom shall be an everlasting kingdom,
and all dominions shall serve and obey them.'

Both the Revelation and Daniel passages have a time frame for this great tribulation in which the devil's agent will prevail over the saints – "a time, times and half a time" or "forty-two months".

The Christian is not to despair, however. The message given by Jesus to the Church in Smyrna will be apropos to the saints of this tribulation time:

Rev. 2:9-11

" 'I know your tribulation and your poverty (but you are rich) and the slander of those who say that they are Jews and are not, but are a synagogue of Satan. [10] Do not fear what you are about to suffer. Behold, the devil is about to throw some of you into prison, that you may be tested, and for ten days you will have tribulation. Be faithful unto death, and I will give you the crown of life. [11] He who has an ear, let him hear what the Spirit says to the churches. The one who conquers will not be hurt by the second death.'

Though there will be a temporary victory by the devil and his forces, he is conquered by the martyred saints as we read in

Rev. 12:11

"And they have conquered him by the blood of the Lamb and by the word of their testimony, for they loved not their lives even unto death."

The Beginning Point of the Great Tribulation

What will be the sign that the Great Tribulation is about to begin? Jesus tells us:

Matthew 24:14-22

And this gospel of the kingdom will be proclaimed throughout the whole world as a testimony to all nations, and then the end will come.

[15] "So when you see the abomination of desolation spoken of by the prophet Daniel, standing in the holy place (let the reader understand), [16] then let those who are in Judea flee to the mountains. [17] Let the one who is on the housetop not go down to take what is in his house, [18] and let the one who is in the field not

turn back to take his cloak. [19] And alas for women who are pregnant and for those who are nursing infants in those days! [20] Pray that your flight may not be in winter or on a Sabbath. [21] For then there will be great tribulation, such as has not been from the beginning of the world until now, no, and never will be. [22] And if those days had not been cut short, no human being would be saved. But for the sake of the elect those days will be cut short.

The Gospel of the kingdom of God through Jesus Christ has to be proclaimed throughout the whole earth first. We see that happening today through TV, radio, internet, missionaries, visions, dreams, and the Bible being translated into practically every language.

The sign of the beginning, however, is the "abomination of desolation" which we have looked at before. This is when the man of lawlessness – the Antichrist, or the Beast, reveals himself in the temple: "who opposes and exalts himself against every so-called god or object of worship, so that he takes his seat in the temple of God, proclaiming himself to be God." (2 Thess. 2:4). When that happens, those in Israel have to flee for their lives to the mountains. This event presupposes that there will be a Jewish temple in Jerusalem, so that has to take place beforehand.

In Jerusalem there is an organization called the "Temple Institute" (www.templeinstitute.org). They have made preparations for the Third Temple by making all the temple furnishings and priestly garments, as well as building up a herd of red heifers for sacrifices. Could it be that the treaty that the Antichrist will make will be to permit the building of the temple on the temple mount?

Daniel 9:27 (NIV)

[27] He will confirm a covenant with many for one 'seven.' In the middle of the 'seven' he will put an end to sacrifice and offering. And on a wing [of the temple] he will set up an abomination that causes desolation, until the end that is decreed is poured out on him".

As noted earlier, contrary to the opinion of many, the "Great Tribulation" is not the last seven year period prior to Christ's return, but rather begins at the midpoint of those last seven years with the abomination of desolation. As we have cited before, the prophet Daniel asks, after hearing that there will be a time of trouble such as has never been before,

Daniel 12:6-13

"How long shall it be till the end of these wonders?" [7] And I heard the man clothed in linen, who was above the waters of the stream; he raised his right hand and his left hand toward heaven and swore by him who lives forever that it would be for a time, times, and half a time, and that when the shattering of the power of the holy people comes to an end all these things would be finished. [8] I heard, but I did not understand. Then I said, "O my lord, what shall be the outcome of these things?" [9] He said, "Go your way, Daniel, for the words are shut up and sealed until the time of the end. [10] Many shall purify themselves and make themselves white and be refined, but the wicked shall act wickedly. And none of the wicked shall understand, but those who are wise shall understand. [11] And from the time that the regular burnt offering is taken away and the abomination that makes desolate is set up, there shall be 1,290 days. [12] Blessed is he who waits and arrives at the 1,335 days. [13] But go your way till the end. And you shall rest and shall stand in your allotted place at the end of the days."

As I wrote earlier, the difference between the 1290 days and the three and a half years, or 1260 days could be that the sacrifices are halted 30 days before the Antichrist commits the abomination that makes desolate – the setting himself up in the temple and proclaiming himself to be God.

While the Bible does not give the location of where this image will be set up, it could be that the false prophet will set up the image of the Antichrist in the temple itself:

Rev. 13:13-15

It performs great signs, even making fire come down from heaven to earth in front of people, [14] and by the signs that it is allowed to work in the presence of the beast it deceives those who dwell on earth, telling them to make an image for the beast that was wounded by the sword and yet lived. [15] And it was allowed to give breath to the image of the beast, so that the image of the beast might even speak and might cause those who would not worship the image of the beast to be slain.

The Bible presents in a fair amount of detail what the world will go through during this time of the Great Tribulation. Most of that detail is recorded in the book of Revelation, which we will look at more carefully in the last section of the book.

The Biblical teaching on the Antichrist, or the Beast, his false prophet (Rev. 13:11-12), the Abomination of Desolation and the Great Tribulation lead us to the next great teaching in the Bible: The Millennium.

14 THE MILLENNIUM

IN CHAPTER 7 I discussed how the seven Jewish festivals relate to Jesus' first and second coming and made an argument for his second coming occurring at the Feast of Trumpets. The subjects of "the rapture" and the "millennial reign of Christ" have been hotly debated topics in Christendom and there are clearly divided beliefs regarding the meaning of these terms and when they will take place. To better understand the discussion of the Rapture, or the Resurrection, the subject of the Millennium will be dealt with first.

The fact that there are so many divergent understandings of what the Bible says regarding these future events indicates that Bible prophesy is not at all a clear, mathematical science. Had the prophecies been crystal clear, all the Jews would have immediately recognized Jesus as the predicted Messiah. Likewise, prophesies regarding Jesus' second coming have spawned many divergent viewpoints. Does this mean that we should then say, "What is the use of studying this subject since it is so unclear?"

We are given an interesting insight at the end of the book of Daniel.

Daniel 12:8-10

"I heard, but I did not understand. Then I said, "O my lord, what shall be the outcome of these things?" [9] He said, "Go your way, Daniel, for the words are shut up and sealed until the time of the end. [10] Many shall purify themselves and make themselves white and be refined, but the wicked shall act wickedly. And none of the wicked shall understand, but those who are wise shall understand."

I believe we are at the time of the end and what had been shut up and sealed before has now been revealed for the wise to understand.

The main prophetical book in the Bible states in its preface:

Rev. 1:3
"Blessed is the one who reads aloud the words of this prophecy, and blessed are those who hear, and who keep what is written in it, for the time is near."

We are to read, (let me say that my understanding greatly increased as I read it aloud), study, seek to understand and obey what Biblical prophecy tells us. That is what this book is all about. May God grant us wisdom and insight to understand what he has dedicated a vast portion of his Word to tell us.

HISTORICAL OVERVIEW

As mentioned, there are many different viewpoints regarding the millennium, the rapture and Jesus' second coming, but I think all Christians and Jews agree on these starting points.

1. The Messiah is King and is coming to judge the living and the dead (Apostles Creed, Nicene Creed).
2. There will be a resurrection of the righteous and the unrighteous.
3. This has not yet happened.

The Christians understand Jesus to be the Messiah who will come a second time. The Jews await the Messiah's first coming. This chapter, while quoting extensively from the Old Testament, will none the less approach the subject from a Christian perspective. The church has understood Bible prophesy and the future coming of Christ in a number of ways throughout history. Some of the major categories are defined under these terms and I will give very simplistic chronologies and definitions of each:

Premillennialism
First Coming of Christ / Church Age / Second Coming of Christ / 1,000 Year Reign

Amillennialism
First Coming of Christ / Church Age = 1,000 Year Reign / Second Coming of Christ

Postmillennialism
First Coming of Christ / Church Age Leads into 1,000 Year Reign / Second Coming of Christ

These three positions respond to three different interpretations of the following passage, though the divergent methods of interpretation affect not only the interpretation of this passage, but also how all prophetic literature is interpreted and what the mission and message of the gospel is.

Rev. 20:1-10

Then I saw an angel coming down from heaven, holding in his hand the key to the bottomless pit and a great chain. [2] And he seized the dragon, that ancient serpent, who is the devil and Satan, and bound him for **a thousand years**, [3] and threw him into the pit, and shut it and sealed it over him, so that he might not deceive the nations any longer, until **the thousand years** were ended. After that he must be released for a little while.

[4] Then I saw thrones, and seated on them were those to whom the authority to judge was committed. Also I saw the souls of those who had been beheaded for the testimony of Jesus and for the word of God, and who had not worshiped the beast or its image and had not received its mark on their foreheads or their hands. They came to life and **reigned with Christ** for **a thousand years**. [5] The rest of the dead did not come to life until **the thousand years** were ended. This is the first resurrection. [6] Blessed and holy is the one who shares in the first resurrection! Over such the second death has no power, but they will be priests of God and of Christ, and they will **reign with him** for **a thousand years**.

[7] And when **the thousand years** are ended, Satan will be released from his prison [8] and will come out to deceive the nations that are at the four corners of the earth, Gog and Magog, to gather them for battle; their number is like the sand of the sea. [9] And they marched up over the broad plain of the earth and surrounded the camp of the saints and the beloved city, but fire came down from heaven and consumed them, [10] and the devil who had deceived them was thrown into the lake of fire and sulfur where the beast and the false

prophet were, and they will be tormented day and night forever and ever.

Premillennialism, begins with a "literal" hermeneutical approach (method of interpreting the Bible). By "literal" it means that each text of scripture is to be interpreted according to its genre. Poetry, historical narrative, didactic, apocalyptic, allegorical literature are each to be understood in light of their literary style and is to be interpreted according to the clear intent of the author given the style in which it was written. "Literal" interpretation does not interpret

Isaiah 55:12
"For you shall go out in joy
and be led forth in peace;
the mountains and the hills before you
shall break forth into singing,
and all the trees of the field shall clap their hands.

as saying that the mountains literally sing and the trees literally clap their hands. These are seen as metaphors. However, the idea is that texts are to be taken at their most literal meaning unless otherwise indicated in the text and unless otherwise to be understood given the genre of literature.

That being said, premillennialism starts with the understanding that the text in Revelation 20 is to be understood literally, not metaphorically, allegorically or symbolically and that Jesus, at his second coming, will reign with the saints on earth for a literal 1,000 years while Satan is bound, after which he will be loosed for a short while.

That position found support among some of the early Church Fathers, including 2nd century Bishop Irenaeus.

Amillennialism starts with a symbolical, figurative or spiritual hermeneutic. It sees promises of political justice, physical health, material prosperity and reign of the Messiah on the throne of David in the Old Testament as being fulfilled not physically, and not to ethnic Israel, but rather spiritually and to spiritual Israel, which they see as the Church. Therefore it sees the millennium not as a literal 1,000 year reign of Christ on the throne of David in Jerusalem, after the second coming, but rather the rule of Christ in the heart of the believer now. The number 1,000 is seen as merely a symbolic number referring to a long period of Christ's rule. They see Christ as already having bound Satan and the described blessings of the millennium as being fulfilled in the age of grace, the gospel, and the church.

This position was first made prominent by St. Augustine in the early 5th century. He adopted the more symbolic approach and this has been the dominant position of the Church until the 20th century.

Postmillennialism today is a minority view. An evangelical proponent, J. Marcellus Kik defines the position this way:

"The *postmil* looks for a fulfillment of the Old Testament prophecies of a glorious age of the church upon earth through the preaching of the gospel under the power of the Holy Spirit. He looks forward to all nations becoming Christian and living in peace one with another. He relates all prophecies to history and time. After the triumph of Christianity throughout the earth he looks for the second coming of the Lord."[68]

The millennium need not be exactly 1,000 years, but will be a long golden age brought about through the preaching of the gospel after which Christ will return.

This viewpoint came to prominence by the Puritans of the 17th century who saw the gospel expanding around the world. They had as their starting point a non-literal hermeneutic coming from the amillennial position and they felt that the power of the gospel could bring global transformation. That viewpoint was greatly diminished by the onslaught of the 1st World War.

The amillennialist and the postmillennialist both believe that Christ will not return to this earth. The Second Coming will bring about the judgment and probable annihilation of the old creation. The purpose of Christ's return is not to rule on earth but to take his Church to be with Himself in heaven and to bring to an end all earthly existence.

Historicism is a school of interpretation which treats the eschatological prophecies of Daniel and Revelation as finding literal earthly fulfillment through the history of the church age and especially in relation to the struggle between the true church and apostasy. Emerging within the

---

[68] J. Marcellus Kik, An Eschatology of Victory (Philadelphia: Presbyterian and Reformed, 1971) p. 4

early church, historicism became a dominant eschatological interpretation in the Protestant-Catholic conflicts of the Reformation. A Historicist approach was taken by Martin Luther and John Calvin.

Preterism is an interpretation of Christian eschatology which holds that most or all of the biblical prophecies concerning the End Times refer to events which have already happened in the first century after Christ's birth. The system also claims that Ancient Israel finds its continuation or fulfillment in the Christian church at the destruction of Jerusalem in A.D. 70. This position was first published by Jesuit Luis De Alcasar during the Catholic Counter Reformation in the early 1600's and later came to be accepted by Protestants, especially by those of the amillennial position. One of the more well known proponents of that position today is R.C. Sproul.

Dispensational Premillennialism was brought to prominence by Irishman John Nelson Darby in the mid 1800s. He brought changes to the up-to-then understood premillennialism. The historicist interpretation was that in chapters 6-18 of Revelation we have a symbolic presentation of the history of the church, the nations, and rulers associated with them. It was commonly held that the prophetic days, whether 1260, 1335 or 2300 were understood as years and the papacy was seen to be the Antichrist. Darby introduced the **futurist** interpretation – that almost all of Revelation was yet future. He saw the prophetic days as literal days rather than years, did not automatically consider the Pope to be the Antichrist and he made popular the idea of a pre-tribulational rapture. In the US, the 1909 Scofield Reference Bible greatly disseminated that viewpoint and the greatest popular books of this generation to expound that position are Hal Lindsey's *The Late Great Planet Earth* and Tim LaHaye and Jerry Jenkins' *Left Behind* Series.

WHY THE DIFFERENT INTERPRETATIONS?

If we have the same Bible, how is it that there are such widely diverse interpretations as to what it is saying? For a more detailed explanation of these divergent views, let me suggest the unabridged version of this book. Another helpful resource is Joel Richardson's DVD series entitled: "Understanding the Times". One of the main components to understand the concept of the millennium is what Jesus and the Old Testament meant by "the gospel of the kingdom."

Joel says, "Understanding Eschatology is very closely tied to our understanding of what is "the gospel of the kingdom" that Jesus preached. We often talk about preaching the "gospel", but Jesus specifically spoke of "the gospel of the kingdom". Is there a difference? Note the following verses:

Matthew 4:23
And he went throughout all Galilee, teaching in their synagogues and proclaiming **the gospel of the kingdom** and healing every disease and every affliction among the people.

Matthew 24:14
And **this gospel of the kingdom** will be proclaimed throughout the whole world as a testimony to all nations, and then the end will come.

WHAT IS THE GOSPEL OF THE KINGDOM?

- The "Day of the Lord" is coming. It is a day of justice and vengeance.
- The return of Messiah from heaven is coming.
- The literal physical resurrection of the dead is coming.
- The Day of Justice for the righteous and oppressed is coming.
- The Day of Judgment against unrighteousness is coming.
- The Day of Salvation for the Remnant of Israel is coming.
- The judgment of all who oppress Israel is coming.
- The judgment of unrighteous leadership throughout the earth is coming.

Psalm 110 A Psalm of David.
"The Lord says to my Lord: 'Sit at my right hand, until I make your enemies your footstool.'
[2] The Lord sends forth from Zion your mighty scepter. Rule in the midst of your enemies!
[5] The Lord is at your right hand; he will shatter kings on the day of his wrath.
[6] He will execute judgment among the nations, filling them with corpses; he will shatter chiefs over the wide earth."

- The restoration of righteous leadership globally is coming.
- Salvation and entrance in the kingdom of heaven comes through repentance and faith in Jesus as Messiah and Son of God.

(The above material has been taken from Joel Richardson's DVD series entitled "Understanding the Times")

I personally embrace the premillennial position and literal approach to interpreting the Bible. I believe there will be a literal 1,000 year reign of Christ with his saints here on earth following his second coming. What does the Bible say about that period of time besides the passage in Revelation 20 cited above? The Bible indicates that Jesus will reign as King on the earth with complete power and justice:

Rev. 19:11-16

Then I saw heaven opened, and behold, a white horse! The one sitting on it is called Faithful and True, and in righteousness he judges and makes war. [12] His eyes are like a flame of fire, and on his head are many diadems, and he has a name written that no one knows but himself. [13] He is clothed in a robe dipped in blood, and the name by which he is called is The Word of God. [14] And the armies of heaven, arrayed in fine linen, white and pure, were following him on white horses. [15] From his mouth comes a sharp sword with which to strike down the nations, and **he will rule them with a rod of iron**. He will tread the winepress of the fury of the wrath of God the Almighty. [16] On his robe and on his thigh he has a name written, **King of kings and Lord of lords.**

Rev. 12:4-5

And the dragon stood before the woman who was about to give birth, so that when she bore her child he might devour it. [5] She gave birth to a male child, **one who is to rule all the nations with a rod of iron**, but her child was caught up to God and to his throne,

Psalm 2:1-9

Why do the nations rage
and the peoples plot in vain?
[2] The kings of the earth set themselves,
and the rulers take counsel together,
against the Lord and against his anointed, saying,
[3] "Let us burst their bonds apart
and cast away their cords from us."
[4] He who sits in the heavens laughs;
the Lord holds them in derision.

[5] Then he will speak to them in his wrath,
and terrify them in his fury, saying,
[6] **"As for me, I have set my King
on Zion, my holy hill."**
[7] I will tell of the decree:
The Lord said to me, "You are my Son;
today I have begotten you.
[8] Ask of me, and I will make the nations your heritage,
and the ends of the earth your possession.
[9] **You shall break them with a rod of iron
and dash them in pieces like a potter's vessel."**

That this ruling the nations with a rod of iron is as yet a future event, is indicated by the context in Revelation 19 above. It shows him at his second coming, at which time he will execute judgment and will rule the nations from that point on with a rod of iron. In the vision that Daniel had regarding the end times he saw this:

Daniel 7:21-22
As I looked, this horn made war with the saints and prevailed over them, [22] until the Ancient of Days came, and judgment was given for the saints of the Most High, and the time came when the saints possessed the kingdom.
Daniel 7:27
And the kingdom and the dominion
and the greatness of the kingdoms under the whole heaven
shall be given to the people of the saints of the Most High;
their kingdom shall be an everlasting kingdom,
and all dominions shall serve and obey them.' (or "Him")

These and many other texts seem to clearly agree with Revelation 20 that states that the saints will rule with Christ here on earth for a thousand years after the return of Christ on earth. These passages are hard pressed to be understood spiritually.

What will that period of time look like? The Bible gives us several glimpses:

Isaiah 2:1-4
The word that Isaiah the son of Amoz saw concerning Judah and Jerusalem.

[2] It shall come to pass in the latter days
that the mountain of the house of the Lord
shall be established as the highest of the mountains,
and shall be lifted up above the hills;
and all the nations shall flow to it,
[3] and many peoples shall come, and say:
"Come, let us go up to the mountain of the Lord,
to the house of the God of Jacob,
that he may teach us his ways
and that we may walk in his paths."
For out of Zion shall go the law,
and the word of the Lord from Jerusalem.
[4] He shall judge between the nations,
and shall decide disputes for many peoples;
and they shall beat their swords into plowshares,
and their spears into pruning hooks;
nation shall not lift up sword against nation,
neither shall they learn war anymore.

Isaiah 9:6-7
For to us a child is born,
to us a son is given;
and the government shall be upon his shoulder,
and his name shall be called
Wonderful Counselor, Mighty God,
Everlasting Father, Prince of Peace.
[7] Of the increase of his government and of peace
there will be no end,
on the throne of David and over his kingdom,
to establish it and to uphold it
with justice and with righteousness
from this time forth and forevermore.
The zeal of the Lord of hosts will do this.

Isaiah 11:1-10
There shall come forth a shoot from the stump of Jesse,
and a branch from his roots shall bear fruit.
[2] And the Spirit of the Lord shall rest upon him,
the Spirit of wisdom and understanding,
the Spirit of counsel and might,

the Spirit of knowledge and the fear of the Lord.
[3] And his delight shall be in the fear of the Lord.
He shall not judge by what his eyes see,
or decide disputes by what his ears hear,
[4] but with righteousness he shall judge the poor,
and decide with equity for the meek of the earth;
and he shall strike the earth with the rod of his mouth,
and with the breath of his lips he shall kill the wicked.
[5] Righteousness shall be the belt of his waist,
and faithfulness the belt of his loins.
[6] The wolf shall dwell with the lamb,
and the leopard shall lie down with the young goat,
and the calf and the lion and the fattened calf together;
and a little child shall lead them.
[7] The cow and the bear shall graze;
their young shall lie down together;
and the lion shall eat straw like the ox.
[8] The nursing child shall play over the hole of the cobra,
and the weaned child shall put his hand on the adder's den.
[9] They shall not hurt or destroy
in all my holy mountain;
for the earth shall be full of the knowledge of the Lord
as the waters cover the sea.

[10] In that day the root of Jesse, who shall stand as a signal for the peoples—of him shall the nations inquire, and his resting place shall be glorious.

Isaiah 40:1-5
Comfort, comfort my people, says your God.

[2] Speak tenderly to Jerusalem,
and cry to her
that her warfare is ended,
that her iniquity is pardoned,
that she has received from the Lord's hand
double for all her sins.
[3] A voice cries:
"In the wilderness prepare the way of the Lord;
make straight in the desert a highway for our God.

[4] Every valley shall be lifted up,
and every mountain and hill be made low;
the uneven ground shall become level,
and the rough places a plain.
[5] And the glory of the Lord shall be revealed,
and all flesh shall see it together,
for the mouth of the Lord has spoken."

Isaiah 40:9-11

Get you up to a high mountain,
O Zion, herald of good news;
lift up your voice with strength,
O Jerusalem, herald of good news;
lift it up, fear not;
say to the cities of Judah,
"Behold your God!"
[10] Behold, the Lord God comes with might,
and his arm rules for him;
behold, his reward is with him,
and his recompense before him.
[11] He will tend his flock like a shepherd;
he will gather the lambs in his arms;
he will carry them in his bosom,
and gently lead those that are with young.

Isaiah 65:17-25

"For behold, I create new heavens
and a new earth,
and the former things shall not be remembered
or come into mind.
[18] But be glad and rejoice forever
in that which I create;
for behold, I create Jerusalem to be a joy,
and her people to be a gladness.
[19] I will rejoice in Jerusalem
and be glad in my people;
no more shall be heard in it the sound of weeping
and the cry of distress.
[20] No more shall there be in it
an infant who lives but a few days,

or an old man who does not fill out his days,
for the young man shall die a hundred years old,
and the sinner a hundred years old shall be accursed.
[21] They shall build houses and inhabit them;
they shall plant vineyards and eat their fruit.
[22] They shall not build and another inhabit;
they shall not plant and another eat;
for like the days of a tree shall the days of my people be,
and my chosen shall long enjoy the work of their hands.
[23] They shall not labor in vain
or bear children for calamity,
for they shall be the offspring of the blessed of the Lord,
and their descendants with them.
[24] Before they call I will answer;
while they are yet speaking I will hear.
[25] The wolf and the lamb shall graze together;
the lion shall eat straw like the ox,
and dust shall be the serpent's food.
They shall not hurt or destroy
in all my holy mountain,"

says the Lord.

That the passage in Isaiah 65 is not referring to the eternal state in heaven, even though God will create new heavens and a new earth is underscored by the fact that there will still be sinners and death.

As many of these passages point out, there will be a time of judgment first and then restoration when the Lord comes:

Isaiah 66:15-16
"For behold, the Lord will come in fire,
and his chariots like the whirlwind,
to render his anger in fury,
and his rebuke with flames of fire.
[16] For by fire will the Lord enter into judgment,
and by his sword, with all flesh;
and those slain by the Lord shall be many.

Zech. 14:2-9
For I will gather all the nations against Jerusalem to battle, and the

city shall be taken and the houses plundered and the women raped. Half of the city shall go out into exile, but the rest of the people shall not be cut off from the city. [3] Then the Lord will go out and fight against those nations as when he fights on a day of battle. [4] On that day his feet shall stand on the Mount of Olives that lies before Jerusalem on the east, and the Mount of Olives shall be split in two .... Then the Lord my God will come, and all the holy ones with him. .... [9] And the Lord will be king over all the earth....

Zech. 14:12, 16-19

And this shall be the plague with which the Lord will strike all the peoples that wage war against Jerusalem: their flesh will rot while they are still standing on their feet, their eyes will rot in their sockets, and their tongues will rot in their mouths.

[16] Then everyone who survives of all the nations that have come against Jerusalem shall go up year after year to worship the King, the Lord of hosts, and to keep the Feast of Booths. [17] And if any of the families of the earth do not go up to Jerusalem to worship the King, the Lord of hosts, there will be no rain on them. [18] And if the family of Egypt does not go up and present themselves, then on them there shall be no rain; there shall be the plague with which the Lord afflicts the nations that do not go up to keep the Feast of Booths. [19] This shall be the punishment to Egypt and the punishment to all the nations that do not go up to keep the Feast of Booths.

The Millennial Temple

There is much longing and anticipation for the construction of the "Third Temple" in Jerusalem. We have seen that for the Antichrist to be revealed, there will have to be a temple in existence in Jerusalem, for he will set himself up in the temple of God proclaiming himself to be God (2 Thess. 2:3-4). The Apostle John is told to measure the temple:

Rev. 11:1-2

Then I was given a measuring rod like a staff, and I was told, "Rise and measure the temple of God and the altar and those who worship there, [2] but do not measure the court outside the temple; leave that out, for it is given over to the nations, and they will trample the holy city for forty-two months.

Will that be the final temple? It seems that it will not be the final temple. There is a description of a temple in Ezekiel (chpts. 40-48) with minute detail, which seems to be too big for the current temple mount location, especially if it is shared with the Dome of the Rock and the Al Aqsa Mosque. The Bible describes great topographical change which will occur at the time of Jesus' return and will most likely cause the destruction of all buildings. Some of the passages cited before indicate this:

Isaiah 40:4
[4] Every valley shall be lifted up,
and every mountain and hill be made low;
the uneven ground shall become level,
and the rough places a plain.

Ezekiel 38:18-22
But on that day, the day that Gog shall come against the land of
Israel, declares the Lord God, my wrath will be roused in my anger.
[19] For in my jealousy and in my blazing wrath I declare, On that
day there shall be a great earthquake in the land of Israel. [20] The
fish of the sea and the birds of the heavens and the beasts of the field
and all creeping things that creep on the ground, and all the people
who are on the face of the earth, shall quake at my presence. And the
mountains shall be thrown down, and the cliffs shall fall, and every
wall shall tumble to the ground. [21] I will summon a sword against
Gog on all my mountains, declares the Lord God. Every man's sword
will be against his brother. [22] With pestilence and bloodshed I will
enter into judgment with him, and I will rain upon him and his hordes
and the many peoples who are with him torrential rains and
hailstones, fire and sulfur.

Rev. 16:17-21
The seventh angel poured out his bowl into the air, and a loud voice
came out of the temple, from the throne, saying, "It is done!" [18]
And there were flashes of lightning, rumblings, peals of thunder, and
a great earthquake such as there had never been since man was on the
earth, so great was that earthquake. [19] The great city was split into
three parts, and the cities of the nations fell, and God remembered
Babylon the great, to make her drain the cup of the wine of the fury of
his wrath. [20] And every island fled away, and no mountains were to
be found. [21] And great hailstones, about one hundred pounds each,

fell from heaven on people; and they cursed God for the plague of the hail, because the plague was so severe.

Zech. 14:2-10

For I will gather all the nations against Jerusalem to battle, and the city shall be taken and the houses plundered and the women raped. Half of the city shall go out into exile, but the rest of the people shall not be cut off from the city. [3] Then the Lord will go out and fight against those nations as when he fights on a day of battle. [4] On that day his feet shall stand on the Mount of Olives that lies before Jerusalem on the east, and the Mount of Olives shall be split in two from east to west by a very wide valley, so that one half of the Mount shall move northward, and the other half southward. [5] And you shall flee to the valley of my mountains, for the valley of the mountains shall reach to Azal. And you shall flee as you fled from the earthquake in the days of Uzziah king of Judah. Then the Lord my God will come, and all the holy ones with him.

[6] On that day there shall be no light, cold, or frost. [7] And there shall be a unique day, which is known to the Lord, neither day nor night, but at evening time there shall be light.

[8] On that day living waters shall flow out from Jerusalem, half of them to the eastern sea and half of them to the western sea. It shall continue in summer as in winter.

[9] And the Lord will be king over all the earth. On that day the Lord will be one and his name one.

[10] The whole land shall be turned into a plain from Geba to Rimmon south of Jerusalem. But Jerusalem shall remain aloft on its site from the Gate of Benjamin to the place of the former gate, to the Corner Gate, and from the Tower of Hananel to the king's winepresses.

This destruction and leveling of mountains and lifting up of valleys will lead to the preparation for the building of the Fourth Temple as described in Ezekiel. Chronologically in Ezekiel, the description of the temple comes after the great battle of Gog and Magog (Ez. 38-39), which, as we shall see later, I believe is the same as the battle of Armageddon. The description of the temple follows in chapters 40-48.

The following passages give a description of Jerusalem being the place where in the millennial period, peoples will come to worship.

Isaiah 2:1-2

The word that Isaiah the son of Amoz saw concerning Judah and Jerusalem.

[2] It shall come to pass in the latter days
that the mountain of the house of the Lord
shall be established as the highest of the mountains,
and shall be lifted up above the hills;
and all the nations shall flow to it,

Isaiah 4:2-6

In that day the branch of the Lord shall be beautiful and glorious, and the fruit of the land shall be the pride and honor of the survivors of Israel. [3] And he who is left in Zion and remains in Jerusalem will be called holy, everyone who has been recorded for life in Jerusalem, [4] when the Lord shall have washed away the filth of the daughters of Zion and cleansed the bloodstains of Jerusalem from its midst by a spirit of judgment and by a spirit of burning. [5] Then the Lord will create over the whole site of Mount Zion and over her assemblies a cloud by day, and smoke and the shining of a flaming fire by night; for over all the glory there will be a canopy. [6] There will be a booth for shade by day from the heat, and for a refuge and a shelter from the storm and rain.

Lest we think these passages are descriptions of heaven, we are told that in the new, heavenly Jerusalem, there will be no temple.

Rev. 21:22-23

And I saw no temple in the city, for its temple is the Lord God the Almighty and the Lamb. [23] And the city has no need of sun or moon to shine on it, for the glory of God gives it light, and its lamp is the Lamb.

However, in the vision of the temple that Ezekiel saw, which up to today has not been built, we see God coming and his glory filling the temple.

Ezekiel 43:1-7

Then he led me to the gate, the gate facing east. [2] And behold, the glory of the God of Israel was coming from the east. And the sound of his coming was like the sound of many waters, and the earth shone with his glory. [3] And the vision I saw was just like the vision that I had seen when he came to destroy the city, and just like the vision that I had seen by the Chebar canal. And I fell on my face. [4] As the glory of the Lord entered the temple by the gate facing east, [5] the Spirit lifted me up and brought me into the inner court; and behold, the glory of the Lord filled the temple.

[6] While the man was standing beside me, I heard one speaking to me out of the temple, [7] and he said to me, "Son of man, this is the place of my throne and the place of the soles of my feet, where I will dwell in the midst of the people of Israel forever. And the house of Israel shall no more defile my holy name . . . "

Zechariah described living water flowing out of Jerusalem to the east and west and the Lord being king over all the earth (Zech. 14:8-9). The angel shows Ezekiel where that water comes from.

Ezekiel 47:1-12

Then he brought me back to the door of the temple, and behold, water was issuing from below the threshold of the temple toward the east (for the temple faced east). The water was flowing down from below the south end of the threshold of the temple, south of the altar. [2] Then he brought me out by way of the north gate and led me around on the outside to the outer gate that faces toward the east; and behold, the water was trickling out on the south side.

[3] Going on eastward with a measuring line in his hand, the man measured a thousand cubits, and then led me through the water, and it was ankle-deep. [4] Again he measured a thousand, and led me through the water, and it was knee-deep. Again he measured a thousand, and led me through the water, and it was waist-deep. [5] Again he measured a thousand, and it was a river that I could not pass through, for the water had risen. It was deep enough to swim in, a river that could not be passed through. [6] And he said to me, "Son of man, have you seen this?"

Then he led me back to the bank of the river. [7] As I went back, I saw on the bank of the river very many trees on the one side and on the other. [8] And he said to me, "This water flows toward the eastern region and goes down into the Arabah, and enters the sea; when the water flows into the sea, the water will become fresh. [9] And wherever the river goes, every living creature that swarms will live, and there will be very many fish. For this water goes there, that the waters of the sea may become fresh; so everything will live where the river goes. [10] Fishermen will stand beside the sea. From Engedi to En-eglaim it will be a place for the spreading of nets. Its fish will be of very many kinds, like the fish of the Great Sea. [11] But its swamps and marshes will not become fresh; they are to be left for salt. [12] And on the banks, on both sides of the river, there will grow all kinds of trees for food. Their leaves will not wither, nor their fruit fail, but they will bear fresh fruit every month, because the water for them flows from the sanctuary. Their fruit will be for food, and their leaves for healing."

Many biblical scholars object to interpreting the temple in Ezekiel as a literal millennial temple because sacrifices will be offered. Jesus has put an end to the sacrificial system, it is argued. However, since there will be mortal humans born during the millennium who will have sin natures, it seems these sacrifices will be memorial offerings. Just as the sacrifices in the Old Testament were a foreshadowing of Christ's atonement, so these will serve the new generations as remembrances of what their atonement cost. They will have to likewise embrace Christ as their personal Lord for their salvation, even though he is present in their midst and ruling the nations.

As we read at the beginning of Revelation 20, the thousand year reign of Christ will be a period of time when Satan will be bound and will not be able to deceive the nations. However, at the end of that time he will be released:

Rev. 20:7-10

And when the thousand years are ended, Satan will be released from his prison [8] and will come out to deceive the nations that are at the four corners of the earth, Gog and Magog, to gather them for battle; their number is like the sand of the sea. [9] And they marched up over the broad plain of the earth and surrounded the camp of the saints and the beloved city, but fire came down from heaven and consumed them, [10] and the devil who had deceived them was thrown into the lake of fire and sulfur where the beast and the false prophet were, and they will be tormented day and night forever and ever.

These verses immediately precede the passage of the final judgment – the "Great White Throne" judgment. The fact that men will still rebel against God's Anointed – the Son of God, who will have reigned with perfect justice, equity and peace, will show the wickedness of men's hearts. Their rebellion is not due to living in a bad environment, or being unfairly treated, or poverty or lack. God will be perfectly righteous in his judgment when he casts them into the lake of fire because their rebellion was due to themselves alone and the evil inherent in their hearts.

15 THE RAPTURE

AS NOTED IN the previous chapter, there are divergent views as to the meaning of the millennium and whether there will be a literal thousand year reign of Christ here on earth or not. The same can be said for the doctrine of the "rapture". There are various beliefs regarding when this event will take place. The word comes from the Latin Vulgate translation of the Greek word "harpazo" which means to be "caught up". It comes from the following passage:

1 Thess. 4:13-18

But we do not want you to be uninformed, brothers, about those who are asleep, that you may not grieve as others do who have no hope. [14] For since we believe that Jesus died and rose again, even so, through Jesus, God will bring with him those who have fallen asleep. [15] For this we declare to you by a word from the Lord, that we who are alive, who are left until the coming of the Lord, will not precede those who have fallen asleep. [16] For the Lord himself will descend from heaven with a cry of command, with the voice of an archangel, and with the sound of the trumpet of God. And the dead in Christ will rise first. [17] Then we who are alive, who are left, will be **caught up** together with them in the clouds to meet the Lord in the air, and so we will always be with the Lord. [18] Therefore encourage one another with these words.

This event happens at the time of the resurrection of believers as the text points out. In another letter Paul tells of the same event:

1 Cor. 15:50-53

I tell you this, brothers: flesh and blood cannot inherit the kingdom of God, nor does the perishable inherit the imperishable. [51] Behold! I tell you a mystery. We shall not all sleep, but we shall all be changed, [52] in a moment, in the twinkling of an eye, at the last trumpet. For the trumpet will sound, and the dead will be raised imperishable, and we shall be changed. [53] For this perishable body must put on the imperishable, and this mortal body must put on immortality.

The question naturally comes, "When will this take place?" This is where there are divergent viewpoints. There are five premillennial views regarding the rapture:

Five Premillennial Views

1. Pre-tribulation View
   Rapture / 7 year Tribulation (seals, trumpets, bowls) / Return of Christ / Millennium / White Throne Judgment / Eternal Kingdom
2. Mid-tribulation View (same as above except rapture occurs in the middle of the tribulation)
3. Pre-Wrath Rapture View (same as above except rapture occurs before the bowls)
4. Post-tribulation View (rapture occurs at the return of Christ at the end of the tribulation)
5. Pan-Tribulation View – it will all pan out

Since well meaning and mature Christians hold to each of these views, should we just throw up our hands and say, "it doesn't matter, whenever it happens will be fine," as the "pan-tribulation" view would suggest?

I believe it is an important question because the faith of many can be seriously shaken if they hold, for example, to a pre-tribulation rapture position and if that does not come to pass, their whole confidence in the Bible and in God may be called into question. While this is admittedly a difficult subject – thus the divergence of views – I think we can come to rule out at least a couple of the positions.

Imminent Return of Christ

One of the pillars of the pre-trib rapture position is that Christ could come at any time. There is nothing that needs to happen before he returns and so he could come even as you are reading this book. This is what is called the "imminent return of Christ." Support for this position comes from the idea that we are waiting for Christ's return and we don't know when it will be:

Matthew 24:36
"But concerning that day and hour no one knows, not even the angels of heaven, nor the Son, but the Father only.

Matthew 24:42
Therefore, stay awake, for you do not know on what day your Lord is coming.

Matthew 24:44
Therefore you also must be ready, for the Son of Man is coming at an hour you do not expect.

Philip. 3:20
But our citizenship is in heaven, and from it we await a Savior, the Lord Jesus Christ,

1 John 3:2-3
Beloved, we are God's children now, and what we will be has not yet appeared; but we know that when he appears we shall be like him, because we shall see him as he is. [3] And everyone who thus hopes in him purifies himself as he is pure.

1 Thess. 5:2
For you yourselves are fully aware that the day of the Lord will come like a thief in the night.

1 Thess. 5:6
So then let us not sleep, as others do, but let us keep awake and be sober.

Titus 2:13
waiting for our blessed hope, the appearing of the glory of our great God and Savior Jesus Christ,

Does the Bible teach, however, that Jesus could come at any time? We will answer that further ahead. But first, let us look at another pillar of the pre-trib rapture position.

Not Destined to Wrath

According to the pre-trib position, the reason the rapture would have to happen before the great tribulation is that the tribulation time is a time of God's wrath being poured out on the earth and since Christians are not destined to wrath, they must be taken away before God's wrath is poured out. The following verses are cited in support of that supposition:

1 Thess. 1:10
and to wait for his Son from heaven, whom he raised from the dead, Jesus who delivers us from the wrath to come.

1 Thess. 5:9
For God has not destined us for wrath, but to obtain salvation through our Lord Jesus Christ,

Rev. 3:7, 10
"And to the angel of the church in Philadelphia write: ....
Because you have kept my word about patient endurance, I will keep you from the hour of trial that is coming on the whole world, to try those who dwell on the earth."

Rapture vs. Second Coming

The pre-trib position sees the resurrection and the catching up of the live believers as something that occurs separately from Christ's second coming. According to this view, the second coming occurs either seven or three and a half years after the rapture. In this view, Christ does not come to the earth for the rapture; he calls the church up to heaven where he is, but he does come to the earth in power and glory at the second coming.

The official position of a number of seminaries and denominations combined with the popular writing of Tim LaHaye, Hal Lindsey and others, make it seem as though this must be the correct Biblical view. But is the pre-tribulation rapture view what the Bible really teaches? Let me suggest that it is not, and I will attempt to show that this particular view cannot be right according to scripture, and seek to propose some alternative views.

The Problem with Imminence

The Bible clearly states that our being gathered together to Christ (the resurrection and the rapture) will not happen before certain other things happen as we pointed out in Chapter 7. Note that the following passage also combines that event with the coming of the Lord as one event comprising "the day of the Lord".

2 Thess. 2:1-8

Now concerning **the coming of our Lord Jesus Christ and our being gathered together to him**, we ask you, brothers, [2] not to be quickly shaken in mind or alarmed, either by a spirit or a spoken word, or a letter seeming to be from us, to the effect that **the day of the Lord** has come. [3] Let no one deceive you in any way. **For that day will not come, unless the rebellion comes first, and the man of lawlessness is revealed**, the son of destruction, [4] who opposes and exalts himself against every so-called god or object of worship, so that he takes his seat in the temple of God, proclaiming himself to be God. [5] Do you not remember that when I was still with you I told you these things? [6] And you know what is restraining him now so that he may be revealed in his time. [7] For the mystery of lawlessness is already at work. Only **he who now restrains it will do so until he is out of the way.** [8] **And then the lawless one will be revealed**, whom the Lord Jesus will kill with the breath of his mouth and bring to nothing by the appearance of his coming.

There are clearly five events that have to take place before Jesus comes and we are gathered together to him:

1. The rebellion (apostasy or falling away)
2. The restrainer of the lawless one will be taken out of the way
3. The man of lawlessness (the Antichrist) will be revealed
4. The temple has to be rebuilt
5. This man of lawlessness takes his seat in the temple of God and proclaims himself to be God.

The last verse above says that the Lord will kill him at the appearance of his coming, so the events listed above have to happen before Jesus comes and we are gathered together to him.

Jesus said clearly that certain things had to happen before the end would come:

1. The gospel would be preached to the whole world
2. The abomination of desolation would occur (the antichrist setting himself up in the temple proclaiming himself to be God) which would usher in
3. The great tribulation
4. Cataclysmic signs in the heavens and on the earth and seas

Matthew 24:14-22

And this gospel of the kingdom will be proclaimed throughout the whole world as a testimony to all nations, and then the end will come.

[15] "So when you see the abomination of desolation spoken of by the prophet Daniel, standing in the holy place (let the reader understand), [16] then let those who are in Judea flee to the mountains. [17] Let the one who is on the housetop not go down to take what is in his house, [18] and let the one who is in the field not turn back to take his cloak. [19] And alas for women who are pregnant and for those who are nursing infants in those days! [20] Pray that your flight may not be in winter or on a Sabbath. [21] For then there will be great tribulation, such as has not been from the beginning of the world until now, no, and never will be. [22] And if those days had not been cut short, no human being would be saved. But for the sake of the elect those days will be cut short.

Matthew 24:29-31

"Immediately after the tribulation of those days the sun will be darkened, and the moon will not give its light, and the stars will fall from heaven, and the powers of the heavens will be shaken. [30] Then will appear in heaven the sign of the Son of Man, and then all the tribes of the earth will mourn, and they will see the Son of Man coming on the clouds of heaven with power and great glory. [31] And he will send out his angels with a loud trumpet call, and they will gather his elect from the four winds, from one end of heaven to the other.

Luke 21:25-28

"And there will be signs in sun and moon and stars, and on the earth distress of nations in perplexity because of the roaring of the sea and the waves, [26] people fainting with fear and with foreboding of what is coming on the world. For the powers of the heavens will be shaken. [27] And then they will see the Son of Man coming in a cloud with power and great glory. [28] **Now when these things begin to take place**, straighten up and raise your heads, because your redemption is drawing near."

The pre-trib position argues that the rapture will take the church away before this tribulation and that this gathering in of the elect at Jesus' second coming will be the gathering in of the "tribulation saints". In other words, there would be two resurrections – one before the tribulation and one after the tribulation.

How Many Resurrections?

Besides the fact that the Bible does not use the term "tribulation saints" to distinguish them from saints from any other time in history, there is a serious flaw with the idea that there will be two resurrections of the righteous – before and after the tribulation. Note the following passages:

Rev. 20:4-6
Then I saw thrones, and seated on them were those to whom the authority to judge was committed. Also I saw the souls of those who had been beheaded for the testimony of Jesus and for the word of God, and who had not worshiped the beast or its image and had not received its mark on their foreheads or their hands. They came to life and reigned with Christ for a thousand years. [5] The rest of the dead did not come to life until the thousand years were ended. **This is the first resurrection**. [6] Blessed and holy is the one who shares in the first resurrection! Over such the second death has no power, but they will be priests of God and of Christ, and they will reign with him for a thousand years.

Who takes part in the first resurrection? Those who had been beheaded for the testimony of Jesus and for the word of God, and who had not worshiped the beast or its image and had not received its mark on their foreheads or their hands.

According to the pre-trib view, the church is resurrected before the beast comes on the scene, before the tribulation begins. This passage clearly states that people who were beheaded (Islam's favorite execution method even today) during the great tribulation will take part in the **first** resurrection. Thus there can be no previous resurrection of the church before the tribulation. The resurrection has to take place either during or after the great tribulation, certainly not pre-tribulation. So when will this take place? Jesus said, "immediately **after** the tribulation of those days…"

It is said that at the beginning, Alexander the Great's soldiers eagerly looked forward to being in battle. The reason was that until they had fought, they were not eligible to have an A tattooed on their arms, signifying that they were in his army. It was a badge of honor. They had to be first tested. God likewise tests us through tribulation.

1 Peter 1:6-7

In this you rejoice, though now for a little while, if necessary, you have been grieved by various trials, [7] so that the tested genuineness of your faith—more precious than gold that perishes though it is tested by fire—may be found to result in praise and glory and honor at the revelation of Jesus Christ.

Following are further passages that speak of the resurrection of the righteous:

Luke 14:14

and you will be blessed, because they cannot repay you. You will be repaid at the resurrection of the just." (There is only one resurrection of the just or righteous).

John 6:39-40

And this is the will of him who sent me, that I should lose nothing of all that he has given me, but raise it up on the last day. [40] For this is the will of my Father, that everyone who looks on the Son and believes in him should have eternal life, and I will raise him up on the last day."

John 6:44

No one can come to me unless the Father who sent me draws him. And I will raise him up on the last day.

John 6:54

Whoever feeds on my flesh and drinks my blood has eternal life, and I will raise him up on the last day.

It does not say "the last day of the church age".

Is there a difference between "raised to life" and "resurrection"? Yes. Raised to life means to be raised from the dead only to die again. Resurrection means being raised from the dead with a new body never to die again.

So how many resurrections are there? The Bible indicates that there are three:

1. Christ
2. The believers
3. The rest of the dead

1 Cor. 15:20-26

But in fact Christ has been raised from the dead, the firstfruits of those who have fallen asleep. [21] For as by a man came death, by a man has come also the resurrection of the dead. [22] For as in Adam all die, so also in Christ shall all be made alive. [23] But each in his own order: Christ the firstfruits, then at his coming those who belong to Christ. [24] Then [*comes*] the end, when he delivers the kingdom to God the Father after destroying every rule and every authority and power. [25] For he must reign until he has put all his enemies under his feet. [26] The last enemy to be destroyed is death.

Jesus – The Prototype of the First Resurrection, the Firstfruits

Rev. 1:5

and from Jesus Christ the faithful witness, **the firstborn of the dead**, and the ruler of kings on earth.

Col. 1:18

And he is the head of the body, the church. He is the beginning, **the firstborn from the dead**, that in everything he might be preeminent.

1 Cor. 15:20

But in fact Christ has been raised from the dead, **the firstfruits** of those who have fallen asleep.

Believers

1 Cor. 15:23

But each in his own order: Christ the firstfruits, then at his coming those who belong to Christ.

Matthew 24:30-31

Then will appear in heaven the sign of the Son of Man, and then all the tribes of the earth will mourn, and they will see the Son of Man coming on the clouds of heaven with power and great glory. [31] And he will send out his angels with a loud trumpet call, and they will gather his elect from the four winds, from one end of heaven to the other.

1 Thess. 4:15-17

For this we declare to you by a word from the Lord, that we who are alive, who are left until the coming of the Lord, will not precede those who have fallen asleep. [16] For the Lord himself will descend from heaven with a cry of command, with the voice of an archangel, and with the sound of the trumpet of God. And the dead in Christ will rise first. [17] Then we who are alive, who are left, will be caught up together with them in the clouds to meet the Lord in the air, and so we will always be with the Lord.

The Dead

1 Corinthians 15:24 (NASB)

24 then *comes* the end, when He hands over the kingdom to the God and Father, when He has abolished all rule and all authority and power.

John 5:28

Do not marvel at this, for an hour is coming when all who are in the tombs will hear his voice

Acts 24:14-15

But this I confess to you, that according to the Way, which they call a sect, I worship the God of our fathers, believing everything laid down by the Law and written in the Prophets, [15] having a hope in

God, which these men themselves accept, that there will be a resurrection of both the just and the unjust.

Daniel 12:2

And many of those who sleep in the dust of the earth shall awake, some to everlasting life, and some to shame and everlasting contempt.

Rev. 20:4-5

Then I saw thrones, and seated on them were those to whom the authority to judge was committed. Also I saw the souls of those who had been beheaded for the testimony of Jesus and for the word of God, and who had not worshiped the beast or its image and had not received its mark on their foreheads or their hands. They came to life and reigned with Christ for a thousand years. [5] **The rest of the dead did not come to life until the thousand years were ended.** This is the first resurrection.

Rev. 20:12-13

And I saw the dead, great and small, standing before the throne, and books were opened. Then another book was opened, which is the book of life. And the dead were judged by what was written in the books, according to what they had done. [13] And the sea gave up the dead who were in it, Death and Hades gave up the dead who were in them, and they were judged, each one of them, according to what they had done.

How Many Second Comings of Christ and How Many Last Trumpets?

The two main "rapture" passages used by the pre-trib position we have cited before:

1 Thess. 4:14-17

For since we believe that Jesus died and rose again, even so, through Jesus, God will bring with him those who have fallen asleep. [15] For this we declare to you by a word from the Lord, that we who are alive, who are left until the coming of the Lord, will not precede those who have fallen asleep. [16] For the Lord himself will descend from heaven with a cry of command, with the voice of an archangel, and with the sound of **the trumpet of God**. And the dead in Christ will rise first. [17] Then we who are alive, who are left, will be caught up together with them in the clouds to meet the Lord in the air, and so we will always be with the Lord.

The picture presented is of Jesus descending personally, visibly and with fanfare, bringing along with him those who have died (fallen asleep) before (vs.14). These dead in Christ will have their bodies resurrected first as Jesus is coming and joined to their spirits or souls that are coming with Jesus. A split second later those believers who are alive are caught up together with them in the clouds **to meet** the Lord in the air. The ESV Study Bible has the following note on vs. 17:

"**to meet.** The Greek term *apantesis* is often used of an important dignitary's reception by the inhabitants of a city, who come out to greet and welcome their honored guest with fanfare and celebration, then accompany him into the city (cf. Matt. 25:6; Acts 28:15; a related term *hypantesis* is used in Matt. 25:1; John 12:13). It may indicate that the subsequent movement of the saints after meeting Christ "in the air" conforms to Christ's direction, thus in a downward motion toward the earth."[69]

The above mentioned uses of the word "to meet" in other passages then seem to contradict the idea of the raptured saints going up to heaven for a period of time and then later returning with Jesus some seven years later. The Acts 28:15 passage relates Paul's coming to Rome. The brothers heard he was coming and "came as far as the Forum of Appius and Three Taverns to meet us." Then they accompanied Paul into the city. The second rapture passage is:

1 Cor. 15:51-53

Behold! I tell you **a mystery**. We shall not all sleep, but we shall all be changed, [52] in a moment, in the twinkling of an eye, at **the last trumpet**. For the trumpet will sound, and the dead will be raised imperishable, and we shall be changed. [53] For this perishable body must put on the imperishable, and this mortal body must put on immortality.

[69] Op. Cit., ESV Study Bible p. 2310

Rapture before the Tribulation and Resurrection After?

There are those who believe that the Church will be raptured before the great tribulation – that is all those believers who are alive at that time so that they will escape the wrath to be poured out on the earth during the tribulation, but that the resurrection of believers who have died all throughout history will not happen until Jesus returns in power and great glory at the end of the tribulation.

What makes that position untenable is that the passage cited above in 1 Thess. 4 indicates that the resurrection happens first, immediately followed by the rapture. So there cannot be a rapture of the Church first followed years later by the resurrection.

One notices that when Jesus himself descends from heaven, his coming will not be a quiet, secret catching away, but there is the cry of command with the voice of an archangel, and the sound of the trumpet of God – the last trumpet. Notice the similarities with what the pre-trib position calls the separate "second coming" and what the mystery being revealed is:

Matthew 24:30-31

Then will appear in heaven the sign of the Son of Man, and then all the tribes of the earth will mourn, and they will see the Son of Man coming on the clouds of heaven with power and great glory. [31] And he will send out his angels with **a loud trumpet call**, and they will gather his elect from the four winds, from one end of heaven to the other.

Rev. 10:7

but that in the days of **the trumpet call** to be sounded by the **seventh angel, the mystery of God would be fulfilled**, just as he announced to his servants the prophets.

Rev. 11:15-18

Then **the seventh angel blew his trumpet**, and there were loud voices in heaven, saying, **"The kingdom of the world has become the kingdom of our Lord and of his Christ, and he shall reign forever and ever."** [16] And the twenty-four elders who sit on their thrones before God fell on their faces and worshiped God, [17] saying,

"We give thanks to you, Lord God Almighty,

who is and who was,
for you have taken your great power
and begun to reign.
[18] The nations raged,
but your wrath came,
and the time for the dead to be judged,
and for rewarding your servants, the prophets and saints,
and those who fear your name,
both small and great,
and for destroying the destroyers of the earth."

The trumpet that the seventh angel blows is the last trumpet and at that trumpet, the mystery of God would be fulfilled, which the 1 Corinthians 15:51 passage tells us is the rapture, or resurrection.

The Bible indicates that when he comes, Jesus will not be alone. He will be accompanied by thousands of angels as well as by the saints – the spirits of those who accompany him to be joined to their resurrected bodies.

Zech. 14:4-5

On that day his feet shall stand on the Mount of Olives that lies before Jerusalem on the east, ... **Then the Lord my God will come, and all the holy ones with him.**

1 Thess. 3:12-13

and may the Lord make you increase and abound in love for one another and for all, as we do for you, [13] so that he may establish your hearts blameless in holiness before our God and Father, **at the coming of our Lord Jesus with all his saints**.

2 Thess. 1:5-10

This is evidence of the righteous judgment of God, that you may be considered worthy of the kingdom of God, for which you are also suffering— [6] since indeed God considers it just to repay with affliction those who afflict you, [7] and to grant relief to you who are afflicted as well as to us, **when the Lord Jesus is revealed from heaven with his mighty angels**

[8] in flaming fire, inflicting vengeance on those who do not know God and on those who do not obey the gospel of our Lord Jesus. [9] They will suffer the punishment of eternal destruction, away from the

presence of the Lord and from the glory of his might, [10] **when he comes on that day to be glorified in his saints,** and to be marveled at among all who have believed, because our testimony to you was believed.

Jude 1:14

It was also about these that Enoch, the seventh from Adam, prophesied, saying, "Behold, **the Lord came with ten thousands of his holy ones,**

The Elect

We read in Matthew 24 that unless the tribulation was cut short, no one would survive, but for the sake of the elect, those days will be cut short. We also saw that the angels will gather God's elect from the one end of heaven to another. Again, in pre-tribulation rapture theology, the elect here are those converted during the tribulation; some say they are the Jews converted during the tribulation. However, who does the Bible say the elect are?

Romans 8:31-33

What then shall we say to these things? If God is for us, who can be against us? [32] He who did not spare his own Son but gave him up for us all, how will he not also with him graciously give us all things? [33] Who shall bring any charge against God's elect? It is God who justifies.

Romans 11:7

What then? Israel failed to obtain what it was seeking. The elect obtained it, but the rest were hardened,

2 Tim. 2:10

Therefore I endure everything for the sake of the elect, that they also may obtain the salvation that is in Christ Jesus with eternal glory.

Titus 1:1

Paul, a servant of God and an apostle of Jesus Christ, for the sake of the faith of God's elect and their knowledge of the truth, which accords with godliness,

1 Peter 1:1
Peter, an apostle of Jesus Christ, To those who are elect exiles of the dispersion in Pontus, Galatia, Cappadocia, Asia, and Bithynia,

Chosen Jews and Gentiles alike who believe in Jesus Christ are the elect. We are the ones who will be gathered when Jesus comes in power and great glory at the last trumpet call.

Resurrection Bodies

Though many of the passages we have looked at speak of us being transformed when Jesus comes, our focus has been more on the timing. What specifically will happen to those who have died in Christ and to those alive in Christ when He comes should not be overlooked.

"We shall all be changed, the dead will be raised imperishable. For this perishable body must put on the imperishable, and this mortal body must put on immortality." (1 Cor. 15:51-53)

Ephes. 1:13
[you] were sealed with the Holy Spirit, who is the guarantee of our inheritance until we acquire possession of it, to the praise of his glory.

Ephes. 4:30
And do not grieve the Holy Spirit of God, by whom you were sealed for **the day of redemption.**

Romans 8:23
And not only the creation, but we ourselves, who have the firstfruits of the Spirit, groan inwardly as we wait eagerly for adoption as sons, **the redemption of our bodies**.

Philip. 3:20-21
But our citizenship is in heaven, and from it we await a Savior, the Lord Jesus Christ, [21] who **will transform our lowly body to be like his glorious body**,

1 John 3:2
Beloved, we are God's children now, and what we will be has not yet appeared; but we know that **when he appears we shall be like**

him, because we shall see him as he is.

When He appears, we will receive immortal bodies that will be just like Jesus' resurrected body. What a wonderful truth for the believer!

What About the Wrath?

We cited arguments earlier by the pre-tribulation rapture position that Christians are not destined for wrath and for that reason, will not go through the tribulation. First, let me say that there are degrees of wrath. Romans 1:18 speaks of God's wrath being revealed now. The severity of the judgments in the seals, trumpets, and bowls of wrath in the book of Revelation increase as they unfold. God's wrath ultimately is the sentence to eternal punishment in hell because of refusal to repent and believe the good news of the Gospel of Jesus Christ. The objects of wrath are also differentiated both temporally – as they were during the ten plagues in Egypt during the time of Moses, and eternally.

As has been mentioned several times, God tells us over and over in his Word that we will suffer persecution, affliction and tribulation. In fact, in the same letter that Paul said (1 Thess. 5:9) "For God has not destined us for wrath, but to obtain salvation through our Lord Jesus Christ," he also said he was sending Timothy to exhort them in the faith (1 Thess. 3:3-4) "that no one be moved by these afflictions. For you yourselves know that we are destined for this. [4] For when we were with you, we kept telling you beforehand that we were to suffer affliction, just as it has come to pass, and just as you know."

But what about the promise to the church in Philadelphia?

Rev. 3:7-13

"And to the angel of the church in Philadelphia write: 'The words of the holy one, the true one, who has the key of David, who opens and no one will shut, who shuts and no one opens.

[8] " 'I know your works. Behold, I have set before you an open door, which no one is able to shut. I know that you have but little power, and yet you have kept my word and have not denied my name. [9] Behold, I will make those of the synagogue of Satan who say that they are Jews and are not, but lie—behold, I will make them come and bow down before your feet and they will learn that I have loved you. [10] **Because you have kept my word about patient endurance, I will keep you from the hour of trial that is coming on the whole world, to try those who dwell on the earth.** [11] I am

coming soon. Hold fast what you have, so that no one may seize your crown. [12] The one who conquers, I will make him a pillar in the temple of my God. Never shall he go out of it, and I will write on him the name of my God, and the name of the city of my God, the new Jerusalem, which comes down from my God out of heaven, and my own new name. [13] He who has an ear, let him hear what the Spirit says to the churches.'

This was a promise to a specific church, one of seven that Jesus directed the Apostle John to write to. There is an interpretive difficulty – how does a letter written 1900 years ago to a historic church in what is today Turkey apply to us today? How do we apply the letters written to the other churches? Interestingly, of the seven churches, only two were not reprimanded by Christ as having something that he was against: The one above – the church of Philadelphia, and the church in Smyrna. I include the letter to that church:

Rev. 2:8-11
"And to the angel of the church in Smyrna write: 'The words of the first and the last, who died and came to life.
[9] " 'I know your tribulation and your poverty (but you are rich) and the slander of those who say that they are Jews and are not, but are a synagogue of Satan. [10] Do not fear what you are about to suffer. Behold, the devil is about to throw some of you into prison, that you may be tested, and for ten days you will have tribulation. Be faithful unto death, and I will give you the crown of life. [11] He who has an ear, let him hear what the Spirit says to the churches. The one who conquers will not be hurt by the second death.'

While the church in Philadelphia is promised to be kept from the hour of trial that will come to try the whole earth, the church in Smyrna is told that the tribulation they are currently suffering will get worse – that some will be thrown in prison and be put to death.

The point is that these letters cannot be taken to be a universal promise to all the church. In other words, applying the promise made to the church in Philadelphia to all Christians at the time of the end when the great tribulation begins does not seem to be a very consistent hermeneutic. One interpretation that may be more consistent is that there will be a part of the church of Christ that will be kept from the hour of trial coming to the whole earth. Perhaps there will be a geographical area in the world that will be relatively unaffected by the onslaught of the Antichrist, or will be protected from some of the natural disasters that will be coming to the earth.

Given this context: "Behold, I will make those of the synagogue of Satan who say that they are Jews and are not, but lie—behold, I will make them come and bow down before your feet and they will learn that I have loved you. [10] Because you have kept my word about patient endurance, I will keep you from the hour of trial that is coming on the whole world, to try those who dwell on the earth. [11] I am coming soon." (Rev. 3:9-11), what would be more consistent, is that the passage refers to the believing Jews who escape Jerusalem at the abomination of desolation and flee to the mountains where they will be protected during the time of tribulation. Note this passage:

Rev. 12:13-17

And when the dragon saw that he had been thrown down to the earth, he pursued the woman who had given birth to the male child. [14] But the woman was given the two wings of the great eagle so that she might fly from the serpent into the wilderness, to the place where she is to be nourished for a time, and times, and half a time. [15] The serpent poured water like a river out of his mouth after the woman, to sweep her away with a flood. [16] But the earth came to the help of the woman, and the earth opened its mouth and swallowed the river that the dragon had poured from his mouth. [17] Then the dragon became furious with the woman and went off to make war on the rest of her offspring, on those who keep the commandments of God and hold to the testimony of Jesus.

Satan tries to destroy those Jews who flee into the wilderness, but is thwarted and they are sustained for the duration of the great tribulation – the "time, and times and half a time." The people they were being persecuted by before this were Jews. That certainly fits the description of reality in Israel today. Messianic Jews are greatly persecuted by the religious, orthodox Jews. "Behold, I will make those of the synagogue of Satan who say that they are Jews and are not, but lie—behold, I will make them come and bow down before your feet and they will learn that I have loved you."

Can you see that happening, after Jesus returns? The surviving Jews in Jerusalem will "look on me whom they have pierced and mourn…" That is when they will realize that the Jews they had formerly persecuted in God's name were the ones that God loved.

Conclusion

So what can we conclude regarding the timing of the resurrection and the rapture? I think we have seen that Jesus' return is not imminent – that certain things have to happen before he will return and we will be resurrected. I think we have also seen that there is not a two stage resurrection – one for the church before the tribulation and one for those converted during the tribulation. Those who die during the tribulation because they refuse to worship the beast and receive his mark will be included in the first resurrection.

All the indications seem to point to the resurrection and rapture as taking place at the end of the great tribulation. That would most likely leave the post-tribulation rapture view as the most viable.

THE END TIME SEQUENCE OF EVENTS: THE BOOK OF REVELATION

PART FOUR

16 THE SEVEN SEALS

DOES THE BIBLE give us an indication of what is next on the prophetic calendar? Is there really a chronological outline of events presented, or is it all piecemeal, like the section before, "Pieces of the Apocalyptic Pie.?" I believe the Book of Revelation outlines for us a chronological glimpse into the future. Jesus revealed to the Apostle John what is to take place. The events are given in three sets of progressively more intense judgments on the earth. There are seven seals, seven trumpets and seven bowls of the wrath of God that will be poured out upon the earth. As I wrote before, volumes have been written on just the Book of Revelation alone and it is not in the scope of this book to give a detailed exegesis of the book, but we will look at some of the broad pictures presented.

The Seven Seals

Rev. 5:1-5

Then I saw in the right hand of him who was seated on the throne a scroll written within and on the back, sealed with seven seals. [2] And I saw a strong angel proclaiming with a loud voice, "Who is worthy to open the scroll and break its seals?" [3] And no one in heaven or on earth or under the earth was able to open the scroll or to look into it, [4] and I began to weep loudly because no one was found worthy to open the scroll or to look into it. [5] And one of the elders said to me, "Weep no more; behold, the Lion of the tribe of Judah, the Root of David, has conquered, so that he can open the scroll and its seven seals."

Jesus is the one found worthy to open the seven seals. The living creatures and twenty-four elders in heaven respond this way:

Rev. 5:9-14

And they sang a new song, saying,

"Worthy are you to take the scroll
and to open its seals,
for you were slain, and by your blood
you ransomed people for God
from every tribe and language and people and nation,
[10] and you have made them a kingdom and priests to our God,
and they shall reign on the earth."

[11] Then I looked, and I heard around the throne and the living creatures and the elders the voice of many angels, numbering myriads of myriads and thousands of thousands, [12] saying with a loud voice, "Worthy is the Lamb who was slain, to receive power and wealth and wisdom and might and honor and glory and blessing!" [13] And I heard every creature in heaven and on earth and under the earth and in the sea, and all that is in them, saying, "To him who sits on the throne and to the Lamb be blessing and honor and glory and might forever and ever!" [14] And the four living creatures said, "Amen!" and the elders fell down and worshiped.

The First Seal – The White Horse and Rider

Rev. 6:1-2

Now I watched when the Lamb opened one of the seven seals, and I heard one of the four living creatures say with a voice like thunder, "Come!" [2] And I looked, and behold, a white horse! And its rider had a bow, and a crown was given to him, and he came out conquering, and to conquer.

Various interpretations are offered as to the identity of this white horse and rider with a crown given him, and the one who goes out to conquer. Another picture is given later in the book of one also on a white horse who comes to conquer:

Rev. 19:11-16

Then I saw heaven opened, and behold, a white horse! The one sitting on it is called Faithful and True, and in righteousness he judges and makes war. [12] His eyes are like a flame of fire, and on his head are many diadems, and he has a name written that no one knows but himself. [13] He is clothed in a robe dipped in blood, and the name by which he is called is The Word of God. [14] And the armies of heaven, arrayed in fine linen, white and pure, were following him on white horses. [15] From his mouth comes a sharp sword with which to strike down the nations, and he will rule them with a rod of iron. He will tread the winepress of the fury of the wrath of God the Almighty. [16] On his robe and on his thigh he has a name written, King of kings and Lord of lords.

The passage above is obviously Jesus, the conquering King as he comes in glory at his second coming. Satan is presented as a counterfeit – a deceiver. A counterfeit tries to copy the real thing. I believe the rider on a white horse in chapter 6 is the Antichrist. It is interesting that some in Islam interpret this passage as referring to their Mahdi.

In their book, *Al Mahdi and the End of Time*, Muhammad ibn Izzat and Muhammad Arif, two well-known Egyptian authors, identify the Mahdi in the Book of Revelation, quoting the hadith narrator Ka'ab al-Ahbar.

In one place, they write,

"I find the Mahdi recorded in the books of the Prophets... For instance, the Book of Revelation says: "And I saw and behold a white horse. He that sat on him [...] went forth conquering and to conquer."

Ibn Izzat and Arif then go on to say: "It is clear that this man is the Mahdi who will ride the white horse and judge by the Qur'an (with justice) and with whom will be men with marks of prostration (zabiba) on their foreheads."[70]

If this rider is indeed the Antichrist, before he is revealed there must be a ten nation coalition from the dragon's seventh head – the last world empire, as we have already seen from passages we have cited earlier (Dan. 2:40-43; 7:19-25; Rev. 13:1-4; 17:7-13).

So before this rider on a white horse appears, I believe that the Muslim Empire with a Caliphate will be reborn, uniting ten regions or

---

[70] Izzat, Arif, Muhammad, Al Mahdi and the End of Time (U.K.: Dar al-Taqwa Ltd. (UK), ISBN 1870582756, 1997) p. 15,16

kingdoms. Already there is a movement to unify Islam by the Organization of the Islamic Conference. As its website states:

"The Organization of the Islamic Conference (OIC) is the second largest inter-governmental organization after the United Nations which has membership of 57 states spread over four continents. The Organization is the collective voice of the Muslim world and ensuring to safeguard and protect the interests of the Muslim world … The Organization has the singular honor to galvanize the Ummah into a unified body and have actively represented the Muslims by espousing all causes close to the hearts of over 1.5 billion Muslims of the world."[71]

As the world has seen, however, Islamic unity is at best precarious and as Daniel's prophecy states about these ten "toes": "As you saw the iron mixed with soft clay, so they will mix with one another in marriage, but they will not hold together, just as iron does not mix with clay." Remember that the word "mixed" in Hebrew is "arab", which characterizes the Arab peoples.

After there is a ten nation confederacy, there will be another "horn", or an "eighth king" who will conquer three of the ten. At some point in time the others will all give him their authority and will submit themselves to him. With further regard to the idea of conquering, Daniel saw the following regarding this final leader:

Daniel 11:40-45
"At the time of the end, the king of the south shall attack him, but the king of the north shall rush upon him like a whirlwind, with chariots and horsemen, and with many ships. And he shall come into countries and shall overflow and pass through. [41] He shall come into the glorious land. And tens of thousands shall fall, but these shall be delivered out of his hand: Edom and Moab and the main part of the Ammonites. [42] He shall stretch out his hand against the countries, and the land of Egypt shall not escape. [43] He shall become ruler of the treasures of gold and of silver, and all the precious things of Egypt, and the Libyans and the Cushites shall follow in his train. [44] But news from the east and the north shall alarm him, and he shall go out with great fury to destroy and devote many to destruction. [45]

[71] The Organization of the Islamic Conference, < http://www.oic-oci.org>

And he shall pitch his palatial tents between the sea and the glorious holy mountain. Yet he shall come to his end, with none to help him.

The Second Seal – the Bright Red Horse and Rider

Rev. 6:3-4
When he opened the second seal, I heard the second living creature say, "Come!" [4] And out came another horse, bright red. Its rider was permitted to take peace from the earth, so that men should slay one another, and he was given a great sword.

As stated earlier, there are increasing conflicts around the globe between nations, tribes, ethnic groups and religions. The rhetoric from leaders in Iran and North Korea along with the many wars and conflicts that the United States and NATO are involved in, to say nothing of the conflicts in Africa and the Middle East, are indicators that peace is taken from the world and there is no realistic hope for peace in sight.

The Third Seal – the Black Horse and Rider

Rev. 6:5-6
When he opened the third seal, I heard the third living creature say, "Come!" And I looked, and behold, a black horse! And its rider had a pair of scales in his hand. [6] And I heard what seemed to be a voice in the midst of the four living creatures, saying, "A quart of wheat for a denarius, and three quarts of barley for a denarius, and do not harm the oil and wine!"

A denarius was what a common laborer would earn in a day. This picture portrays a scarcity of basic foods, likely from famine that causes a laborer to spend all his wages on food for himself and his family. That the drought, a possible cause of this situation, is not very severe and long lasting is indicated by the fact that olives and grapes will not be greatly affected. Indeed, these plants have deep roots and can survive in dry times, whereas grain crops such as corn, wheat and barley have to have rains or irrigation to be able to grow.

In a Scientific American Journal article, the following is said about the seriousness of the water supply in the US.

The Ogallala Aquifer: Saving a Vital U.S. Water Source

The massive underground water source feeds the middle third of the country but is disappearing fast. Can it be conserved?

On America's high plains, crops in early summer stretch to the horizon: field after verdant field of corn, sorghum, soybeans, wheat and cotton. Framed by immense skies now blue, now scarlet-streaked, this 800-mile expanse of agriculture looks like it could go on forever.

It can't.

The Ogallala Aquifer, the vast underground reservoir that gives life to these fields, is disappearing. In some places, the groundwater is already gone. This is the breadbasket of America—the region that supplies at least one fifth of the total annual U.S. agricultural harvest. If the aquifer goes dry, more than $20 billion worth of food and fiber will vanish from the world's markets. And scientists say it will take natural processes 6,000 years to refill the reservoir."[72]

"According to data from the UN's Food and Agriculture Organization (FAO), published Tuesday (June 7, 2011), global food prices have barely budged since April but the big picture remains bleak: the global price for a basket of basic foods is still 37% higher than it was this time last year.

High and volatile food prices are also likely to prevail for the rest of the year, and into 2012, according to the FAO's biannual report on global food markets, also published on Tuesday. The UN agency warns that weather conditions - too much or too little rain - could weaken maize and wheat yields in Europe and North America, and an overall rundown on food inventories is set to tighten global supply."[73]

Other alarming headlines cause serious concern regarding future food shortages:

U.S Bumble bee Population Implodes, Drops 96%: Pollinators of food crops and wild plants are in near catastrophic decline.[74]

---

[72] Jane Braxton Little, "The Ogallala Aquifer: Saving a Vital U.S. Water Source," Scientific American, March 30, 2009

[73] Claire Provost, "The Rising Cost of Food – Get the Data," The Guardian, <http://www.guardian.co.uk/global-development/datablog/2011/jun/07/rising-cost-of-food>

[74] FishOutofWater, "U.S. Bumble Bee Population Implodes, Drops 96%," Daily Kos, Tue Jan 04, 2011 at 06:58 PM PST, <http://www.dailykos.com/story/2011/01/04/933430/-US-Bumble-bee-Population-Implodes,-Drops-96>

U.N. agency warns of further decline in world's bee population without big changes in human behavior

"The bees are needed to pollinate crops that feed the world's growing population. Of the 100 crop species that provide 90% of the world's food, more than 70 are pollinated by bees, the U.N. report said.

"Human beings have fabricated the illusion that in the 21st century they have the technological prowess to be independent of nature," said Achim Steiner, executive director of the U.N.'s environmental program. "Bees underline the reality that we are more, not less dependent on nature's services in a world of close to 7 billion people."[75]

The Fourth Seal – the Pale Horse and Rider

Rev. 6:7-8

When he opened the fourth seal, I heard the voice of the fourth living creature say, "Come!" [8] And I looked, and behold, a pale horse! And its rider's name was Death, and Hades followed him. And they were given authority over a fourth of the earth, to kill with sword and with famine and with pestilence and by wild beasts of the earth.

The term "Hades" is the place where the souls of those who do not believe in Jesus go until the final Day of Judgment. This rider "Death" – the grim reaper, takes a quarter of the earth's population through these various means. As of this writing, there are 6.9 billion people in the world. A quarter of the world's population today would be 1.725 billion people. First, there are wars and violence that take millions – perhaps a major nuclear war. Then comes the slow death of famine after land and crops are destroyed by the ravages of war. Disease and plagues normally follow and when the human population is diminished, the wild animal population grows and attacks humans too weak to defend themselves. If all of the U.S. and the European Union's populations were annihilated, that would only be half of the number of people to die.

---

[75] Jason Straziuso, "LA Unleashed," The Los Angeles Times, March 11,2011 <http://latimesblogs.latimes.com/unleashed/2011/03/un-agency-warns-of-further-decline-in-worlds-bee-population-without-big-changes-in-human-behavior.html>

Peace Treaty

As mentioned before, each prophet was given a partial glimpse of the broader picture and so putting the pieces of the puzzle together is difficult and subject to various interpretations.

We are told in Daniel that this end time Antichrist will make a covenant for the last seven years before Christ's return, but that he will break it halfway through the seven years, which at that point will mark the beginning of the "great tribulation" brought about by the abomination of desolation.

Daniel 9:27

And he shall make a strong covenant with many for one week, and for half of the week he shall put an end to sacrifice and offering. And on the wing of abominations shall come one who makes desolate, until the decreed end is poured out on the desolator."

Matthew 24:15-21

"So when you see the abomination of desolation spoken of by the prophet Daniel, standing in the holy place (let the reader understand),
[16] then let those who are in Judea flee to the mountains. …. [21]
For then there will be great tribulation, such as has not been from the beginning of the world until now, no, and never will be."

When this covenant takes place is not clear in the text in Revelation. We read earlier of the Antichrist conquering in the first seal:

Daniel 11:40-45

"At the time of the end, the king of the south shall attack him, but the king of the north shall rush upon him like a whirlwind, with chariots and horsemen, and with many ships. And he shall come into
countries and shall overflow and pass through. [41] He shall come
into the glorious land. And tens of thousands shall fall,

Those verses that follow tell us that he will take Egypt, Libya and Sudan. But then it says:

[44] But news from the east and the north shall alarm him, and he shall go out with great fury to destroy and devote many to destruction.
[45] And he shall pitch his palatial tents between the sea and the glorious holy mountain.

Admittedly, this is a guess. Could it be that verse 44 above in Daniel 11 refers to the Fourth Seal in Revelation – the Pale horse with the rider named Death who ends up killing a quarter of the earth's population? East and north of "the glorious land" (Israel, vs. 41), could refer to China and Russia. Assuming that the Antichrist had gained control over the Islamic Empire by then, it is conceivable that there could be a war between the "Communist Infidels" and the Muslims in which 1.725 billion people could die.

India, which is predominantly Hindu, with a current population of 1.21 billion and having nuclear weapons and also with a historic animosity toward the Muslim world, could also be the land in the east which engages in battle with the Muslim Empire – of which Pakistan would undoubtedly be a part.

Verse 45, "And he shall pitch his palatial tents between the sea and the glorious holy mountain," (Mediterranean Sea and Jerusalem). This follows the time of great destruction after which he settles in Israel. Could it be that this is the time then, when "he makes a strong covenant with the many"? The context in Daniel suggests that the "many" will include the Jewish people. Could it be that this will initiate the seven year countdown and also be the treaty that enables Israel to build their temple?

This covenant could occur before this first seal of the white horse whose rider goes out to conquer, but it seems to me that in order to have the political clout to be able to execute a treaty, the Antichrist will have had to gain control over the 10 nation coalition which he does not do without a fight.

The Fifth Seal – the Martyred Souls in Heaven

Rev. 6:9-11

When he opened the fifth seal, I saw under the altar the souls of those who had been slain for the word of God and for the witness they had borne. [10] They cried out with a loud voice, "O Sovereign Lord, holy and true, how long before you will judge and avenge our blood on those who dwell on the earth?" [11] Then they were each given a white robe and told to rest a little longer, until the number of their fellow servants and their brothers should be complete, who were to be killed as they themselves had been.

We have included numerous texts that indicate that the Antichrist will make war on the believers in Jesus Christ and many will be put to death. But even before the Antichrist is revealed, many Christians are being put to death for their faith all over the world – especially in Muslim lands. This scene shows them asking God to avenge their blood, but they are to wait until the full number of saints to be killed join them.

The Sixth Seal – A Great Earthquake and Cosmic Cataclysms

Rev. 6:12-17

When he opened the sixth seal, I looked, and behold, there was a great earthquake, and the sun became black as sackcloth, the full moon became like blood, [13] and the stars of the sky fell to the earth as the fig tree sheds its winter fruit when shaken by a gale. [14] The sky vanished like a scroll that is being rolled up, and every mountain and island was removed from its place. [15] Then the kings of the earth and the great ones and the generals and the rich and the powerful, and everyone, slave and free, hid themselves in the caves and among the rocks of the mountains, [16] calling to the mountains and rocks, "Fall on us and hide us from the face of him who is seated on the throne, and from the wrath of the Lamb, [17] for the great day of their wrath has come, and who can stand?"

This massive earthquake moves every mountain and island. In addition there is a shower of meteors or asteroids striking the earth and perhaps the earthquake sets off some volcanoes. One has only to remember the volcano in Iceland in 2010 and how it disrupted air travel for hundreds of thousands of passengers, blackening the sky for those nearby, to get an idea of the sun becoming black as sackcloth and the moon being as though it were in an eclipse – red like blood.

What Happens To God's People?

It is at this point that everyone seems to understand that the cataclysmic events are not happenstance, but rather the outpouring of God the Father and Jesus' wrath and they are filled with terror. They ask the question, "for the great day of their wrath has come, and who can stand?" The question is answered in the passage following in Revelation 7 where there is a picture presented of 144,000 Jews from the twelve tribes being sealed with the seal of God on their foreheads. The seventh seal, which marks the beginning of the seven trumpets of God's wrath being poured out with increased intensity, is put in check until these Jews are sealed.

In the Old Testament, the people of Israel suffered the results of the first three plagues in Egypt – the water turning to blood, the frogs and the gnats - but with the fourth plague of flies and following plagues, God spared his people.

Exodus 8:22-23

"But on that day I will set apart the land of Goshen, where my people dwell, so that no swarms of flies shall be there, that you may know that I am the Lord in the midst of the earth. [23] Thus I will put a division between my people and your people."

So, it seems that God's people will experience the six seals like everyone else, but these 144,000 Jews will be somehow protected from the horrendous things to follow.

Rev. 7:1-4

After this I saw four angels standing at the four corners of the earth, holding back the four winds of the earth, that no wind might blow on earth or sea or against any tree. [2] Then I saw another angel ascending from the rising of the sun, with the seal of the living God, and he called with a loud voice to the four angels who had been given power to harm earth and sea, [3] saying, "Do not harm the earth or the sea or the trees, until we have sealed the servants of our God on their foreheads." [4] And I heard the number of the sealed, 144,000, sealed from every tribe of the sons of Israel:

The winds of judgment are held in check until God's servants are sealed. This is reminiscent of what happened in Ezekiel 9 when God was about to execute the wicked in Jerusalem.

Ezekiel 9:4-10

And the Lord said to him, "Pass through the city, through Jerusalem, and **put a mark on the foreheads of the men who sigh and groan over all the abominations that are committed in it**." [5] And to the others he said in my hearing, "Pass through the city after him, and strike. Your eye shall not spare, and you shall show no pity. [6] Kill old men outright, young men and maidens, little children and women, but touch no one on whom is the mark. And begin at my sanctuary." So they began with the elders who were before the house. [7] Then he said to them, "Defile the house, and fill the courts with the slain. Go out." So they went out and struck in the city. [8] And while they were striking, and I was left alone, I fell upon my face, and cried, "Ah, Lord God! Will you destroy all the remnant of Israel in the outpouring of your wrath on Jerusalem?"

[9] Then he said to me, "The guilt of the house of Israel and Judah is exceedingly great. The land is full of blood, and the city full of injustice. For they say, 'The Lord has forsaken the land, and the Lord does not see.' [10] As for me, my eye will not spare, nor will I have pity; I will bring their deeds upon their heads."

What follows is a picture of another group – one in heaven.

Rev. 7:9-10

After this I looked, and behold, a great multitude that no one could number, from every nation, from all tribes and peoples and languages, standing before the throne and before the Lamb, clothed in white robes, with palm branches in their hands, [10] and crying out with a loud voice, "Salvation belongs to our God who sits on the throne, and to the Lamb!"

Rev. 7:13-14

Then one of the elders addressed me, saying, "Who are these, clothed in white robes, and from where have they come?" [14] I said to him, "Sir, you know." And he said to me, "These are the ones coming out of the great tribulation. They have washed their robes and made them white in the blood of the Lamb.

Remember the question asked by those in terror from the earthquake and falling stars, after recognizing that the day of God's wrath has come? It is, "who can stand?" The implied answer is that the 144,000 can as well as this great multitude that no one could number from all over the world. Standing in the day of God's wrath for these people, however, does not mean that they will not die. This is a picture of an innumerable host who have died during the great tribulation, some undoubtedly martyred for their faith, yet experiencing God's salvation.

The apostle Paul, in the face of his imminent execution for his faith wrote this:

2 Tim. 4:6-8, 18

For I am already being poured out as a drink offering, and the time of my departure has come. [7] I have fought the good fight, I have finished the race, I have kept the faith. [8] Henceforth there is laid up for me the crown of righteousness, which the Lord, the righteous judge, will award to me on that Day, and not only to me but also to all who have loved his appearing. .... The Lord will rescue me from every evil deed and bring me safely into his heavenly kingdom. To him be the glory forever and ever. Amen.

Though his death was imminent, his confidence was that the Lord would rescue him from every evil deed and bring him safely into God's heavenly kingdom. For the Christian, death is not the end and not the greatest evil. It is a new beginning. So, this innumerable host, though perishing during the great tribulation, was saved, and were able to stand, not suffering God's wrath during that tribulation. The heavenly elder goes on to tell John about this group:

Rev. 7:15-17
"Therefore they are before the throne of God,
and serve him day and night in his temple; and he who sits on the throne will shelter them with his presence.
[16] They shall hunger no more, neither thirst anymore;
the sun shall not strike them, nor any scorching heat.
[17] For the Lamb in the midst of the throne will be their shepherd, and he will guide them to springs of living water,
and God will wipe away every tear from their eyes."

The Seventh Seal – The Giving of the Seven Trumpets

Rev. 8:1-5
When the Lamb opened the seventh seal, there was silence in heaven for about half an hour. [2] Then I saw the seven angels who stand before God, and seven trumpets were given to them. [3] And another angel came and stood at the altar with a golden censer, and he was given much incense to offer with the prayers of all the saints on the golden altar before the throne, [4] and the smoke of the incense, with the prayers of the saints, rose before God from the hand of the angel. [5] Then the angel took the censer and filled it with fire from the altar and threw it on the earth, and there were peals of thunder, rumblings, flashes of lightning, and an earthquake.

Christians have gone through the time of the seals – a time of great upheavals and as we saw in the fifth seal, those who have died for their faith are asking God to judge and avenge their blood. Those believers still on earth will be praying that Jesus will come quickly. The prayers of the saints have an effect. It brings about the beginning of the trumpet blasts. In ancient days, the sounding of a trumpet was a warning to the people of imminent danger, much as in many small communities in the US, the sounding of the siren at the fire station warns of an approaching tornado or some sort of danger. Warning people ahead of time of coming danger was a very important thing.

Ezekiel 33:1-6

The word of the Lord came to me: [2] "Son of man, speak to your people and say to them, If I bring the sword upon a land, and the people of the land take a man from among them, and make him their watchman, [3] and if he sees the sword coming upon the land and blows the trumpet and warns the people, [4] then if anyone who hears the sound of the trumpet does not take warning, and the sword comes and takes him away, his blood shall be upon his own head. [5] He heard the sound of the trumpet and did not take warning; his blood shall be upon himself. But if he had taken warning, he would have saved his life. [6] But if the watchman sees the sword coming and does not blow the trumpet, so that the people are not warned, and the sword comes and takes any one of them, that person is taken away in his iniquity, but his blood I will require at the watchman's hand.

The trumpet sound itself is not the sword, but warns of what is to come. So God does not send his wrath without warning people to repent. If they heed the warning they will be saved. Notice again the sounding of the trumpet motif, warning of a great army bringing destruction, which occurs at the end of the bowls of wrath:

Joel 2:1-3, 10-11

Blow a trumpet in Zion; sound an alarm on my holy mountain!
Let all the inhabitants of the land tremble,
for the day of the Lord is coming; it is near,
[2] a day of darkness and gloom,
a day of clouds and thick darkness!
Like blackness there is spread upon the mountains
a great and powerful people;
their like has never been before,
nor will be again after them
through the years of all generations.

[3] Fire devours before them,
and behind them a flame burns.
The land is like the garden of Eden before them,
but behind them a desolate wilderness,
and nothing escapes them. .....
[10] The earth quakes before them;
the heavens tremble.
The sun and the moon are darkened,
and the stars withdraw their shining.
[11] The Lord utters his voice
before his army,
for his camp is exceedingly great;
he who executes his word is powerful.
For the day of the Lord is great and very awesome;
who can endure it?

Is there to be no hope? Can man do anything about the coming destruction? The following verses in Joel give the answer:

Joel 2:12-14
"Yet even now," declares the Lord,
"return to me with all your heart,
with fasting, with weeping, and with mourning;
[13] and rend your hearts and not your garments."
Return to the Lord, your God,
for he is gracious and merciful,
slow to anger, and abounding in steadfast love;
and he relents over disaster.
[14] Who knows whether he will not turn and relent,
and leave a blessing behind him,
a grain offering and a drink offering
for the Lord your God?

The purpose of the sounding of the coming seven trumpets is to call the world to repentance.

17 THE SEVEN TRUMPETS

UP UNTIL THE time of the sixth seal, which was the great earthquake and falling stars, all the previous seals were a result of manmade or caused disasters. Even the high cost of food could likely have been caused by human factors. Beginning with the earthquake, people realize that divine wrath is involved. It becomes even clearer with the trumpets.

In response to the prayers and supplications of the saints on earth, fire from the altar in heaven is thrown to the earth and there are peals of thunder, rumblings, lightning and an earthquake (Rev. 8:1-5). The warning trumpets are not total judgments, they are partial. In chapter 8 of Revelation, the term "a third" is used a dozen times. The bowls of wrath that follow the trumpets will be much more all encompassing.

The First Trumpet

Rev. 8:6-7

Now the seven angels who had the seven trumpets prepared to blow them.

[7] The first angel blew his trumpet, and there followed hail and fire, mixed with blood, and these were thrown upon the earth. And a third of the earth was burned up, and a third of the trees were burned up, and all green grass was burned up.

In June 2011 there were major fires in Canada, southwest USA, Brazil, south central Africa, Russia and northern Australia. Looking at a satellite map of those fires made it not hard to imagine a third of the earth's trees and all the grass being burned up. While many fires are started by the carelessness of some person who throws out a cigarette into dry brush or some camper who doesn't thoroughly put out his camp fire, many fires in forests are started by lightning. The lightning and hail will be so severe, that the blood of many humans and animals will be splattered about as they are struck either by huge hail stones or lightning. The devastation caused by the hail, fire, and blood will be exacerbated by the smoke such fires will produce, to say nothing of the numbers of houses and businesses that will be consumed by these flames.

The Second Trumpet

Rev. 8:8-9

The second angel blew his trumpet, and something like a great mountain, burning with fire, was thrown into the sea, and a third of the sea became blood. [9] A third of the living creatures in the sea died, and a third of the ships were destroyed.

This is very likely a picture of a great volcanic explosion that literally lifts the mountain and throws it into the sea or it could be a large asteroid blazing toward earth as it enters the atmosphere. Whichever, it causes a third of the sea to become blood, killing a third of the sea creatures and destroying a third of the ships.

On a couple of occasions, during visits to Naples, Florida, we were struck with a reddish color in the water, something in the air that caused us to cough and the scene of thousands of dead fish on the beaches. We were told that it was "red tide." According to Wikipedia,

Red tide is a common name for a phenomenon also known as an algal bloom. Some red tides are associated with the production of natural toxins, depletion of dissolved oxygen or other harmful effects, and are generally described as harmful algal blooms. The most conspicuous effects of red tides are the associated wildlife mortalities among marine and coastal species of fish, birds, marine mammals, and other organisms. In the case of Florida red tides, these mortalities are caused by exposure to a potent neurotoxin called brevetoxin which is produced naturally by the marine algae *Karenia brevis*. In high concentrations, its toxin paralyzes the central nervous system of fish so they cannot breathe. Dead fish wash up on Gulf of Mexico beaches. Dense concentrations appear as discolored water, often reddish in color. It is a natural phenomenon, but the exact cause or combination of factors that result in a red tide outbreak are unknown.[76]

A large burning asteroid or lava burning volcano entering the ocean would immediately suck up huge amounts of oxygen in the water, thus killing many sea creatures, in addition to possibly creating the conditions favorable to a "red tide." The impact would create a giant tsunami or tidal wave that would destroy a third of the world's ships. The stench of all those dead sea creatures washing up on shores will be unbearable. The world's commerce and distribution of goods will be irreparably damaged.

The Third Trumpet

Rev. 8:10-11
The third angel blew his trumpet, and a great star fell from heaven, blazing like a torch, and it fell on a third of the rivers and on the springs of water. [11] The name of the star is Wormwood. A third of the waters became wormwood, and many people died from the water, because it had been made bitter.

The world will be able to witness the great star coming to earth, blazing like a torch. Whether it breaks up into many pieces as it enters the atmosphere and thus spreads out to contaminate a third of the rivers and springs or contaminates them in some other way is not clear. The effect is clear, however. Many die because the water is poisoned.

The Fourth Trumpet

Rev. 8:12
The fourth angel blew his trumpet, and a third of the sun was struck, and a third of the moon, and a third of the stars, so that a third of their light might be darkened, and a third of the day might be kept from shining, and likewise a third of the night.

Besides the obvious effect on world temperatures, one can only imagine the increased fear that such phenomena will produce. But while the first four trumpets will cause major worldwide physical problems,

---

[76] "Red Tide," < http://en.wikipedia.org/wiki/Red_tide>

one notes that in each case, only a third has been affected. These are warning shots if you will, urging man to repent of his evil deeds and to embrace the creator God of heaven. The next trumpets introduce a whole new dimension of suffering, caused by a demonic unleashing.

Rev. 8:13
Then I looked, and I heard an eagle crying with a loud voice as it flew directly overhead, "Woe, woe, woe to those who dwell on the earth, at the blasts of the other trumpets that the three angels are about to blow!"

What will have happened up to that point was already a tremendous amount of woe. What could be worse than what the world will have already experienced? What could cause this three times woe?

The Fifth Trumpet – The First Woe

Rev. 9:1-11
And the fifth angel blew his trumpet, and I saw a star fallen from heaven to earth, and he was given the key to the shaft of the bottomless pit. [2] He opened the shaft of the bottomless pit, and from the shaft rose smoke like the smoke of a great furnace, and the sun and the air were darkened with the smoke from the shaft. [3] Then from the smoke came locusts on the earth, and they were given power like the power of scorpions of the earth. [4] They were told not to harm the grass of the earth or any green plant or any tree, but only those people who do not have the seal of God on their foreheads. [5] They were allowed to torment them for five months, but not to kill them, and their torment was like the torment of a scorpion when it stings someone. [6] And in those days people will seek death and will not find it. They will long to die, but death will flee from them.

[7] In appearance the locusts were like horses prepared for battle: on their heads were what looked like crowns of gold; their faces were like human faces, [8] their hair like women's hair, and their teeth like lions' teeth; [9] they had breastplates like breastplates of iron, and the noise of their wings was like the noise of many chariots with horses rushing into battle. [10] They have tails and stings like scorpions, and their power to hurt people for five months is in their tails. [11] They have as king over them the angel of the bottomless pit. His name in Hebrew is Abaddon, and in Greek he is called Apollyon.

The star, or angel in this case, falls from heaven and is given the key to the shaft of the bottomless pit, from which come locusts, quite unlike normal earthly locusts. They have tails and stings like scorpions and are given power to torment people for five months. People will want to die, but not be able to. There is a differentiation, however, in whom they can sting. They will only sting those who do not have the mark of God on their foreheads.

There is some debate as to whether John, writing from a first century perspective, is describing some sort of modern machinery like a helicopter or whether these are demonic creatures unlike anything the world has ever seen before. An argument in favor of it being a description of a modern airborne army is the fact that Revelation 12, the passage describing Satan as the dragon, says this:

Rev. 12:4-5

His tail swept down a third of the stars of heaven and cast them to the earth. And the dragon stood before the woman who was about to give birth, so that when she bore her child he might devour it. [5] She gave birth to a male child, one who is to rule all the nations with a rod of iron, but her child was caught up to God and to his throne,

This is an obvious reference to King Herod's attempt to kill Jesus shortly after his birth when he ordered all the male children two years old and under to be killed in the surrounding area of Bethlehem. It was not an actual dragon, but Satan, using human means to seek to accomplish his designs. The same may be true here.

However, these "locusts" come from the bottomless pit and "they have as king over them the angel of the bottomless pit." Angels do have the ability of taking on human forms, as we saw in the case of the formation of the Nephilim (Gen. 6). What John describes may actually be the forms that these demonic angels coming out of the abyss take – something the world has never seen. We don't have enough information to decide one way or another, but I am sure when it happens, we will all know.

The Sixth Trumpet – The Second Woe

Rev. 9:12-21

The first woe has passed; behold, two woes are still to come.

[13] Then the sixth angel blew his trumpet, and I heard a voice from the four horns of the golden altar before God, [14] saying to the

sixth angel who had the trumpet, "Release the four angels who are bound at the great river Euphrates." [15] So the four angels, who had been prepared for the hour, the day, the month, and the year, were released to kill a third of mankind. [16] The number of mounted troops was twice ten thousand times ten thousand; I heard their number. [17] And this is how I saw the horses in my vision and those who rode them: they wore breastplates the color of fire and of sapphire and of sulfur, and the heads of the horses were like lions' heads, and fire and smoke and sulfur came out of their mouths. [18] By these three plagues a third of mankind was killed, by the fire and smoke and sulfur coming out of their mouths. [19] For the power of the horses is in their mouths and in their tails, for their tails are like serpents with heads, and by means of them they wound.

[20] The rest of mankind, who were not killed by these plagues, did not repent of the works of their hands nor give up worshiping demons and idols of gold and silver and bronze and stone and wood, which cannot see or hear or walk, [21] nor did they repent of their murders or their sorceries or their sexual immorality or their thefts.

Fallen angels, bound at the Euphrates River will be released and somehow, will orchestrate the mobilization of 200 million troops. Again, the question arises as to whether this is a description of humans using modern weapons or whether the fallen angels call up their cohorts who form a non-human army of 200 million. Either way, the result is that a third of the remaining world population is killed. Using today's population figures, that could result in another close to 1.7 billion deaths. The fact that these angels are released at the Euphrates River, which runs through modern Iraq, seems to indicate that the theater of war or the point from which the war will originate will be the Middle East. 2011 and 2012 have seen all kinds of revolutions and unrest in Middle Eastern countries. Iran is involved in a series of war games, testing some of their new missiles. The massacres in Syria has the whole world concerned.

While there are an estimated 1.5 billion Muslims, 1.69 billion Chinese and 1.21 billion Indians, thus making it not inconceivable that a unified Muslim Empire or the Chinese or Indians, or a combination of these countries could field an army of 200 million, logistics will make it a pretty big stretch to be able to field such a human army. During War World II there were only 70 million troops mobilized between all the Allied and Axis forces. If one sees the mobilization of 200 million human troops not localized, but worldwide, it is easier to conceive of this army being human, though directed by evil angelic spirits.

Though the world will be experiencing suffering and carnage never before imagined, people will still not repent of their wicked deeds that are the very cause of the judgment they face. The sins listed are:

1. The works of their hands,

2. Their worship of demons and idols of gold and silver and bronze and stone and wood, which cannot see or hear or walk. As we saw previously, the Bible states that when a person serves an idol, they are worshiping demons (cf. 1 Cor. 10:14-22):

Psalm 106:36-37
They served their idols, which became a snare to them.
They sacrificed their sons and their daughters to the demons;

The first two of the Ten Commandments are:

Exodus 20:3-6
"You shall have no other gods before me.
[4] "You shall not make for yourself a carved image, or any likeness of anything that is in heaven above, or that is in the earth beneath, or that is in the water under the earth. [5] You shall not bow down to them or serve them, for I the Lord your God am a jealous God, visiting the iniquity of the fathers on the children to the third and the fourth generation of those who hate me, [6] but showing steadfast love to thousands of those who love me and keep my commandments.

This is why Evangelical churches are opposed to having images in their churches or statues of Jesus, Mary or the saints. These are idols that the scripture says provoke God to jealousy, and when people pray to them, they, even unknowingly, are praying to demons. This is one of the sins that people will not repent of.

3. Murders,

4. Sorceries – the word in Greek is "pharmakeia" which means pharmacy or medication but also magic arts, or the practice of sorceries or witchcraft. Often drugs are used in these arts. The use of drugs worldwide is well known, as is the practice of sorcery or witchcraft – particularly in Africa and Brazil.

5. Sexual immorality – the word here is "porneia" which means "fornication", but also is the term from which we get pornography. The universal accessibility of pornography through mass media and the internet, the push in schools around the western world to encourage children to consider sexual activity as normative, the rampant sexual activity in Africa and Asia and the militant imposition of the homosexual agenda make this a universal and growing problem.

6. Thefts. Not only is there the common petty theft, but there has been a growing number of white collar thieves who have used Ponzi schemes to bilk people out of billions. There are corporate executives who rob their employees and stock holders out of fortunes. There are governments who purposely devalue currencies which steal people's life savings. There are thieves of every stripe.

None of these disasters will bring people to repentance, however. Is it perhaps because they have not heard the message from God of their need to turn from sin and embrace Jesus as Lord and Savior? We see that God indeed left a witness.

The Third Temple

The thesis has been that Jerusalem is the key to human history because the battle between Satan and God is fought there, with Jesus having dealt the devil a mortal head wound when he died and rose again in order to redeem for God a people from the kingdom of darkness. We have seen that there is still a future battle to be fought over who will be worshiped from the temple in Jerusalem – both God and Satan claim they will be worshiped there. Up to now, however, the seals and trumpets have been silent with regard to Jerusalem. Is it forgotten? Has it been out of the picture?

Just as a novelist with a large cast of characters treats what is happening to them one by one, so here we are taken back to the beginning of this last seven year period of time and are brought up to date on what has been going on in Jerusalem during the time of the seals and trumpets.

Rev. 11:1-3

Then I was given a measuring rod like a staff, and I was told, "Rise and measure the temple of God and the altar and those who worship there, [2] but do not measure the court outside the temple; leave that out, for it is given over to the nations, and they will trample the holy city for forty-two months. [3] And I will grant authority to my two witnesses, and they will prophesy for 1,260 days, clothed in sackcloth."

We have read in Daniel 9 that the Antichrist will make a strong covenant with many for one week. This one week is the 70th week of years, meaning he will make a seven year covenant. Halfway through that 7 year period he will break the treaty, put an end to sacrifice and offering, will commit the "abomination of desolation," repeating what Antiochus Ephiphanes did in 167 B.C., and initiate what Jesus said would be the start of the great tribulation.

Matthew 24:15
"So when you see the abomination of desolation spoken of by the prophet Daniel, standing in the holy place (let the reader understand),

As we have seen, the Apostle Paul tells us that the man of lawlessness will be one

"who opposes and exalts himself against every so-called god or object of worship, so that he takes his seat in the temple of God, proclaiming himself to be God." (2 Thess. 2:4)

The fact that John is told to measure the temple and the altar, though not the outer court which is given over to the nations, and that the Antichrist will sit in the temple of God, stand in the holy place and proclaim himself to be God, means that at some point in time the temple will be rebuilt. While we are not told specifically, it could be that part of the covenant that this Antichrist will make to bring about peace, will be to allow the Jews to build the temple – perhaps in exchange for giving up Jewish authority over Jerusalem, making it a "United Nations World City of Peace" where the followers of the three great monotheistic religions, Jews, Christians and Muslims, can worship together in unity and harmony on the temple mount. That serious Jewish, Muslim and Christian leaders are talking about such a thing shows that it is not some foolish utopian pipe dream in their minds.

Speaker and author Joel Richardson relates in an interview with *World Net Daily* his meeting with Muslim and Jewish leaders:

TROUBLE IN THE HOLY LAND
What? Muslim leader wants Temple rebuilt
Jewish Sanhedrin rabbis unite with Turk on common cause

Posted: August 05, 2009 9:08 pm Eastern

"With the Middle East still in chaos and rumors of war in the air, the idea of rebuilding the Jerusalem Temple on a foundation occupied and administered by Islamic militants might seem fanciful – even preposterous.

But the author of a new book, "The Islamic Antichrist: The Shocking Truth About the Real Nature of the Beast," returned from Turkey recently with news that a prominent Islamic teacher and best-selling author and Jewish Sanhedrin rabbis are hoping to do just that.

In a column penned in WND today, author Joel Richardson reveals the historically unprecedented development.

Adnan Oktar, who uses the pen name of Harun Yahya, is a controversial but highly influential Muslim intellectual and author with more than 65 million of his books in circulation worldwide. Oktar recently met with three representatives from the re-established Jewish Sanhedrin, a group of 71 Orthodox rabbis and scholars from Israel, to discuss how religious Muslims, Jews and Christians can work together on the project.

"The objectives of the alliance include waging a joint intellectual and spiritual battle against the worldwide growing tide of irreligiousness, unbelief and immorality," explains Richardson, who met in Turkey with Oktar. "But even more unusual is their agreement with regard to the need to rebuild the Jewish Temple, a structure that Mr. Oktar refers to as the 'Masjid (Mosque)' or the 'Palace of Solomon.'"

An official statement about the meeting has been published on the Sanhedrin's website. Concluding the statement is the following call:

"Out of a sense of collective responsibility for world peace and for all humanity we have found it timely to call to the World and exclaim that there is a way out for all peoples. It is etched in a call to all humanity: We are all the sons of one father, the descendants of Adam, and all humanity is but a single family. Peace among Nations will be achieved through building the House of G-d, where all peoples will serve as foreseen by King Solomon in his prayers at the dedication of the First Holy Temple. Come let us love and respect one another, and love and honor and hold our heavenly Father in awe. Let us establish a house of prayer in His name in order to worship and serve Him together, for the sake of His great compassion. He surely does not want the blood of His creations spilled, but prefers love and peace among all mankind. We pray to the Almighty Creator, that you hearken to our Call. Together – each according to his or her ability – we shall work towards the building of the House of Prayer for All Nations on the Temple Mount in peace and mutual understanding."

Oktar explained his vision for the rebuilding of Solomon's Temple to Richardson:

"The Palace of Solomon is a historically important palace and rebuilding it would be a very wonderful thing. It is something that any Jew, a Christian or a Muslim should welcome with enthusiasm. Every Muslim, every believer will want to return to those days, to experience those days again and, albeit partially, to bring the beauty of those days back to life."

Oktar added that the Temple of Solomon "will be rebuilt and all believers will worship there in tranquility." During his meeting with the Sanhedrin Rabbis, Oktar expressed his belief that the Temple could be rebuilt in one year:

"It could be done in a year at most. It could be built to the same perfection and beauty. The Torah says it was built in 13 years, if I remember correctly. It could be rebuilt in a year in its perfect form."

Richardson later met with Rabbi Abrahamson and Rabbi Hollander, two of the Sanhedrin representatives who conferred with Oktar. Regarding the rebuilding of the Temple, Rabbi Hollander explained, "The building of the Temple is one of the stages in the Messianic process."

This is not the only similar call to rebuild the Jewish Temple, points out Richardson. Yoav Frankel is an Orthodox Jew who has been deeply involved in interfaith dialogue with Muslims and also envisions a shared Temple Mount. The Interfaith Encounter Association is working on a project called "God's Holy Mountain." It sees the day when the rebuilt Jewish Temple will exist side by side with the Dome of the Rock.

Richardson sees such plans tying in to Barack Obama's calls for internationalizing the city of Jerusalem.

A recent poll showed nearly two-thirds of Israelis back the idea of rebuilding the Temple.

"Meanwhile, the work of the Temple Institute, a group that has openly dedicated itself for years to rebuilding the Jewish Temple goes on," writes Richardson.

It has already created many of the most significant priestly utensils and pieces of furniture necessary for the Temple once it is ready."[77]

So within the first three and a half years of this covenant, it is not unreasonable to expect the third temple to be rebuilt, perhaps even next to the Dome of the Rock which would explain the angel's instruction to John to not measure the court outside the temple; "leave that out, for it is given over to the nations, and they will trample the holy city for forty-two months." The fact that he is told to measure the altar as well as the worshipers in the temple – implying a separation between these worshipers and the nations or Gentiles outside, seems to indicate that this happens before the Antichrist proclaims himself to be God in the temple, which happens three and a half years or forty-two months into the last seven year period of time. At the point of the abomination of desolation, not just the outside courts are given over to the Gentiles, but also the inside of the temple itself.

The Two Witnesses

Not only will the temple be rebuilt, but God will have two extraordinary witnesses in Jerusalem who will call people to repentance and faith.

Rev. 11:3-14

And I will grant authority to my two witnesses, and they will prophesy for 1,260 days, clothed in sackcloth."

[4] These are the two olive trees and the two lampstands that stand before the Lord of the earth. [5] And if anyone would harm them, fire pours from their mouth and consumes their foes. If anyone would harm them, this is how he is doomed to be killed. [6] They have the power to shut the sky, that no rain may fall during the days of their prophesying, and they have power over the waters to turn them into blood and to strike the earth with every kind of plague, as often as they desire. [7] And when they have finished their testimony, the beast that rises from the bottomless pit will make war on them and conquer them and kill them, [8] and their dead bodies will lie in the street of the great city that symbolically is called Sodom and Egypt,

---

[77] "Trouble in the Holy Land," World Net Daily, Aug. 5, 2009, <http://www.wnd.com/index.php?fa=PAGE.view&pageId=105938>

where their Lord was crucified. [9] For three and a half days some from the peoples and tribes and languages and nations will gaze at their dead bodies and refuse to let them be placed in a tomb, [10] and those who dwell on the earth will rejoice over them and make merry and exchange presents, because these two prophets had been a torment to those who dwell on the earth. [11] But after the three and a half days a breath of life from God entered them, and they stood up on their feet, and great fear fell on those who saw them. [12] Then they heard a loud voice from heaven saying to them, "Come up here!" And they went up to heaven in a cloud, and their enemies watched them. [13] And at that hour there was a great earthquake, and a tenth of the city fell. Seven thousand people were killed in the earthquake, and the rest were terrified and gave glory to the God of heaven.

[14] The second woe has passed; behold, the third woe is soon to come.

The reference in verse 4 to these two witnesses being the two olive trees and the two lampstands that stand before the Lord of the earth comes from the Old Testament prophet of Zechariah. He had a vision and asks what the elements of the vision are:

Zech. 4:11-14

Then I said to him, "What are these two olive trees on the right and the left of the lampstand?" .... [13] He said to me, "Do you not know what these are?" I said, "No, my lord." [14] Then he said, "These are the two anointed ones who stand by the Lord of the whole earth."

The context was the rebuilding of the second temple in Jerusalem, and Zerubbabel the governor, and Joshua the high priest, had been charged by the prophet Haggai to rebuild. In this context is the famous verse,

Zech. 4:6

Then he said to me, "This is the word of the Lord to Zerubbabel: Not by might, nor by power, but by my Spirit, says the Lord of hosts.

The rebuilding was not going to be by human power and might, but by the Spirit of God. So too, these two witnesses in Revelation may be involved in the rebuilding of the third temple.

While we are not told who these witnesses are, most believe they will be either Enoch and Elijah or Moses and Elijah. Support for Enoch and Elijah is that neither of them died; they were caught up into heaven and the Bible says that it is appointed for man to die once and after that comes the judgment (Heb. 9:27). So when the Antichrist kills them, it will be their first and only death. In support for Moses and Elijah, the miracles mentioned were the same kind of miracles that both Moses and Elijah performed, including the fact that Elijah prayed that it not rain and it did not rain for three and a half years (James 5:17) – the same as this time period; they were both on the Mount of Transfiguration with Jesus (Mt. 17:1-13) and the last words of the Septuagint and Christian arrangements of the Old Testament were these:

Malachi 4:4-6

"Remember the law of my servant **Moses**, the statutes and rules that I commanded him at Horeb for all Israel.

[5] "Behold, I will send you **Elijah** the prophet before the great and awesome day of the Lord comes. [6] And he will turn the hearts of fathers to their children and the hearts of children to their fathers, lest I come and strike the land with a decree of utter destruction."

We see the timing and God's power in their protection. It is only when they have finished their testimony that the beast who comes from the Abyss is able to kill them. People will be so happy with their death that they will give them the greatest insult – that of not letting their bodies be buried. In Muslim Sharia law, a person is to be buried as soon as possible, preferably before sunset of the day they died. The text says, "For three and a half days some from the peoples and tribes and languages and nations will gaze at their dead bodies and refuse to let them be placed in a tomb," This prophesy is understandable today, in the context of worldwide television, but must have been difficult for people to imagine how it could be 1900 years ago.

One can only imagine the impact on the world when "after the three and a half days a breath of life from God entered them, and they stood up on their feet, and great fear fell on those who saw them. [12] Then they heard a loud voice from heaven saying to them, "Come up here!" And they went up to heaven in a cloud, and their enemies watched them."

TV cameras will be trained on them 24 hours a day and the world will see this event, but instead of it convincing the world that the message of these men of God should be believed as confirmed by their miracles, resurrection, voice from heaven and visible ascension into heaven, the majority of the earth will not respond, but rather turn to someone else who as we will see in the next chapter also rises from the dead.

While many believe these two will be on the scene for the last half of the 7 year period – the time of the great tribulation, the context seems to indicate that they minister in the first half of the last 7 years. In this passage, we have the first of 36 references to the "Beast" in the book of Revelation, who is identified as the Antichrist in chapter 17 (vs. 8-14). Also, following their death, resurrection and ascent to heaven we are told, [14] "The second woe has passed; behold, the third woe is soon to come." The third woe includes the Antichrist's coming to worldwide power – something that up to now has not yet happened. In fact, I believe that "the Beast's" success in killing them, - something which no one else had been able to do - will be part of what catapults him into worldwide acclaim.

The result of their witness, resurrection, ascension and earthquake does cause many in the city to react differently than those unrepentant who were also in terror from the other plagues. These gave glory to the God of heaven.

"The second woe has passed; behold, the third woe is soon to come."

18 THE SEVENTH TRUMPET: THE THIRD WOE

THIS TRUMPET IS dealt with separately because of the significant events that take place during this trumpet call.

There is an interlude between the sixth and seventh trumpets. Revelation 10 tells of seven thunders that sound and as John is about to write what they had said, he is instructed not to write it down. They are to be sealed up. The angel then swears to him that "there would be no more delay, [7] but that in the days of the trumpet call to be sounded by the seventh angel, the mystery of God would be fulfilled, just as he announced to his servants the prophets."(Rev. 10:6-7)

A very important detail is given in this passage. The trumpet call is not just a moment in time. It says, "in the ***days*** of the trumpet call to be sounded by the seventh angel …." There are numerous things that happen during the "days" of the seventh trumpet as we will see.

The obvious question arises from the text above. What is "the mystery of God" that will be revealed in the days of the seventh trumpet?

Mystery of God

There are a couple of passages that use the term "mystery" in a yet future sense.

Romans 11:25-27

Lest you be wise in your own conceits, I want you to understand this **mystery**, brothers: a partial hardening has come upon Israel, until the fullness of the Gentiles has come in. [26] And in this way all Israel will be saved, as it is written,

"The Deliverer will come from Zion,
he will banish ungodliness from Jacob";
[27] "and this will be my covenant with them
when I take away their sins."

Could it be that the mystery that will be fulfilled during the sounding of the seventh trumpet will be the salvation of all Israel? The context certainly refers to a time yet future, when "the fullness of the Gentiles has come in". It also speaks of the Messiah's coming from Zion.

There are two other mysteries mentioned that have yet to be fulfilled:

Ephes. 1:7-10

In him [Christ] we have redemption through his blood, the forgiveness of our trespasses, according to the riches of his grace, [8] which he lavished upon us, in all wisdom and insight

[9] making known to us the **mystery** of his will, according to his purpose, which he set forth in Christ [10] as a plan for the fullness of time, to unite all things in him, things in heaven and things on earth.

The mystery spoken of here is God's plan to unite all things in Christ – things in heaven and things on earth. There is a time frame – "the fullness of time". At the present time, Christ is exalted and reigning in the heavenly realm:

Ephes. 1:19-23

"and what is the immeasurable greatness of his power toward us who believe, according to the working of his great might [20] that he worked in Christ when he raised him from the dead and seated him at his right hand in the heavenly places, [21] far above all rule and authority and power and dominion, and above every name that is named, not only in this age but also in the one to come. [22] And he put all things under his feet and gave him as head over all things to the church, [23] which is his body, the fullness of him who fills all in all."

There is the present age at which time Christ is seated at God's right hand in the heavenly places, but there will be an age to come when he will unite his rule in heaven with his rule on earth at which point every knee will bow and proclaim him to be Lord:

Philip. 2:8-11
"he [Christ] humbled himself by becoming obedient to the point of death, even death on a cross. [9] Therefore God has highly exalted him and bestowed on him the name that is above every name, [10] so that at the name of Jesus every knee should bow, in heaven and on earth and under the earth, [11] and every tongue confess that Jesus Christ is Lord, to the glory of God the Father."

Is this the mystery to be fulfilled during the days of the seventh trumpet call – that of uniting all things in heaven and earth under the Lordship of Christ? It is the view of this author that what is referred to in the passage in Ephesians and Philippians cited above is not what is being referred to in Revelation 10:7. The reason is that these passages seem to refer to an event following the thousand year reign of Jesus on earth. Note this passage:

1 Cor. 15:22-26
"For as in Adam all die, so also in Christ shall all be made alive. [23] But each in his own order: Christ the firstfruits, then at his coming those who belong to Christ. [24] Then comes the end, when he delivers the kingdom to God the Father after destroying every rule and every authority and power. [25] For he must reign until he has put all his enemies under his feet. [26] The last enemy to be destroyed is death."

The last enemy – death – will not be destroyed, nor will Christ destroy every rule, authority and power until the end of the millennial reign when Satan is briefly released to deceive the nations (Rev. 20:7-10).

I believe the mystery referred to in Rev. 10:7 at the seventh trumpet is the one stated below which we alluded to in an earlier chapter:

1 Cor. 15:50-53
"I tell you this, brothers: flesh and blood cannot inherit the kingdom of God, nor does the perishable inherit the imperishable. [51] Behold! I tell you a **mystery**. We shall not all sleep, but we shall all be changed, [52] in a moment, in the twinkling of an eye, **at the last trumpet**. For the trumpet will sound, and the dead will be raised imperishable, and we shall be changed. [53] For this perishable body

must put on the imperishable, and this mortal body must put on immortality."

This is further confirmed by what follows the death and ascension of the two witnesses:

Rev. 11:14-19
"The second woe has passed; behold, the third woe is soon to come.

[15] Then the seventh angel blew his trumpet, and there were loud voices in heaven, saying, "The kingdom of the world has become the kingdom of our Lord and of his Christ, and he shall reign forever and ever." [16] And the twenty-four elders who sit on their thrones before God fell on their faces and worshiped God, [17] saying,

"We give thanks to you, Lord God Almighty,
who is and who was,
for you have taken your great power
and begun to reign.
[18] The nations raged,
but your wrath came,
and the time for the dead to be judged,
and for rewarding your servants, the prophets and saints,
and those who fear your name,
both small and great,
and for destroying the destroyers of the earth."

[19] Then God's temple in heaven was opened, and the ark of his covenant was seen within his temple. There were flashes of lightning, rumblings, peals of thunder, an earthquake, and heavy hail."

That all these events above do not happen the instant that the trumpet is blown is clear by the fact that the third woe still has not yet been revealed. This further confirms that the "days of the trumpet to be sounded by the seventh angel" are exactly that – a period of time – and not a moment in time. In fact, I believe it will be a period of at least three and a half years.

In examining the various rapture viewpoints, we stated that one view is that it will occur at the mid-tribulation point. This view erroneously defines the great tribulation as being a seven year period of time and so the idea is that it will occur at the midway point. The fact that the seventh trumpet is sounded at about the midway point would seem to support this position. There is another factor that makes this position attractive.

It is during the seventh trumpet that the great tribulation begins. The seventh trumpet also introduces the seven bowls of the wrath of God:

Rev. 15:1
Then I saw another sign in heaven, great and amazing, seven angels with seven plagues, which are the last, for with them the wrath of God is finished.

Rev. 16:1
Then I heard a loud voice from the temple telling the seven angels, "Go and pour out on the earth the seven bowls of the wrath of God."

Could it be that the believers in Christ are raptured at this time, prior to the outpouring of wrath on the earth and prior to the great tribulation? Those holding the mid-tribulation rapture view would like to think that is the case. We shall see if the scripture supports that view as we go along.

The Third Woe

Rev. 8:13
Then I looked, and I heard an eagle crying with a loud voice as it flew directly overhead, "Woe, woe, woe to those who dwell on the earth, at the blasts of the other trumpets that the three angels are about to blow!"

After the sounding of the fifth trumpet it says:

Rev. 9:12
The first woe has passed; behold, two woes are still to come.

After the sixth trumpet, the measuring of the temple and the two witnesses we read:

Rev. 11:14-15

The second woe has passed; behold, the third woe is soon to come. [15] Then the seventh angel blew his trumpet, ..."

The first two woes are clearly identified with the fifth and sixth trumpets and the third woe is clearly associated with the seventh trumpet, but so much happens during the seventh trumpet, what could it be? Could the third woe be the whole outpouring of the seven bowls of wrath?

The very next chapter tells us what the third woe is. Chapter 12 of Revelation gives us a compressed view of history, from the time of Satan's rebellion to the time of Christ's second coming. It is important to know because it sets the stage for the third woe.

Rev. 12:1-6

And a great sign appeared in heaven: a woman clothed with the sun, with the moon under her feet, and on her head a crown of twelve stars. [2] She was pregnant and was crying out in birth pains and the agony of giving birth. [3] And another sign appeared in heaven: behold, a great red dragon, with seven heads and ten horns, and on his heads seven diadems. [4] His tail swept down a third of the stars of heaven and cast them to the earth. And the dragon stood before the woman who was about to give birth, so that when she bore her child he might devour it. [5] She gave birth to a male child, one who is to rule all the nations with a rod of iron, but her child was caught up to God and to his throne, [6] and the woman fled into the wilderness, where she has a place prepared by God, in which she is to be nourished for 1,260 days.

A brief explanation of the imagery in this passage is in order. The woman seems to be Israel as personified by Mary. The reason she is not Mary per se is that vs. 6 pictures the woman as fleeing into the wilderness where God will nourish her for 1260 days. The context that follows shows that this is as yet a future event. It is the three and a half year period of the great tribulation introduced by the seventh trumpet. There will be those Jews who will heed Jesus' warning that when they see the abomination of desolation, that they should immediately flee Judah and Jerusalem into the wilderness because it will initiate a time of tribulation such as the world has never seen.

The red dragon, as the following verses will show, is the devil. Sometime either before or shortly after creation, he swept a third of the angels with him in the rebellion against God and they have been his agents on earth ever since. The child that is born refers to Jesus, who will rule the nations with a rod of iron. The dragon, or Satan, seeks to devour the child as soon as it is born, which is what the devil did through King Herod when he ordered all the male children in Bethlehem two years old and younger to be killed. The child being caught up to heaven and to his throne refers to Christ's ascension to heaven after his earthly ministry.

At the risk of interrupting the flow of thought regarding the third woe, let me comment on the astrological picture presented in this text. Genesis 1:14 tells us that God created the lights in the sky to "be for signs and for seasons, and for days and years …" The above text speaks of two signs appearing in heaven, one of a woman and the other of a dragon with seven heads (Rev. 12:1, 3).

F.A. Larson has done an excellent study and DVD presentation on the astrological phenomena present at the time of Christ's birth entitled, "The Star of Bethlehem".[78] He posits that what drew the Magi to travel from Persia to Israel in search of the baby, born King of the Jews (Mt. 2) was an alignment of Jupiter, planet of Kings, along with Venus, the Mother planet in the constellation of Virgo, the virgin maiden, following close behind the constellation of Leo, the lion made up of 12 stars (Jesus was of the royal tribe of Judah associated with the lion – Gen. 49:8-12). This alignment with the sun and the moon at Virgo's feet took place at the time of Rosh Hashana, the Feast of Trumpets, or the Jewish New Year which corresponds to our September, in 3 BC. Larson believes that was the day of Jesus' conception. The birth, he believes, took place on June 17, 2 BC when Jupiter and Venus briefly came together to form the brightest "star" in the sky, and most likely the "star" that the Magi had seen. He believes that another phenomenon took place on December 25, 2 BC which was when Jupiter seemed to stop in the sky as it went into retrograde. That, he believes was the day the Magi visited Jesus in Bethlehem.

The text speaks of a second sign that appeared in heaven – a great red dragon with seven heads. At this time in 3-2 BC, the constellation Hydra, the seven-headed water serpent, was at the side of Virgo. It seems that God has written history in the skies. In fact, Psalm 19 states:

---

[78] http://bethlehemstar.com/

Psalm 19:1-4
To the choirmaster. A Psalm of David.
The heavens declare the glory of God,
and the sky above proclaims his handiwork.
[2] Day to day pours out speech,
and night to night reveals knowledge.
[3] There is no speech, nor are there words,
whose voice is not heard.
[4] Their measuring line goes out through all the earth,
and their words to the end of the world.

The words and signs in the sky were what spoke to the non-Jewish Magi and told them of the King who was being born. Now, to return to the third woe.

The following verses introduce a scene yet future or recently fulfilled for reasons I will show:

Rev. 12:7-17
Now war arose in heaven, Michael and his angels fighting against the dragon. And the dragon and his angels fought back, [8] but he was defeated and there was no longer any place for them in heaven. [9] And the great dragon was thrown down, that ancient serpent, who is called the devil and Satan, the deceiver of the whole world— he was thrown down to the earth, and his angels were thrown down with him. [10] And I heard a loud voice in heaven, saying, "Now the salvation and the power and the kingdom of our God and the authority of his Christ have come, for the accuser of our brothers has been thrown down, who accuses them day and night before our God. [11] And they have conquered him by the blood of the Lamb and by the word of their testimony, for they loved not their lives even unto death. [12] Therefore, rejoice, O heavens and you who dwell in them! **But woe to you**, O earth and sea, for the devil has come down to you in great wrath, because he knows that his time is short!"

[13] And when the dragon saw that he had been thrown down to the earth, he pursued the woman who had given birth to the male child. [14] But the woman was given the two wings of the great eagle so that she might fly from the serpent into the wilderness, to the place where she is to be nourished for **a time, and times, and half a time.** [15] The serpent poured water like a river out of his mouth after the woman, to sweep her away with a flood. [16] But the earth came to

the help of the woman, and the earth opened its mouth and swallowed the river that the dragon had poured from his mouth. [17] Then the dragon became furious with the woman and went off to make war on the rest of her offspring, on those who keep the commandments of God and hold to the testimony of Jesus.

The third woe is identified as the devil and his angels being cast down to earth and the wrath that he will unleash because he knows his time is short.

Some theologians believe that Satan was cast out of heaven when Jesus died and rose from the dead. However Daniel, in the Old Testament, along with another clue in Paul's writings, seem to corroborate this event as taking place sometime prior to the last half of the seven year period.

Daniel 11:44-12:1

But news from the east and the north shall alarm him, and he shall go out with great fury to destroy and devote many to destruction. [45] And he shall pitch his palatial tents between the sea and the glorious holy mountain. Yet he shall come to his end, with none to help him.

"At that time shall arise **Michael**, the great prince who has charge of your people. And there shall be a time of trouble, such as never has been since there was a nation till that time. But at that time your people shall be delivered, everyone whose name shall be found written in the book.

Daniel 12:6-7

And someone said to the man clothed in linen, who was above the waters of the stream, "How long shall it be till the end of these wonders?" [7] And I heard the man clothed in linen, who was above the waters of the stream; he raised his right hand and his left hand toward heaven and swore by him who lives forever that it would be for **a time, times, and half a time**, and that when the shattering of the power of the holy people comes to an end all these things would be finished.

At the time that this figure mentioned in Daniel 11 is living in Israel, whom we have identified as the Antichrist, Michael will arise. It will be followed by a time of trouble such as Israel has never seen, but those Jews (your people – Daniel's people) whose names are written in the book (of life) will be delivered. Those will be the ones who flee to the wilderness, I believe. A time frame is given – "a time, times and a half a time" which we have seen refers to three and a half years, or 1260 days or 42 months.

This text seems to be speaking of the same event mentioned in Revelation where Michael, fights against Satan and his angels and casts him down to the earth which then begins the devil's fury which will be for a period of "a time, times and a half a time."

Paul in his letter to the Thessalonians refers to someone who is restraining the man of lawlessness from being revealed. While this is personal conjecture, I believe the restrainer is Michael, the angel who protects the people of Israel. When he is removed, the Antichrist is revealed.

2 Thess. 2:3-10

Let no one deceive you in any way. For that day will not come, unless the rebellion comes first, and the man of lawlessness is revealed, the son of destruction, [4] who opposes and exalts himself against every so-called god or object of worship, so that he takes his seat in the temple of God, proclaiming himself to be God. [5] Do you not remember that when I was still with you I told you these things? [6] And you know what is restraining him now so that he may be revealed in his time. [7] For the mystery of lawlessness is already at work. Only he who now restrains it will do so until he is out of the way. [8] And then the lawless one will be revealed, whom the Lord Jesus will kill with the breath of his mouth and bring to nothing by the appearance of his coming. [9] The coming of the lawless one is by the activity of Satan with all power and false signs and wonders, [10] and with all wicked deception for those who are perishing, because they refused to love the truth and so be saved.

The Dragon's Wrath Revealed

What does Satan do once he is thrown down to the earth? It says he pursues the woman who had given birth to the male child. That means he will pursue the Jewish people. There will be, as said before, a remnant of Jews who will escape into the wilderness and just as Satan tried to kill Jesus through Herod, so he will try to kill this remnant through a flood, but the earth will open its mouth and the river that is sent to sweep the people away will be swallowed up by the earth.

When I was growing up, we spent a few days in Arizona and I remember playing on one side of a dry river bed and my friend playing on the other side. It was a clear day, but all of a sudden, a wall of water came rushing down the river bed. Apparently, there had been rain up in the mountains. There was no time for me to get across. It was very scary for me as I had no idea how I was going to get on the other side where civilization was. Fortunately, a mile or so downstream there was a bridge and I was able to walk to it and cross. Indeed, in 2011 we saw a terrible video of a family in India that was swept over some waterfalls to their death when a wall of water came rushing down the stream and they were caught in the middle before they could get to the side. The wilderness where these Jews will escape to will have canyons and it could be Satan will have a torrent of water come to sweep them away, but his plan will be thwarted.

This will cause him to become furious with the Jews and he will go off to make war on the rest of their offspring – those who keep the commandments of God and hold to the testimony of Jesus - in other words, the Christians.

The following is pure speculation on my part, but I believe plausible speculation. The Mayan Calendar predicted the end of an age taking place at the end of the 13th b'ak'tun of the Mayan Long Count Calendar which took place on December 21, 2012. In simple terms, the precession of the Earth's axis through one circuit of the twelve constellations of the Zodiac takes approximately 26,000 years and December 21, 2012 marked the end of this rotation. This did not mark the end for them, rather it marked the beginning of an age when their feathered serpent god, Kukulkán or known as Quetzalcoatl to the Aztecs, would return to earth.

February 2012 to 2013 is known as the Year of the Dragon in China. More specifically, the Water Dragon. Could it be possible that 2012 was the time when the war with Michael and his angels took place in the heavens with Satan and his angels, and the dragon, that ancient serpent was cast down to earth with his angels? The text in Revelation 12 talks about the serpent pouring water out of his mouth to sweep away the woman, who flees to the wilderness. Could all this be written for us in the stars as Hydra, the seven headed water serpent is there ready to devour Virgo, the woman, not only when Jesus was born, but also again, at the time when the end is at hand?

There was no visible catastrophic event that took place on December 21, 2012, but just as most human beings were oblivious to the greatest event in history, God taking on human form, even though the event was written in the skies, so possibly another momentous event has taken place with most all of us being completely unaware of its occurrence.

If this speculation on my part is true, then we are told, "But woe to you, O earth and sea, for the devil has come down to you in great wrath, because he knows that his time is short!"

Satan's Agent

It is at this point in the book of Revelation that the final Antichrist is revealed. He was mentioned briefly in the context of the two witnesses, but it is here, immediately following Satan's being cast out of heaven and coming to earth with great wrath, that we see this person introduced.

We have seen in the past that the way Satan and God operate is through people. Satan has used world leaders and empires down through the ages to do his bidding in seeking to destroy the people of God. His ultimate instrument is what has been known as the Antichrist. In the chapter on the Antichrist, we noted the similarities of the description of Satan, the dragon and the Antichrist, the Beast (Rev. 12:3; 13:1-2):

Rev. 13:2

And the beast that I saw was like a leopard; its feet were like a bear's, and its mouth was like a lion's mouth. And to it the dragon gave his power and his throne and great authority.

There is an event that draws everyone's attention to this beast and causes all to marvel:

Rev. 13:3-4

One of its heads seemed to have a mortal wound, but its mortal wound was healed, and the whole earth marveled as they followed the beast. [4] And they worshiped the dragon, for he had given his authority to the beast, and they worshiped the beast, saying, "Who is like the beast, and who can fight against it?"

We have spoken before about the fact that the "beast" may be both an empire and a person. He is said to have ten horns that have crowns – referring to a ten nation or ten region alliance. We have also spoken about the possibility of this resurrection referring to the resurrection of the Islamic Empire with the reestablished Caliphate as well as the personal resurrection of the Antichrist.

Picture the following possible scenario. I offer a caveat. While all that the scriptures say is true, the details and order of certain events I present in this scenario are purely speculation, though I believe a very possible speculation.

The two witnesses have been tormenting the earth for three and a half years, preaching repentance and judgment – not popular messages. They are sending plagues on the earth and withholding rain. Anyone who would try to harm them would be consumed by fire coming out of their mouths. Finally, they are killed by this beast:

Rev. 11:7

And when they have finished their testimony, the beast that **rises from the bottomless pit** will make war on them and conquer them and kill them,

Is this the same beast – the Antichrist we are talking about in Chapter 13? Yes. Chapter 17 clarifies:

Rev. 17:7-8

But the angel said to me, "Why do you marvel? I will tell you the mystery of the woman, and of the beast with seven heads and ten horns that carries her. [8] The beast that you saw was, and is not, and is about **to rise from the bottomless pit** and go to destruction. And the dwellers on earth whose names have not been written in the book of life from the foundation of the world will marvel to see the beast, because it was and is not and is to come.

Rev. 17:11-14

As for the beast that was and is not, it is an eighth but it belongs to the seven, and it goes to destruction. [12] And the ten horns that you saw are ten kings who have not yet received royal power, but they are to receive authority as kings for one hour, together with the beast. [13] These are of one mind and hand over their power and authority to the beast. [14] They will make war on the Lamb, and the Lamb will conquer them, for he is Lord of lords and King of kings, and those with him are called and chosen and faithful."

While this Antichrist has been on the scene for at least three and a half years, people do not know, follow or worship him in the first half of the last seven year period. It is he who makes the covenant with many, but does not have the worldwide following and worship until midway through those seven years, when Satan, being cast down from heaven, empowers him, perhaps as no one in history up to this time has been empowered before. He most likely becomes fully possessed by Satan or is Satan personified. Remember, the Bible says that Satan presents himself as an angel of light. He will not be one who has an evil face with horns, pitchfork and tail.

Two things will catapult him to worldwide fame. While the order of events is not clear, you can imagine what will happen. The two witnesses perform with miraculous powers evident to the whole world. No one can kill them. They say they are messengers of God. Then, this world renown leader, who brokered a peace treaty with Israel and the Muslim world by permitting Israel to build their temple on the temple mount, forces the Jews to cease offering sacrifices in the temple. This would occur 1290 days before Christ's return:

Daniel 12:11

And from the time that the regular burnt offering is taken away and the abomination that makes desolate is set up, there shall be 1,290 days.

In the thirty days following the cessation of the sacrifices, perhaps there is an assassination attempt by a zealous Jew on this leader. He receives a mortal head wound and appears to be dead.

He then comes back to life and 30 days after the sacrifices had been stopped, he succeeds in killing the two witnesses – something no one else has been able to do. This he does 1260 days or three and a half years after these two witnesses had begun their ministry. With these hated men dead and their bodies left in the streets as a trophy of his triumph over them, this "beast" goes to the temple that very day and proclaims himself to be God.

2 Thess. 2:4

who opposes and exalts himself against every so-called god or object of worship, so that he takes his seat in the temple of God, proclaiming himself to be God.

The world goes wild in celebration with the two witnesses finally being killed and everyone marvels at this man who was able to kill them.

2 Thess. 2:9-11

"The coming of the lawless one is by the activity of Satan with all power and false signs and wonders, [10] and with all wicked deception for those who are perishing, because they refused to love the truth and so be saved. [11] Therefore God sends them a strong delusion, so that they may believe what is false,"

The fact that he seemed to be raised from the dead and all of a sudden has miraculous powers, makes the world readily believe and worship him.

Rev. 13:3-4
One of its heads seemed to have a mortal wound, but its mortal wound was healed, and the whole earth marveled as they followed the beast. [4] And they worshiped the dragon, for he had given his authority to the beast, and they worshiped the beast, saying, "Who is like the beast, and who can fight against it?"

The Apostasy (a.k.a. The Rebellion)

This worldwide acclaim of the beast will be what the Bible calls the rebellion or apostasy. His outrageous claims will be believed.

Rev. 13:5-6
And the beast was given a mouth uttering haughty and blasphemous words, and it was allowed to exercise authority for forty-two months. [6] It opened its mouth to utter blasphemies against God, blaspheming his name and his dwelling, that is, those who dwell in heaven.

This entering the temple and proclaiming himself to be God, will be accepted by most people. In fact, Jesus said

Matthew 24:24
"For false christs and false prophets will arise and perform great signs and wonders, so as to lead astray, if possible, even the elect."

Millions of people claiming to be Christians will embrace him as the Christ. Many Jews likewise will see him as their Messiah and more than a billion Muslims will see him as their Mahdi. The fact that what he says denies the tenants of the Christian faith will be overlooked, much as those today disregard what the Bible says about homosexuality and a host of other teachings.

There will be a great rebellion or falling away from the Christian faith at this time.

2 Thess. 2:1-3

Now concerning the coming of our Lord Jesus Christ and our being gathered together to him, we ask you, brothers, [2] not to be quickly shaken in mind or alarmed, either by a spirit or a spoken word, or a letter seeming to be from us, to the effect that the day of the Lord has come. [3] Let no one deceive you in any way. For that day will not come, unless the rebellion comes first, and the man of lawlessness is revealed, the son of destruction,

His taking his seat in the temple, proclaiming himself to be God will be what is called by Daniel and Jesus "the abomination of desolation" and marks the beginning of the great tribulation. Anyone who has heard or read what Jesus said and is living in Israel will need to flee immediately.

Matthew 24:15-22

"So when you see the abomination of desolation spoken of by the prophet Daniel, standing in the holy place (let the reader understand), [16] then let those who are in Judea flee to the mountains. [17] Let the one who is on the housetop not go down to take what is in his house, [18] and let the one who is in the field not turn back to take his cloak. [19] And alas for women who are pregnant and for those who are nursing infants in those days! [20] Pray that your flight may not be in winter or on a Sabbath. [21] For then there will be great tribulation, such as has not been from the beginning of the world until now, no, and never will be. [22] And if those days had not been cut short, no human being would be saved. But for the sake of the elect those days will be cut short.

This will begin the final three and a half year period of great tribulation. Those Jews who manage to escape to the wilderness will be protected from Satan's pursuit of them as we saw earlier and they will be nourished there in the desert for that three and a half year period of time (Rev. 12:13-16).

This Antichrist will not be operating alone. The third member of this unholy trinity is called the false prophet, who will join him and will likewise have miraculous powers:

Rev. 16:13-14

"And I saw, coming out of the mouth of the dragon and out of the mouth of the beast and out of the mouth of the false prophet, three unclean spirits like frogs. [14] For they are demonic spirits, performing signs ...."

Rev. 13:11-18
Then I saw another beast rising out of the earth. It had two horns like a lamb and it spoke like a dragon. [12] It exercises all the authority of the first beast in its presence, and makes the earth and its inhabitants worship the first beast, whose mortal wound was healed. [13] It performs great signs, even making fire come down from heaven to earth in front of people, [14] and by the signs that it is allowed to work in the presence of the beast it deceives those who dwell on earth, telling them to make an image for the beast that was wounded by the sword and yet lived. [15] And it was allowed to give breath to the image of the beast, so that the image of the beast might even speak and might cause those who would not worship the image of the beast to be slain. [16] Also it causes all, both small and great, both rich and poor, both free and slave, to be marked on the right hand or the forehead, [17] so that no one can buy or sell unless he has the mark, that is, the name of the beast or the number of its name. [18] This calls for wisdom: let the one who has understanding calculate the number of the beast, for it is the number of a man, and his number is 666.

The Culmination of Satan's Objective

As we have seen over and over in this book, Satan has had his sight set on being worshiped on Mt. Zion. Remember the texts:

Isaiah 14:13-14 (NIV)
13 You said in your heart, "I will ascend to heaven; I will raise my throne above the stars of God; I will sit enthroned on the mount of assembly, on the utmost heights of the sacred mountain. [Zaphon] 14 I will ascend above the tops of the clouds; I will make myself like the Most High."

Psalm 48:1-2 (NIV)
1 Great is the Lord, and most worthy of praise, in the city of our God, his holy mountain.
2 It is beautiful in its loftiness, the joy of the whole earth. Like the utmost heights of Zaphon is Mount Zion, the city of the Great King.

There is no mistaking his objective. Just as those who worship Jesus Christ, God's Son, also worship God the Father, so those who worship the beast, the Antichrist, also worship Satan.

The job of the false prophet will be to make everyone on earth worship the beast.

Like Mohammed who would behead those who refused to say the *shahada*, acknowledging Allah as God and he as Allah's prophet, or use economic coercion by forcing non-Muslims to pay the *Jizya* tax, so the Antichrist will make a strong incentive for people to worship him. Though not completely clear, the following taken from the passage mentioned in Revelation 13 seems to imply that the false prophet will call down fire from heaven to consume those who refuse to worship the beast. "It exercises all the authority of the first beast in its presence, and makes the earth and its inhabitants worship the first beast, whose mortal wound was healed. [13] It performs great signs, even making fire come down from heaven to earth in front of people,"

Certainly the end result of death is what the image of the beast calls for when people refuse to worship.

> "[14] and by the signs that it is allowed to work in the presence of the beast it deceives those who dwell on earth, telling them to make an image for the beast that was wounded by the sword and yet lived. [15] And it was allowed to give breath to the image of the beast, so that the image of the beast might even speak and might cause those who would not worship the image of the beast to be slain." (Rev. 13:14-15)

Whether there will be only one image, perhaps located in the temple, or images set up all over the world before which people will have to worship is not stated. The worldwide economic incentive is stated. Unless people have the mark of the beast, signifying their allegiance and worship of him, they will not be able to buy or sell.

Today, with almost universal reliance on the banking and credit card system, it is easy to envision this scenario. Without the mark, people's ATM and credit cards will be blocked. Banks will not give them cash. People's checking and savings accounts and safety deposit boxes will be seized or frozen, just as they are able to do today with the accounts of some public heads of state whom the world community has judged to be worthy of being ousted and pursued.

As we have mentioned, most of the world will be deceived and will willingly worship the Antichrist and happily receive his mark. For those who are not deceived however, when confronted with the choice of either having their head cut off or receiving the mark and worshiping the beast, they will choose to say the words and receive the mark. Many will probably think, "what difference does it make? I don't really believe in this man, but if it will make the establishment happy and save my life and allow me to do business and carry on with my life normally, it doesn't matter what I say."

While most of the people from other religions will go along with it, the number one target for this unholy trinity – the dragon, the beast and the false prophet – will be Christians and God-fearing Jews. They will resist and there will be a war against them.

Rev. 13:7-10

Also it [the beast] was allowed to make war on the saints and to conquer them. And authority was given it over every tribe and people and language and nation, [8] and all who dwell on earth will worship it, everyone whose name has not been written before the foundation of the world in the book of life of the Lamb that was slain. [9] If anyone has an ear, let him hear:

[10] If anyone is to be taken captive,
to captivity he goes;
if anyone is to be slain with the sword,
with the sword must he be slain.

Here is a call for the endurance and faith of the saints.

Six hundred years previous to John's vision, Daniel also saw that this beast would prevail against the saints for a three and a half year period as we have cited on a number of occasions previously (Dan. 7:20-25). Again, it is important to remember that this coming to power occurs at the seventh trumpet, after the earlier seven seals and trumpets.

Muslim Eschatology

As we have seen before, the Muslims also believe there will be a false Messiah, or rather a false Mahdi. Here is another Muslim description of this "Dajjal" (spelling as written in the following texts):

Identifying the Dajjaal

The Dajjal will claim that he is Allah. He will perform mighty acts to convince people of his claim. But, every true believer, whether literate or illiterate, will be able to read the word kafir on his forehead, as stated by Prophet Muhammad (Sallallaahu Alayhi Wasallam). He (Sallallaahu Alayhi Wasallam) has also described his physical appearance as: short, fat, red-faced, bow-legged, with curly hair and one-eyed. One of his eyes is extinguished, and is neither protruding nor deep-seated, but resembles a floating grape. "If you are confused, know that your Lord is not one-eyed, and that no one will be able to see the Lord [in this world]." (paraphrased from Bukhari, Muslim, Ahmad and Abu Dawud). And in the narration related by Muslim and Bukhari, the Prophet (Sallallaahu Alayhi Wasallam) told us that, "There has never been a Prophet who did not warn his people against the one-eyed Dajjal. Verily he is one-eyed and your lord is not one eyed. On his forehead will be written the letters Kaf, Fa', Ra, i.e., the root letters for 'kafir' or 'unbeliever')." These words will actually be written between his eyes on the forehead.

The Dajjaal – a man created by Allaah, who will appear at the end of time because of something that makes Allaah angry. He will spread corruption on earth and will claim divinity, calling on people to worship him. They will be tested by the extraordinary powers that Allaah will grant him, such as causing rain to fall, reviving the earth with vegetation and extracting the treasures of the earth. He will be a young man with a ruddy complexion, short of stature, with curly hair. He will be one-eyed; his right eye will be flat and his other eye will have a thick piece of flesh over it. Written between his eyes will be the word "Kaafir" (disbeliever). Most of those who follow him will be Jews. He will meet his end at the hands of 'Eesa ibn Maryam (Jesus the son of Mary) who will kill him with a spear in Lod, which is in Palestine.[79]

One notices that Jesus is the one who will kill this one-eyed Dajjal. We have seen in other texts before, who the Muslims think Jesus is and what he will do. Jesus' second coming is not referred to in the Quran, but some of the Hadiths speak of it. Jesus is seen as subordinating himself to the Mahdi. He is said to kill the Jews, the swine, break the cross (destroy the symbol of Christianity) and revert the world to Islam. The following is what Muslim writings have to say on Jesus:

---

[79]Imam Ibn Katheer, " Dajjal, The False Messiah"

II. Hadhrat Isa's (A.S.) Descension The Physical Features of Hadhrat Isa (A.S.)

He will resemble the famous Sahabi (A.S.) Hadhrat Urwa bin Masoodi (R.A.). He will be of average height and red and white in colour. His hair spread to the shoulders, straight, neat and shining as after a bath. On bending his head, it will seem as if pearls are falling. He will have an armour on his body. He will be wearing two pieces of cloth light yellow in color.

His Descension

He will descend on a Jamaat (group) that will be righteous at the time and comprising of 800 men and 400 women. The people will be preparing for war at the time against Dajjal (the anti-Christ). It will be time for Fajr prayers, and Imam Mahdi will be the Amir (leader). From the darkness of the dawn, a sound will suddenly be heard that "one who listens to your pleas has come" -- the righteous people will look everywhere and their eyes will fall on Isa (A.S.). Briefly, at the time of Fajr, Isa (A.S.) will descend. When descending, Isa (A.S.)'s hands will be on the shoulders of two angels (according to another source (Kab Abrar), a cloud will carry him). On their insistence Hadhrat Isa will introduce himself. He will inquire about their enthusiasm and thoughts on Jihad against Dajjal. Hadhrat Isa (A.S.) will descend on the eastern side near the Minaret in Damascus (or in Baitul-Muqaddus by Imam Mahdi). At the time Imam Mahdi will have proceeded forward to lead the Fajr Salaat. The Iqamat of the Salaat would have been said (already recited) and Imam Mahdi will call Hadhrat Isa (A.S.) for Imamat (to lead the prayer), but he (Hadhrat Isa (A.S.)) will instead tell Imam Mahdi to lead the prayer since the Iqamat of that Salaat has already been said for him. Thus Imam Mahdi will lead the prayer, and Hadhrat Isa (A.S.) will follow him. After the ruku, he will make this statement: "Allah has killed Dajjal and the Muslims have appeared."

The Killing of Dajjal (anti-Christ) and the Victory of the Muslims

After the completion of Fajr Salaat (congregational dawn prayers), Hadhrat Isa (A.S.) will open the door behind him where Dajjal accompanied by 70,000 Yahudis (Jews) will be. He will indicate with his hand to move away between him (Hadhrat Isa (A.S.)) and Dajjal. Dajjal will then see Hadhrat Isa (A.S.). At that time every Kafir on whom the breath of Hadhrat Isa (A.S.) will reach, will die. His breath will reach up to the distance of his eyesight. The Muslims will then come down from the mountains and break loose on the army of Dajjal. There will be war, Dajjal will retreat, and Hadhrat Isa (A.S.) will pursue Dajjal. Hadhrat Isa (A.S.) will have two flexible swords and one shield with him and with these he will kill Dajjal at the Gate of Hudd. He will show the Muslims the blood of Dajjal which will get on his shield. Eventually the Yahudis will be selected and killed. The swine will be killed and the cross broken. People will revert to Islam. Wars will end, and people will return to their respective countries. One Jamaat (group) of Muslims will remain in his service and companionship.

Hadhrat Isa (A.S.) will go to Fajr Rawha and perform Haj or Umrah (or both) from there. He will also go to the grave of Rasulullah (Sallallahu Alayhi Wasallam) and present his greetings and Rasulullah (Sallallahu Alayhi Wasallam) will reply. People will live comfortable lives. The wall of Yajooj and Majooj (Gog and Magog) will then break.

III. **The Blessings of Hadhrat Isa (Jesus) (A.S.)**

1 Hadhrat Isa (A.S.) will descend and stay on earth.
2 His descension will be in the last era of the Ummat.
3 He will be a just ruler and a fair judge.
4 His ummat will be the Khalifa (deputies) of Rasulullah (Sallallahu Alayhi Wasallam).
5 He will act himself and instruct others on the Qur'an and Hadith (Shariat/Tradition of Islam).
6 He will lead people in Salaat (Prayer).
7 He will stay on earth for a period of 40 years after descending. The will be the best era of the Ummat after the first era of Islam.
8 Allah will protect his companions from Jahannam.
9 Those who will save the Deen of Islam by associating themselves with Hadhrat Isa (A.S.) will be amongst the most loved by Allah Ta'ala.
10 During this period all other religions and mazhabs besides Islam

will perish, hence there will be no kuffaars (non-believers) in the world.

11 Jihad will be stopped.

12 No Khiraaj will be taken.

13 Nor Jizya (protection tax) money from the kafirs (non-believers)

14 Wealth and property will be in surplus to such an extent that there will be no one to accept the wealth of the other (everyone will be independent).

15 Receiving Zakaat (Alms-giving, Charity to poor) and Saadaqa will be discarded (as there will be no poor to receive them!).

16 The people will love the sajda (prostration to God) more than the world and what it consists of.

17 All types of Deeni (religious) and worldly blessings will descend on earth (many halaal (lawful) things will be created).

18 There will be peace, harmony and tranquility during the time of Hadhrat Isa (A.S.)'s stay in the world.

19 There will be no animosity for a period of seven years, even between two persons.

20 All hearts will be free from miserliness, envy, hatred, malice and jealousy.

21 For a period of forty years no one will fall ill or die.

22 Venom will be taken out of all venomous animals.

23 Snakes and scorpions will not harm anyone to the extent that if a child put his hand in its mouth, he will not be harmed.

24 Will animals will not harm anyone.

25 If a man will pass a lion, he will not be troubled or harmed, or even if any girl will open its mouth to test if it will do anything.

26 The camels will graze among lions, cheetahs with cattle and the jackals with goats.

27 The fertility of the land will increase to such an extent that even if a seed is planted in a hard rock, it will sprout.

28 A pomegranate will be so huge that a jamaat will be able to eat it and the people will use its peel as shade.

29 There will be so much barakaat (blessing) in milk that a camel will suffice for a huge jamaat, a cow for a tribe and a goat for a family.

30 **In short, life will be most pleasant after the descension of Jesus (A.S.).**

His Marriage, Death and Deputies

After his descension on earth, Hadhrat Isa (A.S.) will marry. He will have children, and he will remain on earth 19 years after marriage. He will pass away and Muslims will perform his Janaza Salaat and bury him net to Rasulullah (Sallallahu Alayhi Wasallam). (Tirmidhi)[80]

Reference is made to Jews being killed at the time that Jesus comes. Here is a famous quote:

Abu Huraira reported Allah's Messenger (may peace be upon him) as saying: The last hour would not come unless the Muslims will fight against the Jews and the Muslims would kill them until the Jews would hide themselves behind a stone or a tree and a stone or a tree would say: Muslim, or the servant of Allah, there is a Jew behind me; come and kill him; but the tree Gharqad would not say, for it is the tree of the Jews.[81]

As we have seen in a previous chapter, though there are some similarities between what Muslim theology says about Jesus and the Biblical account, the main tenants of Christianity are denied – the Trinity, the deity of Christ and his atoning death and resurrection among many other things.

As has been alluded to before, from a Christian perspective, the Mahdi will be the Antichrist and Isa will be the false prophet. Together they will stir up the Muslim world to kill the Jews and rid the world of all other religions. An interesting question arises. In Muslim eschatology,

"The Dajjal will claim that he is Allah. He will perform mighty acts to convince people of his claim."

What will Muslims do when their Mahdi performs signs and wonders and sets himself up in the temple and proclaims himself to be God? Will they be persuaded? Will they change their theology? Will they take the mark of allegiance he will require?

---

80 Mufti Afzal Hoosein Elias, Hadhrat Esa (Alaihis Salaam): The Truth Revealed and Major Signs of Qiyamat, "Jesus (Isa) A.S. in Islam, and his Second Coming" <http://www.islam.tc/prophecies/jesus.html>

81 Book 041, Number 6985: Sahih Muslim:

19 AN INTERLUDE: THE CALM BEFORE THE STORM

BETWEEN THE SOUNDING of the seventh trumpet and the outpouring of the seven bowls of wrath on the earth there is an interlude during which time John sees various things that will take place during this last three and a half years.

The 144,000 and the Lamb

Immediately after introducing the dragon (Rev. 12), the beast, the second beast or false prophet and the mark of the beast (Rev. 13), John sees Jesus, the lamb on Mt. Zion – Jerusalem, standing with the 144,000 who had been sealed in chapter 7. It is not clear if this is a scene on the earthly Mt. Zion or if this is in the heavenly Mt. Zion (Heb. 12:22).

Rev. 14:1-5
"Then I looked, and behold, on Mount Zion stood the Lamb, and with him 144,000 who had his name and his Father's name written on their foreheads. [2] And I heard a voice from heaven like the roar of many waters and like the sound of loud thunder. The voice I heard was like the sound of harpists playing on their harps, [3] and they were singing a new song before the throne and before the four living creatures and before the elders. No one could learn that song except the 144,000 who had been redeemed from the earth. [4] It is these who have not defiled themselves with women, for they are virgins. It is these who follow the Lamb wherever he goes. These have been

redeemed from mankind as firstfruits for God and the Lamb, [5] and in their mouth no lie was found, for they are blameless."

They had been sealed before the seven trumpets were sounded and perhaps were Jews who came to faith in Yeshua in the first half of the last seven year period through the testimony of the two witnesses before the seventh trumpet was sounded. If the scene is earthly Jerusalem, Jesus apparently comes and appears to them on Mount Zion. Was this to strengthen and encourage them for the great tribulation that was about to be unleashed on the world? Note the verses that follow in the chapter:

Rev. 14:12-13

Here is a call for the endurance of the saints, those who keep the commandments of God and their faith in Jesus. [Greek: "commandments of God and the faith of Jesus."]

[13] And I heard a voice from heaven saying, "Write this: Blessed are the dead who die in the Lord from now on." "Blessed indeed," says the Spirit, "that they may rest from their labors, for their deeds follow them!"

Remember, the seventh trumpet has just sounded. The bowls of wrath are about to be poured out on the earth. The last three and a half years of great tribulation are about to begin. The Antichrist has just killed the two witnesses and has proclaimed himself to be God in the temple. The 144,000 believers in the Messiah may even be there on the temple mount when he enters the temple. If however the scene described is in heaven, it is a picture of these Jewish believers who will be martyred during the last three and a half years and are with the Lamb in heaven.

The world is wild with rejoicing because he has killed these two witnesses and their bodies are still in the street. He is about to initiate his insistence on everyone worshiping him and receiving his mark.

God does not leave the world without a witness, however. In the first three and a half years, there were the two witnesses in Jerusalem. Now there are 144,000 Jewish believers standing on Mt. Zion. The church is still present in the world. The Antichrist has proclaimed himself to be God and is basking in the worldwide acclamation when a few days later the world's unbridled joy over this new leader – god – messiah, who has succeeded in killing the hated two witnesses, is brought to a sobering end. The two witnesses rise from the dead after three and a half days of lying dead in the street. A voice everyone can hear calls them up into heaven and they ascend in view of the entire world.

God is patient and gracious and in spite of the open rebellion against him, he will not leave the world without a witness. They have just witnessed the resurrection and ascension of the witnesses and before God begins to pour out his bowls of wrath on the world, he makes sure everyone is aware of what is at stake.

Three angels give three warnings to the earth to prepare them for what is to come and warn them to turn from their sin and embrace the gospel.

Rev. 14:6-11

Then I saw another angel flying directly overhead, with an eternal gospel to proclaim to those who dwell on earth, to every nation and tribe and language and people. [7] And he said with a loud voice, "Fear God and give him glory, because the hour of his judgment has come, and worship him who made heaven and earth, the sea and the springs of water."

That the book of Revelation has been laying out for us a chronological order of events is further supported by the phrase, "because the hour of his judgment has come." Up to this point, the catastrophes have been warnings - a call to repent, to flee from God's eternal wrath. The pouring out of the bowls of wrath initiate the hour of his judgment.

Notice the emphasis on worshiping "him who made heaven and earth, the sea and the springs of water." An almost universal determination today is to make sure any teaching of God creating the universe is silenced. Evolution is supreme. No mention of God can be made in the classroom and even those who would say there must be an intelligent designer or design for us to have what we have are silenced by lawsuits or losing their jobs. Note the primary issue that brings God's wrath even today on humanity:

Romans 1:18-32

For the wrath of God is revealed from heaven against all ungodliness and unrighteousness of men, who by their unrighteousness suppress the truth. [19] For what can be known about God is plain to them, because God has shown it to them. [20] For his invisible attributes, namely, his eternal power and divine nature, have been clearly perceived, ever since the creation of the world, in the things that have been made. So they are without excuse. [21] For although they knew God, they did not honor him as God or give thanks to him, but they became futile in their thinking, and their foolish hearts were darkened. [22] Claiming to be wise, they became fools, [23] and exchanged the glory of the immortal God for images resembling mortal man and birds and animals and reptiles.

[24] Therefore God gave them up in the lusts of their hearts to impurity, to the dishonoring of their bodies among themselves, [25] because they exchanged the truth about God for a lie and worshiped and served the creature rather than the Creator, who is blessed forever! Amen.

[26] For this reason God gave them up to dishonorable passions. For their women exchanged natural relations for those that are contrary to nature; [27] and the men likewise gave up natural relations with women and were consumed with passion for one another, men committing shameless acts with men and receiving in themselves the due penalty for their error.

[28] And since they did not see fit to acknowledge God, God gave them up to a debased mind to do what ought not to be done. [29] They were filled with all manner of unrighteousness, evil, covetousness, malice. They are full of envy, murder, strife, deceit, maliciousness. They are gossips, [30] slanderers, haters of God, insolent, haughty, boastful, inventors of evil, disobedient to parents, [31] foolish, faithless, heartless, ruthless. [32] Though they know God's decree that those who practice such things deserve to die, they not only do them but give approval to those who practice them.

God is jealous of our acknowledgment that he is the creator, and humanity is equally determined today that he will not be acknowledged as creator. But before the bowls of wrath are poured out on the earth, an angel calls people from every nation, tribe, language and people to "Fear God and give him glory, because the hour of his judgment has come, and worship him who made heaven and earth, the sea and the springs of water."

[8] Another angel, a second, followed, saying, "Fallen, fallen is Babylon the great, she who made all nations drink the wine of the passion of her sexual immorality." (Rev. 14:8)

The next angel warns what will happen to Babylon. Babylon has always represented the city that proudly and defiantly rebels against God. It was where Nimrod built the tower of Babel. It later became the great capital city of Nebuchadnezzar. In the New Testament, it was the code name for Rome. Some believe that the literal city of Babylon in Iraq will be rebuilt to become the headquarters of the Antichrist and will be the city destroyed, as we shall see in chapters 17-18 of Revelation. Others believe it is speaking of Rome, as the headquarters of the Roman Catholic Church and former seat of the pagan Roman Empire. There are other possibilities we will look at in more detail as we study those chapters.

[9] And another angel, a third, followed them, saying with a loud voice, "If anyone worships the beast and its image and receives a mark on his forehead or on his hand, [10] he also will drink the wine of God's wrath, poured full strength into the cup of his anger, and he will be tormented with fire and sulfur in the presence of the holy angels and in the presence of the Lamb. [11] And the smoke of their torment goes up forever and ever, and they have no rest, day or night, these worshipers of the beast and its image, and whoever receives the mark of its name." (Rev. 14:9-11)

This warning to not worship the beast or receive its mark is given before that has begun to be widely required. This is why I believe the great tribulation is just about to begin at this point and the Antichrist has just been revealed. The warning is not sent out long after the fact – long after the requirement to worship and receive the mark is in practice. The warning is given at the beginning, so that all will have to weigh carefully what they are doing. It will not be a mark forced on people. Those who receive the mark and worship the beast will not do so out of ignorance. It will be a willful turning away from God's warning which somehow the whole world will hear.

It is after these warnings that the verses cited below come:

Rev. 14:12-13

Here is a call for the endurance of the saints, those who keep the commandments of God and their faith in Jesus.

[13] And I heard a voice from heaven saying, "Write this: Blessed are the dead who die in the Lord from now on." "Blessed indeed," says the Spirit, "that they may rest from their labors, for their deeds follow them!"

There is a certain blessedness promised to those who die in the Lord from that point forward. What point is it? It is from the point of the beginning of the great tribulation, the point from which the hour of judgment on the earth begins. There is no indication that the believers will escape this time, or be taken from the world scene by a rapture before this begins. Otherwise, why would there be a call for endurance and promise of blessedness for those believers who die during this time?

The Two Harvests

During this interlude between the sounding of the seventh trumpet and the pouring out of the bowls of wrath, a picture is given of two harvests, both of which I believe will happen during the days of the seventh trumpet which will also be during the time of the seven bowls. The first harvest seems to be Jesus harvesting the ripe grain which seems to allude back to the parable of the weeds:

Matthew 13:30
Let both grow together until the harvest, and at harvest time I will tell the reapers, Gather the weeds first and bind them in bundles to be burned, but gather the wheat into my barn.' "

Rev. 14:14-16
Then I looked, and behold, a white cloud, and seated on the cloud one like a son of man, with a golden crown on his head, and a sharp sickle in his hand. [15] And another angel came out of the temple, calling with a loud voice to him who sat on the cloud, "Put in your sickle, and reap, for the hour to reap has come, for the harvest of the earth is fully ripe." [16] So he who sat on the cloud swung his sickle across the earth, and the earth was reaped.

A Pre-tribulation Rapture?

The pre-trib. rapture position, as we have stated before, believes the rapture will occur before the last seven years, mistakenly identifying the whole period of time as the "great tribulation". Likewise, the mid-trib. rapture position could use this passage as supporting their position. Again, however, this passage comes before the beginning of the great tribulation, though midway through the last seven years. In Marvin Rosenthal's book, *The Pre-Wrath Rapture of the* Church, he takes into account that this is not halfway through the great tribulation, but he believes the rapture will occur at this point which he calls "the pre-wrath rapture."[82] Is this a passage supporting the rapture – the resurrection of believers and those alive being caught up to God before the bowls of wrath are poured out?

As much as I would like to think so, the context indicates to us that this is not the case. Along with what has just been stated about believers patiently enduring, the verses immediately following indicate the second of the two harvests. This second harvest we see later in Revelation 16 and 19 occurring after Jesus' second coming. A hermeneutic supporting the harvest of the believers as occurring before the bowls of wrath are poured out would have to, if one wants to be consistent, also posit the second harvest of the wicked as also occurring at that time, which Revelation 19 shows us is not the case.

Rev. 14:17-20

Then another angel came out of the temple in heaven, and he too had a sharp sickle. [18] And another angel came out from the altar, the angel who has authority over the fire, and he called with a loud voice to the one who had the sharp sickle, "Put in your sickle and gather the clusters from the vine of the earth, for its grapes are ripe." [19] So the angel swung his sickle across the earth and gathered the grape harvest of the earth and threw it into the great winepress of the wrath of God. [20] And the winepress was trodden outside the city, and blood flowed from the winepress, as high as a horse's bridle, for 1,600 stadia.

Again, in this interlude before the bowls of wrath are poured out, John sees the two harvests that will be taking place during the days of the seventh trumpet, which as we have seen, are the last three and a half years. The second harvest is an incredible bloodbath outside Jerusalem. Blood flows for 184 miles, or close to 300 kilometers. Interestingly, 300 kilometers is about the distance between Gaza's border with Egypt and Israel's northern border with Lebanon. This great winepress of the wrath of God is language from the Old Testament in Isaiah 63:1-6 and Joel 3:9-16 which we will look at when we get to the specific context of this bloodbath in Revelation 16 and 19.

---

[82] Marvin Rosenthal, *The Pre-Wrath Rapture of the Church* (Nashville, TN: Thomas Nelson Publishers, 1990)

Seven Last Plagues – Bowls of Wrath

During this interlude, John sees what is about to happen:

Rev. 15:1

Then I saw another sign in heaven, great and amazing, seven angels with seven plagues, which are the last, for with them the wrath of God is finished.

He also sees those who, during the following outpouring of these plagues, will conquer the beast and will be in heaven.

Rev. 15:2-4

And I saw what appeared to be a sea of glass mingled with fire—and also those who had conquered the beast and its image and the number of its name, standing beside the sea of glass with harps of God in their hands. [3] And they sing the song of Moses, the servant of God, and the song of the Lamb, saying,

"Great and amazing are your deeds,
O Lord God the Almighty!
Just and true are your ways,
O King of the nations!
[4] Who will not fear, O Lord,
and glorify your name?
For you alone are holy.
All nations will come
and worship you,
for your righteous acts have been revealed."

Like the vision of the two harvests, this scene of those who conquered the beast is yet future.

Now, after all the warnings, the full judgment and wrath is about to begin. These bowls of wrath will be poured out on the earth over the last three and a half year period of time.

Rev. 15:5-8

After this I looked, and the sanctuary of the tent of witness in heaven was opened, [6] and out of the sanctuary came the seven angels with the seven plagues, clothed in pure, bright linen, with golden sashes around their chests. [7] And one of the four living creatures gave to the seven angels seven golden bowls full of the wrath of God who lives forever and ever, [8] and the sanctuary was filled with smoke from the glory of God and from his power, and no one could enter the sanctuary until the seven plagues of the seven angels were finished.

20 THE BOWLS OF WRATH

Rev. 16:1

Then I heard a loud voice from the temple telling the seven angels, "Go and pour out on the earth the seven bowls of the wrath of God."

We saw earlier, that these are the last:

Rev. 15:1

Then I saw another sign in heaven, great and amazing, seven angels with seven plagues, which are the last, for with them the wrath of God is finished.

The First Bowl

Rev. 16:2

So the first angel went and poured out his bowl on the earth, and harmful and painful sores came upon the people who bore the mark of the beast and worshiped its image.

This plague affects only those who have worshiped the beast and received his mark. It could be like so many things in medical history; what is promoted as being harmless and having no side effects, after a period of time, the real consequences come to light. This plague may be the body's natural reaction to having received the mark. The sores are not just painful, but also harmful – in what way we are not told.

The Second Bowl

Rev. 16:3
The second angel poured out his bowl into the sea, and it became like the blood of a corpse, and every living thing died that was in the sea.

The second trumpet had turned one third of the sea to blood and a third of the sea creatures and ships perished because of the burning mountain falling into the sea. In this case, all sea creatures die. Dead sea life of every kind will wash up on the shores. The stench will be unimaginable. The livelihood of all those involved in the seafood industry will be affected. It is likely that disease will begin to spread from the coastlines.

The Third Bowl

Rev. 16:4-7
The third angel poured out his bowl into the rivers and the springs
of water, and they became blood. [5] And I heard the angel in charge
of the waters say,
"Just are you, O Holy One, who is and who was,
for you brought these judgments.
[6] For they have shed the blood of saints and prophets,
and you have given them blood to drink.
It is what they deserve!"
[7] And I heard the altar saying,
"Yes, Lord God the Almighty,
true and just are your judgments!"

The third trumpet had poisoned a third of the rivers and springs. Now it seems all of them become blood. An angel acknowledges God's right and justice in this horrific plague. He is giving them what they deserve for how they shed the blood of the saints and prophets.

We are reminded of:

Romans 12:19:
Beloved, never avenge yourselves, but leave it to the wrath of God, for it is written, "Vengeance is mine, I will repay, says the Lord."

Those who have experienced catastrophes know how one of the first things to happen is that the grocery stores are emptied out within hours. There will be a worldwide shortage of potable water and people will begin to die of thirst.

The Fourth Bowl

Rev. 16:8-9

The fourth angel poured out his bowl on the sun, and it was allowed to scorch people with fire. [9] They were scorched by the fierce heat, and they cursed the name of God who had power over these plagues. They did not repent and give him glory.

Those who lived in Europe in 2003 will remember the summer heat wave that claimed 40,000 lives. That will pale in comparison with what is presented here. People will know that God is the one who has power over these plagues, but instead of seeking him, repenting and giving him glory, they will curse him. This extreme heat will be a foretaste of the suffering that will await them in the lake of fire.

All during this time, the Antichrist will be waging his war against Jews and Christians, either executing them – by beheading as the text says in chapter 20:4, or imprisoning them. It would not be surprising that the Christians would be treated with special vehemence because they may be blamed as the cause of these plagues.

The Fifth Bowl

Rev. 16:10-11

The fifth angel poured out his bowl on the throne of the beast, and its kingdom was plunged into darkness. People gnawed their tongues in anguish [11] and cursed the God of heaven for their pain and sores. They did not repent of their deeds.

The fourth trumpet had darkened a third of the sun, moon and stars. This bowl plunges the Antichrist's throne and kingdom into darkness. What causes this darkness we are not told. However, immediately preceding Christ's return, the sun and moon will not give their light.

Matthew 24:29-30

"Immediately after the tribulation of those days the sun will be darkened, and the moon will not give its light, and the stars will fall from heaven, and the powers of the heavens will be shaken. [30] Then will appear in heaven the sign of the Son of Man, and then all the tribes of the earth will mourn, and they will see the Son of Man coming on the clouds of heaven with power and great glory."

If a cataclysm is not in view with the fifth bowl, one possible reason for the kingdom to be plunged into darkness is that the scorching heat of the previous plague will cause widespread power outages or blackouts. The world's power companies will be taxed beyond their capacities as everyone uses their air conditioners and fans in an effort to keep cool. The summer of 2012 saw more than half of the population of India experience a blackout. Getting power grids back on line can sometimes take weeks depending on many factors. The effects of the previous plagues – that of the sores because of the mark, dead sea creatures, water shortages and heat may still be continuing, which explains why people will be gnawing their tongues in anguish and cursing God because of their pain and sores. They will continue to be unrepentant.

The language is not clear as to whether this is a worldwide phenomenon or just in the Antichrist's immediate middle eastern kingdom. Of course, the Middle East is normally hotter than the rest of the world and so one can see the above scenario happening in a more localized area.

The Sixth Bowl

Rev. 16:12-16

The sixth angel poured out his bowl on the great river Euphrates, and its water was dried up, to prepare the way for the kings from the east. [13] And I saw, coming out of the mouth of the dragon and out of the mouth of the beast and out of the mouth of the false prophet, three unclean spirits like frogs. [14] For they are demonic spirits, performing signs, who go abroad to the kings of the whole world, to assemble them for battle on the great day of God the Almighty. [15] ("Behold, I am coming like a thief! Blessed is the one who stays awake, keeping his garments on, that he may not go about naked and be seen exposed!") [16] And they assembled them at the place that in Hebrew is called Armageddon.

This bowl is not the battle itself, but is the assembling of the nations in Israel for the final battle. Much is written in the Bible concerning this great conflagration. First, let's look at some of the details. The bowl is poured out on the river Euphrates in Iraq, and the effect is that the water is dried up. Already, the water level of the river is very low. An April 12, 2011 article states:

> "A UN press release on World Water Day, marked on March 22, quotes a recent international report warning that "the Tigris and Euphrates rivers could completely dry up by 2040 because of the compounded effect of climate change, reduced upstream supply, and [an] increase in domestic and industrial use."[83]

What is the purpose of the angel drying up the river? It says, "to prepare the way for the kings from the east." The Euphrates river begins in eastern Turkey, makes its way through Syria and flows through the middle of Iraq. Countries east of the Euphrates are parts of Turkey, Syria, and Iraq, along with Iran, all the "stan" countries (Afghanistan, Pakistan, Kazakhstan, etc.), India, China and many more.

Out of the mouths of the unholy trinity – the dragon (Satan), the beast (the Antichrist) and the false prophet, come three demonic spirits like frogs. They have the ability to perform miraculous signs and persuade the kings of the whole earth to assemble at a place called Armageddon. In Hebrew, Har-Megiddo means Mount Megiddo which today is a tell, a mound of ruins where many cities have been built, one atop the other in the vast Jezreel Valley. The valley is a place where great battles have been fought. It is in northern Israel, about a hundred kilometers north of Jerusalem.

What is the purpose of gathering all these nations together? The text says, "to assemble them for battle on the great day of God the Almighty." The demonic spirits persuade the kings to gather, but God is the one gathering them for his purpose.

The fact that Jesus has not yet come and the rapture has not yet taken place is seen by the language used by God to believers still on earth at this time:

> [15] ("Behold, I am coming like a thief! Blessed is the one who stays awake, keeping his garments on, that he may not go about naked and be seen exposed!") Rev. 16:15

The language of "I am coming like a thief!" directed toward believers

---

[83] "Iraq Grapples With Water Shortages, Pollution," <http://crisisboom.com/2011/04/12/euphrates-river-dry/>

is the language pre-trib. rapture people use to defend their position that the rapture occurs before the tribulation, but here we see it being used in the context of the sixth bowl of wrath being poured out on the earth.

Besides this battle of Armageddon, the Bible speaks of another group, Gog and Magog in Ezekiel 38-39, that gather for battle against Israel. The same name is used for the battle after the thousand year reign of Christ when Satan is released for a short while in Revelation 20:7-9. Could all these battles be one and the same battle by different names, or are they referring to different events?

The Mother of All Battles

Saddam Hussein popularized the Arabic expression "mother of all battles" when he used it in 1990 following his invasion of Kuwait. He threatened Desert Storm troops with "the mother of all battles" if they tried to invade Iraq. Wikipedia defines the term this way:

> "**The mother of all...** has become a stock phrase in English-language public discourse and popular culture. It implies the largest or most significant example of a class, which completely overshadows all other cases in the class. For example, "the mother of all battles" would imply the largest, most destructive, most significant battle ever fought."[84]

Indeed, this battle of Armageddon will be the "mother of all battles." It is the most written about battle in the Bible and as we look at the various scripture passages, I think you will see that it is the same battle as that of Gog and Magog in Ezekiel. We will look at that in more detail in chapter 22.

First, we see that it is the last battle, before the millennial reign of Christ. The kings are assembled "for battle on the great day of God the Almighty." We saw the description of it in

Rev. 14:19-20

"So the angel swung his sickle across the earth and gathered the grape harvest of the earth and threw it into the great winepress of the wrath of God. [20] And the winepress was trodden outside the city, and blood flowed from the winepress, as high as a horse's bridle, for 1,600 stadia."

---

[84] "The Mother of All," <http://en.wikipedia.org/wiki/The_mother_of_all>

Notice the theme of blood and winepress in the following passages:

Isaiah 63:1-6

Who is this who comes from Edom,
in crimsoned garments from Bozrah,
he who is splendid in his apparel,
marching in the greatness of his strength?
"It is I, speaking in righteousness, mighty to save."
[2] Why is your apparel red,
and your garments like his who treads in the winepress?
[3] "I have trodden the winepress alone,
and from the peoples no one was with me;
I trod them in my anger
and trampled them in my wrath;
their lifeblood spattered on my garments,
and stained all my apparel.
[4] For the day of vengeance was in my heart,
and my year of redemption had come.
[5] I looked, but there was no one to help;
I was appalled, but there was no one to uphold;
so my own arm brought me salvation,
and my wrath upheld me.
[6] I trampled down the peoples in my anger;
I made them drunk in my wrath,
and I poured out their lifeblood on the earth."

God is seen as the one who treads on the winepress of his wrath and has the blood of the peoples splattered on his garments. It is the time of his vengeance and redemption, vengeance on his enemies and redemption of his people.

The prophet Joel records the coming "day of the Lord" with language similar to that used by Jesus in

Matthew 24:29-31

"Immediately after the tribulation of those days the sun will be darkened, and the moon will not give its light, and the stars will fall from heaven, and the powers of the heavens will be shaken. [30] Then will appear in heaven the sign of the Son of Man, and then all the tribes of the earth will mourn, and they will see the Son of Man coming on the clouds of heaven with power and great glory. [31] And he will send out his angels with a loud trumpet call, and they will gather his elect from the four winds, from one end of heaven to the other.

Joel 2:30-32
"And I will show wonders in the heavens and on the earth, blood
and fire and columns of smoke. [31] The sun shall be turned to
darkness, and the moon to blood, before the great and awesome day
of the Lord comes. [32] And it shall come to pass that everyone who
calls on the name of the Lord shall be saved. For in Mount Zion and
in Jerusalem there shall be those who escape, as the Lord has said,
and among the survivors shall be those whom the Lord calls.
Joel 3:1-3
"For behold, in those days and at that time, when I restore the
fortunes of Judah and Jerusalem, [2] I will gather all the nations and
bring them down to the Valley of Jehoshaphat. And I will enter into
judgment with them there, on behalf of my people and my heritage
Israel, because they have scattered them among the nations and have
divided up my land, [3] and have cast lots for my people, and have
traded a boy for a prostitute, and have sold a girl for wine and have
drunk it.
Joel 3:9-16
Proclaim this among the nations:
Consecrate for war;
stir up the mighty men.
Let all the men of war draw near;
let them come up.
[10] Beat your plowshares into swords,
and your pruning hooks into spears;
let the weak say, "I am a warrior."
[11] Hasten and come,
all you surrounding nations,
and gather yourselves there.
Bring down your warriors, O Lord.
[12] Let the nations stir themselves up
and come up to the Valley of Jehoshaphat;
for there I will sit to judge
all the surrounding nations.
[13] Put in the sickle,
for the harvest is ripe.

Go in, tread, for the winepress is full.
The vats overflow,
  for their evil is great.
[14] Multitudes, multitudes,
  in the valley of decision!
For the day of the Lord is near
  in the valley of decision.
[15] The sun and the moon are darkened,
  and the stars withdraw their shining.
[16] The Lord roars from Zion,
  and utters his voice from Jerusalem,
  and the heavens and the earth quake.
But the Lord is a refuge to his people,
  a stronghold to the people of Israel.

Again, language is used of a harvest: "Put in the sickle, for the harvest is ripe. Go in, tread, for the winepress is full. The vats overflow, for their evil is great." All the surrounding nations are gathered together in what is here called "the Valley of Jehoshaphat" which is called the valley of decision. The description of the sun, moon and stars are the same as what Jesus said would take place immediately after the tribulation of those days and we see that the resurrection / rapture takes place likewise at his coming after the tribulation when he comes to do battle.

Many other passages use the term, "day of the Lord" to refer to the time of God's judgment at the last battle. Isaiah uses this expression:

Isaiah 13:4-13
The sound of a tumult is on the mountains
  as of a great multitude!
The sound of an uproar of kingdoms,
  of nations gathering together!
The Lord of hosts is mustering
  a host for battle.
[5] They come from a distant land,
  from the end of the heavens,
the Lord and the weapons of his indignation,
  to destroy the whole land [or *earth*].
[6] Wail, for the day of the Lord is near;
  as destruction from the Almighty it will come!
[7] Therefore all hands will be feeble,

and every human heart will melt.
[8] They will be dismayed:
pangs and agony will seize them;
they will be in anguish like a woman in labor.
They will look aghast at one another;
their faces will be aflame.
[9] Behold, the day of the Lord comes,
cruel, with wrath and fierce anger,
to make the land [or *earth*] a desolation
and to destroy its sinners from it.
[10] For the stars of the heavens and their constellations
will not give their light;
the sun will be dark at its rising,
and the moon will not shed its light.
[11] I will punish the world for its evil,
and the wicked for their iniquity;
I will put an end to the pomp of the arrogant,
and lay low the pompous pride of the ruthless.
[12] I will make people more rare than fine gold,
and mankind than the gold of Ophir.
[13] Therefore I will make the heavens tremble,
and the earth will be shaken out of its place,
at the wrath of the Lord of hosts
in the day of his fierce anger.

Other allusions:

Psalm 2:1-3
Why do the nations rage
and the peoples plot in vain?
[2] The kings of the earth set themselves,
and the rulers take counsel together,
against the Lord and against his anointed, saying,
[3] "Let us burst their bonds apart
and cast away their cords from us."

Psalm 110:1,2, 5-6 A Psalm of David.
The Lord says to my Lord:
"Sit at my right hand,
until I make your enemies your footstool."

[2] The Lord sends forth from Zion
your mighty scepter.
Rule in the midst of your enemies!
[5] The Lord is at your right hand;
he will shatter kings on the day of his wrath.
[6] He will execute judgment among the nations,
filling them with corpses;
he will shatter chiefs over the wide earth.

Isaiah 24:21-23
On that day the Lord will punish
the host of heaven, in heaven,
and the kings of the earth, on the earth.
[22] They will be gathered together
as prisoners in a pit;
they will be shut up in a prison,
and after many days they will be punished.
[23] Then the moon will be confounded
and the sun ashamed,
for the Lord of hosts reigns
on Mount Zion and in Jerusalem,
and his glory will be before his elders.

Micah 4:11-13
Now many nations
are assembled against you,
saying, "Let her be defiled,
and let our eyes gaze upon Zion."
[12] But they do not know
the thoughts of the Lord;
they do not understand his plan,
that he has gathered them as sheaves to the threshing floor.
[13] Arise and thresh,
O daughter of Zion,
for I will make your horn iron,
and I will make your hoofs bronze;
you shall beat in pieces many peoples;
and shall devote their gain to the Lord,
their wealth to the Lord of the whole earth.

Zech. 12:2-3
"Behold, I am about to make Jerusalem a cup of staggering to all the surrounding peoples. The siege of Jerusalem will also be against Judah. [3] On that day I will make Jerusalem a heavy stone for all the peoples. All who lift it will surely hurt themselves. And all the nations of the earth will gather against it.

But, we must not get ahead of ourselves. The sixth bowl is the gathering of these armies to Israel. We will talk about the actual battle when we get to chapter 22. Then we will also deal with the question of "Gog and Magog."

The Seventh Bowl

Rev. 16:17-21
The seventh angel poured out his bowl into the air, and a loud voice came out of the temple, from the throne, saying, "It is done!" [18] And there were flashes of lightning, rumblings, peals of thunder, and a great earthquake such as there had never been since man was on the earth, so great was that earthquake. [19] The great city was split into three parts, and the cities of the nations fell, and God remembered Babylon the great, to make her drain the cup of the wine of the fury of his wrath. [20] And every island fled away, and no mountains were to be found. [21] And great hailstones, about one hundred pounds each, fell from heaven on people; and they cursed God for the plague of the hail, because the plague was so severe.

In any great fireworks display, the finale is the most spectacular when the biggest, loudest and most brilliant fireworks are all set off together. So, in this last bowl of wrath, there is the most spectacular outpouring of God's power and wrath. There is a tremendous lightning and thunder storm – perhaps the greatest in history. The earthquake is the greatest since man has been on earth. It is a worldwide quake, since it says that the cities of the nations fell. Every island disappears and the mountains are no more. Jerusalem, the great city, is split into three parts. Massive, hundred pound hailstones fall killing many and inflicting tremendous damage. But another major event happens with the outpouring of this seventh bowl. It says, "and God remembered Babylon the great, to make her drain the cup of the wine of the fury of his wrath."

With all this, again, instead of repenting, they curse God.

21 BABYLON THE GREAT

THAT THE DESTRUCTION of Babylon is reserved for the end, and the fact that two chapters in Revelation are dedicated to it shows the importance of this event. It is the culminating battle in which the city of proud, defiant, independent man, used by Satan to combat God and his people, is destroyed, while the city of God – Jerusalem, with the armies of the world gathered against it is delivered by Jesus himself.

There are numerous interpretations regarding what "Babylon the great" is. Before dealing with some of those views, it is better to read the text first.

Rev. 17:1-6

Then one of the seven angels who had the seven bowls came and said to me, "Come, I will show you the judgment of the great prostitute who is seated on many waters, [2] with whom the kings of the earth have committed sexual immorality, and with the wine of whose sexual immorality the dwellers on earth have become drunk." [3] And he carried me away in the Spirit into a wilderness, and I saw a woman sitting on a scarlet beast that was full of blasphemous names, and it had seven heads and ten horns. [4] The woman was arrayed in purple and scarlet, and adorned with gold and jewels and pearls, holding in her hand a golden cup full of abominations and the impurities of her sexual immorality. [5] And on her forehead was written a name of mystery: "Babylon the great, mother of prostitutes and of earth's abominations." [6] And I saw the woman, drunk with the blood of the saints, the blood of the martyrs of Jesus.

The passage is full of symbols. However, many of the symbols are explained in the passage. For example, one would wonder, "who or what this prostitute is?" The last verse of the chapter tells us:

Rev. 17:18
And the woman that you saw is the great city that has dominion over the kings of the earth."

Besides the woman, we see that she is seated on a scarlet beast that had seven heads and ten horns. Again, we are told what the beast is. Picking up with verse 6:

Rev. 17:6-14
And I saw the woman, drunk with the blood of the saints, the blood of the martyrs of Jesus.
When I saw her, I marveled greatly. [7] But the angel said to me, "Why do you marvel? I will tell you the mystery of the woman, and of the beast with seven heads and ten horns that carries her. [8] The beast that you saw was, and is not, and is about to rise from the bottomless pit and go to destruction. And the dwellers on earth whose names have not been written in the book of life from the foundation of the world will marvel to see the beast, because it was and is not and is to come. [9] This calls for a mind with wisdom: the seven heads are seven mountains on which the woman is seated; [10] they are also seven kings, five of whom have fallen, one is, the other has not yet come, and when he does come he must remain only a little while. [11] As for the beast that was and is not, it is an eighth but it belongs to the seven, and it goes to destruction. [12] And the ten horns that you saw are ten kings who have not yet received royal power, but they are to receive authority as kings for one hour, together with the beast. [13] These are of one mind and hand over their power and authority to the beast. [14] They will make war on the Lamb, and the Lamb will conquer them, for he is Lord of lords and King of kings, and those with him are called and chosen and faithful."

We have looked at this passage a number of times. Briefly, the beast with seven heads represents the seven kings or kingdoms that Satan has used to oppose God and his people through much of human history. We mentioned that the five which had already fallen by John's time were Egypt, Assyria, Babylon, Media-Persia and Greece. The one that was during John's time was Rome. The one that had not yet come I have argued, is the Muslim empire.

"The beast that you saw was, and is not, and is about to rise from the bottomless pit and go to destruction. As for the beast that was and is not, it is an eighth but it belongs to the seven, and it goes to destruction." This is what I have suggested is the revived Muslim Empire which will also have, I believe, a leader who will experience a mortal wound and be revived or resurrected. The ten horns are ten kings who will give their support and power to this Antichrist and they will make war against the Lamb – Jesus Christ. This revived Muslim Empire has not yet been revived and this individual has not yet been revealed (as of Jan. 5, 2013).

There is an important clue regarding this city, Babylon. It says, "This calls for a mind with wisdom." Only one other time is this phrase used in Revelation:

Rev. 13:18

This calls for wisdom: let the one who has understanding calculate the number of the beast, for it is the number of a man, and his number is 666.

That would seem to indicate that the clue given will not be easily understood by everyone. What is the clue? "This calls for a mind with wisdom: the seven heads are seven mountains on which the woman is seated; [10] they are also seven kings . . ." The seven heads do not have just one significance. The city is said to be on seven mountains.

Of the list of 51 cities that claim to be built on seven hills (Wikipedia), the more interesting ones for this context are Rome, Jerusalem, Istanbul, Athens and Mecca. Interestingly, Babylon itself was built on a plain.

Rome

Traditionally, most Bible scholars have seen Rome to be the obvious city John is referencing here. During his lifetime, Rome was "the great city that has dominion over the kings of the earth." Many kings prostituted themselves through Emperor worship, bribery and every other means imaginable to curry Rome's favor. It was also a very sexually immoral city, a city full of pagan idols and the city most responsible for the death of Christians. It was also known as the city on seven hills. In fact, Plutarch referred to a national festival called "Septimontium" – the feast of the seven-hilled city. The names of the seven hills were Capitolinus, Palatinus, Aventinus, Esquilinus, Coelius,

Viminalis, and Quirinalis.

After the rise of Protestantism, many saw not only Rome, but specifically the Vatican, the seat of the Roman Catholic Church, as the great Prostitute, drunk with the blood of the saints, the blood of the martyrs of Jesus. The Roman Church has through the centuries persecuted to the death those who believed in the five "sola" declarations of the reformers: *sola scriptura, sola fide, sola gratia, solus Christus, soli Deo gloria* (scripture alone, faith alone, grace alone, Christ alone and glory to God alone).

In opposition to these, the Church has stood for the scripture not being sufficient, but that the Church and Tradition have equal authority as the scriptures; faith alone is not sufficient, it has to be added to works; grace alone is not sufficient, merit is likewise a necessary ingredient; Christ alone is not enough – one needs the grace of Mary, the Saints and the institution of the Church for salvation; and God alone is not glorified, but rather Mary and the Saints often, in practice, receive equal or greater glory and praise.

We mentioned in the chapter on the Antichrist the Prophecy of the Popes which I will include here again in its translated form:

"In the final persecution of the Holy Roman Church, there will sit [i.e., as Pope] Peter the Roman, who will pasture his sheep in many tribulations: and when these things are finished, the city of seven hills will be destroyed, and the terrible judge will judge his people. The End."

This prophecy would seem to support the idea of Rome being Babylon the Great. Yet while Rome was and is a good type of the Babylon referred to in this text for many reasons, there are several arguments against Rome, and specifically against the Roman Catholic Church being what is referred to in this passage. I believe that it is entirely possible that Rome could be destroyed as well, not as "**The** Babylon the Great" but rather as a type, just as Antiochus Epiphanes was a type of the Antichrist.

Why do I believe Rome to be only a type of the real Prostitute? First of all, Rome is on hills, not mountains, as the Greek text indicates. Secondly, the Vatican is not built on one of the seven hills in the original city, but across the Tiber River on the *Collis Vaticanus* (Vatican hill). In addition, the Spirit takes John away into a wilderness. Rome is definitely not in a wilderness, but rather in a well watered green area. The passage says that this calls for a mind with wisdom. Rome is the obvious choice for anyone. Could wisdom lead us to another city that fits the description?

More information is needed before drawing a conclusion.

Rev. 17:15-18

And the angel said to me, "The waters that you saw, where the prostitute is seated, are peoples and multitudes and nations and languages. [16] And the ten horns that you saw, they and the beast will hate the prostitute. They will make her desolate and naked, and devour her flesh and burn her up with fire, [17] for God has put it into their hearts to carry out his purpose by being of one mind and handing over their royal power to the beast, until the words of God are fulfilled. [18] And the woman that you saw is the great city that has dominion over the kings of the earth."

More detail is given in chapter 18 of Revelation, but first a summary. The "prostitute" in Greek is the word "pornee" and the same root word used for the "sexual immorality" that the kings of the earth commit with her. It is the word from which we get pornography, but is generally the idea of fornication. This is significant as it is differentiated from the idea of adultery. Often in the Bible sexual immorality is a symbol of spiritual unfaithfulness (cf. Ezekiel 16:15-43). God accused Israel in the Old Testament of spiritual adultery when they worshiped idols, because they were wed to God in a covenant relationship but were whoring after other gods.

Fornication, on the other hand, does not imply a covenant relationship on either of the parts. It is between unmarried persons. This means that the city referred to here, and the kings involved with her, are not those who have had a relationship with the God of the Bible. That would seem to rule out Jerusalem as one of the options. It would also seem to rule out the Roman Catholic Church, as their activity would be termed adultery rather than fornication since the Church by creed has espoused Christ.

The prostitute is seated on many waters. The angel explained, "The waters that you saw, where the prostitute is seated, are peoples and multitudes and nations and languages." This city is a multinational, multicultural, multilingual city and has worldwide influence. The woman is arrayed in purple and scarlet and adorned with gold, jewels and pearls – symbols of great wealth and royalty. She has a golden goblet full of abominations and the impurities of her fornication. On her forehead is written a name of mystery: "Babylon the great, mother of prostitutes and of earth's abominations."

One of the other cities built on seven hills is Athens. While it has exerted worldwide influence over humanity by spreading its language and culture, it does not seem to be the city that has been known for its widespread killing of the saints. While it has seen a great wealth and former glory, today it is not a city of wealth or worldwide influence.

We have discounted Babylon – it is built on a plain, and we have set aside Jerusalem, Rome and Athens as likely possibilities. That leaves Istanbul and Mecca.

Istanbul

Istanbul, known previously as Byzantium and later Constantinople, is the second largest city on the continent of Europe, behind only Moscow, with a greater metropolitan population of 12.6 million. It became the capital of the Roman Empire (330-395) under Constantine, who through the Edict of Milan in 313 proclaimed tolerance of all religions, after which Christianity came to be the religion of the state under Theodosius I in 391. The city then became the capital of the Eastern Roman (Byzantine) Empire (395–1204 and 1261–1453), the Latin Empire (1204–1261), and the Ottoman Empire (1453–1922). While Ankara is today the capital of Turkey, Istanbul is the city of most influence.

During the reign of Constantius II, the Hagia Sophia Cathedral was inaugurated in 360 and remained the largest Christian cathedral in the world for one thousand years until 1453 when the Muslim Caliph turned it into a mosque. The older part of the city is said to be built on seven hills, each of which has a mosque built on top. While Istanbul was the seat of the Muslim Caliphate for nearly five hundred years, it was a fairly tolerant city with Jews, Christians and Muslims living in relative harmony. Because of that, it is hard to describe the city as being drunk with the blood of the saints. It is also not a city in the wilderness.

Mecca

That leaves us with Mecca. Missionary Samuel Zwemer described the city from his personal time there in the 1890s. "The sacred Mosque, Masjid al Haram with the Ka'aba as its center, is located in the middle of the city. Mecca lies in a hot, sandy valley, absolutely without verdure and surrounded by rocky, seven barren hills, destitute of trees or even shrubs. The valley is about 300 feet wide and 4,000 feet long, and slopes towards the south. Al-Ka'aba (the Cube) or Beit Allah (House of Allah)

is located in the bed of the valley."[85] The mountains are listed as follows:[86]
Jabal Quba
Jabal Al-Qinaa
Jabal Li Aali
Jabal Jifan
Jabal Jiyad
Jabal Abi Qubais
Jabal Hindi

With Mecca, we see that it is in a wilderness and that it has seven hills or mountains. While much seems to favor Mecca as the anti-type of which Babylon is the type, if one is to be honest, we have to say that at best it is still an educated guess. Much can change in a very short period of time, but at this point in time, it seems to me that Mecca best fulfills the description of Babylon. Before comparing the details listed in Revelation 17, let us look at the next chapter where more information is given.

Rev. 18:1-24
After this I saw another angel coming down from heaven, having great authority, and the earth was made bright with his glory. [2] And he called out with a mighty voice,

"Fallen, fallen is Babylon the great!
She has become a dwelling place for demons,
a haunt for every unclean spirit,
a haunt for every unclean bird,
a haunt for every unclean and detestable beast.
[3] For all nations have drunk
the wine of the passion of her sexual immorality,
and the kings of the earth have committed immorality with her,
and the merchants of the earth have grown rich from the power of her luxurious living."
[4] Then I heard another voice from heaven saying,

---

[85] Samuel M. Zwemer, The influence of Animism on Islam, <http://www.bible.ca/islam/library/Zwemer/Animism/chapt8.htm>
[86] <**meccaseven**mountains.blogspot.com/.../project-**mecca**-alert-woman-riding.html>

"Come out of her, my people,
lest you take part in her sins,
lest you share in her plagues;
[5] for her sins are heaped high as heaven,
and God has remembered her iniquities.
[6] Pay her back as she herself has paid back others,
and repay her double for her deeds;
mix a double portion for her in the cup she mixed.
[7] As she glorified herself and lived in luxury,
so give her a like measure of torment and mourning,
since in her heart she says,
'I sit as a queen,
I am no widow,
and mourning I shall never see.'
[8] For this reason her plagues will come in a single day,
death and mourning and famine,
and she will be burned up with fire;
for mighty is the Lord God who has judged her."

[9] And the kings of the earth, who committed sexual immorality
and lived in luxury with her, will weep and wail over her when they
see the smoke of her burning. [10] They will stand far off, in fear of
her torment, and say,

"Alas! Alas! You great city,
you mighty city, Babylon!
For in a single hour your judgment has come."

[11] And the merchants of the earth weep and mourn for her, since
no one buys their cargo anymore, [12] cargo of gold, silver, jewels,
pearls, fine linen, purple cloth, silk, scarlet cloth, all kinds of scented
wood, all kinds of articles of ivory, all kinds of articles of costly
wood, bronze, iron and marble, [13] cinnamon, spice, incense, myrrh,
frankincense, wine, oil, fine flour, wheat, cattle and sheep, horses and
chariots, and slaves, that is, human souls.

[14] "The fruit for which your soul longed
has gone from you,
and all your delicacies and your splendors
are lost to you,

never to be found again!"
[15] The merchants of these wares, who gained wealth from her, will stand far off, in fear of her torment, weeping and mourning aloud,

[16] "Alas, alas, for the great city
that was clothed in fine linen,
in purple and scarlet,
adorned with gold,
with jewels, and with pearls!
[17] For in a single hour all this wealth has been laid waste."

And all shipmasters and seafaring men, sailors and all whose trade is on the sea, stood far off [18] and cried out as they saw the smoke of her burning,

"What city was like the great city?"
[19] And they threw dust on their heads as they wept and mourned, crying out,

"Alas, alas, for the great city
where all who had ships at sea
grew rich by her wealth!
For in a single hour she has been laid waste.
[20] Rejoice over her, O heaven,
and you saints and apostles and prophets,
for God has given judgment for you against her!"

[21] Then a mighty angel took up a stone like a great millstone and threw it into the sea, saying,

"So will Babylon the great city be thrown down with violence,
and will be found no more;
[22] and the sound of harpists and musicians, of flute players and trumpeters,
will be heard in you no more,
and a craftsman of any craft
will be found in you no more,
and the sound of the mill
will be heard in you no more,
[23] and the light of a lamp

will shine in you no more,
and the voice of bridegroom and bride
will be heard in you no more,
for your merchants were the great ones of the earth,
and all nations were deceived by your sorcery.
[24] And in her was found the blood of prophets and of saints,
and of all who have been slain on earth."

Rev. 19:1-5
After this I heard what seemed to be the loud voice of a great multitude in heaven, crying out,

"Hallelujah!
Salvation and glory and power belong to our God,
[2] for his judgments are true and just;
for he has judged the great prostitute
who corrupted the earth with her immorality,
and has avenged on her the blood of his servants."

[3] Once more they cried out,

"Hallelujah!
The smoke from her goes up forever and ever."
[4] And the twenty-four elders and the four living creatures fell down and worshiped God who was seated on the throne, saying, "Amen. Hallelujah!" [5] And from the throne came a voice saying,

"Praise our God, all you his servants,
you who fear him, small and great."

The metaphor used in Revelation of this city is that of a prostitute, with whom people, in particular kings, commit sexual immorality. The language is similar in some respects to a passage in Zechariah, in which a woman is personified as "Wickedness".

Zech. 5:5-11
Then the angel who talked with me came forward and said to me, "Lift your eyes and see what this is that is going out." [6] And I said, "What is it?" He said, "This is the basket that is going out." And he said, "This is their iniquity in all the land." [7] And behold, the leaden

cover was lifted, and there was a woman sitting in the basket! [8] And he said, "This is Wickedness." And he thrust her back into the basket, and thrust down the leaden weight on its opening.

[9] Then I lifted my eyes and saw, and behold, two women coming forward! The wind was in their wings. They had wings like the wings of a stork, and they lifted up the basket between earth and heaven. [10] Then I said to the angel who talked with me, "Where are they taking the basket?" [11] He said to me, "To the land of Shinar, to build a house for it. And when this is prepared, they will set the basket down there on its base."

This "woman" closed in a basket with a leaden cover, is taken to the land of Shinar – Babylon, where a house is built for it and it is set down on a base.

While Zechariah ministered (beginning in 520 B.C.) in the period following the return to Israel from the Babylonian captivity, and much of what he wrote had to do with the immediate situation of rebuilding Jerusalem and the need to rebuild the temple, a large part of his prophesies have to do with both the first and second coming of the Messiah. Could this vision above refer to the future end time Babylon – the great prostitute?

Spiritual Seduction

The most sacred site for the Muslims is the Ka'bah (also spelled Kaaba), or black cube at the center of the Grand Mosque in Mecca.

"The **Black Stone** (called الحجر الأسود *al-Hajr al-Aswad* in Arabic) is a Muslim relic, which according to Islamic tradition dates back to the time of Adam and Eve. Historical research claims that the Black Stone marked the Kaaba as a place of worship during pre-Islamic pagan times.[1] It is the eastern cornerstone of the Kaaba, the ancient stone building towards which Muslims pray, in the center of the Grand Mosque in Mecca, Saudi Arabia.[2] The Stone is a dark rock, polished smooth by the hands of millions of pilgrims, that has been broken into a number of fragments cemented into a silver frame in the side of the Kaaba. Although it has often been described as a meteorite, this hypothesis is still under consideration.[3]
Muslim pilgrims circle the Kaaba as part of the Tawaf ritual of the Hajj. Many of them try, if possible, to stop and kiss the Black Stone, emulating the kiss that Islamic tradition records that it received from

the Islamic Prophet Muhammad.[4] If they cannot reach it, they point to it on each of their seven circuits around the Kaaba. [5]

The Black Stone was revered well before the preaching of Islam by Muhammad. By the time of Muhammad, it was already associated with the Kaaba, a pre-Islamic shrine that was revered as a sacred sanctuary and a site of pilgrimage. In her book, *Islam: A Short History*, Karen Armstrong asserts that the Kaaba was dedicated to Hubal, a Nabatean deity, and contained 360 idols which either represented the days of the year, or were effigies of the Arabian pantheon.

The Black Stone, in Muslim belief, originated in the time of Adam. According to the Hadith, "it descended from Paradise whiter than milk, but the sins of the sons of Adam made it black".[19] According to belief, an angel spoke to the great prophet Abraham, and told him to institute the rite of the stone in the hajj at Mecca.[20]

Islamic tradition holds that the Stone fell from Heaven to show Adam and Eve where to build an altar, which became the first temple on Earth. Muslims believe that the stone was originally pure and dazzling white, but has since turned black because of the sins of the people.[21] Adam's altar and the stone were said to have been lost during Noah's Flood and forgotten. Ibrahim was said to have later found the Black Stone at the original site of Adam's altar when the angel Jibrail revealed it to him.[9] Ibrahim ordered his son Ismael - who is an ancestor of Muhammad - to build a new temple, the Kaaba, in which to embed the Stone."[87]

When one looks at pictures of the Kaaba (cf. www.google.com, "kaaba black stone"), one notices that the Kaaba is on a base, or pedestal. The fragments of stone cemented inside a silver frame on one of the corners of the Kaaba is the object that Muslims try to kiss. The angel told Zechariah that the woman in the basket was "Wickedness" and it was taken to the land of Shinar – the land of Babylon. For the Jewish and Christian reader, it does not require a great stretch of the imagination to see the female symbolism in the object that is kissed and connect the Kaaba with the passage cited in Zechariah 5 above.

Within the metaphor of the prostitute representing a city, so those

---

[87] "Black Stone,"< http://en.wikipedia.org/wiki/Black_Stone>

who have sexual relations with her symbolize a spiritual union with the prostitute. Various online pictures of the Kaaba show kings, princes, presidents and world leaders awaiting their turn to kiss the black stone, which is an important aspect in Muslim worship, though Muslims are quick to point out that they are not involved in idolatry by this act.

The city is a place of strong spiritual influence:

Rev. 18:2

"Fallen, fallen is Babylon the great!
She has become a dwelling place for demons,
a haunt for every unclean spirit,
a haunt for every unclean bird,
a haunt for every unclean and detestable beast.

We have mentioned that there are 57 countries that are members of the Organization of the Islamic Conference (OIC). The kings and leaders of each of these nations are obligated to make their pilgrimage to Mecca to worship Allah.

This prostitute is seen to not only seduce kings but also intoxicate the peoples:

Rev. 17:1-2

"…. I will show you the great prostitute …. with whom the kings of the earth have committed sexual immorality, and with the wine of whose sexual immorality the dwellers on earth have become drunk."

Those who are drunk come under the influence of alcohol. The people come under the inebriating influence of this prostitute, causing them to do things they normally would not do.

We saw in earlier chapters how the Israelites would sacrifice their children alive in the fire to the pagan gods around them. So also, many Muslim families willingly sacrifice their children to Allah as suicide bombers.

Rev. 17:6

"And I saw the woman, drunk with the blood of the saints, the blood of the martyrs of Jesus."

Islam has been and is the greatest opponent of the Christian faith. Just in the Anglican St. George's Church in Baghdad, some 200 have been killed in the first six months of 2011. Anglican Canon Andrew

White said that in the year 2010, he baptized 13 Muslims; within a week, 11 of them were murdered.[88] Millions of Christians throughout the Muslim world have been put to death since Mohammed began his religion.

Economic Seduction

This is a city that lives in luxury and buys all kinds of luxurious items. It is a city that enriches many, particularly the merchants and the shipping industry.

Rev. 18:3
"… the merchants of the earth have grown rich from the power of her luxurious living."

Rev. 18:7
"… she glorified herself and lived in luxury, …. in her heart she says, 'I sit as a queen, I am no widow, and mourning I shall never see.'

Rev. 18:9
"And the kings of the earth, who committed sexual immorality and lived in luxury with her, will weep and wail over her when they see the smoke of her burning."

Rev. 18:11-19
"And the merchants of the earth weep and mourn for her, since no one buys their cargo anymore, [12] cargo of gold, silver, jewels, pearls, fine linen, purple cloth, silk, scarlet cloth, all kinds of scented wood, all kinds of articles of ivory, all kinds of articles of costly wood, bronze, iron and marble, [13] cinnamon, spice, incense, myrrh, frankincense, wine, oil, fine flour, wheat, cattle and sheep, horses and chariots, and slaves, that is, human souls."

Even though slavery is outlawed in all countries in the world today, it is estimated that there are more slaves today than at any other time in history, with the number being estimated at 27 million people.[89]

---

[88] Felicia Mann, "Despite 200 Murders, Iraqi Church Grows Strong," Charisma Magazine, 02 June, 2011

[89] "Slavery," <http://en.wikipedia.org/wiki/Slavery>

[14] "The fruit for which your soul longed
has gone from you,
and all your delicacies and your splendors
are lost to you,
never to be found again!"
[15] The merchants of these wares, who gained wealth from her, will
stand far off, in fear of her torment, weeping and mourning aloud,

[16] "Alas, alas, for the great city
that was clothed in fine linen,
in purple and scarlet,
adorned with gold,
with jewels, and with pearls!
[17] For in a single hour all this wealth has been laid waste."

And all shipmasters and seafaring men, sailors and all whose trade is
on the sea, stood far off [18] and cried out as they saw the smoke of
her burning,

"What city was like the great city?"
[19] And they threw dust on their heads as they wept and mourned,
crying out,

"Alas, alas, for the great city
where all who had ships at sea
grew rich by her wealth!
For in a single hour she has been laid waste.

The country known today for the most extreme opulent living seems to be Saudi Arabia. It is the world's largest oil exporting nation and other than oil, pretty much imports everything else. The excesses of spending by the Saudi royal family are legendary. Kings and leaders of nations, including many US presidents have received generous personal gifts – some in the millions of dollars, for favoring Saudi Arabia[90]

Merchants have made enormous sums of money by selling every imaginable luxury object to the Saudi wealthy, including a rare diamond studded Mercedes SL 600 worth $4.8 million. It is Saudi Prince Waleed Bin Talal's 38th car after owning the best cars available.

The ship owners have also made out fabulously, both those with big

[90] Joel Richardson, *Understanding the Times*, DVD sessions 3-4

tankers shipping oil around the world and cargo ships bringing merchandise into the country. While there are six major ports in Saudi Arabia, besides those for oil, the one at Jeddah, located 39 miles (63 km) from Mecca, is the most important one.

"Jeddah Islamic Port is the major port for Saudi Arabia and the capital of the Makkah Province. Located on the country's central western coast on the Red Sea west of Mecca, Jeddah is one of Saudi Arabia's largest cities and the diplomatic country's capital, home to many foreign embassies and the country's ministry of foreign affairs. Jeddah Islamic Port is the gateway to the holy city of Mecca. More than 3.4 million people live in the Jeddah Islamic Port and city.

At one time, the city's economy depended on pilgrims and fishing. With long history of trading, Jeddah (also spelled Jiddah) is home to many of the most successful businesses and merchants in the world. Today, it is Saudi Arabia's commercial capital. It is also well-positioned between the Africa and the Middle East, making it a commercial center for the subcontinent as well. It is also the country's third busiest industrial city.

Jeddah Islamic Port is strategically located at the crossroads of the east-west international shipping route. Serving the holy cities of Medina and Mecca, almost 60% of Saudi Arabia's ocean-going imports come through Jeddah Islamic Port."[91]

As with the building of the Tower of Babel, ever increasingly high skyscrapers tend to be a symbol of man's independence and pride. Having a $4.8 million diamond studded Mercedes is child's play compared to the project that Prince Waleed Bin Talal is currently creating and leading. The project that was formerly called the "Mile High Tower" (1.6 km) is now known as the "Kingdom Tower" and has been downsized to at least 1,000 meters high (3,281 ft.) because of poor soil. It will be the first kilometer high building and will be at least 568 ft (173 m) taller than the Burj Khalifa in Dubai. On August 2, 2011, it was publicly announced that a contract had been signed by Saudi Bin Ladin Group (SBG), construction was going to start soon, and that the tower was expected to take 63 months (5 years, 3 months) to

91 "Jeddah Islamic Port", <http://www.worldportsource.com/ports/SAU_Jeddah_Islamic_Port_281.php>

complete.[92]

The Reason for the Destruction

Yet in spite of Mecca being the city toward which all Muslims pray, the text says:

Rev. 17:16-17
"And the ten horns that you saw, they and the beast will hate the prostitute. They will make her desolate and naked, and devour her flesh and burn her up with fire,"

The natural explanation is that these leaders will hate this city and will burn it up. It is no secret that much of the Muslim world harbors animosity toward Saudi Arabia. They are seen to be collaborators with the West. They have even given Israel permission to fly over their air space and refuel if necessary, if they attack Iran. They are seen to be corrupt.

On a spiritual level, however, Satan's plan is that he will be worshiped in Jerusalem, not Mecca. Once he has achieved that goal, he wants undivided attention to his throne and agent on Mt. Zion, not in Mecca.

While it will be the beast, inspired by the dragon and the ten kings under his authority who will burn up the city, the real reason for its destruction is that they will be fulfilling God's purpose by bringing judgment to the city that has so vehemently stood against the God of the Bible and his people.

"[17] for God has put it into their hearts to carry out his purpose by being of one mind and handing over their royal power to the beast, until the words of God are fulfilled."

We see that God's purpose is judgment:

Rev. 17:1
Then one of the seven angels who had the seven bowls came and said to me, "Come, I will show you the judgment of the great prostitute who is seated on many waters,

[92] "Kingdom Tower", <
http://en.wikipedia.org/wiki/Kingdom_Tower_(Jeddah)>

Rev. 18:6

Pay her back as she herself has paid back others,
and repay her double for her deeds;
mix a double portion for her in the cup she mixed.

Rev. 18:8

For this reason her plagues will come in a single day,
death and mourning and famine,
and she will be burned up with fire;
for mighty is the Lord God who has judged her."

Rev. 18:10

They will stand far off, in fear of her torment, and say,

"Alas! Alas! You great city,
you mighty city, Babylon!
For in a single hour your judgment has come."

Rev. 18:20

Rejoice over her, O heaven,
and you saints and apostles and prophets,
for God has given judgment for you against her!"

Rev. 19:1-2

After this I heard what seemed to be the loud voice of a great multitude in heaven, crying out,
"Hallelujah!
Salvation and glory and power belong to our God,
[2] for his judgments are true and just;
for he has judged the great prostitute …."

But why this judgment?

This is the city with whom the kings of the earth have committed sexual immorality, with whom the dwellers on earth have become drunk with the wine of her immorality. She is the mother of prostitutes, and of earth's abominations. She is drunk with the blood of the martyrs of Jesus. She is a dwelling place for demons. She has lived in pride, arrogance and luxury. She has deceived the world by her sorcery and in her was found the blood of prophets and of saints and of all who have been slain on earth.

This is why God uses his very enemies to accomplish his purpose in destroying this great city that has dominion over the kings of the earth.

Rev. 18:21

Then a mighty angel took up a stone like a great millstone and threw it into the sea, saying,

"So will Babylon the great city be thrown down with violence,
and will be found no more;

".... The smoke from her goes up forever and ever." (19:3)

During the first Iraq war, Saddam Hussein set on fire a number of oil fields in Kuwait that took weeks to put out. The smoke was suffocating. One can picture the non-stop blaze that a small nuclear bomb would create if dropped on a city that sits atop oil reserves. As the text says, "the smoke from her goes up forever and ever."

While Isaiah was speaking of Nebuchadnezzar's Babylon in the following text, it may also be one of those passages that have a double fulfillment:

Isaiah 13:19-20

And Babylon, the glory of kingdoms,
the splendor and pomp of the Chaldeans,
will be like Sodom and Gomorrah
when God overthrew them.
[20] It will never be inhabited
or lived in for all generations;
no Arab will pitch his tent there;
no shepherds will make their flocks lie down there.

Warning to God's People

God does not leave the world without a warning. In particular he tells his people to come out of the city.

Rev. 18:4-5

Then I heard another voice from heaven saying,

"Come out of her, my people,
lest you take part in her sins,

lest you share in her plagues;
[5] for her sins are heaped high as heaven,
and God has remembered her iniquities.

It is forbidden for any non-Muslim to enter the city of Mecca, so the question naturally arises, "How can there be a warning for God's people to come out if there are no people of God in her? Reports have been abounding of Muslims being converted to Christ in various parts of the world. Many have had angelic visitations, some have even had Jesus appear to them; others have had dreams or visions. It is not unreasonable to imagine that even in the city of Mecca, the grace of God is able to break through the darkness and bring Muslims to embrace Jesus as the Son of God who died for their sins and rose again. However, they are warned to flee lest they take part in the sins of the city and share in her plagues, just as God warned Lot and his family to flee Sodom before it was destroyed.

There is a principle that God does nothing without first giving a warning through his prophets:

Amos 3:6-7
Is a trumpet blown in a city,
and the people are not afraid?
Does disaster come to a city,
unless the Lord has done it?
[7] "For the Lord God does nothing
without revealing his secret
to his servants the prophets.

The destruction of this city seals the transfer of religious allegiance from Mecca to Jerusalem where the Antichrist has his throne and where his image is standing in the temple. And if this prophecy has a dual fulfillment like so many others, Rome also may be destroyed and the religious allegiance of Catholics will be transferred from Rome to the Antichrist in Jerusalem as well.

His end is imminent, however.

22 ARMAGEDDON AND GOG AND MAGOG

IN CHAPTER 20 we looked at the bowls of judgment. The sixth bowl of wrath saw the gathering of nations to a place in Israel called Armageddon, or in the valley of Megiddo or Jezreel. This is in preparation for the final great battle. We alluded to the question as to whether this is the same battle as that referred to in Ezekiel when he speaks of "Gog and Magog." As we look at the passages, I believe we will see they are the same event with different details added.

Demonic spirits have persuaded the nations of the world to send their armies to Israel. Jerusalem will be taken. It is not stated how long it will be occupied.

Rev. 16:12-16

The sixth angel poured out his bowl on the great river Euphrates, and its water was dried up, to prepare the way for the kings from the east. [13] And I saw, coming out of the mouth of the dragon and out of the mouth of the beast and out of the mouth of the false prophet, three unclean spirits like frogs. [14] For they are demonic spirits, performing signs, who go abroad to the kings of the whole world, to assemble them for battle on the great day of God the Almighty. [15] ("Behold, I am coming like a thief! Blessed is the one who stays awake, keeping his garments on, that he may not go about naked and be seen exposed!") [16] And they assembled them at the place that in Hebrew is called Armageddon.

Zech. 14:1-3

Behold, a day is coming for the Lord, when the spoil taken from you will be divided in your midst. [2] For I will gather all the nations against Jerusalem to battle, and the city shall be taken and the houses plundered and the women raped. Half of the city shall go out into exile, but the rest of the people shall not be cut off from the city. [3] Then the Lord will go out and fight against those nations as when he fights on a day of battle.

Zech. 14:12-15

And this shall be the plague with which the Lord will strike all the peoples that wage war against Jerusalem: their flesh will rot while they are still standing on their feet, their eyes will rot in their sockets, and their tongues will rot in their mouths.

[13] And on that day a great panic from the Lord shall fall on them, so that each will seize the hand of another, and the hand of the one will be raised against the hand of the other. [14] Even Judah will fight against Jerusalem. And the wealth of all the surrounding nations shall be collected, gold, silver, and garments in great abundance. [15] And a plague like this plague shall fall on the horses, the mules, the camels, the donkeys, and whatever beasts may be in those camps.

Those who have seen the movie series, "Raiders of the Lost Ark" will remember what happened to the soldiers who looked into the Ark of the Covenant. I do not know if the producers of the movie got their inspiration from this passage in Zechariah 14, but the film showed the glory and power coming out of the Ark causing the people's eyes and flesh to melt off their bodies before they could fall to the ground.

Some have speculated that what is described is the effect of some modern day weapon. Thermo baric weapons (heat and pressure) use the principle of exploding fuel or oxygen in the air which first sucks all the oxygen out of an area – perhaps enough to suck the flesh off a human. However, its succeeding shock waves and conflagration would burn up all the clothing and this text says they will be able to collect the garments of the dead enemies. A neutron bomb, or "enhanced radiation weapon" (ERW) is, as Leonid Brezhnev once said, a "capitalist bomb" because it is designed to destroy people while preserving property. Whether God chooses to use human technology or does something completely new with his own display of power, we cannot say with certainty. What is clear is that there will be millions of dead, both of humans and animals.

Perhaps another word is in order again about Bible interpretation. I have mentioned that the writers may have been writing based on what the reality of war was in their day, thus the mention of mules, camels, horses and donkeys in the enemy's camp. However, there exist today nuclear and non-nuclear electromagnetic pulses (EMP) which can be detonated in the atmosphere resulting in the destruction of computer and electronic equipment. Such a weapon would make modern weaponry and transportation unusable, thus forcing armies to revert to animal and strictly mechanical means.

Another possibility is a repeat of the solar storm of 1859. NASA's website describes what happened this way:

> In scientific circles where solar flares, magnetic storms and other unique solar events are discussed, the occurrences of September 1-2, 1859, are the star stuff of legend. Even 144 years ago, many of Earth's inhabitants realized something momentous had just occurred. Within hours, telegraph wires in both the United States and Europe spontaneously shorted out, causing numerous fires, while the Northern Lights, solar-induced phenomena more closely associated with regions near Earth's North Pole, were documented as far south as Rome, Havana and Hawaii, with similar effects at the South Pole.
>
> What happened in 1859 was a combination of several events that occurred on the Sun at the same time. If they took place separately they would be somewhat notable events. But together they caused the most potent disruption of Earth's ionosphere in recorded history. "What they generated was the perfect space storm," says Bruce Tsurutani, a plasma physicist at NASA's Jet Propulsion Laboratory.[93]

Similar, but much smaller coronal mass ejections have occurred in the last several decades, knocking out power grids and communications systems. NASA scientists believe a perfect storm like that of 1859 could happen again, and be even more intense than that one. Such an event could likewise destroy much, if not all electrical and electronic equipment.

Rev. 19:17-19

Then I saw an angel standing in the sun, and with a loud voice he called to all the birds that fly directly overhead, "Come, gather for the great supper of God, [18] to eat the flesh of kings, the flesh of captains, the flesh of mighty men, the flesh of horses and their riders, and the flesh of all men, both free and slave, both small and great."

93<**http://science.nasa.gov/science-news/science-at-nasa/2003/23oct_superstorm/**

[19] And I saw the beast and the kings of the earth with their armies gathered to make war against him who was sitting on the horse and against his army.

Gog and Magog

But what about the war spoken of in Ezekiel? Some Biblical scholars believe it will happen at the beginning of the last seven year period of time. Others feel it is just at the end of the millennium. As we have noted before, often biblical prophecies have double or multiple fulfillments, such as the "abomination of desolation." This, I believe, is another example of a prophecy that will have a double fulfillment: the first at Christ's return and the second at the end of the millennium period.

Ezekiel 38:1-6

The word of the Lord came to me: [2] "Son of man, set your face toward Gog, of the land of **Magog**, the chief prince of **Meshech** and **Tubal**, and prophesy against him [3] and say, Thus says the Lord God: Behold, I am against you, O Gog, chief prince of Meshech and Tubal. [4] And I will turn you about and put hooks into your jaws, and I will bring you out, and all your army, horses and horsemen, all of them clothed in full armor, a great host, all of them with buckler and shield, wielding swords. [5] **Persia, Cush, and Put** are with them, all of them with shield and helmet; [6] **Gomer** and all his hordes; **Beth-togarmah** from the uttermost parts of the north with all his hordes— many peoples are with you.

The text identifies a prince – Gog - whom God says he is against. He is identified as being of the land of Magog, the chief prince of Meshech and Tubal. God will bring their armies, along with a number of allies - the picture is that of putting hooks in their jaws to bring them out - to what the following verses identify as Israel. Who are these peoples that 6th century B.C. prophet Ezekiel is talking about?

First century A.D. historian Josephus wrote: "Magog founded those that from him were named Magogites, but who are by the Greeks called Scythians."[94]

[94] Flavius Josephus, The Works of Flavius Josephus. *Antiquities of the Jews*, Bk 1, ch. 6

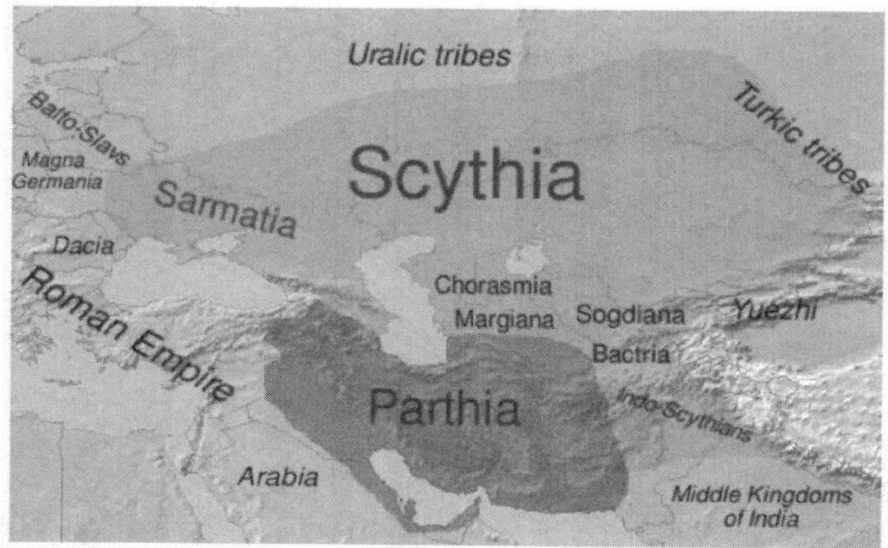

Scythia-Parthia 100 BC
95

The modern territories covered by the 1st century BC Scythians are the Ukraine, southern Russia, Georgia, Armenia, Azerbaijan, Kazakhstan, Uzbekistan, Kyrgyzstan, Tajikistan, Turkmenistan, Afghanistan and Pakistan.

While most of this area is predominantly Muslim today, it is well known that non-Islamic Russia has become an important ally of Iran and Syria, furnishing Iran with nuclear materials and technology and selling large quantities of weapons and training to both countries. Putin's visit in October 16, 2007 marked the first visit of a Russian head of state to Tehran since Stalin in 1943. During several previous wars against Israel, the USSR aided Arab nations with weapons and military advisors.

However, "Meshek, Tubal, Gomer and Beth Togarmah can be identified with real 8th and 7th century peoples, kings or kingdoms of Anatolia, modern Turkey."[96]

In addition to these northern peoples listed, Persia, Cush and Put are with them. Persia is of course, Iran, east of Israel. Cush has been identified as the area south of Egypt, or what is today northern Sudan. Put refers to the north African area of Libya. Hordes of people will come from north, east and south to attack Israel.

---

[95] Cam Rea, "From Parthia to Gothica", < http://britam.org/PARTHIANS.html>

[96] Daniel I. Block, The Book of Ezekiel: chapters 25-48. (Eerdmans 1998), p. 439

The biblical text continues:

Ezekiel 38:7-16
"Be ready and keep ready, you and all your hosts that are assembled about you, and be a guard for them. [8] After many days you will be mustered. In the latter years you will go against the land that is restored from war, the land whose people were gathered from many peoples upon the mountains of Israel, which had been a continual waste. Its people were brought out from the peoples and now dwell securely, all of them. [9] You will advance, coming on like a storm. You will be like a cloud covering the land, you and all your hordes, and many peoples with you.

[10] "Thus says the Lord God: On that day, thoughts will come into your mind, and you will devise an evil scheme [11] and say, 'I will go up against the land of unwalled villages. I will fall upon the quiet people who dwell securely, all of them dwelling without walls, and having no bars or gates,' [12] to seize spoil and carry off plunder, to turn your hand against the waste places that are now inhabited, and the people who were gathered from the nations, who have acquired livestock and goods, who dwell at the center of the earth. [13] Sheba and Dedan and the merchants of Tarshish and all its leaders will say to you, 'Have you come to seize spoil? Have you assembled your hosts to carry off plunder, to carry away silver and gold, to take away livestock and goods, to seize great spoil?'

[14] "Therefore, son of man, prophesy, and say to Gog, Thus says the Lord God: On that day when my people Israel are dwelling securely, will you not know it? [15] You will come from your place out of the uttermost parts of the north, you and many peoples with you, all of them riding on horses, a great host, a mighty army. [16] You will come up against my people Israel, like a cloud covering the land. In the latter days I will bring you against my land, that the nations may know me, when through you, O Gog, I vindicate my holiness before their eyes.

The text speaks of the people of Israel having been gathered from many peoples and nations to the land of Israel and that they are prosperous. They turned the land from being a continual waste to being inhabited. All of this has happened so far.

At the time of this invasion, they are restored from war and living securely and peacefully in unwalled villages. Perhaps this will be due to the peace treaty brought about by the Antichrist. A big motive for this invasion is to carry off the wealth of the people. Today, Israel far exceeds its neighbors in wealth and per capita income. Recent discoveries of vast natural gas deposits and huge aquifers in the desert will give Israel even greater riches. There may be discoveries of larger oil fields in the future than have been discovered thus far. The text speaks of seizing their gold and silver among other things as one of the motivations for this invasion. Today, with the world's currencies being in trouble, many have invested in gold and silver as a hedge against inflation.

The names Sheba, Dedan and Tarshish are mentioned. Sheba is the area of Yemen, Dedan in Saudi Arabia and Tarshish is in Turkey. These armies will cover the land of Israel like a cloud. But God is not surprised. In fact, it is he who brings them against Israel. Why? "In the latter days I will bring you against my land, that the nations may know me, when through you, O Gog, I vindicate my holiness before their eyes."

Ezekiel 38:17-23

"Thus says the Lord God: Are you he of whom I spoke in former days by my servants the prophets of Israel, who in those days prophesied for years that I would bring you against them? [18] But on that day, the day that Gog shall come against the land of Israel, declares the Lord God, my wrath will be roused in my anger. [19] For in my jealousy and in my blazing wrath I declare, On that day there shall be a great earthquake in the land of Israel. [20] The fish of the sea and the birds of the heavens and the beasts of the field and all creeping things that creep on the ground, and all the people who are on the face of the earth, shall quake at my presence. And the mountains shall be thrown down, and the cliffs shall fall, and every wall shall tumble to the ground. [21] I will summon a sword against Gog on all my mountains, declares the Lord God. Every man's sword will be against his brother. [22] With pestilence and bloodshed I will enter into judgment with him, and I will rain upon him and his hordes and the many peoples who are with him torrential rains and hailstones, fire and sulfur. [23] So I will show my greatness and my holiness and make myself known in the eyes of many nations. Then they will know that I am the Lord.

Again, recall the description of the seventh and last bowl of wrath:

Rev. 16:17-21

The seventh angel poured out his bowl into the air, and a loud voice came out of the temple, from the throne, saying, "It is done!" [18] And there were flashes of lightning, rumblings, peals of thunder, and a great earthquake such as there had never been since man was on the earth, so great was that earthquake. [19] The great city was split into three parts, and the cities of the nations fell, and God remembered Babylon the great, to make her drain the cup of the wine of the fury of his wrath. [20] And every island fled away, and no mountains were to be found. [21] And great hailstones, about one hundred pounds each, fell from heaven on people; and they cursed God for the plague of the hail, because the plague was so severe.

Both texts mention the massive earthquake, such that the mountains will be thrown down or be no more. There is the mention of lightning, fire, hailstones – about one hundred pounds each. This seems to be describing the same event.

There is an event that I believe happens simultaneously with Jesus' coming in person during this Armageddon / Gog Magog battle.

The Rapture

In the text immediately preceding Christ's return in Revelation 19 we have this interlude:

Rev. 19:6-11

Then I heard what seemed to be the voice of a great multitude, like the roar of many waters and like the sound of mighty peals of thunder, crying out,

"Hallelujah!
For the Lord our God
the Almighty reigns.
[7] Let us rejoice and exult
and give him the glory,
for the marriage of the Lamb has come,
and his Bride has made herself ready;
[8] it was granted her to clothe herself
with fine linen, bright and pure"—

for the fine linen is the righteous deeds of the saints.

[9] And the angel said to me, "Write this: Blessed are those who are invited to the marriage supper of the Lamb." And he said to me, "These are the true words of God." [10] Then I fell down at his feet to worship him, but he said to me, "You must not do that! I am a fellow servant with you and your brothers who hold to the testimony of Jesus. Worship God." For the testimony of Jesus is the spirit of prophecy.

[11] Then I saw heaven opened, and behold, a white horse! The one sitting on it is called Faithful and True, and in righteousness he judges and makes war. …"

This marriage of the Lamb is the language Jesus used to describe his coming:

Matthew 25:1-13

"Then the kingdom of heaven will be like ten virgins who took their lamps and went to meet the bridegroom. [2] Five of them were foolish, and five were wise. [3] For when the foolish took their lamps, they took no oil with them, [4] but the wise took flasks of oil with their lamps. [5] As the bridegroom was delayed, they all became drowsy and slept. [6] But at midnight there was a cry, 'Here is the bridegroom! Come out to meet him.' [7] Then all those virgins rose and trimmed their lamps. [8] And the foolish said to the wise, 'Give us some of your oil, for our lamps are going out.' [9] But the wise answered, saying, 'Since there will not be enough for us and for you, go rather to the dealers and buy for yourselves.' [10] And while they were going to buy, the bridegroom came, and those who were ready went in with him to the marriage feast, and the door was shut. [11] Afterward the other virgins came also, saying, 'Lord, lord, open to us.' [12] But he answered, 'Truly, I say to you, I do not know you.' [13] Watch therefore, for you know neither the day nor the hour.

The Timing

As we have stated before, it is after the tribulation, immediately after these cataclysmic events of the world's greatest earthquake, lightning, thunder, hailstones, a meteor shower, the sun and moon not giving their light, that Jesus comes with the souls of his saints and his angels and the resurrection takes place and those believers still alive will be raptured or transformed.

Matthew 24:29-31

"Immediately after the tribulation of those days the sun will be darkened, and the moon will not give its light, and the stars will fall from heaven, and the powers of the heavens will be shaken. [30] Then will appear in heaven the sign of the Son of Man, and then all the tribes of the earth will mourn, and they will see the Son of Man coming on the clouds of heaven with power and great glory. [31] And he will send out his angels with a loud trumpet call, and they will gather his elect from the four winds, from one end of heaven to the other.

Rev. 19:11-16

Then I saw heaven opened, and behold, a white horse! The one sitting on it is called Faithful and True, and in righteousness he judges and makes war. [12] His eyes are like a flame of fire, and on his head are many diadems, and he has a name written that no one knows but himself. [13] He is clothed in a robe dipped in blood, and the name by which he is called is The Word of God. [14] And the armies of heaven, arrayed in fine linen, white and pure, were following him on white horses. [15] From his mouth comes a sharp sword with which to strike down the nations, and he will rule them with a rod of iron. He will tread the winepress of the fury of the wrath of God the Almighty. [16] On his robe and on his thigh he has a name written, King of kings and Lord of lords.

Returning to the text in Ezekiel, God continues his message:

Ezekiel 39:1-20

"And you, son of man, prophesy against Gog and say, Thus says the Lord God: Behold, I am against you, O Gog, chief prince of Meshech and Tubal. [2] And I will turn you about and drive you forward, and bring you up from the uttermost parts of the north, and lead you against the mountains of Israel. [3] Then I will strike your bow from your left hand, and will make your arrows drop out of your right hand. [4] You shall fall on the mountains of Israel, you and all your hordes and the peoples who are with you. I will give you to birds of prey of every sort and to the beasts of the field to be devoured. [5] You shall fall in the open field, for I have spoken, declares the Lord God. [6] I will send fire on Magog and on those who dwell securely in the coastlands, and they shall know that I am the Lord.

This again is the same language used in Revelation 19 in the context of Jesus coming to slay the nations:

Rev. 19:17-21

[17] Then I saw an angel standing in the sun, and with a loud voice he called to all the birds that fly directly overhead, "Come, gather for the great supper of God, [18] to eat the flesh of kings, the flesh of captains, the flesh of mighty men, the flesh of horses and their riders, and the flesh of all men, both free and slave, both small and great." [19] And I saw the beast and the kings of the earth with their armies gathered to make war against him who was sitting on the horse and against his army. [20] And the beast was captured, and with it the false prophet who in its presence had done the signs by which he deceived those who had received the mark of the beast and those who worshiped its image. These two were thrown alive into the lake of fire that burns with sulfur. [21] And the rest were slain by the sword that came from the mouth of him who was sitting on the horse, and all the birds were gorged with their flesh.

Continuing in Ezekiel 39:

[7] "And my holy name I will make known in the midst of my people Israel, and I will not let my holy name be profaned anymore. And the nations shall know that I am the Lord, the Holy One in Israel. [8] Behold, it is coming and it will be brought about, declares the Lord God. That is the day of which I have spoken.

We see the theme reiterated that God wants the world to know that He is the Lord. They have profaned his name, have refused to acknowledge him as Creator, or have worshiped a false god and not Yahováh, the God of Abraham, Isaac and Jacob.

[9] "Then those who dwell in the cities of Israel will go out and make fires of the weapons and burn them, shields and bucklers, bow and arrows, clubs and spears; and they will make fires of them for seven years, [10] so that they will not need to take wood out of the field or cut down any out of the forests, for they will make their fires of the weapons. They will seize the spoil of those who despoiled them, and plunder those who plundered them, declares the Lord God.

[11] "On that day I will give to Gog a place for burial in Israel, the Valley of the Travelers, east of the sea. It will block the travelers, for

there Gog and all his multitude will be buried. It will be called the Valley of Hamon-gog. [12] For seven months the house of Israel will be burying them, in order to cleanse the land. [13] All the people of the land will bury them, and it will bring them renown on the day that I show my glory, declares the Lord God. [14] They will set apart men to travel through the land regularly and bury those travelers remaining on the face of the land, so as to cleanse it. At the end of seven months they will make their search. [15] And when these travel through the land and anyone sees a human bone, then he shall set up a sign by it, till the buriers have buried it in the Valley of Hamon-gog. [16] (Hamonah is also the name of the city.) Thus shall they cleanse the land.

[17] "As for you, son of man, thus says the Lord God: Speak to the birds of every sort and to all beasts of the field, 'Assemble and come, gather from all around to the sacrificial feast that I am preparing for you, a great sacrificial feast on the mountains of Israel, and you shall eat flesh and drink blood. [18] You shall eat the flesh of the mighty, and drink the blood of the princes of the earth—of rams, of lambs, and of he-goats, of bulls, all of them fat beasts of Bashan. [19] And you shall eat fat till you are filled, and drink blood till you are drunk, at the sacrificial feast that I am preparing for you. [20] And you shall be filled at my table with horses and charioteers, with mighty men and all kinds of warriors,' declares the Lord God.

It seems clear from the similar language and details that the invasion of Gog and Magog is the same as the battle of Armageddon (Rev. 16:12-16) and is the last battle spoken of in Revelation 19 above. Jesus comes with his angels and the glorified saints to wage war against those who have opposed him and worshiped the dragon, the beast and the false prophet.

It is the time of vengeance mentioned before by Paul:

2 Thess. 1:5-10

This is evidence of the righteous judgment of God, that you may be considered worthy of the kingdom of God, for which you are also suffering— [6] since indeed God considers it just to repay with affliction those who afflict you, [7] and to grant relief to you who are afflicted as well as to us, when the Lord Jesus is revealed from heaven with his mighty angels

[8] in flaming fire, inflicting vengeance on those who do not know God and on those who do not obey the gospel of our Lord Jesus. [9] They will suffer the punishment of eternal destruction, away from the presence of the Lord and from the glory of his might, [10] when he comes on that day to be glorified in his saints, and to be marveled at among all who have believed, because our testimony to you was believed.

Contrary to the belief of some theological positions, this does not usher in the eternal state. We see from the text in Ezekiel that the weapons gathered will provide fuel for seven years and it will take seven months to bury all the dead. Likewise, this description is not referring to the Gog and Magog following the Millennial reign of Christ because immediately after that battle, the final judgment takes place and the eternal new heavens and new earth are created. In this passage, the time required to bury the dead and the weapons being used for fuel for seven years does not fit in with the last Gog and Magog scenario. Ezekiel goes on to speak of the effect that this great battle will have on the surviving world and on Israel.

Ezekiel 39:21-24

"And I will set my glory among the nations, and all the nations shall see my judgment that I have executed, and my hand that I have laid on them. [22] The house of Israel shall know that I am the Lord their God, from that day forward. [23] And the nations shall know that the house of Israel went into captivity for their iniquity, because they dealt so treacherously with me that I hid my face from them and gave them into the hand of their adversaries, and they all fell by the sword. [24] I dealt with them according to their uncleanness and their transgressions, and hid my face from them.

This corresponds to the language of the passage we have previously cited in Romans and Zechariah:

Romans 11:25-27

Lest you be wise in your own conceits, I want you to understand this mystery, brothers: a partial hardening has come upon Israel, until the fullness of the Gentiles has come in. [26] And in this way all Israel will be saved, as it is written,

"The Deliverer will come from Zion,

he will banish ungodliness from Jacob";
[27] "and this will be my covenant with them
when I take away their sins."

Zech. 14:12-17

And this shall be the plague with which the Lord will strike all the peoples that wage war against Jerusalem: their flesh will rot while they are still standing on their feet, their eyes will rot in their sockets, and their tongues will rot in their mouths.

[13] And on that day a great panic from the Lord shall fall on them, so that each will seize the hand of another, and the hand of the one will be raised against the hand of the other. [14] Even Judah will fight against Jerusalem. And the wealth of all the surrounding nations shall be collected, gold, silver, and garments in great abundance. [15] And a plague like this plague shall fall on the horses, the mules, the camels, the donkeys, and whatever beasts may be in those camps.

[16] Then everyone who survives of all the nations that have come against Jerusalem shall go up year after year to worship the King, the Lord of hosts, and to keep the Feast of Booths. [17] And if any of the families of the earth do not go up to Jerusalem to worship the King, the Lord of hosts, there will be no rain on them.

God speaks through Ezekiel of his future plan for Israel. He not only will bring all of the surviving ones to salvation, but will also gather all of the Jews from around the world back to their land.

Ezekiel 39:25-29

"Therefore thus says the Lord God: Now I will restore the fortunes of Jacob and have mercy on the whole house of Israel, and I will be jealous for my holy name. [26] They shall forget their shame and all the treachery they have practiced against me, when they dwell securely in their land with none to make them afraid, [27] when I have brought them back from the peoples and gathered them from their enemies' lands, and through them have vindicated my holiness in the sight of many nations. [28] Then they shall know that I am the Lord their God, because I sent them into exile among the nations and then assembled them into their own land. I will leave none of them remaining among the nations anymore. [29] And I will not hide my face anymore from them, when I pour out my Spirit upon the house of Israel, declares the Lord God."

Marriage Supper of the Lamb

We have read of the call to prepare for the marriage of the Lamb in Revelation 19 just prior to Christ's glorious return. When and where will this supper take place and who will be included? The parable Jesus told of the ten virgins in Matthew 25 indicate that the supper comes after the bridegroom has come for his bride, which would mean that it takes place after Christ has come in power and glory and the angels have gathered the elect from around the world and they are joined with their glorified bodies.

Where this will take place is indicated in Isaiah.

Isaiah 25:6

On this mountain the Lord of hosts will make for all peoples
  a feast of rich food, a feast of well-aged wine,
of rich food full of marrow, of aged wine well refined.

The texts that use the language "this mountain" consistently refer to Jerusalem or Zion.

Rev. 19:9

And the angel said to me, "Write this: Blessed are those who are invited to the marriage supper of the Lamb." And he said to me, "These are the true words of God."

So who are those blessed to be invited? Who is the bride, the wife of the Lamb? There are those who identify Israel with the bride of Christ and the Church as the body of Christ. They argue that only the Jews will be at this marriage supper of the Lamb as they are the bride.

From the following passages, it seems clear that while two metaphors are used, that of the bride and that of the body of Christ, they refer to the same group which are comprised of all saints, Jews and Gentiles, from Adam to the time of Christ's return and perhaps even those who respond shortly after his return.

In the context of the Roman centurion's faith, Jesus said,

Matthew 8:11-12

I tell you, many will come from east and west and recline at table with Abraham, Isaac, and Jacob in the kingdom of heaven, [12] while the sons of the kingdom will be thrown into the outer darkness. In that place there will be weeping and gnashing of teeth."

The text cited just above in Isaiah 25:6 says this feast will be for all peoples, implying not just Israel.

Paul, in writing to a Gentile church said this,

2 Cor. 11:1-3

I wish you would bear with me in a little foolishness. Do bear with me! [2] I feel a divine jealousy for you, for I betrothed you to one husband, to present you as a pure virgin to Christ. [3] But I am afraid that as the serpent deceived Eve by his cunning, your thoughts will be led astray from a sincere and pure devotion to Christ.

In another passage, he mixes the metaphors of husband and wife, referring to Christ and the Church with the Church being the body of Christ.

Ephes. 5:22-32

Wives, submit to your own husbands, as to the Lord. [23] For the husband is the head of the wife even as Christ is the head of the church, his body, and is himself its Savior. [24] Now as the church submits to Christ, so also wives should submit in everything to their husbands.

[25] Husbands, love your wives, as Christ loved the church and gave himself up for her, [26] that he might sanctify her, having cleansed her by the washing of water with the word, [27] so that he might present the church to himself in splendor, without spot or wrinkle or any such thing, that she might be holy and without blemish. [28] In the same way husbands should love their wives as their own bodies. He who loves his wife loves himself. [29] For no one ever hated his own flesh, but nourishes and cherishes it, just as Christ does the church, [30] because we are members of his body. [31] "Therefore a man shall leave his father and mother and hold fast to his wife, and the two shall become one flesh." [32] This mystery is profound, and I am saying that it refers to Christ and the church.

It seems clear from the various texts, that all resurrected and raptured saints will be included in this marriage supper of the Lamb, to be held in Jerusalem, after Christ's glorious return. As alluded to earlier, what is not clear is whether those mortal people who pass the first judgment after Christ's return will be included or not. That leads us to the next chapter.

23 THE JUDGMENTS

JESUS' COMING IN glory will be a return to bring wrath and judgment, destroying all the armies that have gathered against him and his people and to establish his earthly kingdom.

Rev. 19:15

From his mouth comes a sharp sword with which to strike down the nations, and he will rule them with a rod of iron. He will tread the winepress of the fury of the wrath of God the Almighty.

But what of those who survive the battle – those who remained home? It says he will rule them with a rod of iron. Will there be any judgment for those who did not participate in the battle? Revelation 20 tells us of a final judgment before the great white throne of God, but that is after the one thousand year period of Christ's earthly rule. What about before then? Will there be a judgment for those who enter into the thousand year millennium? It seems to be the case. Admittedly these are difficult passages to interpret. Many Bible scholars interpret these passages to be referring to the one final judgment mentioned above, but it seems to me that there are at least four separate judgments spoken of in the Bible. Let us look at what may be the first one.

THE SHEEP AND GOATS JUDGMENT

Matthew 16:27

For the Son of Man is going to come with his angels in the glory of his Father, and then he will repay each person according to what he has done.

Jude 1:14-15

It was also about these that Enoch, the seventh from Adam, prophesied, saying, "Behold, the Lord came with ten thousands of his holy ones, [15] to execute judgment on all and to convict all the ungodly of all their deeds of ungodliness that they have committed in such an ungodly way, and of all the harsh things that ungodly sinners have spoken against him."

Matthew 19:27-28

Then Peter said in reply, "See, we have left everything and followed you. What then will we have?" [28] Jesus said to them, "Truly, I say to you, in the new world, when the Son of Man will sit on his glorious throne, you who have followed me will also sit on twelve thrones, judging the twelve tribes of Israel.

Matthew 25:31-46

"When the Son of Man comes in his glory, and all the angels with him, then he will sit on his glorious throne. [32] Before him will be gathered all the nations, and he will separate people one from another as a shepherd separates the sheep from the goats. [33] And he will place the sheep on his right, but the goats on the left. [34] Then the King will say to those on his right, 'Come, you who are blessed by my Father, inherit the kingdom prepared for you from the foundation of the world. [35] For I was hungry and you gave me food, I was thirsty and you gave me drink, I was a stranger and you welcomed me, [36] I was naked and you clothed me, I was sick and you visited me, I was in prison and you came to me.' [37] Then the righteous will answer him, saying, 'Lord, when did we see you hungry and feed you, or thirsty and give you drink? [38] And when did we see you a stranger and welcome you, or naked and clothe you? [39] And when did we see you sick or in prison and visit you?' [40] And the King will answer them, 'Truly, I say to you, as you did it to one of the least of these my brothers, you did it to me.'

[41] "Then he will say to those on his left, 'Depart from me, you cursed, into the eternal fire prepared for the devil and his angels. [42] For I was hungry and you gave me no food, I was thirsty and you gave me no drink, [43] I was a stranger and you did not welcome me, naked and you did not clothe me, sick and in prison and you did not

visit me.' [44] Then they also will answer, saying, 'Lord, when did we see you hungry or thirsty or a stranger or naked or sick or in prison, and did not minister to you?' [45] Then he will answer them, saying, 'Truly, I say to you, as you did not do it to one of the least of these, you did not do it to me.' [46] And these will go away into eternal punishment, but the righteous into eternal life."

What can we gather from these passages that is clear? First, it is important to note that there will be a judgment. We will all stand before God to give account for our lives sooner or later. Second, we see that Jesus will be the judge. Third, the basis for judgment will be the person's deeds, or lack thereof. Fourth, the timing of this judgment will be after Jesus returns in glory with his angels and when he sits on his glorious throne. Finally, all the earth - every person left alive, will appear at this judgment and there will be only two categories – sheep and goats and two destinations – Christ's kingdom and eternal life, and eternal punishment.

It seems pretty straight forward until we begin to fit details together. First, let us look at who will not be in this judgment. They will not be the redeemed from Adam to the moment when Jesus who had died appears. They will be the resurrected saints that the angels gather from the four corners of the earth when Christ comes. They will not be the ones still alive who were believers in Jesus at the time of his coming because they will have been raptured, or caught up and transformed with glorified bodies to meet Christ in the air as he comes. All these previously dead and the alive believers will reign with Christ for the thousand years.

So who makes up the rest of the mortal worldwide population that will be included in this judgment? Who are the ones over whom Jesus will reign with a rod of iron accompanied by the immortal saints with glorified bodies? Will any unbelievers in Christ enter the millennial kingdom?

First, we see that the judgment will be universal – all the nations. By then, if Christ's return comes soon, the current 7 billion worldwide population will have been reduced to 3 billion or fewer (a fourth of the world dies in the fourth seal and a third dies in the sixth trumpet), not counting the numbers to die from all the other wars, plagues and persecution and those who will die in the final battle. Most likely the number will be much smaller than 3 billion. In fact, Jesus said,

Matthew 24:21-22
For then there will be great tribulation, such as has not been from the beginning of the world until now, no, and never will be. [22] And if those days had not been cut short, no human being would be saved. But for the sake of the elect those days will be cut short.

So those who appear before Jesus in this judgment will be the survivors of the great tribulation and will be those who had not believed in Christ before his second coming.

There will be two categories of people in the judgment – sheep and goats – righteous and unrighteous. But if all the righteous believers in Christ are raptured when he comes, then who are these additional righteous who will be called sheep after his coming?

The Sheep

I believe there will be three groups of people who will comprise this "sheep" group. The first group will be the Jews.

It is evident from various texts we have looked at previously in Zechariah 12-14 and Romans 11 that all the Jews alive at the time of Christ's return and who were not previously believers in Yeshua (Jesus) will be converted and come to embrace him as their Messiah after his return.

Zech. 12:9-13:1
And on that day I will seek to destroy all the nations that come against Jerusalem.

[10] "And I will pour out on the house of David and the inhabitants of Jerusalem a spirit of grace and pleas for mercy, so that, when they look on me, on him whom they have pierced, they shall mourn for him, as one mourns for an only child, and weep bitterly over him, as one weeps over a firstborn.

"On that day there shall be a fountain opened for the house of David and the inhabitants of Jerusalem, to cleanse them from sin and uncleanness."

Romans 11:25-27
Lest you be wise in your own conceits, I want you to understand this mystery, brothers: a partial hardening has come upon Israel, until the fullness of the Gentiles has come in. [26] And in this way all Israel will be saved, as it is written,

"The Deliverer will come from Zion,
he will banish ungodliness from Jacob";
[27] "and this will be my covenant with them
when I take away their sins."

With a worldwide population of Jews being only 15 million in 2010 and many of them will be killed during the great tribulation, the number of Jews who come to faith in their Messiah will be relatively small, by worldwide population standards. We have already seen texts that say that God will gather them all to the promise land and that the twelve Apostles will sit on twelve thrones with Jesus judging the twelve tribes of Israel.

The second group who will make up the sheep will be those Gentiles who had not worshiped the beast and had not received his mark and just as there will be Jews who will embrace Christ after his visible return, so these Gentiles will likewise embrace Christ after his return and prior to this judgment.

This leads us to the question as to when this judgment will be. We are told it will be when Christ returns and is sitting on his glorious throne. We touched in an earlier chapter the passage in Daniel 12 that refers to three periods of time:

Daniel 12:6-7

And someone said to the man clothed in linen, who was above the waters of the stream, "How long shall it be till the end of these wonders?" [7] And I heard the man clothed in linen, who was above the waters of the stream; he raised his right hand and his left hand toward heaven and swore by him who lives forever that it would be for a time, times, and half a time, and that when the shattering of the power of the holy people comes to an end all these things would be finished.

This refers to three and a half years, or forty-two months or 1260 days, as the times are given in various other passages in Daniel, Matthew and Revelation. But then there is the enigmatic addition of two more time periods, of which I have dealt in a previous chapter:

Daniel 12:11-12

And from the time that the regular burnt offering is taken away and the abomination that makes desolate is set up, there shall be 1,290 days. [12] Blessed is he who waits and arrives at the 1,335 days.

There is a total of 75 days between the 1260 days and the 1335 days. I mentioned that that is the exact period of time between the Feast of Trumpets, or Rosh Hashanah, and Chanukkah, the festival celebrating the re-dedication or purifying of the temple. If Jesus were to return on the Feast of Trumpets ("the last trumpet"), it could be that the battle of Armageddon, the conversion of the Jews and all the activities leading up to Jesus' sitting on his glorious throne could take place in the 75 day period of time. The judgment could take place either shortly before the end of this time when the temple is rededicated, at the time of the rededication, or shortly thereafter.

Isaiah presents an interesting picture, at the end of his book, of what will happen from the time of Christ's return to this time of judgment. The fact that this passage relates to a relatively short period of time is borne out by the last verse, in which all the nations and tongues will come to Jerusalem and see Christ's glory (vs. 18), and they will see the still as yet unburied bodies of those who Christ destroyed in the great battle of Armageddon (vs. 24).

Isaiah 66:15-24

"For behold, the Lord will come in fire,
and his chariots like the whirlwind,
to render his anger in fury,
and his rebuke with flames of fire.
[16] For by fire will the Lord enter into judgment,
and by his sword, with all flesh;
and those slain by the Lord shall be many.

[17] "Those who sanctify and purify themselves to go into the gardens, following one in the midst, eating pig's flesh and the abomination and mice, shall come to an end together, declares the Lord.

[18] "For I know their works and their thoughts, and the time is coming to gather all nations and tongues. And they shall come and shall see my glory, [19] and I will set a sign among them. And from them I will send survivors to the nations, to Tarshish, Pul, and Lud, who draw the bow, to Tubal and Javan, to the coastlands afar off, that have not heard my fame or seen my glory. And they shall declare my glory among the nations. [20] And they shall bring all your brothers from all the nations as an offering to the Lord, on horses and in chariots and in litters and on mules and on dromedaries, to my holy mountain Jerusalem, says the Lord, just as the Israelites bring their

grain offering in a clean vessel to the house of the Lord. [21] And some of them also I will take for priests and for Levites, says the Lord.

[22] "For as the new heavens and the new earth
that I make
shall remain before me, says the Lord,
so shall your offspring and your name remain.
[23] From new moon to new moon,
and from Sabbath to Sabbath,
all flesh shall come to worship before me,
declares the Lord.

[24] "And they shall go out and look on the dead bodies of the men who have rebelled against me. For their worm shall not die, their fire shall not be quenched, and they shall be an abhorrence to all flesh."

The text seems to say that surviving Jews, who embrace the Messiah, will be sent to the nations around – to those who had not heard of His fame or seen His glory, and they will declare the Lord's glory among these nations. These Gentiles will then bring surviving Jews from their lands to Jerusalem, as an offering to the Lord. From these Jews, the Lord will take some of them to be priests and Levites. It says that all flesh will come to worship before the Lord. And as they are there, they will see the remains of those who rebelled against the Messiah.

Again, this text seems to indicate that there will be those who did not know God before the Lord's coming, but will hear of his glory, embrace him and will come to worship him. Could the phrase, "all flesh shall come to worship before me" indicate that only sheep will be entering the millennial kingdom? Is it saying that those who are goats, who do not worship, will not be in the millennial kingdom?

There is a third group that I believe will be included with the sheep. Most commentators, in an effort to emphasize other scripture passages that teach that salvation is not by works, but by grace through faith in Christ, say that the basis on which everyone is judged – which is based on how they treated "one of the least of these my (Jesus') brothers," is an outward evidence of a genuine inward faith. While that may be true, we have already seen the difficulty with these people being believers before Christ's return. Had they been believers, they would not be at this judgment since they would already be in their glorified bodies.

I believe an example of this third group would be a Gentile Roman officer in the Bible by the name of Cornelius.

Acts 10:1-5
At Caesarea there was a man named Cornelius, a centurion of what was known as the Italian Cohort, [2] a devout man who feared God with all his household, gave alms generously to the people, and prayed continually to God. [3] About the ninth hour of the day he saw clearly in a vision an angel of God come in and say to him, "Cornelius." [4] And he stared at him in terror and said, "What is it, Lord?" And he said to him, "Your prayers and your alms have ascended as a memorial before God. [5] And now send men to Joppa and bring one Simon who is called Peter. …

Though a devout, generous, praying, God-fearing man, Cornelius did not know God. However, his seeking after God caused God to make sure that he would hear the message from Peter, who would explain to him the way to know God. When he did hear, he gladly responded.

Likewise, I believe that there will be many, who, though not knowing Jesus Christ, will be people who know in their spirits that the Antichrist is evil and they will refuse to worship him and will refuse to receive his mark. They may become the rebels, the underground resistance movement, and though they do not have a personal faith in Christ, they aid those Jews or Christians who are being persecuted by the Antichrist and his regime. They risk their own lives to feed, give drink, clothe and visit in prison those children of God who refuse to worship the beast. Indeed, in a similar vein to this passage on the sheep and what they did, Jesus said:

Matthew 10:40-42
"Whoever receives you receives me, and whoever receives me receives him who sent me. [41] The one who receives a prophet because he is a prophet will receive a prophet's reward, and the one who receives a righteous person because he is a righteous person will receive a righteous person's reward. [42] And whoever gives one of these little ones even a cup of cold water because he is a disciple, truly, I say to you, he will by no means lose his reward."

I believe that like Cornelius, God will reward them by allowing them to enter Jesus' kingdom and will as well, show them the way to salvation, which may even occur at that judgment hour. Perhaps another passage that may have some bearing on this is:

Romans 2:5-16

But because of your hard and impenitent heart you are storing up wrath for yourself on the day of wrath when God's righteous judgment will be revealed.

[6] He will render to each one according to his works: [7] to those who by patience in well-doing seek for glory and honor and immortality, he will give eternal life; [8] but for those who are self-seeking and do not obey the truth, but obey unrighteousness, there will be wrath and fury. [9] There will be tribulation and distress for every human being who does evil, the Jew first and also the Greek, [10] but glory and honor and peace for everyone who does good, the Jew first and also the Greek. [11] For God shows no partiality.

[12] For all who have sinned without the law will also perish without the law, and all who have sinned under the law will be judged by the law. [13] For it is not the hearers of the law who are righteous before God, but the doers of the law who will be justified. [14] For when Gentiles, who do not have the law, by nature do what the law requires, they are a law to themselves, even though they do not have the law. [15] They show that the work of the law is written on their hearts, while their conscience also bears witness, and their conflicting thoughts accuse or even excuse them [16] on that day when, according to my gospel, God judges the secrets of men by Christ Jesus.

In my view, these sheep are among the elect – from before the foundation of the earth, who had not yet come to the moment of regeneration before Christ's glorious return. Just as Jesus said:

John 10:14-16

I am the good shepherd. I know my own and my own know me, [15] just as the Father knows me and I know the Father; and I lay down my life for the sheep. [16] And I have other sheep that are not of this fold. I must bring them also, and they will listen to my voice. So there will be one flock, one shepherd.

He called people sheep who had not yet been converted – he spoke of them in the future tense. It was not that they were goats and were later converted to sheep. He calls them sheep all along. However the opposite is also true. The reason the Pharisees did not believe is because they were not sheep.

John 10:24-28 (NIV)
[24] The Jews gathered around him, saying, "How long will you keep us in suspense? If you are the Christ, tell us plainly."
[25] Jesus answered, "I did tell you, but you do not believe. The miracles I do in my Father's name speak for me,
[26] but you do not believe because you are not my sheep.
[27] My sheep listen to my voice; I know them, and they follow me.
[28] I give them eternal life, and they shall never perish; no one can snatch them out of my hand.

Those Jews were goats and not sheep. Had they been sheep, they would have listened to his voice. In the same way, there will be those at this judgment day who though not yet believing in Christ, were sheep and perhaps at this judgment were for the first time exposed to his voice.

The Goats

Who are the goats in this separation and judgment day? Their judgment is immediate, severe and eternal. They neither inherit nor enter into the immediate millennial kingdom nor the eternal one.

Matthew 25:41
"Then he will say to those on his left, 'Depart from me, you cursed, into the eternal fire prepared for the devil and his angels.

<u>The Worshipers of the beast</u>

Though not stated in this text, perhaps because the revelation regarding the beast and his mark would not be given for another sixty years, it makes sense that all those who had worshiped the beast and received his mark and survived to this point will be numbered among the goats. We had read earlier the warning given to the earth before the institution of the worship and mark of the beast.

Rev. 14:9-11
And another angel, a third, followed them, saying with a loud voice, "If anyone worships the beast and its image and receives a mark on his forehead or on his hand, [10] he also will drink the wine of God's wrath, poured full strength into the cup of his anger, and he will be tormented with fire and sulfur in the presence of the holy

angels and in the presence of the Lamb. [11] And the smoke of their torment goes up forever and ever, and they have no rest, day or night, these worshipers of the beast and its image, and whoever receives the mark of its name."

The Unrighteous

We would naturally assume that those practicing the lists of sins mentioned in the Bible would also fall in the category of goats. Here are some of the lists:

Romans 1:18-32

For the wrath of God is revealed from heaven against all ungodliness and unrighteousness of men, who by their unrighteousness suppress the truth. [19] For what can be known about God is plain to them, because God has shown it to them. [20] For his invisible attributes, namely, his eternal power and divine nature, have been clearly perceived, ever since the creation of the world, in the things that have been made. So they are without excuse. [21] For although they knew God, they did not honor him as God or give thanks to him, but they became futile in their thinking, and their foolish hearts were darkened. [22] Claiming to be wise, they became fools, [23] and exchanged the glory of the immortal God for images resembling mortal man and birds and animals and reptiles.

[24] Therefore God gave them up in the lusts of their hearts to impurity, to the dishonoring of their bodies among themselves, [25] because they exchanged the truth about God for a lie and worshiped and served the creature rather than the Creator, who is blessed forever! Amen.

[26] For this reason God gave them up to dishonorable passions. For their women exchanged natural relations for those that are contrary to nature; [27] and the men likewise gave up natural relations with women and were consumed with passion for one another, men committing shameless acts with men and receiving in themselves the due penalty for their error.

[28] And since they did not see fit to acknowledge God, God gave them up to a debased mind to do what ought not to be done. [29] They were filled with all manner of unrighteousness, evil, covetousness, malice. They are full of envy, murder, strife, deceit, maliciousness. They are gossips, [30] slanderers, haters of God, insolent, haughty,

boastful, inventors of evil, disobedient to parents, [31] foolish, faithless, heartless, ruthless. [32] Though they know God's decree that those who practice such things deserve to die, they not only do them but give approval to those who practice them.

1 Cor. 6:9-10

Do you not know that the unrighteous will not inherit the kingdom of God? Do not be deceived: neither the sexually immoral, nor idolaters, nor adulterers, nor men who practice homosexuality, [10] nor thieves, nor the greedy, nor drunkards, nor revilers, nor swindlers will inherit the kingdom of God.

Galatians 5:19-21

Now the works of the flesh are evident: sexual immorality, impurity, sensuality, [20] idolatry, sorcery, enmity, strife, jealousy, fits of anger, rivalries, dissensions, divisions, [21] envy, drunkenness, orgies, and things like these. I warn you, as I warned you before, that those who do such things will not inherit the kingdom of God.

Rev. 21:8

But as for the cowardly, the faithless, the detestable, as for murderers, the sexually immoral, sorcerers, idolaters, and all liars, their portion will be in the lake that burns with fire and sulfur, which is the second death."

Rev. 22:15

Outside are the dogs and sorcerers and the sexually immoral and murderers and idolaters, and everyone who loves and practices falsehood.

The last verse in Romans 1 says that people who practice these kinds of things know God's decree that they deserve to die, so it will be no surprise for them to hear Jesus' sentence of judgment. However, there will be people who will be very surprised on that judgment day.

<u>The Surprised</u>

They are not judged because of a lifestyle of gross and obvious sins, but rather because of what they did <u>not</u> do. They did not feed, give drink, welcome, clothe or minister to the Jews or Christians – "the least of these my brothers." And as they did not do these things to them, they did not do it to Jesus. "And these will go away into eternal punishment, but the righteous into eternal life." There may be people who resisted the Antichrist and did not receive his mark, and were generally good people (not perfect as no one is perfect), but because they did not aid God's people – they may have just wanted to avoid the risk of helping those being hunted down by the State – their judgment is the same as those who actively rebelled against God and his laws.

Another group of surprised people will be those who claimed to have done ministry for God in Jesus' name, but had never had a personal relationship with Christ resulting in obedience.

Matthew 7:21-23

"Not everyone who says to me, 'Lord, Lord,' will enter the kingdom of heaven, but the one who does the will of my Father who is in heaven. [22] On that day many will say to me, 'Lord, Lord, did we not prophesy in your name, and cast out demons in your name, and do many mighty works in your name?' [23] And then will I declare to them, 'I never knew you; depart from me, you workers of lawlessness.'

In the same discourse in which Jesus revealed this future judgment, he related some parables to illustrate who would be included in the kingdom and who would not. Again, in the first one, those who are shut out are very surprised.

Matthew 25:1-13

"Then the kingdom of heaven will be like ten virgins who took their lamps and went to meet the bridegroom. [2] Five of them were foolish, and five were wise. [3] For when the foolish took their lamps, they took no oil with them, [4] but the wise took flasks of oil with their lamps. [5] As the bridegroom was delayed, they all became drowsy and slept. [6] But at midnight there was a cry, 'Here is the bridegroom! Come out to meet him.' [7] Then all those virgins rose and trimmed their lamps. [8] And the foolish said to the wise, 'Give us some of your oil, for our lamps are going out.' [9] But the wise answered, saying, 'Since there will not be enough for us and for you, go rather to the dealers and buy for yourselves.' [10] And while they were going to buy, the bridegroom came, and those who were ready went in with him to the marriage feast, and the door was shut. [11] Afterward the other virgins came also, saying, 'Lord, lord, open to us.'

[12] But he answered, 'Truly, I say to you, I do not know you.' [13] Watch therefore, for you know neither the day nor the hour.

Jesus makes the point that people need to be prepared for his return at any time. Those who think they will have plenty of time to prepare later, will be unprepared when the time comes and will be shut out of the kingdom.

The Unproductive

The other parable is about the talents.

Matthew 25:14-15
"For it will be like a man going on a journey, who called his servants and entrusted to them his property. [15] To one he gave five talents, to another two, to another one, to each according to his ability. Then he went away.

Jesus relates that two of the servants put the money to work and produced more. The third, however, did nothing with what he was entrusted.

When the master returned to settle accounts – referring to the time Jesus returns, his response was the same for the first two:

Matthew 25:20-21
And he who had received the five talents came forward, bringing five talents more, saying, 'Master, you delivered to me five talents; here I have made five talents more.' [21] His master said to him, 'Well done, good and faithful servant. You have been faithful over a little; I will set you over much. Enter into the joy of your master.'

Not so the third one.

Matthew 25:24-30
He also who had received the one talent came forward, saying, 'Master, I knew you to be a hard man, reaping where you did not sow, and gathering where you scattered no seed, [25] so I was afraid, and I went and hid your talent in the ground. Here you have what is yours.' [26] But his master answered him, 'You wicked and slothful servant! You knew that I reap where I have not sowed and gather where I scattered no seed? [27] Then you ought to have invested my money

with the bankers, and at my coming I should have received what was my own with interest. [28] So take the talent from him and give it to him who has the ten talents. [29] For to everyone who has will more be given, and he will have an abundance. But from the one who has not, even what he has will be taken away. [30] And cast the worthless servant into the outer darkness. In that place there will be weeping and gnashing of teeth.'

The third servant is called wicked and slothful. His wrong view of his master's character caused him to be afraid, which then kept him from putting to work what he was entrusted with. There will be many at judgment day who will share the fate of that man because of their wrong view of God and how that affects their lives and actions.

Jesus relates a similar parable on another occasion and ties it in to the appearance of the kingdom of God:

Luke 19:11-27

As they heard these things, he proceeded to tell a parable, because he was near to Jerusalem, and because they supposed that the kingdom of God was to appear immediately. [12] He said therefore, "A nobleman went into a far country to receive for himself a kingdom and then return. [13] Calling ten of his servants, he gave them ten minas, and said to them, 'Engage in business until I come.' [14] But his citizens hated him and sent a delegation after him, saying, 'We do not want this man to reign over us.' [15] When he returned, having received the kingdom, he ordered these servants to whom he had given the money to be called to him, that he might know what they had gained by doing business. [16] The first came before him, saying, 'Lord, your mina has made ten minas more.' [17] And he said to him, 'Well done, good servant! Because you have been faithful in a very little, you shall have authority over ten cities.' [18] And the second came, saying, 'Lord, your mina has made five minas.' [19] And he said to him, 'And you are to be over five cities.' [20] Then another came, saying, 'Lord, here is your mina, which I kept laid away in a handkerchief; [21] for I was afraid of you, because you are a severe man. You take what you did not deposit, and reap what you did not sow.' [22] He said to him, 'I will condemn you with your own words, you wicked servant! You knew that I was a severe man, taking what I did not deposit and reaping what I did not sow? [23] Why then did you not put my money in the bank, and at my coming I might have collected it with interest?' [24] And he said to those who stood by, 'Take the mina from him, and give it to the one who has the ten minas.' [25] And they said to him, 'Lord, he has ten minas!' [26] 'I tell you that to everyone who has, more will be given, but from the one who has not, even what he has will be taken away. [27] But as for these enemies of mine, who did not want me to reign over them, bring them here and slaughter them before me.' "

Thus, at the end of this age there is a separating of people – sheep from goats – a judgment that determines not only who can enter into the kingdom of God, but also determines eternal destinies.

"And these will go away into eternal punishment, but the righteous into eternal life."

THE JUDGMENT OF BELIEVERS

What about the saints? Will they never have to give account for their lives? Did Christ's atonement on the cross mean that they would never be judged? Paul did say:

Romans 8:1
There is therefore now no condemnation for those who are in Christ Jesus.

While Christians will never be condemned for their sins or have to pay for them, there will be a judgment that will determine the rewards they will receive and the responsibilities they will have in the millennial kingdom. The parable of the minas above speaks of Jesus giving authority over cities, commensurate with the level of faithfulness they had displayed in putting the resources to work that he had entrusted to them. I believe this will be a literal reward given during the millennium, and the extent of one's scope of authority will be determined by how we lived with what God had given us while alive.

Another passage that speaks of a judgment of believers is:

1 Cor. 3:8-15
He who plants and he who waters are one, and each will receive his wages according to his labor. [9] For we are God's fellow workers. You are God's field, God's building.

[10] According to the grace of God given to me, like a skilled master builder I laid a foundation, and someone else is building upon it. Let each one take care how he builds upon it. [11] For no one can lay a foundation other than that which is laid, which is Jesus Christ. [12] Now if anyone builds on the foundation with gold, silver, precious stones, wood, hay, straw— [13] each one's work will become manifest, for the Day will disclose it, because it will be revealed by fire, and the fire will test what sort of work each one has done. [14] If the work that anyone has built on the foundation survives, he will receive a reward. [15] If anyone's work is burned up, he will suffer loss, though he himself will be saved, but only as through fire.

Many times in the gospels Jesus spoke of rewards: rewards for those persecuted for his sake, those who give, pray and fast with genuine motives, and for those who love their enemies and lend. Paul also spoke often of rewards and his concern that he not be disqualified from receiving certain rewards.

1 Cor. 9:16-17

For if I preach the gospel, that gives me no ground for boasting. For necessity is laid upon me. Woe to me if I do not preach the gospel! [17] For if I do this of my own will, I have a reward, but not of my own will, I am still entrusted with a stewardship.

1 Cor. 9:24-27

Do you not know that in a race all the runners compete, but only one receives the prize? So run that you may obtain it. [25] Every athlete exercises self-control in all things. They do it to receive a perishable wreath, but we an imperishable. [26] So I do not run aimlessly; I do not box as one beating the air. [27] But I discipline my body and keep it under control, lest after preaching to others I myself should be disqualified.

Often, rewards are spoken of as crowns.

2 Tim. 4:8

Henceforth there is laid up for me the crown of righteousness, which the Lord, the righteous judge, will award to me on that Day, and not only to me but also to all who have loved his appearing.

Those who endure trials for the sake of Christ are promised the crown of life:

James 1:12
Blessed is the man who remains steadfast under trial, for when he has stood the test he will receive the crown of life, which God has promised to those who love him.

Rev. 2:10
Do not fear what you are about to suffer. Behold, the devil is about to throw some of you into prison, that you may be tested, and for ten days you will have tribulation. Be faithful unto death, and I will give you the crown of life.

Rev. 3:10-11
Because you have kept my word about patient endurance, I will keep you from the hour of trial that is coming on the whole world, to try those who dwell on the earth. [11] I am coming soon. Hold fast what you have, so that no one may seize your crown.

In speaking to elders of the Church, Peter says:

1 Peter 5:4
And when the chief Shepherd appears, you will receive the unfading crown of glory.

It seems from these texts that the time for receiving these crowns and rewards will be when Christ appears – some time shortly after his second coming. Indeed, in the last few words of the Bible Jesus says:

Revelation 22:12 (NASB)
12 "Behold, I am coming quickly, and My reward *is* with Me, to render to every man according to what he has done.

THE MILLENNIUM

We dealt at some length with the Millennial reign of Christ in Chapter 14, so I will not reiterate much at this point. God reveals to Isaiah:

Isaiah 65:17
"For behold, I create new heavens
and a new earth,
and the former things shall not be remembered
or come into mind.

Lest we think this is referring to the eternal state, the following verses say this:

Isaiah 65:20-25
No more shall there be in it
an infant who lives but a few days,
or an old man who does not fill out his days,
for the young man shall die a hundred years old,
and the sinner a hundred years old shall be accursed.
[21] They shall build houses and inhabit them;
they shall plant vineyards and eat their fruit.
[22] They shall not build and another inhabit;
they shall not plant and another eat;
for like the days of a tree shall the days of my people be,
and my chosen shall long enjoy the work of their hands.
[23] They shall not labor in vain
or bear children for calamity,
for they shall be the offspring of the blessed of the Lord,
and their descendants with them.
[24] Before they call I will answer;
while they are yet speaking I will hear.
[25] The wolf and the lamb shall graze together;
the lion shall eat straw like the ox,
and dust shall be the serpent's food.
They shall not hurt or destroy
in all my holy mountain,"
says the Lord.

In the millennial reign of Christ, there will be a reordering of nature. People will live for hundreds of years, but they will die. They will bear children. People will still be sinners, though Satan will be bound for the thousand year millennium and unable to deceive or tempt people. These are not things that will happen in the eternal heavenly state.

Those sheep, the righteous ones separated out in the first judgment, will be the ones to inhabit and repopulate the earth. Christ will rule from Jerusalem and those saints from Adam on who were resurrected at his coming or alive and transformed with glorified bodies at his appearance, will rule with him for that thousand year period of time.

Rev. 20:6

Blessed and holy is the one who shares in the first resurrection! Over such the second death has no power, but they will be priests of God and of Christ, and they will reign with him for a thousand years.

As is true today, so it will be then. Children do not always accept the faith of their parents. While all who enter the millennial kingdom will be believers and worship Christ the king, not all their offspring will do so.

There will be those individuals and peoples who will over time refuse to come and worship the King in Jerusalem.

Zech. 14:16-19

Then everyone who survives of all the nations that have come against Jerusalem shall go up year after year to worship the King, the Lord of hosts, and to keep the Feast of Booths. [17] And if any of the families of the earth do not go up to Jerusalem to worship the King, the Lord of hosts, there will be no rain on them. [18] And if the family of Egypt does not go up and present themselves, then on them there shall be no rain; there shall be the plague with which the Lord afflicts the nations that do not go up to keep the Feast of Booths. [19] This shall be the punishment to Egypt and the punishment to all the nations that do not go up to keep the Feast of Booths.

Jesus himself will be reigning on earth with perfect peace, justice and equity. Satan and his demons will have no influence. The environment will be practically perfect, and yet, even as Adam and Eve, in a perfect environment did not remain faithful to God, but rebelled against him, so also, on the day of the final Judgment, God will be perfectly just in his judgment because it will be evident that man's sin and rebellion is not due to outward, external circumstances, but rather a personal and individual matter of the heart. God will give man an opportunity to choose at the end of the perfect world order, who they want to follow.

Rev. 20:7-10

And when the thousand years are ended, Satan will be released from his prison [8] and will come out to deceive the nations that are at the four corners of the earth, Gog and Magog, to gather them for battle; their number is like the sand of the sea. [9] And they marched up over the broad plain of the earth and surrounded the camp of the saints and the beloved city, but fire came down from heaven and consumed them, [10] and the devil who had deceived them was thrown into the lake of fire and sulfur where the beast and the false prophet were, and they will be tormented day and night forever and ever.

THE JUDGMENT OF ANGELS

In an earlier chapter we saw that Satan in his rebellion took with him a third of the angelic host (Rev. 12:4). Some of these angels are already confined because of their intermarriage with humans:

Jude 1:6-7

And the angels who did not stay within their own position of authority, but left their proper dwelling, he has kept in eternal chains under gloomy darkness until the judgment of the great day— [7] just as Sodom and Gomorrah and the surrounding cities, which likewise indulged in sexual immorality and pursued unnatural desire, serve as an example by undergoing a punishment of eternal fire.

2 Peter 2:4

For if God did not spare angels when they sinned, but cast them into hell and committed them to chains of gloomy darkness to be kept until the judgment;

The context of the judgment on those angels is that of unnatural sexual relations, with Sodom and Gomorrah serving as similar examples.

Just as humanity will be judged, so likewise the fallen angels will be judged. It is not clearly stated when this will take place. Jude says it will be "the judgment of the great day." That could refer either to the "Day of the Lord" which generally takes in all the events of the final outpouring of wrath on the earth when Jesus returns, or it could refer to the final judgment. A passage in Isaiah seems to indicate that it will happen when Jesus comes to reign on earth.

Isaiah 24:1

Behold, the Lord will empty the earth and make it desolate,
and he will twist its surface and scatter its inhabitants.

Isaiah 24:5-6
The earth lies defiled
under its inhabitants;
for they have transgressed the laws,
violated the statutes,
broken the everlasting covenant.
[6] Therefore a curse devours the earth,
and its inhabitants suffer for their guilt;
therefore the inhabitants of the earth are scorched,
and few men are left.

Isaiah 24:19-23
The earth is utterly broken,
the earth is split apart,
the earth is violently shaken.
[20] The earth staggers like a drunken man;
it sways like a hut;
its transgression lies heavy upon it,
and it falls, and will not rise again.
[21] **On that day the Lord will punish**
the host of heaven, in heaven,
and the kings of the earth, on the earth.
[22] They will be gathered together
as prisoners in a pit;
they will be shut up in a prison,
and after many days they will be punished.
[23] Then the moon will be confounded
and the sun ashamed,
for the Lord of hosts reigns
on Mount Zion and in Jerusalem,
and his glory will be before his elders.

The chapter speaks in the language we have seen in this book of great judgment; much of the earth will be destroyed in a worldwide earthquake. "On that day the Lord will punish the host of heaven, in heaven, and the kings of the earth, on the earth." Afterwards it speaks of the Lord reigning on Mount Zion and in Jerusalem. We have already seen evidence of the first judgment of humanity which occurs shortly after Christ's return. Here, it includes the host of heaven – or angels, in judgment at that time as well.

Since Satan will be bound for those thousand years, it makes sense that his angels will also be bound and will have been judged. It says, "They will be gathered together as prisoners in a pit; they will be shut up in a prison, and after many days they will be punished." Possibly they will be judged and bound like Satan and whether they will be released for a short time with him after the thousand years or not, we do not know. However, their fate is sure. They will be cast in the lake of fire, created for the devil and his angels.

Amazingly, however, it will not be just God who judges them. Paul is speaking to Christians.

1 Cor. 6:3

Do you not know that we are to judge angels? How much more, then, matters pertaining to this life!

Just as the twelve apostles will sit on twelve thrones judging Israel with Jesus, so all the glorified and resurrected saints will participate in this judging of angels, most likely at the close of this age, before the millennial kingdom is fully ushered in.

THE GREAT WHITE THRONE JUDGMENT

The final judgment is before God the Father almighty. It follows the thousand year millennium and final rebellion.

Rev. 20:7-15

And when the thousand years are ended, Satan will be released
from his prison [8] and will come out to deceive the nations that are at
the four corners of the earth, Gog and Magog, to gather them for
battle; their number is like the sand of the sea. [9] And they marched
up over the broad plain of the earth and surrounded the camp of the
saints and the beloved city, but fire came down from heaven and
consumed them, [10] and the devil who had deceived them was
thrown into the lake of fire and sulfur where the beast and the false
prophet were, and they will be tormented day and night forever and
ever.

[11] Then I saw a great white throne and him who was seated on it.
From his presence earth and sky fled away, and no place was found
for them. [12] And I saw the dead, great and small, standing before
the throne, and books were opened. Then another book was opened,

which is the book of life. And the dead were judged by what was written in the books, according to what they had done. [13] And the sea gave up the dead who were in it, Death and Hades gave up the dead who were in them, and they were judged, each one of them, according to what they had done. [14] Then Death and Hades were thrown into the lake of fire. This is the second death, the lake of fire. [15] And if anyone's name was not found written in the book of life, he was thrown into the lake of fire.

Again, there will be those raised up for this judgment who will be surprised. There will be those who were Jesus' neighbors, those who ate and drank with him and followed him around while he was on the earth.

Luke 13:23-30

And someone said to him, "Lord, will those who are saved be few?" And he said to them, [24] "Strive to enter through the narrow door. For many, I tell you, will seek to enter and will not be able. [25] When once the master of the house has risen and shut the door, and you begin to stand outside and to knock at the door, saying, 'Lord, open to us,' then he will answer you, 'I do not know where you come from.' [26] Then you will begin to say, 'We ate and drank in your presence, and you taught in our streets.' [27] But he will say, 'I tell you, I do not know where you come from. Depart from me, all you workers of evil!' [28] In that place there will be weeping and gnashing of teeth, when you see Abraham and Isaac and Jacob and all the prophets in the kingdom of God but you yourselves cast out. [29] And people will come from east and west, and from north and south, and recline at table in the kingdom of God. [30] And behold, some are last who will be first, and some are first who will be last."

Jesus was speaking in this context specifically to the Jews to whom he ministered. Even though they are the chosen people, many of them will be cast out into hell, while many Gentiles will fellowship with the great Hebrew men of God like Abraham, Isaac and Jacob.

While everyone will be judged by their deeds, and be condemned, only those whose names are written in the book of life will not be condemned. They are the ones whose evil deeds were atoned for by Jesus, whose redemption they appropriated by repentance and faith in Him.

24 THE NEW JERUSALEM

JUST AS THE kingdom of God unfolds in stages, so God's plan for this earth unfolds in stages. For the millennial period, God creates new heavens and a new earth (Isaiah 65:17), but as we have seen, it is not the final creative act, since sin and death will still exist during that time (Is. 65:17-25). Following the final judgment, however, there will be another new heaven and earth, replacing the current earth with its seas, and the holy city Jerusalem will come out of heaven.

Rev. 21:1-8

Then I saw a new heaven and a new earth, for the first heaven and the first earth had passed away, and the sea was no more. [2] And I saw the holy city, new Jerusalem, coming down out of heaven from God, prepared as a bride adorned for her husband. [3] And I heard a loud voice from the throne saying, "Behold, the dwelling place of God is with man. He will dwell with them, and they will be his people, and God himself will be with them as their God. [4] He will wipe away every tear from their eyes, and death shall be no more, neither shall there be mourning nor crying nor pain anymore, for the former things have passed away."

[5] And he who was seated on the throne said, "Behold, I am making all things new." Also he said, "Write this down, for these words are trustworthy and true." [6] And he said to me, "It is done! I am the Alpha and the Omega, the beginning and the end. To the thirsty I will give from the spring of the water of life without payment. [7] The one who conquers will have this heritage, and I will be his God and he will be my son. [8] But as for the cowardly, the

faithless, the detestable, as for murderers, the sexually immoral, sorcerers, idolaters, and all liars, their portion will be in the lake that burns with fire and sulfur, which is the second death."

The New Jerusalem

Rev. 21:9-27

Then came one of the seven angels who had the seven bowls full of the seven last plagues and spoke to me, saying, "Come, I will show you the Bride, the wife of the Lamb." [10] And he carried me away in the Spirit to a great, high mountain, and showed me the holy city Jerusalem coming down out of heaven from God, [11] having the glory of God, its radiance like a most rare jewel, like a jasper, clear as crystal. [12] It had a great, high wall, with twelve gates, and at the gates twelve angels, and on the gates the names of the twelve tribes of the sons of Israel were inscribed— [13] on the east three gates, on the north three gates, on the south three gates, and on the west three gates. [14] And the wall of the city had twelve foundations, and on them were the twelve names of the twelve apostles of the Lamb.

[15] And the one who spoke with me had a measuring rod of gold to measure the city and its gates and walls. [16] The city lies foursquare; its length the same as its width. And he measured the city with his rod, 12,000 stadia. Its length and width and height are equal. [17] He also measured its wall, 144 cubits by human measurement, which is also an angel's measurement. [18] The wall was built of jasper, while the city was pure gold, clear as glass. [19] The foundations of the wall of the city were adorned with every kind of jewel. The first was jasper, the second sapphire, the third agate, the fourth emerald, [20] the fifth onyx, the sixth carnelian, the seventh chrysolite, the eighth beryl, the ninth topaz, the tenth chrysoprase, the eleventh jacinth, the twelfth amethyst. [21] And the twelve gates were twelve pearls, each of the gates made of a single pearl, and the street of the city was pure gold, transparent as glass.

[22] And I saw no temple in the city, for its temple is the Lord God the Almighty and the Lamb. [23] And the city has no need of sun or moon to shine on it, for the glory of God gives it light, and its lamp is the Lamb. [24] By its light will the nations walk, and the kings of the earth will bring their glory into it, [25] and its gates will never be shut by day—and there will be no night there. [26] They will bring into it the glory and the honor of the nations. [27] But nothing unclean will

ever enter it, nor anyone who does what is detestable or false, but only those who are written in the Lamb's book of life.

This city is where the Bride of Christ, the wife of the Lamb will dwell, along with the Triune God. The gates, named after the twelve tribes of Israel and the foundation stones, named after the twelve apostles, represent the makeup of the Bride – saints from both Jews and Gentiles, or put in another way, Old Testament and New Testament believers.

It is a city of extraordinary beauty, made with materials that man through the ages has considered most precious. But for those materials to be appreciated there needs to be a strong light and that is provided by the glory of God. His radiance will cause all the jewels, gold and pearls to shine with all their brilliance and glory.

The city is also a perfect cube, after which was patterned the perfect cube of the Holy of Holies in the temple. The city measures some 1,380 miles or 2,221 km. on each side, making it more than 2.6 billion cubic miles, or almost 11 billion cubic kilometers in volume. There will be plenty of room for the Bride of the Lamb, who will be able to live in a different dimension than the three dimensional earth. The walls are 216 feet or 64.8 meters high (or wide, as some commentators believe), or equivalent to an 18 lane highway. The word used for the material of the walls – jasper – is most likely a clear or translucent quartz type stone in various colors, or could even be diamond. The radiance of God will shine through the walls creating an unimaginable beauty. Just as the Holy of Holies in the temple was a perfect cube, completely covered in gold, so this perfect cube of a city, where God and his people dwell, will be of pure gold.

The River and Tree of Life

Rev. 22:1-21

Then the angel showed me the river of the water of life, bright as crystal, flowing from the throne of God and of the Lamb [2] through the middle of the street of the city; also, on either side of the river, the tree of life with its twelve kinds of fruit, yielding its fruit each month. The leaves of the tree were for the healing of the nations. [3] No longer will there be anything accursed, but the throne of God and of the Lamb will be in it, and his servants will worship him. [4] They will see his face, and his name will be on their foreheads. [5] And night will be no more. They will need no light of lamp or sun, for the Lord God will be their light, and they will reign forever and ever.

[6] And he said to me, "These words are trustworthy and true. And the Lord, the God of the spirits of the prophets, has sent his angel to show his servants what must soon take place. "

[7] "And behold, I am coming soon. Blessed is the one who keeps the words of the prophecy of this book."

[8] I, John, am the one who heard and saw these things. And when I heard and saw them, I fell down to worship at the feet of the angel who showed them to me, [9] but he said to me, "You must not do that! I am a fellow servant with you and your brothers the prophets, and with those who keep the words of this book. Worship God."

[10] And he said to me, "Do not seal up the words of the prophecy of this book, for the time is near. [11] Let the evildoer still do evil, and the filthy still be filthy, and the righteous still do right, and the holy still be holy."

[12] "Behold, I am coming soon, bringing my recompense with me, to repay everyone for what he has done. [13] I am the Alpha and the Omega, the first and the last, the beginning and the end."

[14] Blessed are those who wash their robes, so that they may have the right to the tree of life and that they may enter the city by the gates. [15] Outside are the dogs and sorcerers and the sexually immoral and murderers and idolaters, and everyone who loves and practices falsehood.

[16] "I, Jesus, have sent my angel to testify to you about these things for the churches. I am the root and the descendant of David, the bright morning star."

[17] The Spirit and the Bride say, "Come." And let the one who hears say, "Come." And let the one who is thirsty come; let the one who desires take the water of life without price.

[18] I warn everyone who hears the words of the prophecy of this book: if anyone adds to them, God will add to him the plagues described in this book, [19] and if anyone takes away from the words of the book of this prophecy, God will take away his share in the tree of life and in the holy city, which are described in this book.

[20] He who testifies to these things says, "Surely I am coming soon." Amen. Come, Lord Jesus!

[21] The grace of the Lord Jesus be with all. Amen.

25 HOW TO PREPARE FOR THE APOCALYPSE

IF YOU ARE alive when these events begin to take place, you will go through this Apocalypse. Is there a way to prepare for it? Is there a way to escape it?

The first thing to understand is that as bad as this coming time of judgment will be, it pales into insignificance compared to the eternal judgment of the lake of fire. The Bible does tell us how to escape that judgment. In fact, all along, Jesus extends an invitation, even to the very end of this book:

Rev. 22:12-17

"Behold, I am coming soon, bringing my recompense with me, to repay everyone for what he has done. [13] I am the Alpha and the Omega, the first and the last, the beginning and the end."

[14] Blessed are those who wash their robes, so that they may have the right to the tree of life and that they may enter the city by the gates. [15] Outside are the dogs and sorcerers and the sexually immoral and murderers and idolaters, and everyone who loves and practices falsehood.

[16] "I, Jesus, have sent my angel to testify to you about these things for the churches. I am the root and the descendant of David, the bright morning star."

[17] The Spirit and the Bride say, "Come." And let the one who hears say, "Come." And let the one who is thirsty come; let the one who desires take the water of life without price.

Jesus invites all to come - to come and drink of the water of life. It is not something a person can pay for, earn or merit. It is free. In the Old Testament the invitation was given:

Isaiah 55:1-3
"Come, everyone who thirsts, come to the waters;
and he who has no money,
come, buy and eat!
Come, buy wine and milk
without money and without price.
[2] Why do you spend your money for that which is not bread,
and your labor for that which does not satisfy?
Listen diligently to me, and eat what is good,
and delight yourselves in rich food.
[3] Incline your ear, and come to me;
hear, that your soul may live;
and I will make with you an everlasting covenant,
my steadfast, sure love for David.

Jesus, during the Feast of Sukkoth, or Feast of Tabernacles or Booths, repeated that invitation:

John 7:37-39
On the last day of the feast, the great day, Jesus stood up and cried out, "If anyone thirsts, let him come to me and drink. [38] Whoever believes in me, as the Scripture has said, 'Out of his heart will flow rivers of living water.' " [39] Now this he said about the Spirit, whom those who believed in him were to receive, for as yet the Spirit had not been given, because Jesus was not yet glorified.

The invitation is to come, but come to where? Jesus says, "Come to me." What does coming to Jesus involve? The passage in Isaiah further clarifies:

Isaiah 55:6-7
"Seek the Lord while he may be found;
call upon him while he is near;
[7] let the wicked forsake his way,
and the unrighteous man his thoughts;
let him return to the Lord, that he may have compassion on him,
and to our God, for he will abundantly pardon.

The first step is repentance, turning from our sin. The second step is given in Jesus' invitation to come: "Whoever believes in me, as the Scripture has said, 'Out of his heart will flow rivers of living water.' " [39] Now this he said about the Spirit, whom those who believed in him were to receive . . . " What does believing in Jesus mean? It involves believing in who he is and what he did. It entails trusting in him to apply what he did for our cleansing and forgiveness.

John 3:16
"For God so loved the world, that he gave his only Son, that whoever believes in him should not perish but have eternal life.

The passage above in Revelation said, "Blessed are those who wash their robes, so that they may have the right to the tree of life and that they may enter the city by the gates."

How does one wash their robes? A passage cited much earlier in the book of Revelation tells us:

Rev. 7:9-10, 13-14
After this I looked, and behold, a great multitude that no one could number, from every nation, from all tribes and peoples and languages, standing before the throne and before the Lamb, clothed in white robes, with palm branches in their hands, [10] and crying out with a loud voice, "Salvation belongs to our God who sits on the throne, and to the Lamb!"

Then one of the elders addressed me, saying, "Who are these, clothed in white robes, and from where have they come?" [14] I said to him, "Sir, you know." And he said to me, "These are the ones coming out of the great tribulation. They have washed their robes and made them white in the blood of the Lamb.

As we, by repentance and faith, trust in Christ's death for our sins, his shed blood washes us clean. He takes upon himself all our sins and credits to us his perfect righteousness. It is a free gift.

2 Cor. 5:21
For our sake he made him to be sin who knew no sin, so that in him we might become the righteousness of God.

Paul summarizes the gospel:

1 Cor. 15:1-9

Now I would remind you, brothers, of the gospel I preached to you, which you received, in which you stand, [2] and by which you are being saved, if you hold fast to the word I preached to you— unless you believed in vain.

[3] For I delivered to you as of first importance what I also received: that Christ died for our sins in accordance with the Scriptures, [4] that he was buried, that he was raised on the third day in accordance with the Scriptures, [5] and that he appeared to Cephas, then to the twelve. [6] Then he appeared to more than five hundred brothers at one time, most of whom are still alive, though some have fallen asleep. [7] Then he appeared to James, then to all the apostles. [8] Last of all, as to one untimely born, he appeared also to me. [9] For I am the least of the apostles, unworthy to be called an apostle, because I persecuted the church of God.

Romans 10:9-10

because, if you confess with your mouth that Jesus is Lord and believe in your heart that God raised him from the dead, you will be saved. [10] For with the heart one believes and is justified, and with the mouth one confesses and is saved.

Friend, if you have never taken that step of coming to Jesus, let me urge you to do so right now. You can pray this prayer, if it is a true expression of your heart's desire.

"Lord Jesus Christ, I come to you in this moment. I forsake my sin and ask you to forgive me. I believe that you are the Son of God and that you died on the cross, bearing my sin, so that I could be forgiven. I believe that you rose from the dead. I receive you now as Lord and Savior of my life. Amen."

If you, in praying this prayer, were genuinely turning from sin and turning to God, he has heard you and accepted you. In fact, he has adopted you into his family.

John 1:11-12

He came to his own, and his own people did not receive him. [12] But to all who did receive him, who believed in his name, he gave the right to become children of God,

John 5:24

Truly, truly, I say to you, whoever hears my word and believes him who sent me has eternal life. He does not come into judgment, but has passed from death to life.

He will give you the right to drink from the river of life and eat from the tree of life in the New Jerusalem and you will live forever in the presence of God! There is no better news!

For Those Who Are In the Family

Once you are in the family of God, now what? We have read that the Antichrist will wage war against the saints and will prevail against them. Some will be put in prison, some put to death. Is a Christian to remain passive and just allow whatever is to happen, come?

While many will be caught and some will be called upon to suffer for the name of Christ, Jesus' admonition to flee the city of Jerusalem and Judea when they see the abomination of desolation taking place to a place of refuge and protection gives us the idea that God does not want us to just passively wait to be killed.

While a book can be written on this subject, I will just mention a few key points that will help the believer be prepared for what is to come.

Learn to Live By Faith

Christians who live by sight and not by faith will be sitting ducks. Over and over Jesus said in the gospels: "Your faith has saved you." The word most commonly used for "saved" is *sozo*, which encompasses the idea of eternal salvation as well as healing, provision and as well as protection. Learn to trust God for the everyday details of life now, so that it will be second nature later. Even for simple things like finding a parking place – ask God to provide and trust him to do so.

Learn to Hear God's Voice

God is a God of communication and he communicates through various means. The first is through his Word. He also speaks through his Holy Spirit, angels, visions and dreams. Notice the various ways God spoke to Philip in this passage:

Acts 8:26-40

Now an angel of the Lord said to Philip, "Rise and go toward the south to the road that goes down from Jerusalem to Gaza." This is a desert place. [27] And he rose and went. And there was an Ethiopian, a eunuch, a court official of Candace, queen of the Ethiopians, who was in charge of all her treasure. He had come to Jerusalem to worship [28] and was returning, seated in his chariot, and he was reading the prophet Isaiah. [29] **And the Spirit said** to Philip, "Go over and join this chariot." [30] So Philip ran to him and heard him reading Isaiah the prophet and asked, "Do you understand what you are reading?" [31] And he said, "How can I, unless someone guides me?" And he invited Philip to come up and sit with him. [32] Now the passage of the Scripture that he was reading was this:

"Like a sheep he was led to the slaughter
and like a lamb before its shearer is silent,
so he opens not his mouth.
[33] In his humiliation justice was denied him.
Who can describe his generation?
For his life is taken away from the earth."

[34] And the eunuch said to Philip, "About whom, I ask you, does the prophet say this, about himself or about someone else?" [35] Then Philip opened his mouth, and beginning with this Scripture he told him the good news about Jesus. [36] And as they were going along the road they came to some water, and the eunuch said, "See, here is water! What prevents me from being baptized?" [37]

[38] And he commanded the chariot to stop, and they both went down into the water, Philip and the eunuch, and he baptized him. [39] And when they came up out of the water, **the Spirit of the Lord carried Philip away**, and the eunuch saw him no more, and went on his way rejoicing. [40] But **Philip found himself at Azotus**, and as he passed through he preached the gospel to all the towns until he came to Caesarea.

An angel spoke to Philip, the Holy Spirit spoke to him, and he was even supernaturally transported by the Spirit of God from the eunuch's location, to Azotus.

Reports abound from around the world of God doing supernatural things: all manner of healings, people being raised from the dead, whole villages having dreams in which Jesus appears to them, leading them to seek someone who can tell them the message of Christ. There have been reports of people being transported from one place to another.

Learn to Live in the Kingdom of God

As we have stated before, this present world is under the dominion of Satan and is cursed because of man's rebellion. Jesus came to establish the kingdom of God, which operates with different laws. Jesus demonstrated what the kingdom of God is like, by casting out demons, healing the sick, multiplying food to feed multitudes, walking on water, commanding storms to cease, raising the dead and so forth. The kingdom of God reality supersedes the natural laws of this sin cursed order. Jesus did not just come to demonstrate this reality as the only one in history to be able to do this. He told his disciples, and by extension, us:

John 14:12-14
"Truly, truly, I say to you, whoever believes in me will also do the works that I do; and greater works than these will he do, because I am going to the Father. [13] Whatever you ask in my name, this I will do, that the Father may be glorified in the Son. [14] If you ask me anything in my name, I will do it.

Begin by first believing that God's plan and intention is for us to operate in this kingdom of God reality today, that it was not just something for Jesus and the Apostles. Then, by faith, begin to operate in these works. Extraordinary times of evil will require extraordinary manifestations of the power of God.

Know that there may come a time when your boldness for Christ will call you to pay with your life, in spite of any miraculous signs God may do through you. Stephen, the first Christian martyr was a man full of God's power:

Acts 6:8-10
And Stephen, full of grace and power, was doing great wonders and signs among the people. [9] Then some of those who belonged to the synagogue of the Freedmen (as it was called), and of the Cyrenians, and of the Alexandrians, and of those from Cilicia and Asia, rose up and disputed with Stephen. [10] But they could not withstand the wisdom and the Spirit with which he was speaking.

In spite of his power, he was seized and brought to trial. It says this of him:

Acts 6:15
And gazing at him, all who sat in the council saw that his face was like the face of an angel.

He made his defense, led by the Holy Spirit. God wanted him to confront the leaders of Israel with their rebellion against him. Here is how he wrapped up his discourse:

Acts 7:51-60
"You stiff-necked people, uncircumcised in heart and ears, you always resist the Holy Spirit. As your fathers did, so do you. [52] Which of the prophets did not your fathers persecute? And they killed those who announced beforehand the coming of the Righteous One, whom you have now betrayed and murdered, [53] you who received the law as delivered by angels and did not keep it."
[54] Now when they heard these things they were enraged, and they ground their teeth at him. [55] But he, full of the Holy Spirit, gazed into heaven and saw the glory of God, and Jesus standing at the right hand of God. [56] And he said, "Behold, I see the heavens opened, and the Son of Man standing at the right hand of God." [57] But they cried out with a loud voice and stopped their ears and rushed together at him. [58] Then they cast him out of the city and stoned him. And the witnesses laid down their garments at the feet of a young man named Saul. [59] And as they were stoning Stephen, he called out, "Lord Jesus, receive my spirit." [60] And falling to his knees he cried out with a loud voice, "Lord, do not hold this sin against them." And when he had said this, he fell asleep.

The Bible speaks of Jesus sitting at the right hand of God, but at that moment, he was standing there, intently watching this testimony of his servant and ready to personally welcome him home. He would receive Stephan with those great words, "Well done, good and faithful servant. Enter into the joy of your Lord."

Likewise, we must be ready, as prophesied in the scripture, to combat and conquer Satan:

Rev. 12:11
And they have conquered him by the blood of the Lamb and by the

word of their testimony, for they loved not their lives even unto death.

A Prophetic Psalm for the End Time

At times we tend to interpret some of the Psalms metaphorically, rather than literally. One such Psalm, perhaps, is Psalm 46. In light of what the Bible says will take place in the future, notice how the Psalm makes what I believe to be literal references to what has been prophesied for the future. What is the response of the believer? "We will not fear ..." The end of the Psalm addresses what has been the theme throughout human history. Who will be worshiped? God assures us of the answer.

Psalm 46:1-11

To the choirmaster. Of the Sons of Korah. According to Alamoth. A Song.

God is our refuge and strength,
a very present help in trouble.
[2] Therefore we will not fear though the earth gives way,
though the mountains be moved into the heart of the sea,
[3] though its waters roar and foam,
though the mountains tremble at its swelling. Selah
[4] There is a river whose streams make glad the city of God,
the holy habitation of the Most High.
[5] God is in the midst of her; she shall not be moved;
God will help her when morning dawns.
[6] The nations rage, the kingdoms totter;
he utters his voice, the earth melts.
[7] The Lord of hosts is with us;
the God of Jacob is our fortress. Selah
[8] Come, behold the works of the Lord,
how he has brought desolations on the earth.
[9] He makes wars cease to the end of the earth;
he breaks the bow and shatters the spear;
he burns the chariots with fire.
[10] "Be still, and know that I am God.
I will be exalted among the nations,
I will be exalted in the earth!"

[11] The Lord of hosts is with us;
the God of Jacob is our fortress.

Selah

Satan coveted God's place, gambled big, has had a long, seemingly winning streak, but will meet his destruction because God is God. My friend, I hope and pray that you are not like Satan, taking a big gamble with your life only to come to the bitter end with no hope and no second chance. Jesus calls you to come now to the river of life. God calls you to know that **He** is God and to exalt him willingly.

ABOUT THE AUTHOR

Dan Pinckney is an ordained minister and has served as a missionary and pastor in Quito, Ecuador, Washington, D.C., Rome, Italy and Munich, Germany. His wife Iara, is from Rio de Janeiro, Brazil and they have a son in his 20's. He may be contacted at comingapoc@hotmail.com.

Made in the USA
Charleston, SC
17 April 2015